Cinema Is the
Strongest Weapon

Cinema Is the Strongest Weapon

Race-Making and Resistance in Fascist Italy

LORENZO FABBRI

UNIVERSITY OF MINNESOTA PRESS

MINNEAPOLIS • LONDON

This book is freely available in an open access edition thanks to TOME (Toward an Open Monograph Ecosystem)—a collaboration of the Association of American Universities, the Association of University Presses, and the Association of Research Libraries—and the generous support of the College of Liberal Arts at the University of Minnesota, Twin Cities. Learn more at the TOME website, available at openmonographs.org.

Chapter 7 was originally published as "Queer Neorealism: Luchino Visconti's *Ossessione* and the *Cinema* Conspiracy against Fascism," *Screen* 60, no. 1 (Spring 2019): 1–24. Portions of the Conclusion are adapted from "Neorealism as Ideology: Bazin, Deleuze, and the Avoidance of Fascism," *The Italianist* 35, no. 2 (2015): 182–201, https://doi.org/10.1179/0261434015Z.000000000115.

Published by the University of Minnesota Press
111 Third Avenue South, Suite 290
Minneapolis, MN 55401–2520
http://www.upress.umn.edu

Available as a Manifold edition at manifold.umn.edu

ISBN 978-1-5179-1083-9 (hc)
ISBN 978-1-5179-1084-6 (pb)

Library of Congress record available at https://lccn.loc.gov/2023012198.

Printed on acid-free paper

The University of Minnesota is an equal-opportunity educator and employer.

Race! It is a feeling.

—Benito Mussolini

.

Contents

Preface and Acknowledgments. Fascism and Us   ix

Introduction. Race War through Other Media   1

1. The Government of the Ungovernable:
   Race and Cinema in Early Italian Film Novels   33

2. Workers Entering the Military-Industrial Complex:
   Pirandello's and Ruttman's *Acciaio*   59

3. White, Red, Blackshirt: Blasetti's Ecofascist Realism   81

4. The Shame of Escapism: Camerini's Anthropological
   Machines   109

5. The White Italian Mediterranean: De Robertis, Rossellini,
   and Fascism's Melodramatic Imperialism   135

6. De Sica's Genre Trouble: Laughing Fascism Away?   169

7. Queer Antifascism: Visconti's *Ossessione* and the *Cinema*
   Conspiracy against Ethno-Nationalism   199

   Conclusion. On Neorealism: The Ends of the Resistance
   and the Birth of an Area   229

   Notes   249

   Index   275

Preface and Acknowledgments

Fascism and Us

In the wake of Nazi Fascism's collapse, Italy and Germany reckoned with their atrocious shared pasts in very different ways. In Nuremberg, the trials set up by the Allied forces would summon the most prominent members of the Nazi state apparatus and oblige a whole people to appear before the concentration camps. Italy's explosive sociopolitical situation and its status as a border zone between East and West, the Global North and the Global South, contributed to preventing a similarly public—although incomplete—confrontation with history. Due to the country's particular geopolitical role, after the execution of Benito Mussolini and the Allied takeover of Italy, the pressure to return to normal life mounted: it was time to let go of the revolutionary passions and radical ambitions that had characterized the years of the resistance and the civil war. It was time to cease addressing Fascism, overcome divisions, move on, and return to normality. In portraying the Italian people as Mussolini's victims rather than his accomplices, postwar national culture and film favored this process of normalization and geopolitical realignment based on a suppression of memory and responsibility, and introduced into the global public imagination the account of Fascism elaborated by liberal philosopher Benedetto Croce during the Nazi occupation of the country. In influential political speeches as well as impactful opinion pieces in the *New York Times* and *Il Giornale di Napoli,* the public intellectual had in fact argued there was no need to arraign fascist Italy, insofar as Mussolini's dictatorship had been a mere parenthesis in the country's life, the effect of a foreign virus that had spread across Italy after World War I and temporally compromised an otherwise healthy body politic.[1]

Croce's treatment of Italian Fascism resonates eerily with how mainstream public discourse has framed the resurgence of right-wing extremism in countries like Italy or the United States a full century after Mussolini's rise to power. The popular support for explicitly racist and discriminatory agendas was and is still often painted as an abjection into which the population is bullied, tricked, or fooled. This is not a mere oversight. As Claudio Fogu argues, the avoidance of the systemic reasons behind people's embrace of the radical right is a move that exorcises more transformative engagements with the trajectories of Western history under racial capitalism.[2] And while there are still glimmers of hope that the current fascist new wave will be addressed rather than avoided, the Blackshirt Ventennio was quickly bracketed as a momentary insanity from which a brutalized nation, through incredible sacrifices, had redeemed itself. The partisans' insurrection against Nazi Fascism came to stand for a collective recovery from the fascist madness and was presented as evidence that Italians were ultimately *brava gente,* "good people" who—under the influence of a few deranged individuals—had just lost their minds for a while. By displacing guilt for the regime onto a few contaminating agents, this mythology compartmentalized Fascism and obfuscated its structural connection to the imaginaries and processes upon which the Italian nation-state was founded in the late nineteenth century.

The geopolitically convenient tale about Fascism that Croce articulated and that neorealism projected worldwide underwent severe scrutiny in the 1970s, when—in a context of radical sociopolitical turmoil—a new generation in national auteur cinema challenged sedimented ways of feeling about Italy. Films such as *Il conformista* (*The Conformist,* 1970), *Il portiere di notte* (*The Night Porter,* 1974), *Salò o le 120 giornate di Sodoma* (*Salò, or the 120 Days of Sodom,* 1975), or *Pasqualino Settebellezze* (*Seven Beauties,* 1975) disrupt the *brava gente* narrative by exposing Italians as a people hostage to deviant desires and repugnant pleasures. Informed by Herbert Marcuse's Freudo-Marxism, Bernardo Bertolucci, Liliana Cavani, Pier Paolo Pasolini, and Lina Wertmüller resort to sexualized tropes of evil to reveal the "sins of the fathers" and stage the nation's disturbing fascination with Fascism.[3] Besides establishing questionable links between fascist rule, nonconforming sexual practices, and mental illness, in staging Fascism as an abjection, the account of the regime proposed after 1968 continues to other it as an abomination.

Notwithstanding their differences, the post–World War II "good people" legend and the "sick folks" discourse articulated by Italian film in the 1970s resort to a medical and ableist imaginary to understand Fascism because they perceive it as a perversion, not a manifestation, of national history and identity. In treating a historical phenomenon as an exception—a pathology—neither framework can ultimately confront what is most frightening about Mussolini's rule: the banality of its evil. The millions of Italians who performed Fascism were not a "basket of deplorables," mentally ill, depraved, or sadistic. They were, for the most part, unexceptional, considerate, sane, upright, trivial, banal individuals. Thus emerges a host of unanswered questions that "the worst" in Italian history still challenges us to address: Why did ordinary citizens, folks who found no pleasure in inflicting or receiving pain, collaborate with colonialism, white supremacy, antisemitism, chemical warfare, and totalitarianism? How did such toxicity become so widespread? Upon what memories and imaginaries was this deadly normality undergirded? In which media forms and forms of affect was it couched?

These are not easy questions to take up, especially when pondering national history also entails pausing on the story of one's own family. My grandfather, born in 1918, was drafted into the military just before Italy's entry into World War II. He was first deployed in Greece, then sent to Africa after the end of the Balkans Campaign. After the 1943 armistice, Corrado refused to follow Mussolini to Salò and stayed in the Royal Army, this time battling the Nazi occupation of Italy and the Italian Social Republic puppet state. Wounded on the battlefield, he was captured by the Nazis and transferred to Dachau. Having survived the detention camp, in the 1950s Corrado fell in love with a single mother who had served as a partisan courier during the resistance and became a father to her daughter, my mom. My grandfather died a few short months after I was born, so I never had the chance to ask him the questions I have about his implication with the regime. But I did ask my grandmother, when I was perhaps fifteen, why nonno Corrado initially had fought for Fascism: Why didn't he defect or something? Babi served under Mussolini, she said, because he felt that by doing so he was serving his people.

Cinema Is the Strongest Weapon: Race-Making and Resistance in Fascist Italy is an attempt to get to the root of the fears and anxieties, hopes and desires, resentments and attachments, expectations and aspirations that shaped my grandfather's commitment to Fascism, which was also the commitment of too many Italian men and women. Now, as always, the questions of why normal folks become involved with nefarious sociopolitical projects for the sake of their people—and thus what it means to be a people—are crucial ones to raise.

I wouldn't have been able to ask the questions in this book without a community around me. Writing *Cinema Is the Strongest Weapon* has been a struggle at times, and I could not have made it through without Jennifer Row by my side.

At Cornell University, Timothy Campbell, Karen Pinkus, Kevin Attell, and Naoki Sakai were fundamental interlocutors in the early phases of this project. I will always cherish the year I spent at the Society for the Humanities, and the inspiring conversations in the A.D. White House with Timothy Murray, Vivian Choi, Bishnu Ghosh, Bhaskar Sarkar, Antoine Traisnel, and Ingrid Diran. Without the warmth and brilliance of Elisabeth Fay, Andrea Righi, Simona Antonacci, Caroline Ferraris-Besso, Elizabeth Wijaya, Michela Baraldi, and Mark Wilson, my Ithaca winters would have been incredibly gloomier.

At the University of Minnesota, Susanna Ferlito, Cesare Casarino, Joseph Farag, Maggie Hennefeld, Travis Workman, Sugi Ganeshananthan, Sonali Pahwa, Ainsley Boe, and Jason McGrath have been perfect colleagues—I am very lucky for the community I have found in the Twin Cities. Invited lectures at the University of Notre Dame (thank you, Charles Leavitt!) and at Rutgers University provided me key opportunities to talk through my ideas. Valeria Dalle Donne from the Cineteca di Bologna, Tracy Bergstrom from the Wagstaff Archive at the University of Notre Dame, Laura Ceccarelli at the Centro Sperimentale di Cinematografia, and Matteo Zannone and Paola Angelucci from the Archivio Storico Instituto Luce in Rome all provided invaluable help in navigating archival resources. Marie McDonough's feedback was essential for nuancing my intervention, and I am very grateful for all the time she spent on my manuscript. Editorial assistance from Sarah Watkins and Mariam Wassif was crucial to get this book ready for publication, and chapter 6 was translated into English thanks to generous support from Amanda Minervini. I am the most obliged to the De Benedetti and Muzi family for opening their home to me during Covid-19 to access playwright Aldo De Benedetti's private archive. I also feel fortunate for the support that, in different phases of writing, I received from Noa Steimatsky, Karl Schoonover, Alessia Ricciardi, and Dana Renga. Special thanks go to Rhiannon Welch, for the generosity and graciousness of her comments on early versions of my argument.

But my biggest *grazie* is owed to my family . . . Jennie, Daniela, Annalisa, Giorgio, Franco, Vittorio: your support is what makes everything—not only this book—possible.

Race War through Other Media

"Cinema is the strongest weapon." "Truth functions as a weapon."

Can these two claims, made by Benito Mussolini and Michel Foucault, respectively, be read together? In the context of weaponized post-truths and against the backdrop of a global reactionary cycle, might they be useful for articulating the impact that media have on our histories and in our lives, as well as for strategizing alternative forms of life and history?

CINEMA IS THE STRONGEST WEAPON

Rome, November 10, 1937. The groundbreaking ceremony for the new headquarters of the L'Unione Cinematografica Educativa (LUCE) Institute, the public corporation devoted to the production of newsreels and educational films, is scheduled for the afternoon. The previous spring, a few feet away, on the day celebrating the mythical founding of ancient Rome, Benito Mussolini inaugurated the Cinecittà public studios. Soon the Centro Sperimentale di Cinematografia (Experimental Center of Cinematography)—the first state-funded film school in the West—will begin construction just across the street. This transformation of Rome's eastern outskirts into a monumental film production hub bears witness to a major shift in Fascism's attitude toward popular culture, and narrative cinema in particular. Although in fact Mussolini's rise to power dates back to 1922, it is only in the early 1930s that that the regime became invested in the film industry, orchestrating—through financial stimuli, policy interventions, and infrastructure development—the comeback of Italian cinema from its post–World War I crisis.[1] In a sense, then, the 1937 inauguration of the LUCE construction yard in Piazza di Cinecittà also constitutes a celebration of the rebirth of Italian film as fascist national cinema.

For the occasion, Cinecittà Square has been transformed into a giant open-air theater, with VIP boxes from which personalities from show business and party leaders can comfortably enjoy the ceremony. Benito Mussolini himself will break ground for the LUCE headquarters. But the site is also a set. There are Italian flags and fascist banners everywhere; army officers and policemen in dress uniform; an askari, a native soldier serving in Italian East Africa's multiethnic colonial police; a delegation of construction workers; schoolgirls wearing white, and members of the Opera Nazionale Balilla, the fascist youth organization, in their black shirts; common people bustling in excitement. Movie cameras are everywhere, eager to capture Mussolini's grand arrival and the impression he will make on the crowd. The motorcade makes its way through the construction site. Mussolini steps out of his Alfa Romeo. Cinecittà Square explodes with joy.

The Duce salutes the armed forces, greets the people in attendance and the construction workers, then ventures down the walkway leading to the pit where he will lay the foundation stone. Once he signs the act of foundation, Mussolini places it in a white marble shrine. Father Tacchi Venturi, the liaison between Italy and the Vatican, consecrates the shrine before lowering it into the ground and giving one last blessing to the imposing film hub being erected in the capital of the fascist empire. Dominating the scene, on the berm surrounding the construction site, is a thirty-five-foot cutout of Mussolini himself behind a movie camera, peering through the viewfinder and posing as a consummate director. Spelled out in white capital letters beneath the larger-than-life icon is the infamous motto "Cinema is the strongest weapon," followed by a reproduction of the Duce's own signature (Figure 1).

The suggestive equivalency, a riff on the Leninist claim that film constitutes the most relevant of the arts, is often evoked in surveys of the fascist mediascape. Its staging at Piazza di Cinecittà in November 1937 is featured, for instance, on the cover of two influential treatments of popular culture during the Ventennio: David Forgacs's edited volume *Rethinking Italian Fascism* and Ruth Ben-Ghiat's *Fascist Modernities*.[2] Notwithstanding their prominent display of the slogan and precise histories of fascist media, not even these prominent studies significantly consider the meaning of the cinematographic apparatus's assimilation to a weapon. Is it a catchy propagandistic slogan? An analogy? Or can such a claim be taken literally? If cinema is

FIGURE I. A gigantic cutout of Mussolini peering behind the movie camera looms over the crowds. Photograph taken during the groundbreaking ceremony of the new headquarters of the LUCE Institute on November 10, 1937. Copyright Archivio Storico Istituto LUCE Cinecittà.

really a weapon, which sort of weapon might it be? How does this weapon work? In which confrontation, battle, fight, or war would it be deployed?

Jacqueline Reich and Piero Garofalo's *Re-viewing Fascism* suggests some answers to these questions: "When Benito Mussolini proclaimed 'Cinema is the strongest weapon,'" the back cover of their edited book reads, "he was only telling half of the story." According to Reich and Garofalo, Mussolini's announcement of the weaponization of cinema was, in essence, false posturing. Reich in particular supports this claim by arguing that Fascism differed from Nazism in that it never sought to hegemonize national culture and it lacked a precise ideology to begin with.[3] For Reich, Mussolini did not merely fail to exert control over the arts; he never sought to control the cultural industry as he lacked a set worldview or vision of Italy to impose upon it. Considering this context of ideological confusion and nonhegemonized media, how can one take seriously Mussolini's proclamation that cinema is a weapon? In "Mussolini at the Movies," Reich does not mention Antonio Gramsci, Jacques Lacan, or Louis Althusser. Nevertheless, given her insistence on the anti-ideological and nonhegemonic nature of fascist command, Reich's intervention constitutes an important challenge to the possibility of viewing Italian cinema under Fascism through the lens of Marxist ideology critique—that is, a challenge to the foundational framework for the development of the discipline of film studies in the 1970s.

The discussion of cinema as an apparatus of ideological warfare dates precisely to that juncture, when journals such as *Cahiers du Cinéma* and *Screen* took notice of Althusser's blend of Gramsci and Lacan. What was particularly generative about a text like "Ideology and Ideological State Apparatuses" was its granting culture and the imaginary of a greater impact on historical dynamics than the economic functionalism of orthodox Marxism.[4] Notably, Althusser highlighted how capitalist rule cannot be assured by violence and repression alone but rather must be supplemented by subjects' quasi-voluntary servitude to state power. For Althusser, this servitude to the capitalist state—"consent," in Gramsci's terms—is brokered by acting on collective consciousness and carried out through institutions that, under the state's control, articulate a fake representation of life under capitalism that rationalizes even its most exploitative and abhorrent features.[5] This is the realm of ideological warfare. The weapons through which this conflict is fought are apparatuses that, by trapping individuals in an inauthentic rendering of reality, persuade them to preserve the current economic, political, and social relations. Althusser contends that it is only after overcoming the worldview imposed upon them by the state that individuals will become free to fight for better lives.

Applied to the study of filmic textuality, Althusser's framework led to brilliant analyses of the "reality effect" through which the cinema hides its ideological operations and achieves the illusion of audiovisual referentiality. In discussing the basic function of the cinematographic apparatus, Jean-Louis Baudry, for instance, famously described the movie theater as a Platonic cave that captures spectators in a web of deceptive projections, and spectators as disembodied larval beings who cannot but recognize/misrecognize themselves and their world when hailed by the screen.[6] Even more strongly than Althusser's original ideology critique, apparatus theory makes political progress dependent on aware mental processes and the liberation of the collective consciousness from state-sanctioned truths about the world.

In the 1990s, Barbara Spackman, Karen Pinkus, Marcia Landy, and Simonetta Falasca-Zamponi—among others—drew upon the post-Althusserian Marxism of Slavoj Žižek and Ernesto Laclau to elaborate a more embodied, sensorial, and haptic take on how capitalist rule was secured in fascist Italy. Yet even their innovative interventions in this last instance uphold the framework that Victoria de Grazia articulated in her key book *The Culture of Consent*: since behaviors are consequences of conscious beliefs, coming to grips with Fascism, coming to terms with the fascistization of the national masses, entails studying the ideas and discourses that the regime convinced the Italian population to hold.[7]

Reich takes a completely different route. She rejects altogether the very terms of ideology critique and apparatus theory. In this regard, "Mussolini at the Movies" is another important confirmation of what media archaeologies by Tom Gunning, Miriam Hansen, Giuliana Bruno, and Jonathan Crary also unearthed: with its generalizations about cinema's basic function and mode of functioning, a model based on ideology, hegemony, consent, and consciousness does not stand the test of film history.[8] Reich is correct when she concludes that Fascism did not work ideologically, that it was never preoccupied with articulating a rational, somehow consistent worldview that could legitimize the abject lives Italians were living. Mussolini was always more interested in commanding how national subjects acted than in influencing what they thought or believed. His admiration for Gustave Le Bon's "crowd psychology" is well documented, but also well known is his appreciation of Fascism as an electrifying network of myths rather than as a precise doctrine or ideology. The regime treated the population as flesh to be emotionally moved, not as disincarnate eyes and ears to be rationally shown and told. Given what new archival research has revealed about film production in Italy between 1922 and 1943, it is truly a stretch to posit that entertainment cinema under the regime functioned as a weapon of hegemony in the way that ideological state apparatuses work in Althusser. However, Reich's conclusion that Fascism was uncommitted to weaponizing cinema and popular culture might be further nuanced.

Can it be that in fascist Italy, film and media were deployed in a battle that was not ideological or carried out through ideas or consciousness? After rejecting traditional explanations of fascist command based on hegemony or consent, the Blackshirt Ventennio still needs to be made sense of, so as to avoid the risk of dismissively archiving it as madness. The inauguration of the LUCE construction site is one such crucial scene because it provides important cues to how Fascism ruled through film as well as to the war in which cinema was weaponized.

A central absence in this primal scene of fascist cinema is that of the king: the head of the Italian state, Victor Emmanuel III, is nowhere to be found. The stage is left to the ministers of the executive branch and foremost to the leader of the government, Benito Mussolini. The DUX sign present on the scene announces that the prime minister is literally responsible for guiding the people forward. The schoolgirls and the Balilla squad evoke the new nation that the Duce has been fathering. Father Tacchi Venturi attests to the closeness between Mussolini's government of the people and the spiritual power exercised by the Catholic pastorate over its flock: it is with the Church's blessing that Mussolini is laying the foundations for a renewed Italian cinema. There are the armed forces—police and army—representing the security apparatus that has been instrumental in advancing Mussolini's fight to redress Italian lives. The Blackshirt militia, another great asset for the fascist disciplining of the body politic, is also present on the scene. But above all, there are the Italian people—industrious, energetic, united, and enthusiastic—who have come together to celebrate Mussolini. They have gathered because, as his gigantic cutout attests, the Duce is quite familiar with the movie camera; he understands film, and based on his expertise he has been restructuring the cinematographic apparatus. The cranes looming beyond Mussolini's photographic reproduction indicate that much more is being erected under fascist power. In the focal point of the scene, the motto identifying film as a weapon is set between a team of construction workers and a line of police in dress uniforms, framing cinema simultaneously as a tool of nation building and a device of social control. The askari remains still, yet the part this character plays in this show of remediation is key (Figure 2). Standing in front of a mobile projection truck that will bring national film to the margins of the nation and to the colonies, this Black African body is exhibited as living proof of cinema's force to reclaim even those lives that have been racialized as most backward. But through his radical difference vis-à-vis everyone else on site, a difference that the newsreel constructs through montage and camera movements, the African soldier also conveys that the Italians assembled here are a non-Black, not-colonized, and not-backward body politic: they are a modern people with an imperial reach, a people that under Mussolini had invaded Ethiopia and were readying to take on the world.

FIGURE 2. An askari, dressed in fine military garb, stands in front of a mobile projection truck. Istituto LUCE Newsreel, November 11, 1937. Copyright Archivio Storico Istituto LUCE Cinecittà.

I am so drawn to this carefully staged performance as its mise-en-scène and emblems conjure a weaponization of media that eschews the horizons of ideology critique and apparatus theory. Through its figures of race, gender, and class; by means of its attention to natality, colonialism, and reproductive futurity; in light of its emphasis on the symbiotic relation between the Dux, the church, the common people, and the police, the inauguration of LUCE connects the cinema with the constellation of practices and machines that Michel Foucault associates with the realm of biopolitical warfare—that is, with the struggle undertaken by modern colonial-capitalist states to govern and put to work their subjects not thanks to consent building or persuasion but by exerting direct control over individuals' biological and affective existence, that is, without going through the mediation of cognition or conscious mental processes.

While "Italian theory" has often presented biopolitical warfare as a homogenizing enterprise, Alexander Weheliye's *Habeas Viscus* insists on the need to take notice of the raced, gendered, and classed dimension of bio-politics, so as to better appreciate its structural complicity with the machi-nations of racial capitalism. Working in the tradition of Black feminism and arguing against Giorgio Agamben, Weheliye shows that the appara-tuses of biopolitics are not interested in producing undifferentiated bare lives; they bring into existence the specific embodiments of race and gen-der that the capitalist-patriarchal-colonial order requires to sustain itself. For this precise reason, biopolitical rule—Weheliye concludes—is intrinsi-cally discriminatory and differential. As Jonathan Xavier Inda also argues, the biopolitical state is not concerned with protecting life in general but always with securing particular ways of being a body, with subjects that are made live, let die, *or killed* on the basis of the naturalized socio-racial group wherein they have been profiled.[9] Biopolitical warfare should be thus more precisely understood as the battle to create different forms of what, via Weheliye, we could dub racialized assemblages, raced forms of living that have been implanted with a distinct set of abilities, duties, norms, desires, pleasures, and commitments—with the ultimate goal of maximiz-ing socioeconomic (re)productivity. Under biopolitics, differences do not disappear but are instead exploited to guarantee the reproduction of what bell hooks dubs "imperialist, white supremacist, capitalist patriarchy."[10]

In Piazza di Cinecittà, on November 10, 1937, biopolitics and biopolitical warfare are everywhere. The newsreel of the event shows a set that is also a construction site. It puts on display a diverse mass of people assembled thanks to the technologies of fascist governance. It presents the Duce as the leader able to bind together—while carefully separating—white Ital-ians and Black Africans, men and women, the rich and the poor, the elites and the masses. Simultaneously, the newsreel also remediates cinema as the most reliable apparatus for fulfilling Fascism's project of unifying and putting to work a population that had been considered for so long impos-sible to discipline. The metaphor of cinema as a weapon starts to make more sense when one considers this emphasis on the medium's ability to gather an ordered Italy. In Piazza di Cinecittà, the cinematographic appa-ratus is ultimately cast as a device that, by means of color, soundscape, light-ing, montage, camera angles, camera movements, frame composition, and mise-en-scène, could refashion a diverse multitude of living beings into the docile gendered racial assemblage Fascism demanded them to be. National

cinema, on this occasion, stages itself as the fundamental asset in the struggle to determine the species of subjects that Italians are and the kind of
nation that Italy is.

"Cinema is the strongest weapon" is then no empty slogan. It is a guiding thread that can be used to investigate the apparatus's contributions
to fascist efforts to make a racially proper Italian assemblage and also to
the revolt against Blackshirt state racism. It is an answer, in its own way,
to the vexed question "What Is Cinema?"—an answer that affords alternative genealogies of the medium and prompts us to reconsider how
audiovisual forms bore on modern Italy's national history, so as to possibly
better evaluate how media impact our transnational, postmodern here
and now.

The history of modern Italy—the history of Italy as a modern capitalist
nation-state—begins in the second half of the nineteenth century, with a
series of wars waged by the House of Savoy against Prussia, the Austro-
Hungarian Empire, the Bourbons, and the Pontifical States with the intent
of turning the peninsula, Sicily, and Sardinia into one united kingdom. Yet,
as Rhiannon Welch traces in her brilliant *Vital Subjects,* the Risorgimento
promise of a unified national space and a pacified national society was still
to be achieved when Fascism rose to power.[11] The country was rife with
differences and fractures that felt insurmountable, and since the turn of
the century national political culture and literature alike betrayed growing
societal concerns about how long this Kingdom of Italy was going to survive if it kept existing in such a fraught and conflictual state. Welch connects the anxious nationalism and sense of disjointedness haunting early
twentieth-century Italy to the entangled economic order, political system,
and racial imaginary that characterized the liberal nation.

Building upon Gramsci, scholars such as Jane Schneider, Nelson Moe,
Pasquale Verdicchio, and Miguel Mellino have contested the traditional
apologetic tone of previous writing on the Risorgimento, suggesting that
the so-called liberation of Italy as carried out under the hegemony of the
Savoy family (which originated from France) and of northern liberal elites
should be considered part of a larger colonial project of territorial expansion, resource extraction, and forced subjugation of urban and rural masses
racialized as quasi-African.[12] Expanding on this tradition of thought, Welch
argues that the tears in the national fabric that were so disconcerting for
public opinion were caused by capitalist exploitation but were understood

to be the consequences of the population's heterogeneous racial background and specifically by the pernicious presence in the country of a pathological breed. If we look at Cesare Lombroso's *L'uomo delinquente* (*The Criminal Man*)—the most vivid manifestation of the bipartisan racism characteristic of the liberal postunification order (Lombroso was a socialist)—we see that the founder of Italian racial anthropology does not even consider Italy as one singular lifeworld but rather as a series of incompatible ethnic folds, each characterized by a different social reality and a different stage of civilization.[13]

A noble minority of Italians shared the blood, customs, and whiteness of other north European stocks, while a multitude of darker and shorter Italians—the indolent, backward peasants and the delinquent, wayward proletarians—constituted a threat to society as they were biologically disposed to delinquency. This kind of gaze reiterated mainstream French, German, English, and U.S. anti-southern stereotypes about an insurmountable biocultural divide between northern and Mediterranean Europes and manifested itself in a regime of quasi-segregation where subaltern Italians were symbolically and materially excluded from belonging in the nation they were toiling to sustain. A very strict color line divided the upper classes from the popular masses, and the existence of a sort of minoritized majority, of an unassimilated proletarian multitude, worked against the grain of the historical project that liberalism was pursuing: turning Italy into a great modern European nation-state. As David Theo Goldberg and Walter Mignolo imply, in the imaginary of the time, "becoming modern" for a Western territorial formation entailed both evolving into a compact sociopolitical assemblage *and* rising to the rank of colonial power.[14] After the conquest of Eritrea in 1890, the 1896 loss against Ethiopia at Adwa as well as the social unrest—regicide, strikes—that marked turn-of-the-century Italy signaled thus to the ruling blocs that modernizing Italy was going to be a strenuous struggle. The relative economic growth and social peace characterizing the early twentieth century, a period that also included the colonization of Libya (1911), only postponed the confrontation with the structural problem afflicting the Kingdom of Italy under liberal rule and which manifested in the aftermath of World War I: the state had not enough of a firm grip over its subjects, and its mix of paternalism, laxism, and authoritarianism was not sufficient to manage conflicts between social parts and hence assure the survival of a modern, that is, colonial and capitalist, Italy.[15] As I specify in chapter 1, the feeling was that something new, something different was needed to secure the country's intersectional system of exploitation at home and abroad.

There is indeed a paradigmatic shift that marks the passage from liberal laissez-faire state governmentality to fascist biopolitical interventionism. This threshold from liberal to fascist history is constituted by the systemic realization that an Italian modernity—which one should understand not merely as the industrialization of the country but also the internal colonization of the population and its deployment for colonial expansion—would be unsustainable as long as the current racial order, governmental logic, and political technologies dominated Italy. Liberalism's divisive elitism, coupled with its extractive capitalism and hands-off approach to government, were ultimately considered obstacles to the mobilization of the country, the urban and rural masses especially, for building a strong bourgeois nation and global empire.

Hence, on the one hand, it is important to historicize Mussolini's rule as something that grew out of the sociopolitical order that liberalism opened up in the wake of Italy's unification—that is, the colonial-capitalist order. On the other hand, the commitment to read Fascism in context, to write a *longue durée* genealogy of the Blackshirt regime and exorcise the "parenthesis" trope, should not entail a disregard for the innovative aspects of fascist rule, for the fact that Mussolini's advent constituted an event in national history that radically changed how Italy was put together and pushed it, as Suzanne Stewart-Steinberg argues, in a postliberal direction.[16]

A central aspect of the postliberal state that Fascism arranged was its totalitarian dimension, the more aggressive and capillary ways in which it bid on individual bodies and the body politic alike. Violence was not a last recourse but rather a fundamental political technology as, for Fascism and its supporters, authentic Italian living was under attack from internal and external enemies who had compromised the health of the nation and, fostering conflicts, were preventing Italy from being the organized totality it was destined to be. But violence was only one of the tools through which to intervene in collective life. Repression was to be supplemented by a global and far-reaching effort to enable one strong united Italian ethno-nation.

The fascist totalitarian rearticulation of sovereignty coincided, in fact, with a rejection of the divisive and division-fostering ethnic racism of the liberal era. There were not two ethnically distinct and ethically incompatible racial groups in Italy; Italians were one race, and under Mussolini they will rise again, the regime assured, leading to what Gaia Giuliani brilliantly describes as the gradual recoloring of Italy.[17] Blackness and backwardness were displaced outside the country, in the Africa that Fascism promised to civilize and turn into an asset that would feed the starving Italian masses. Simultaneously, these national masses underwent a process of whitening as they stopped being reproached as the threatening racial Other within. Mussolini not only silenced those evoking biological fractures keeping the country divided by establishing that Italians were a specific, singular bio-spiritual unicum; he also elevated the industrial and agrarian masses who had been earlier profiled as quasi-African to the status of true Italians, the ones the new government was fighting for and with. Articulating a grittier version of white supremacy, an anti-elitist populist white supremacy cater-ing to subaltern classes, the regime hailed Italy as a proletarian and rural sea-bound people that were ready to work hard, and even go to war, to reclaim the place in history and in the world that they deserved.

Italians were, after all, the glorious race that had birthed Western civili-zation, the regime claimed through references to the Roman Empire, the Church, and the Renaissance. Thus, for Fascism, even if Italy could not make claims to phenotypical whiteness, even if Italians could not flaunt the sort of white modernity exhibited by northern European countries, Italy had to be granted the respect, the prestige, but also the colonial supremacy that white nations were entitled to. Italians' contributions to world cul-ture, history, and the arts made them a race peer to, if not superior to, phenotypically white and nominally more modern European nations. For too long this great stock was prevented from showcasing its prowess, inge-nuity, and industriousness—that is, from deploying its specific iteration of whiteness. But now, thanks to Fascism, Italy might complete the rebirth started with the Risorgimento wars, correcting incongruous behavior and freeing itself from the yoke of racially inappropriate projects of commu-nity and belonging. What was bringing Italian life down was not racial dif-ference (the myth of the "two Italies") but biological degeneration caused by foreign influence and internal decay.

To effect the body politic's resurgence and the ethno-nation's most autochthonous potentialities, Fascism launched a series of massive social health campaigns that had the objective of reclaiming the general condi-tion of the population, so as to make Italy bigger, stronger, more pro-ductive, and more competitive on the world stage. The Battle for Births—promoting natalism, imposing taxes on bachelors, and offering economic and employment advantages to prolific couples—was meant to reverse the depopulation trend of the liberal years (mass migration, World War I, the flu pandemic) and provide Italy with the hands and wombs it needed to birth its glorious future. The Battle for Land cleared and reclaimed vast marshland areas and committed to provide new homes and fields to Italians living in hunger and neglect. The Battle for Grain ramped up cereal production, feeding a growing Italy while making it food independent. The Racial Laws from 1938 relaunched the war to protect the true people, forbidding interracial relations with Jewish Italians and Black colonized subjects in order to exorcise the risk of transnational solidarities and keep the biological body of the ethno-nation pure. They also excluded Jewish Italians from participating in public life to defend society from their pernicious influence. But there was an even more fundamental battle that Fascism was fighting.

Many centuries of external rule, the liberal catastrophe, and then the Red Scare had developed in Italian bodies an obstinate resilience against taking up the commitments and responsibilities, desires and lifestyles that, according to the regime, were proper to the Italian race. As he explicated in a 1933 interview, for Mussolini, a race was not only a biological reality but also an emotion, meaning that for a collectivity of individuals to behave as a race, as a smooth-working sociopolitical assemblage, these individuals had to feel that they were part of a single organism whose survival was dependent on the cooperation of all its components.[18] The regime's concern was that Italians did not feel like one race, and without this sentiment of belonging to a common history, project, and destiny—to be one and the same, notwithstanding all the localisms and differences—the fascist care for the nation's biological body would backfire. In line with Romanticism's antirationalistic understanding of how social bonds and communities are formed, building upon liberal-era theorizations of the relationship between embodiment and subjection, the regime was convinced that acting on people's feelings would have a more significant impact on how they behaved than precise ideologies or even new formulations of racial identity. Thus, among the battles that the regime took up, there was also the fight to implant in the body politic affects and emotions that would lead the Italian masses to behave as the sort of race Fascism had been claiming they were. Already on the eve of the March on Rome, Mussolini clarified that the war to redress national life that the Blackshirts were taking up was going to be conducted by means of a diverse array of political strategies and governmental apparatuses, through violence and religion but also through politics and the arts. The regime's involvement in the rebirth of Italian cinematographic art ought to be understood, I hold, precisely against the backdrop of this multimedia biopolitical effort to *fare razza*—to make race, to intervene on the biological *and* spiritual body of the nation so as to breed the life-forms necessary for heteronormative, capitalist, and colonial Italy, that is, for a whitened and modernized nation, to reproduce itself.[19]

Without a doubt, the regime's 1930s commitments to the film industry were not exclusively a matter of governance and geopolitics. In the post-1929 context of economic stagnation and credit crisis, the support for national film was meant to stimulate the gross national product by enabling a virtuous circle between the consumption and production of "made in Italy" narratives. But the investment in cinema was also motivated by the desire to turn recreational activities into occasions for disciplining what was considered a recalcitrant race in need of much schooling. Just as board games were used to form children into fascist and colonialist subjects, cinema was eyed as a resource to form a people still in its infancy. In this regard, James Hay highlights how the regime's interest in commercial filmmaking reveals the essential link between government and media, power and leisure, that would define the final decade of Fascism's political laboratory.[20]

The traditional outlook on fascist media holds that the regime benefited especially from escapist films distracting the public from the dreariness of life under Mussolini. Notwithstanding the radical differences in their frameworks, influential readers of Italian cinema such as André Bazin, Millicent Marcus, and Gilles Deleuze conjure a direct relation between fascist command and escapist cinema—especially popular rom-coms from the 1930s modeled on coeval Hungarian stage plays and Hollywood hits.[21] Replete with images of opulence and liberality, cinema under Fascism has often been presented as a device of mass distraction, a way to provide spectators with a dream-space where they could forget about all the prohibitions and limitations that the regime imposed on them in real life. In his "Sex in the Cinema," Forgacs highlights a structural analogy between this account of the labor of cinematic figuration during the Ventennio and worn-out descriptions of the Ventennio itself. Both Fascism and its cinema are understood in line with what has been dubbed the "repressive hypothesis," that is, through ideology critique's claim that power is exercised mainly through restrictions, denials, and erasures.[22] Whereas Fascism is reduced to a violent dictatorship betraying true Italian identity, fascist cinema is described as an apparatus denying access to true Italian reality. But, Forgacs concludes, there is a double fallacy at play here: first, in the idea that there are realities and identities independent from circuits of power-knowledge-affect; and second, that Fascism operated through political technologies that falsified these preexisting realities and identities.

To correct these oversights, "Sex in the Cinema" stresses the necessity to devote more attention to the productive dimension of both the regime and its media, so as to appreciate their long-lasting impact on Italians' behaviors and dispositions. Expanding on Forgacs's effort to bridge Gramsci and Foucault, central questions of this book are: Can the feelings harnessed by cinema under the regime help us account for—though not justify or excuse—Italians' widespread collaboration with Fascism? Might a connection be established between the forms of affect that mainstream cinema concocted and the life-forms that Mussolini battled to assemble? In *Fascist Modernities* and *Italian Fascism's Empire Cinema,* Ben-Ghiat shows that realism had an especially important nation- and empire-building function in fascist culture, as this genre—in both literature and film—came to be invested with the function of modeling how "real" Italians ought to live, love, and die.[23] Further interrogating Ben-Ghiat's argument, *Cinema Is the Strongest Weapon* ponders how the different iterations of realism—respectively elaborated by Walter Ruttmann, Alessandro Blasetti, Mario Camerini, Francesco De Robertis, and Roberto Rossellini—mattered to Italy's peculiar racial whiteness by mediating the sense of everyone's place, role, and job in the nation-empire the regime strived to create.

Considering the Italian and fascist reliance on feelings for making race, my approach to realism and the cinematic apparatus privileges their affective affordances—their power to arrange intense audiovisual experiences about national reality by capturing bodies in oppressive deployments of gender, class, and community. Especially in scholarship about Italian cinema, realism and melodrama have been read in opposition, with—as Catherine O'Rawe argues—melodrama being dismissed as the womanly, overaffected, and degraded "other" vis-à-vis masculine and sober realism. Following Linda Williams, I show that realism, as any cinematic register, works melodramatically, that is, by triggering emotions in the spectatorial body. Accordingly, I pay particular attention to how, paraphrasing Williams, reality effects can be deployed to harness racial affects. I am keen in this regard to show how filmmaking strategies usually hailed as tokens of an honest, immediate, ethical cinema (for instance: long takes, location shooting, and use of nonprofessional actors) arranged exploitative simulations of national life that confirmed the sensation of a sociopolitical organism on the brink and thus strengthened the regime's rule over the body politic.[24] Turning Italian locations—factories, waterfalls, cities, the swamp, the countryside, and the Mediterranean sea—into battlefields between proper and improper lives, the works I discuss articulate affective geographies of fear and hope that deliver the people to Mussolini and subject them to the project of an ordered, greater Italy. It is for this reason that I treat even films that are not explicitly about empire or race as machines that are complicit with Fascism's plans of internal colonization and external colonialism.

Shelleen Greene has already started to unpack the fundamental role that cinema plays in enabling deployments of Italian racial identity that negotiate the country's relation to global white supremacy. Greene's pivotal *Equivocal Subjects* advances the study of Italian cinema's involvement with race and racism by focusing on racialization processes that, similarly to those described by Edward Said in *Orientalism,* specify the features of whiteness through a dialectical opposition with spaces and peoples racialized as Other.[25] In this book, I take notice of a different cinematic modality of making a white race: not by opposition but by accumulation. By doing so, I extend to the study of Italian film culture the framework articulated by Richard Dyer in his groundbreaking book *White*: accept that race is a key apparatus in the development of modern history, accept that the modern world is a racial world, and thus see racialization at work even in movies that do not feature Black people, works that do not explicitly thematize racial difference but rather deal with, for instance, Italian life. It is unquestionable that whiteness is predicated on racial difference: in order for white people to exist, Blackness needs to be a fact; nonwhite people ought to be woven into existence as well. Yet, in seeing whiteness only when the specter of Blackness is conjured, one runs the risk of upholding the traditional color-blindness of film and media studies and missing how, racism being a structural phenomenon, "whiteness reproduces itself in all texts all of the time."[26] It is precisely in order to account for the unmarked but ubiquitous production of white lives upon which Western modern history is predicated that *Cinema Is the Strongest Weapon* recognizes a systemic effort to thicken spectators' racialized sense of self in the host of seemingly apolitical films featuring common Italian workers, peasants, teachers, nurses, mothers, fathers, delivery boys, and salesgirls that characterize fascist cinema.

In writing about "fascist cinema," I do not imply that the regime attempted a takeover of film production within the country. We have seen with Reich that hegemony was not a central feature of fascist rule, and Hay confirms that the regime, to govern, relied heavily on initiatives and players that were not under state control. Although Mussolini fashioned himself as a director, the fascist state acted more in the guise of a producer financing "worthy" scripts and filmmakers. When Fascism tried to force a synchronization between the cinematographic apparatus and the other technologies of biopolitical governance it relied on to assemble a white body politic, things did not go well. The lack of success of films like Giovanni Forzano's *Camicia nera* (*Blackshirt*, 1933), one of the few fiction films produced by LUCE, and Walter Ruttmann's concurrent *Acciaio* (*Steel*), a film strongly desired by the fascist apparatus I discuss in chapter 2, attests how the regime was more adept at fostering ideal conditions for cinema to do its part than at imposing projects and directors on production companies.

This relative independence of the film industry from what Marla Stone dubs the "patron state" left room for some tactical maneuvering of the cinematographic apparatus.[27] Indeed, it was not only the Blackshirts who were invested in film. With the Centro Sperimentale di Cinematografia, Fascism had created a state-of-the-art facility where young Italians could learn how to make movies. But knowledge is power, and the very training they were imparted also allowed them to experiment with film form and elaborate alternative deployments of the apparatus. Aware that no political system—even the most complete totalitarianism—is ever able to eliminate resistance, in this book I do not only examine cinema's contributions to fascist history. I also analyze how, starting with the end of the 1930s, cinema was occupied by groups unhappy with fascist life, who sought to disrupt what, thanks to Lauren Berlant, one might describe as the "cruel optimism" that bound the people to the regime.[28]

Fascist Italy, for me, is hence not only an admonitory tale; it is also an archive of resistance. After looking at how representations of Italians at work enabled racialized ways of feeling that contributed to Mussolini's social eugenics efforts, imperial projects, and colonial violence, *Cinema Is the Strongest Weapon* eschews excavating skeletons from the closet of memory, in favor of narrating the stories of the defiant gay, Communist, Jewish, and quasi-feminist Italians who, in fascist Italy, acted like the media activists of today: they infiltrated the culture industry, redeployed audiovisual forms, and shouldered the cinematographic apparatus as a weapon of resistance against fascist race-making. They engaged, in other words, in what Gramsci might have considered a "war of position" against Mussolini's

rule—a conflict that takes place within the realm of cultural fantasies, to
pave the way for real changes in sociopolitical life.[29]

In approaching the fascist mediascape as the battlefield of an aesthetic-
political conflict between different projects of national identity, I achieve
—ideally—two results. On the one hand, my book contributes to the
ongoing endeavors to push the study of Italian visual culture outside an
area studies model and reposition it at the forefront of global discussions
on the relation between power systems, media forms, and subject formations. By reading Mussolini's regime as an attempt to secure the capitalist-
colonial order in Italy, I "deprovincialize Fascism," so to speak, and situate
what happened then and there in a transnational history of racial capitalism that is also and still our history.

On the other hand, *Cinema Is the Strongest Weapon* furthers the turn to
the body in film theory and cultural studies associated with the waning of
ideology critique, by considering the role that formal processes of affective
mediation play in practices of state governance and state racism as well
as in progressive efforts to defy the destructive white normality that biopolitics enables. It is true that feminist theorists—Silvia Federici and Sara
Ahmed, among others—have indeed done groundbreaking work on the
politics of emotion.[30] However, the importance of mediated feelings for
racialization processes is an aspect of biopolitical governance that seems to
me still fairly understudied and yet key for understanding the historical
reality in which we live. We often forget that Foucault's analytics of biopower, a theory in which media and affects play a crucial but unacknowledged role, stems precisely from the question of how to resist burgeoning
new iterations of state racism and fascism.

TRUTH FUNCTIONS AS A WEAPON

The 1970s marked a decisive shift in Foucault's research trajectory. After
the failure of the 1968 protests, in a climate of generalized counterrevolution, with state-enforced violence on the rise in France and the United
States, Foucault grew concerned about ever more invasive strategies of
social control and the ways that state institutions always more decisively
discriminated between lives that matter and disposable bodies. In this regard,
Brady Thomas Heiner documents how at the basis of Foucault's political thought there might be a disavowed appropriation of African American
radicalism. Can it be a mere coincidence that Foucault started developing
his analytics of power after a trip to northern California during which he

became acquainted with the theories and practices developed by the Black Panther Party (BPP)? There are two aspects of the BPP's framework that are particularly germane to Foucault's own critique of state power: the identification of racism as a crucial means of state governance rather than a mere superstructure, and the acknowledgment that Fascism is not a phenomenon relegated to the past but rather a reality inscribed at the very heart of modern capitalism.[31] According to Heiner, it is precisely the Black experience of the (white) United States as a racial quasi-fascist state that forms the basis for Foucault's so-called biopolitical turn. The preoccupation with how institutions produce and hierarchize embodied subjects would lead Foucault to emphasize, in his late work on the ancient "care of the self," the need to experiment with systems of existence that withdraw from the state and the network of its governmental apparatuses. In the 1970s, this concern materialized in the effort to develop an understanding of power and of state sovereignty that avoided the limitations that Foucault recognized in Marxism. One of the first major results of this confrontation with Marxist theory is *Discipline and Punish*.[32]

Notwithstanding the absence of explicit references to "Ideology and Ideological State Apparatuses," there is little doubt that Foucault's intervention from 1975 constitutes a reaction to Althusser. In his 1970 essay, as mentioned, Althusser stressed the importance of consent for the capitalist states' government. In response, *Discipline and Punish* holds that political power does not necessarily need persuasion or cognitive legitimation to be effective. This is the case because the state—to safeguard the capitalist mode of production—prominently relies on technologies that bear directly upon bodies' materiality, potentialities, and forces: bodies to be surveilled, bodies to be measured, bodies to be trained, bodies to be maimed, bodies to be healed. For *Discipline and Punish,* embodiment, not ideology, is the ultimate foundation of the modern state's authority. Foucault deemed the explanation of subjection developed by Althusser (and consequently his political proposal) to be too close to the social contract model, since it overstated the impact of people's ideas, opinions, and intentions on sociopolitical dynamics and underemphasized the importance of the material conditions of their bodily existence. However, Foucault's skepticism about consent building does not necessary entail dismissing mediation as a relevant site for the manufacture of docile capitalist subjects.

I have always been troubled by three passages in *Discipline and Punish.* The first is when Foucault characterizes the Enlightenment discourse (rights, egalitarian framework) as the "bright side" of discipline, implying a correlation between forms of cultural imaginaries and modes of social control. The second is when Foucault insists that the transition from early hands-off modern sovereignty to biopolitics also entailed a shift in the state's code of social acceptability and in the ways that the people felt about kings and queens: the monarchy now cared about the people; it was not to be feared. In the third, Foucault connects the reappraisal of the penal apparatus in nineteenth-century France with the coeval mass circulation, in newspapers and popular literature, of panicked stories seeking to tear apart the solidarity that existed between delinquents and the lower social strata. These passages are as important as they are troubling because they reintroduce in the margins of *Discipline and Punish* something that the book's radical anti-Althusserian stance repeatedly and explicitly excludes: that representation and mediation matter even in disciplinary societies; that signs, truths, narratives, fables, spectacles, and other symbolic forms affecting people's dispositions play an important role in modern society.

In this regard, consider the 1974 interview in *Cahiers du Cinéma* between Foucault and Pascal Bonitzer, Serge Daney, and Serge Toubiana—younger members of the journal's editorial board eager to move away from the uncompromising Marxism-Leninism of Jean-Louis Comolli and Jean Narboni.[33] Responding to questions about the representation of World War II and the resistance in contemporary French cinema, Foucault offers broader considerations on the relation between politics and media. First, he notes the importance of a whole host of apparatuses that reprogram popular memory and naturalize specific relationships between social forces for contemporary state governance. As examples of these *appareils* supporting state power, Foucault mentions schools but also media: popular literature and cheap books, television, and the cinema. Second, Foucault argues that classic Marxism, in light of its economic functionalism and historical determinism, neglects the "affective, erotic attachment" that state formations harness in their subjects through rituals and other political technologies. This is particularly evident for Foucault in Marxism's description of Nazi Fascism as a repressive dictatorship; this definition, he observes, leaves out the enormous issue of power's seductiveness, of the relationship between state power, capitalism, and the desires of the masses. How is the state's grip on how people live—on how they govern themselves and others, on what they do to themselves and others—engendered?

This question is not something that Foucault ever believed to have completely figured out. Alessandro Fontana and Mauro Bertani comment that Foucault never wrote his definitive statement on power, and that he discussed the issue mainly in interviews and seminars, precisely because he felt that his research on the foundations of state never quite came together.[34] However, in his 1976 course at the Collège de France, *"Society Must Be Defended,"* Foucault does provide glimpses of an alternative (to) apparatus theory, one that recognizes the importance of mediation for state command and capitalist rule—as Althusser did—but parts ways with ideology critique's cognitivism. In so doing, he presents a theory of power that enmeshes state authority not with ideological apparatuses and persuasion but rather with the racialization of media and affects.

Foucault opens *"Society Must Be Defended"* by admitting he was experiencing an impasse. In the first session, he announces that he will use the seminar as an opportunity to pause on some problems that he has been working on for quite some time but that he still considers insufficiently elaborated. Foucault seems frustrated that his different research projects remain fragmentary, as if he were trying to piece together parts of a larger mechanism he could not quite figure out. Remarks on the birth of prisons and penal procedures and on the history of madness and psychiatric power, elements for a genealogy of modern sexuality, considerations on technologies of normalization and the treatment of the "abnormal": Foucault's local critiques and local attacks were couched in the larger context of the "insurrection of subjugated knowledges," a period in which intellectuals opposed the practices of medicine, psychiatry, criminology, and so forth by giving voice to systems of experience that official discourses disqualified as too naive or irrational to matter. The knowledge of the patient, of the prisoner: these were marginalized experiences that stood in opposition to state-sanctioned truths and their power effects. After all, Foucault suggests, we are destined to live and die in certain ways by the state's discourses and truths—so it made sense to oppose state government by invoking powerful counterdiscourses and countertruths about history, reality, and society.[35]

Why not go on like this? Why not keep accumulating fragments and raising localized challenges to established power-knowledge-affect networks? Because the political situation had changed, and the field of struggle no longer looked quite the same as before. *"Society Must Be Defended"* and Foucault's theorization of biopolitics come "after": after the 1960s, after the experience of antipsychiatry, after Foucault's involvement with prison liberation struggles, after the realization that racism did not end with decolonization and the civil rights movement, after the establishment in France of a conservative government resulting from the alliance between neoliberal capital and xenophobic factions of the Right. Amid intellectuals' commitment to enable a common front with the wretched of the earth, the people had embraced the counterrevolution and condoned even the most egregious forms of state violence. How could this happen? How had the state defeated the insurrection and secured the capitalist order? Foucault's dilemmas in *"Society Must Be Defended"* are the same raised by Gramsci after the defeat of the red biennium and the rise of Mussolini: Why do the people, even and especially the subaltern, side with the bosses, with those who have ruined them and are the "overseers of capitalist exploitation"?[36] Foucault had been working in the perspective that politics was war continued by other means. Now, in retreat, there was a need to review the battlefield, understand better the skirmishes at hand, so as to strategize more effective tactics of engagement. In suggesting that the racialization of sensibility that accompanied the birth of the great European nation-states in the early modern period is still the event one must contend with in order to confront sovereignty in the present, Foucault allows us to see that the war going on in society is a race war, and thus that the fundamental battle to take up is that against racism.

Commenting on the new world histories composed by French and English historians starting from the late sixteenth century, Foucault notes that the Europe of the time suddenly became populated by races no one had written about before. The Franks, the Gauls, the Celts, the Angles, and the Saxons: new peoples, new ancestors, new victors, and new vanquished appeared in memory, history, and reality. Foucault admonishes readers not to jump to conclusions and assume that these stories were "the sad brainchild of a few intellectuals who were indeed marginalized long ago," gloomy texts reaching only "nostalgic aristocrats or scholars in a library."[37] The new forms of historical imagination were quite popular, circulating not only among a declining aristocracy but also among the emerging bourgeoisie and humble people resentful of their abusive rulers. This historical discourse was not interested in judging the past but rather sought to revive the forgotten battles from which the order of the present had originated.

In telling their war tales, Edward Coke and John Lilburne in England or Henri de Boulainvilliers and Nicolas Fréret in France paired erudite knowledge of historical facts with mythological elements linked to different European ancestries—elements that Foucault characterizes as quite clumsy. And yet clumsiness should not be mistaken for ineffectiveness. These new histories of the past were generating new ways of experiencing the world; they were generating a society dominated by racial fears and racial allegiances so strong as to defy all other existing bonds and kinships.

The basic elements of European life (somatic, linguistic, and religious differences) were suddenly rewritten through the narrative frame of an army of opposing races, incompatible and distinct biospiritual organisms fighting each other for survival. Tales of the victories of the ancient giants; of the twilight of the gods; of invaders at the borders, or sleeper cells already present in the homeland; of the rights and privileges of the authentic national people being flouted by cunning invaders; mythologies of kings who were forgotten in inaccessible caves; of a plot to rekindle war and drive out the usurpers; of the monstrous other hiding among the innocent and of the armored knights who would come and save them: these discourses were appropriated by the new historians as building blocks to mediate a novel experience of the world. This was an experience of marginalization and bitterness, of terror, of conspiracy, but also an experience marked by a thirst for vengeance and the most extravagant expectations about the future. The discourse of history functioned thus, Foucault suggests, as a machine generating hopes and fears, attachments and resentments, as an apparatus where the anxiety over what and who was to come was intertwined with the longing for "the emperor of the last years, the *dux novus,* the new leader, the new guide, the new Führer; the idea of the fifth monarchy, the third empire or the Third Reich, the man who will be both the beast of the Apocalypse and the savior of the poor."[38]

Foucault's jump cut from the reinvention of race in seventeenth-century Europe to twentieth-century Nazi Fascism is extreme and has been rightly criticized for creating an implicit hierarchy of mass massacres, prioritizing one horrific manifestation of state racism over other abhorrent iterations of racial violence, such as slavery and settler or extractive colonialism.[39] Yet with this provocative gesture connecting the birth of modern Europe with what is usually perceived as the "worst" in Western history, Foucault flags something crucial: state racism is not the result of a sudden malaise that abruptly attacked the West but rather a possibility inscribed in the racialized imaginary and racializing affects that took over proto-capitalist and proto-colonial Europe.

In this regard, Ann Laura Stoler emphasizes that a key merit of Foucault's genealogies of biopolitics is that they confuted the scapegoat theory of race. Scapegoat theories imply that racism originates under economic and social distress. For Foucault, instead, racial violence is not the exception but the rule: "the expression of an underlying discourse of permanent social war" that is integral to nation-states in their entanglement with capitalist exploitation and colonial appropriation. In fact, the biopolitical state, the state that produces the sort of lives that racial capitalism requires, can only take root within an environment both framed and experienced as the strife between authentic and inauthentic heritages, between—to use Timothy Campbell's terminology—proper and improper lives.[40]

What, ultimately, does "biopolitics" name? Biopolitics does not refer to a strategy of government confined in time and space. Rather, it signals a particular form of relationality forged between the state and its subjects in a variety of geographical localities and historical realities. Although there are dramatic differences in the specific geohistorical iterations of biopolitics and in the forms of feeling that sustain them, one cannot ignore the consistent structural inscription of racial antagonism in the political systems and technologies of Western modernity. Notwithstanding prominent differences in strategy and modus operandi, the machines and interventions of modern state power are connected to one fundamental and unquestionable horizon of expectations: that the responsibility of the state, the task of politics, or the duty of the sovereign is to protect the authentic national people, the productive and docile subjects, by immunizing the community against presumed bioracial threats posed by internal or external enemies. But if states are intrinsically racial states, then national subjects are intrinsically racial subjects: they are the subjects whom state racism will defend against others and the subjects who will wage state racism against others.

Consequently, for Foucault the birth of modern statehood does not coincide with a glorious moment of pacification but with the inception of a new form of war. This war is not a war happening exclusively at the borders of the state, to protect the "natural" shape of the country. It is a war that takes place at the heart of the nation, to ensure the survival of the true people—of the right breed of body politic. At the origins of the great European nation-states, hence, there is no universalism, no ecumenism, whether religious, philosophical, or juridical. There is only a generalized and subterranean racism affording the full rights to live only to the bodies that contribute to sociopolitical reproduction. Indeed, as soon as the state is invested with the task of policing and protecting life, as soon as it becomes the broker of individual identities, the manager of bodily productive and reproductive forces, the state acquires the prerogative of discriminating, neutralizing, and suppressing all noncompliant modes of being a subject. As we read at the end of *"Society Must Be Defended,"* the fundamental truth under biopolitics, under contemporary state power, is that we are under attack and that everyone needs to do their part to make the nation healthier and the state stronger.

Before concrete biopolitical warfare and real biopolitical machines, there are accounts of a society in a state of siege. Before subjects who kill and die for the state, there is an impersonal horizon of social bellicosity. Before actual race wars, there are conspiracy theories and fake news about the threatening Other looming in. It is for this reason that in the time of biopolitics—which is our time—Foucault contends that truth cannot evade relationships of force and is deployed exclusively as a weapon, insofar as the announcement of the existential danger faced by society constitutes a call to arms that unifies, compacts, coalesces, and mobilizes.[41] What is under attack is not things but a way of life, not a territory but the population, and the people who receive the news about the impending threat are themselves crucial characters in the story being told: this is their history that is unfolding, and on their actions the future depends. Under biopolitics, the truth thus functions as a weapon because it conjures a reality where men and women ought to take a stance, claim a side of the race line, and fight for the survival of the authentic national people with whom they now identify.

Truth "est un plus de force," Foucault writes: truth is a supplementary force with its own specificity. The specific force of truth consists in its capacity to choreograph movements and emotions, to orchestrate affects and actions, to assimilate and redeploy. As it was for Friedrich Nietzsche, for Foucault "the truth" is something that has to do with the body, with experiences of subjugation and subjectification, with resentments and investments, rather than with the abstract realm of consciousness, persuasion, and consent. Accordingly, the force of true discourse is the force of a ritual: it is the force to fascinate, terrorize, and mobilize; the force to dazzle and to bind; the force to impose obligations on the living. It is the force to

make bodies feel. Ultimately, what is truth's audiovisual force to affect existences and capture them in racialized ways of seeing and talking if not
discourse's biopower—its power to form, inform, and reform life?

In this regard, it might indeed be a missed opportunity that still relatively few scholars have used Foucault's treatment of the affective thrust of
biopolitical truth-weapons to investigate audiovisual media's bearings on
our racial histories. In a still-relevant 2009 essay in *Screen,* Lee Grieveson
argues that ideology critique continues to dominate film and media studies precisely due to the field's lack of engagement with Foucault. A few
years later, Mark Hansen echoed Grieveson's conclusions, specifying that
Gilles Deleuze is to blame for the missed encounter between Foucault and
media scholarship as well as for apparatus theory's enduring prominence
in the exploration of audiovisual forms' impact on forms of identity and
subjectivity.[42]

In his "Postscript on the Societies of Control," Deleuze stressed how, in
a postdisciplinary universe, power invests the body beneath the level of
consciousness and interpellation, transforming the stable subjects produced
by the ideological apparatuses of the past into the fluid, flexible, divided,
and precarious beings of late capitalism. Hansen argues that Deleuze's
emphasis on the disappearance of the subject and the rise of bodies without identity might have contributed to foreclosing a possible path "from
Foucault's theorization of discipline to a media-theoretical appreciation for
his final work on governance and subjectification."[43] It is true, Deleuze's dismissal of subjectivity as a relevant category for reading the present favored
a cleavage in film and media research between the study of old media's
subjects and the study of new media's affects, between attention to structures of identity and attention to the body, between a focus on representation and a focus on the haptic—as if the only way of overcoming the
disembodied formal readings of apparatus theory consisted of chronicling
immediate bodily sensations. What remains to be fully considered regarding the affective turn in media scholarship field is how, by harnessing affects
and affecting bodies, language—including film language—also modulates
specific subject positions.

The situation has changed in significant ways since Grieveson's and
Hansen's reviews of the field. In a *Cinema Journal* essay from 2018, Hunter
Hargraves writes about a new generation of film and media scholars making
innovative arguments about embodied representation, tracing the relation
between the cinema's affects, its forms, and its politics in both historically

specific and speculative ways. Paola Bonifazio's *Schooling in Modernity* is to date the most generative contribution in this direction.[44] Influenced by Antonio Negri's analysis of information capitalism, Bonifazio traces how post–World War II Italian educational films eased the population into the forms of living most appropriate for the new geopolitical order and the concurrently burgeoning consumerist economy.

Throughout its analysis of the biopolitical dimension of educational cinema, *Schooling in Modernity* reads for history—the history of Italy, the history of Italian affects, the history of Italian identity, and the history of the nation's industrial apparatus. But it only cursorily reads for film form. Bonifazio's approach and mine differ in distance of reading in addition to treating a different set of archives. *Cinema Is the Strongest Weapon* couples cinema historiography with closer engagements with filmic texts to accentuate how, by means of its forms, the cinema affects the people and how this *formal force to affect* is paramount for grasping the apparatus's contribution to racialized identity politics and biopolitical warfare. Like Eugenie Brinkema's *The Forms of the Affects*, *Cinema Is the Strongest Weapon* is interested in recognizing the specific forms of affect that film forms afford.[45] But whereas Brinkema confines her analysis to the realm of filmic textuality, tentatively and provisionally I relate the forms of affect generated by cinema to extracinematic formations: to figures of Italian subjectivity, intimacy, sociality, history, and state racism.

The brilliance of apparatus theory—the wisdom of Comolli, Baudry, Laura Mulvey, Teresa de Lauretis, Kaja Silverman, and Stephen Heath— consisted in treating cinema simultaneously as a language *and* as a weapon, as art *and* power, as form *and* force. It is true that the way out of its impasses is not to divorce affectivity from formalism, signification, and mediation. But neither is it to retreat, as Brinkema does, into the realm of deconstruction and dismiss, in the name of "reading," the very legitimacy of twinning aesthetics and politics. Rather, in my view at least, the way out is to take seriously Foucault's conclusion that the modern subject of state biopower and of capitalist-colonial economy is a historical formation that emerges in the folds of racialized truths, media, and affects.

Remember that Foucault began *"Society Must Be Defended"* by asking what it meant that modern politics was the continuation of war by other means. He obliquely arrives at the conclusion that biopolitics, the fight to produce a compliant body politic, is the continuation of race wars through other political technologies. Yet given his own emphasis on the importance of truth regimes and practices of mediation for biopolitical command, might we also venture to conclude that politics is race war continued through other media?

Moving from the Gutenberg galaxy to the Lumière galaxy, from the media environment in which biopolitical sovereignty originated in early modern Europe to that where Fascism sprouted in the twentieth century, *Cinema Is the Strongest Weapon* ponders the cinematographic apparatus as a powerful affect-generating device that, by amplifying the sensation of an ongoing race war and conjuring ecofascist landscapes of community and belonging, played a crucial role in Mussolini's bid on Italy and Italians. But before addressing film's deployment as a tool of government under the regime, I take a step back to connect the weaponization of cinema as a technology to make and manage race in fascist Italy to prefascist discussions of the impact that the new medium could have in the new nation's existence.

In chapter 1, "The Government of the Ungovernable," I consider two early film novels—Gualtiero Fabbri's *Al Cinematografo* (*At the Movies*, 1907) and Luigi Pirandello's *Quaderni di Serafino Gubbio operatore* (*Shoot! The Notebooks of Serafino Gubbio, Cinematograph Operator*, 1915)—to show that already in liberal Italy, film started to be remediated into a political weapon that, by shooting (down) the wicked desires that were considered to be compromising the population's racial health, could save the country from the perceived threats of decay and self-annihilation. Through this genealogy, I establish that Fascism is not an unexpected disease that took over Italy but a phenomenon that has deep roots in Italian sociopolitical history. I further document how the imbrication of cinema and race is "structural" as it dates to the first years of the film in Italy. As a popular saying from the turn of the century promised, "Italy is made, now it is time to make Italians." It is precisely against the backdrop of this anxiety to fashion authentic national subjects, that is, racially appropriate Italians, that Fabbri's and Pirandello's novels stage cinema's power to remake lives.

Chapters 2, 3, and 4 examine representations of labor that characterize national film at the moment of its rebirth and beyond to explore how, by capturing Italians at work, directors such as Ruttmann, Blasetti, and Camerini endeavored to employ the nation in the regime's plans of social normalization and imperial expansion. Drawing upon Furio Jesi, Fredric Jameson, and Emmanuel Levinas, in this cluster I unpack the relationship between labor as a film subject and the subjectification of Italian labor to Fascism. Ruttmann's 1933 *Acciaio* (which was based on a scenario by Pirandello); Blasetti's *Sole!* (*Sun*, 1929), *Terra madre* (*Mother Land*, 1931), and *Vecchia guardia* (*Old Guard*, 1935); and Camerini's *Rotaie* (*Rails*, 1930), *Gli uomini che mascalzoni . . .* (*What Scoundrels Men Are!*, 1932), *Il signor Max* (*Mr. Max*, 1937), and *I grandi magazzini* (*Department Store*, 1939) are in fact all busy sanctioning hard work, (re)productivity, and obedience as core features of Italian racial identity, that is, of Blackshirt whiteness. Yet these films put to work different forms of affect, different film forms, to enable sociopolitical docility. Thus, in these chapters, I also map the contrasting audiovisual strategies and affective registers that Italian realism mobilized in support of fascist command.

Chapter 5, "The White Italian Mediterranean," moves from the Italian land to the sea surrounding the fascist ethno-nation to investigate how the paradigm through which national reality was rendered and fascist rule sustained changed in conjunction with Italy's entry into World War II. In earlier fascist realist films, the enemies of the Blackshirt race came from within, in the guise of either improper Italian desires or improper Italian Italians. Navy Captain Francesco De Robertis's *Uomini sul fondo* (*S.O.S Submarine*, 1940) and *La nave bianca* (*The White Ship*, 1941) by De Robertis and Rossellini instead pitch the danger as coming from without—amplifying by means of "corpo-realism" the embodied sensation of a body politic being choked to death, of an innocent but victimized Italian race that had to do whatever it took to protect itself against the threats lurking in Mediterranean waters. I demonstrate this precise way of feeling about Italy and the sea in the coda to this chapter through Rossellini's *Un pilota ritorna* (*A Pilot Returns*, 1942) and *L'uomo dalla croce* (*The Man with the Cross*, 1943), the perfect launching pad for what I describe as the regime's melodramatic imperialism.

Chapter 6 turns to the romantic comedies that Vittorio De Sica authored, with the crucial input of Italian Jewish playwright Aldo De Benedetti, under Fascism. These pre-neorealist, pre–Cesare Zavattini films by De Sica have been traditionally overlooked in postwar film criticism as juvenile concessions to the industry of mass distraction. But if the postwar assessment of these popular rom-coms is correct, why did Giuseppe De Santis—a filmmaker member of the underground Communist Party actively involved in the resistance against Mussolini—quite enthusiastically praise De Sica's seemingly frivolous genre fictions? Is there more to these rom-coms than—

possibly blinded by virtue of Bazin's pro-realist prejudices—we have been able to see? Taking my cue from Agamben's discussion of comedy as anti-disciplinarian register, in "De Sica's Genre Trouble," I rely on Henri Bergson and Walter Benjamin to show how laughter can be appropriated to fight sexism and racism, to challenge heteronormativity and the status quo.

In chapter 7, "Queer Antifascism," I reconstruct the ways in which *Ossessione* (*Obsession*, 1943)—the film that ensued from the collaboration between Luchino Visconti and the Communist cell that infiltrated the journal *Cinema*—brought together realism and melodrama to conjure the dramatic urgency of adopting "foreign" lifestyles in order for Italians to avoid more pain, more deaths. In the classic formula of Italian cinema, the conversion to the gendered norms of tradition is staged as the cure for a race in crisis. In *Ossessione,* on the contrary, redemption comes in the guise of a withdrawal from conventional sociosexual values, suggesting that in order to truly overcome a destructive present, the nation had to transcend the borders of heteronormativity and reproductive futurity.

Cinema Is the Strongest Weapon closes with a panoramic shot of liberated Italy, discussing the role that postwar national cinema played and might still play in foreclosing more transformative confrontations with what the regime was, why it took root in Italy, and how it ended. First, I highlight a shared component in Bazin's and Deleuze's treatments of neorealism— their emphasis on postwar Italian film as a liberation of cinema—as a revo-lutionary, antinarrative, speculative register that breaks away from the deceitful and inauthentic film forms of the past. Then, I suggest that neo-realism is still such a central reference in Italian cultural history precisely because its zero-degree aesthetic streamlines the convenient feeling of a nation at its year zero, of a redeemed, brutalized, and childlike people finally set free from fascist madness and ready to return to its real self, to go back to work. Fascism had been formally defeated; the exploitation of cinema as a key apparatus for governing our racial histories and racialized bodies was far from over.

Ultimately, then, this book tells the story of a struggle—the struggle between incompatible modes of capturing and projecting the truth about a nation, between alternative projects of national identity and belonging. What I hope emerges from this study is a theory of media that directly bears on our understanding of biopolitical command and of the fight against it, not only in fascist Italy. By reconstructing how the cinematographic appa-ratus amplified truths and affects that had a decisive bearing on national life, I aim to provide an insight on affective mediation as a crucial battlefield for racial capitalism, a sphere we need to survey with care in order to reckon with biopolitical states' ongoing endeavors to control who we are and how we are together—what we live for and what we die for.

A concern raised about Foucault's genealogies of biopolitics and state racism is that they might foreclose the possibility of resistance, as they stress power's capacity to redirect and assimilate even the most radical attacks on its authority. But by highlighting the primacy of the medial over the political, by showing that knowledge production happens in society and that the state can only reappropriate it, Foucault is far from negating resistance: on the contrary, he redefines its scale and space. For Foucault, we cannot start from the state to change society; we need to start from society to change the state. We need to start from what Foucault, through Deleuze, had dubbed the "minor," from the mediated affects in which we move and that move us, so as to effect new practices of care of the self and others.[46] Revisiting Mussolini's regime in the light of race management and biopolitical warfare, and biopolitics in the light of the fascist weaponization of media for governing the Italian race, *Cinema Is the Strongest Weapon* concludes that "to resist" entails mediating attachments and investments that could project us beyond the affective horizon undergirding modern sovereignty: that society is under attack from the racial enemy that comes from within and without, and that state power will help the people on the brink of extinction.

Therefore, this book shows, if we wish to prevent history from repeating itself, we need to challenge the racialized backdrop against which our national lives and histories unfold. This means taking up not only Donald Trump's or Giorgia Meloni's fascisms but also the "fascism in all of us," the racism in *our* affects and *our* media that are weaponized so easily for the worst.[47]

1 The Government of the Ungovernable

Race and Cinema in Early Italian Film Novels

In *Dialectic of Enlightenment*, Max Horkheimer and Theodor W. Adorno satirize the disappointment of a tourist who, arriving in Italy, discovers that the picture-perfect destination she was expecting exists only in the press and onscreen.[1] From the very first years of the Italian nation-state, Italians were made aware of an even more disappointing nonexistence: their own. The first mention I could find of Massimo d'Azeglio's apocryphal phrase "Fatta l'Italia, bisogna fare gli Italiani" (After making Italy, we must make Italians) dates to only six years after the foundation of the Kingdom of Italy (1861), and, since then, lamentations over the ungovernability of the Italian people—our resistance to becoming the right kind of subjects— have become a common refrain in national cultural history.

Examining the pervasiveness of tropes of incompleteness in Italian public discourse, Stephanie Malia Hom suggests that in many respects the country might still be working through the tension that defined its foundations.[2] At the origins of the Italian state lay, on the one hand, the ruling blocs' will to govern and their ambition to reorganize a recalcitrant population into a productive but docile body politic; and, on the other hand, their awareness of the challenges involved with transforming the Italian multitudes into their desired ordered assemblage. As a matter of fact, at the end of the unification wars, instead of celebrating the end of a long liberation process and the birth of a new era in Italy's history, the classes in power found themselves unhinged by the realization that the battle to control the territory and pacify the population was far from over. Amid these concerns about the state of the nation, Suzanne Stewart-Steinberg shows, postunification Italian literature made crucial contributions to elaborating the body as the key site to act upon for disciplining a people that were imagined to exist in a dysfunctional state of perpetual childishness, akin to the allegorical figure of Pinocchio.[3] Following the Lumière brothers' tour of Italy in 1899, cinema as well was involved in these discussions: could this wondrous new technology contribute in some way to the urgent and complicated effort of making functional Italians?

In this chapter, by examining Gualtiero Fabbri's *Al Cinematografo* and Luigi Pirandello's *Quaderni di Serafino Gubbio operatore*, literally "At the movies" and "Notebooks of Serafino Gubbio camera operator," respectively, I document how early twentieth-century film culture amplified racialized anxieties about Italy's social health but also built up the usefulness of film in a context of national disjointedness and sociopolitical volatility.[4] Pairing a frustration with liberal Italy with an investment in the cinema as an apparatus that—through its capacity to generate new feelings and desires in the population—might finally conjure a proper body politic, Fabbri's and Pirandello's novels stage the new medium's power to affect national life and, in so doing, prepare its subsequent deployment as a weapon to make and manage race under Mussolini. The point here is not to "denounce" as racist or para-fascist Italian postunification, prefascist film culture, but to show that from the very first years of Italian cinema, articulating the apparatus's relation with individual and collective existence also meant tracking its imbrication with racial matters. Since, as Aaron Gillette and Shelleen Greene trace, in early twentieth-century Italy, behavior was understood as a manifestation of race, the very project of making Italians was intrinsically a racial enterprise.[5] By making film interface with this project, Fabbri and Pirandello could not avoid involving the apparatus with the changing racialized imaginaries of the time.

REMEDIATING THE APPARATUS:
FABBRI'S *AL CINEMATOGRAFO* (1907)

Italian film production started picking up the pace immediately after the Lumière brothers' tour of the country; it seized a prominent position on the world market in a few short years. This situation has always puzzled historians. How does one explain the fact that a late and marginal cinema managed to grow so quickly and play such a critical role in the global history of film? For Luca Giuliani, the incredible success of Italian film was determined—counterintuitively, if compared to what happened in France or the United States—by the outdated technologies, lack of regulations, poor funding, disinterest from the state, and industrial disorganization. As often happens in the Global South, "poverty" in Italy was not a limitation but a resource, fostering a sort of do-it-yourself (DIY) mentality that brought about a generative horizon of experimentation and innovation.[6]

But it was not only film production that was characterized by an incredible liveliness. As soon as a film industry started to materialize in Italy, there emerged in public debate the urgency to norm the cinema, define a proper use of the camera, and articulate the medium's specificities vis-à-vis other technologies and diversions. Writers started to make references to the motion pictures in their works, a variegated host of popular and scholarly film journals appeared, and newspapers were keen to feature think pieces on the cinema as well. No other country could boast a comparable early paratextual investment in thinking film, John Welle observes. The first article on the new medium, "La filosofia del cinematografo" (The philosophy of cinema), was published by a well-known intellectual, Giovanni Papini, in a well-read newspaper, *La stampa,* in 1907. That year also saw the release of *Al Cinematografo,* which might be the first example in world literature of what Gavriel Moses defines as the film novel, a subgenre of speculative fiction in which the "repercussions of this new twentieth-century medium are explored through the means of narrative."[7]

Al Cinematografo is the result of the encounter between two eccentric, forgotten players in the formative years of Italian film: Pietro Tonini and Gualtiero Fabbri. Tonini was a prominent distributor and the owner of a state-of-the-art movie theater in Milan, the Marconi. He was a tireless promoter of the cinema, and of his cinema most of all. We know, for instance, that Tonini set up an automatic shoeshine in the waiting room of the Marconi and gave portable barometers to spectators so they could plan their next movie outing according to the weather. In 1907, Tonini launched a literary contest to publish a novella that would rebrand the motion pictures in the public sphere, dispelling the prejudices surrounding this new form of entertainment. Gualtiero Fabbri's text was judged as the most apt to showcase cinema's respectability—to demonstrate that it was not merely a leisure appropriate for the lower people but also appealing for "the more evolved social class," as Tonini writes in the preface to *Al Cinematografo,* using the hierarchizing language of evolutionary biology to mark class differences.[8]

Fabbri, a writer, historian, polemist, and traveling preacher for the Methodist Episcopal Church, was from Bologna. After authoring *Al Cinematografo*, Fabbri, a firm believer in the educational value of film, went on to become one of the few Italian film theorists whose influence extended beyond national borders. In his history of Russian film, Jay Leyda mentions that for the whole silent era, international production companies relied heavily on Fabbri's 1910 "rules for the perfect screenplay."[9] Fabbri continued to be an important voice throughout the 1910s, and in 1923 he received an honorary doctorate from the University of Los Angeles. He died in 1929 in a convent in southern Italy, where he had retired after converting to Catholicism.

We owe the bulk of our information about Tonini and Fabbri to the invaluable research of Sergio Raffaelli, who in the 1990s rediscovered *Al Cinematografo* and curated the reprint of the work that "ushered cinema into literature."[10] After selling more than forty thousand copies thanks to Tonini's promotional efforts, the novella sank quickly into oblivion. This is not surprising. From a literary point of view, *Al Cinematografo* is forgettable. But where the text's artistic merits are slim, its documentary value is remarkable. With its frequent and verbose descriptive sections—attributed by Raffaelli to Tonini—*Al Cinematografo* is a time capsule bringing us back to the invention of Italian cinema. The novella often reads as reportage: of the changing patterns of mass consumption, of the plots of the most successful films of the time, of the movie-going experience, of the composition of the public, and even of the formulas used by ushers to lure passersby into their venues. But this text does more than merely shed light on the realities of early film exhibition. It also attests to an emerging regime of power-knowledge-affect about the apparatus that would become engrained in national film culture and practice until, at least, neorealism. If, as Francesco Casetti argues, cinema is the privileged technology for mediating modern experience, one cannot overlook the fact that modern experience in Italy is an experience marked by racialized anxieties about the state of the nation.[11] By speculating on the technology of cinema, *Al Cinematografo* thus also articulates how the new medium could resolve the racial problems that were supposedly afflicting Italy.

In transitional moments in media history, new technologies of mediation establish their legitimacy by articulating how they refashion, ameliorate, and overcome older apparatuses. This is a dynamic that Jay David Bolter and Richard Grusin call "remediation."[12] Remediation, they explain, is the way in which one medium presents itself—or is presented—as re-forming or improving upon another. Remediation can be understood as a process of cultural negotiation where the affordances of a new technology are adjudicated by juxtaposing it with previous media. Bolter and Grusin focus on the claims to authenticity that new media advance. However, some forms of remediation are focused not on measuring a new technology's capacity to reproduce reality but on assessing its power to change it. In the case of *Al Cinematografo,* cinema is remediated as a generative apparatus that, unlike the sterile attractions from the nineteenth century, can resolve collective existence and birth healthier national subjects.

To promote cinema's social benefits, *Al Cinematografo* features the first time at the movies of Gastone Fedi, a card player and theater critic who is accustomed to enjoying the frivolous lifestyle of a member of high society. Fedi is not a bad person; he simply has yet to find his path in life. Like a host of characters from turn-of-the-century Italian literature, Fedi exists in the balance between failure and success, redemption and perdition, "absolute virtue and absolute vice."[13] He is particularly irresolute the evening we meet him. Bored out of his mind and experiencing a sort of midlife crisis, Fedi is reviewing his options for the night—assembling a sort of atlas of the emotions and entertainments the city offers. He could go to the social club to play cards, but people are quite immature there. The theater, with its trite stories and overblown passions, is not appealing to him. Fedi could join a salon, but gatherings at private houses are dull, and they are only good for arranging marriages of convenience. Similar to what happens in cosmoramas, Fedi comments, there is a lot to see, but things get boring pretty quickly. Cafés do not work either because the environment there is degenerate and loathsome and fake. Brothels are expensive, and besides, after his fair number of encounters with seamstresses and vedettes, Fedi has had enough of this kind of woman and sets his sights on someone of "nobler stature" (22). The public night classes offered by the local university are worthless, so there is no point in attending them. Since it is still too early to go to bed, one could always stay out and embrace the experience of getting lost in the busy streets. As a matter of fact, Fedi is quite fond of the spectacle of the crowd flowing through the city at night, under the moonlike light of colossal electric lamps. But he also likens the human maelstrom to something out of Dante Alighieri's *Inferno,* and—unlike Charles Baudelaire's *flâneurs*—Fedi fears getting mixed up in such bedlam. Walking the city in desperate need of "something new" (14), Fedi stumbles into one of the movie halls that have been becoming increasingly popular in Italy.[14]

Should he cross the threshold? Fedi hesitates. Cinema might not be an appropriate venue for someone of his rank. A providential vision evaporates all doubts: a heavenly creature, "a blonde Virgin Mary" (18) entering the theater. The young woman feels like a ray of sun in the dark, cold city night. This fair-skinned and blue-eyed apparition is named Olga, and she is at the movies with her little brother, maid, and grandfather—a man whom Fedi had already singled out in the crowd for his wise gray beard, noble demeanor, and elongated, very symmetrical face. What makes Olga so attractive and her grandfather so dignified is evidently their whiteness. Without much subtlety, *Al Cinematografo* colors them as Nordic: Olga is an old Scandinavian name meaning "saint," and Fabbri's description of her and her grandfather is strewn with physiognomic markers associated with tropes of Aryan whiteness and racial superiority, including skin tone, eyes, and hair but also cranial morphology. Fedi finds comfort in the fact that elite Italians of such noble stock, and not only the "popolino" (populace) and the less evolved classes, appreciate film; thus, in search of new stimuli and experiences, he decides to follow Olga and her family inside. A new world opens up to his sight. Fabbri exploits the narrative device of Fedi's discovery of the movies as an occasion to stage, but also sell, cinema.

The first thing that *Al Cinematografo* takes notice of is the stark contrast between the Italians who go to the movies and the ones who do not, between the ordered public attending the cinema and the disordered multitude swarming the city. Outside there is confusion, anonymity, and darkness, but in the movie hall shines a collection of respectable shapes and faces—a humanity that is diverse in its composition and yet peacefully shares a place and an experience (18). As he steps into the movie hall, Fedi cannot tell whether he is among the upper, middle, or lower classes; he is simply among the people and feels connected to each and all of them. There are humble clerks, young professionals, refined retirees, city dwellers and visitors from the countryside, workers and industrialists, soldiers, army officers, and policemen. Whereas the salon, the club, and the café are segregated spaces accessible only to certain segments of the population, the movies welcome all honest people, regardless of their background. Moreover, picture houses abolish the architectural separation between classes enforced in Italian stage theaters.

This sense of commonality has beneficial effects on the nation as a whole, *Al Cinematografo* explains, as it facilitates a feeling of unity. However, at the movies, people not only learn to be together; they also learn from each other. The prolonged interaction with the bourgeoisie and aristocracy instills in the less civil social strata a keener sense of moderation: one of the virtues of the cinematographic milieu is to suppress obscene gestures and profanity. At the same time, the presence of commoners transmits some bodily vitality to the higher classes and pushes them toward more relaxed mores. A couple from the countryside, for example, is kissing in the dark, but no one minds as long as they control themselves. The cinema audience is quite evolved, the novella approvingly concludes by means of Fedi's reflections. Such liberality renders the movie theater a stimulating place that nevertheless shuns excesses. There is a lively exchange between age groups, genders, and classes, yet no one at the end oversteps. This is also the case because films put people in their place.

After insisting on the movie theater as a transformative space that allows the nation to assemble, *Al Cinematografo* turns to featuring the specific improvements film inspires in the spectators. Whereas Fabbri relies on Fedi to show that, at the movies, the multiform Italian body politic gathers, he resorts to Professor Giusti, Olga's grandfather, to unpack for Fedi—and thus for the reader—the beneficial impact that the forms flickering on the screen have on modern living. Again, the articulation of film's power to affect life is carried out through a comparison with the theater. The first thing that Fedi needs to keep in mind, Giusti insists, is that films make a more profound and lasting impression on the public than plays. Giusti takes the example of Valparaiso: the Chilean city made the very wise decision to program public screenings of highly moral films, and after only one week of projections the city enjoyed a sharp decrease in crime, drunkenness, and loitering. The Italian government should take notice of cinema's power to change lives and, Giusti proposes, fully integrate this incredible new technology in its school system.

Guido Cincotti has emphasized that Italian film was born under the sign of the Risorgimento, in the sense that domestic cinema took hold within the context of an ongoing struggle for unity.[15] Giusti's reference to film's deployment as a tool of reeducation in another newly independent country like Chile implicitly situates the cinema against the backdrop of new states' nation-building efforts. But the imbrication of the cinematographic apparatus with the Risorgimento's project becomes fully manifest in *Al Cinematografo* when people are ushered into the movie hall and the lights go out.

The screen is filled with Filoteo Alberini's *La presa di Roma* (*The Capture of Rome*, 1905)—the first feature film produced in Italy, an epic reenactment of the 1870 annexation of Rome that was originally screened for an audience of thousands outdoors, next to the widely mythologized point of entry of the Italian Royal Army into the city still ruled by the Church.[16] The spectators, Fedi expounds, are stunned as the mythic heroes of the battle of Porta Pia appear, larger than life, before them. When the liberation army begins its final assault against the papal army, chanting "long live Italy, long live Rome," the emotion is pulled to a fever pitch. Fedi cannot stay still or silent. He is in awe. He explodes: "For goodness' sake, this is a patriotic spectacle, moral and educational par excellence" (27). His heart is throbbing with national pride. In this regard, it is important to highlight that Professor Giusti likens the effects of the cinema on a national people still in its early years to those of Edmondo De Amicis's patriotic young adult book *Cuore* (*Heart*, 1866). The reference to De Amicis's best seller, a keystone of Italian postunification culture, accomplishes two goals. First, it reiterates the effort to promote the cinema as a governmental technology capable of bringing together a people whom the Kingdom of Italy and its liberal elites had failed to unite. Second, the allusion clarifies that the labor of cinematic subjectification is performed rhetorically and affectively, by moving souls and modulating regimes of embodiment via discursive forms. In fact, *Cuore* constitutes the most blatant example of a nation-building effort advanced by working the people's bodies rather than relying on "juridically binding formulations of citizenship," as happened in other national contexts.[17] In *Al Cinematografo*, as in *Cuore*, emotivity is "regenerative and redemptive" (39); the transformation of the people starts from touching their hearts.

Yet films touch spectators in different ways; they trigger a variegated array of feelings. The films in the program in *Al Cinematografo* thereby become occasions to clarify how the different *genres* of the cinema affect the people and thus regenerate the nation. Giusti prizes social melodramas as especially beneficial for the collectivity: French films such as *The Strike* (1904), *The Poor Mother* (1906), or *The Good Judge* (1906) teach, through tears, the value of moderation and collaboration between classes, preventing social conflicts from erupting into violence. Documentaries expand people's horizons by introducing them to foreign realities, as happens in the case of the extraordinary film capturing the efforts of "one white hunter and thirty negroes" to hunt down hippos along the Zambezi River in the "Black continent" (50). Historical reenactments, like the film about Venetian history titled *Canal grande,* excite spectators' national pride; a crime film like *The Wreckers of the Limited Express* (1906) offers a moving example of heroism; comedies make one laugh while also imparting moral lessons—as Giusti argues while introducing to Fedi another French movie, *The Hen That Laid the Golden Eggs* (1905).

A powerful confirmation of cinema's power to redeem life comes with the last film in the program in *Al Cinematografo.* With its celestial soundscape, the religious parable *The Birth of Jesus* (1906) guides the public toward pure love and authentic good, as Giusti articulates to Fedi. And in the case of the young bon vivant, pure love and authentic good coincide with doing one's own part for Italy's future: put down roots, start a family, procreate an elite lineage. Inspired by Jesus's self-sacrifice for the collectivity, Fedi—who was once an unabashed bachelor and enjoyed the presence of lesser women—promises eternal love to Olga, such a perfect white beauty, and kisses her "ardentemente" (passionately) on the forehead (78). The cinema is indeed, to paraphrase Fedi, a place where unbelievable emotions and ineffable experiences are orchestrated.

The problem is that film cannot touch everyone; there are individuals that it simply cannot regenerate or save. We already know that the city is a dangerous place. At the beginning of *Al Cinematografo,* an older lady has her wallet stolen steps away from the cinema's entrance. Later, a gang of thugs assaults Fedi and the Giusti family as they walk home after their night out. Fedi had noticed and confronted this group earlier that evening. Taking advantage of the darkness, they were molesting Italian women—Olga included—and harassing them with all sorts of indecent proposals. Fedi intervened and kicked them out of the theater. In reviewing their aspect, attitude, and demeanor, *Al Cinematografo* characterizes this group of unrestrained Italians who do not belong at the movies as a different breed of subjects threatening the smooth reproduction of authentic national life. Fabbri profiles these other Italians as a "genìa" (45)—genus, lineage, or ethnicity—whose deviation from national norms is materialized in their primitive fashion choices. Fabbri stresses that they style themselves *"alla bula"* (45), a mysterious locution that I believe constitutes a derogatory reference to the costumes of the Bula people of South Sudan. In fact, in *La mala vita a Roma,* a fascinating 1897 first-person dramatized ethnology of

Rome's underground ("mala vita" literally means bad life, and by extension organized crime), Alfredo Niceforo and Scipio Sighele use the expression *alla bula* to flag the backward, primitive, and pathologically hypersexualized codes of conduct adopted by the Italian capital's masses.[18]

Niceforo and Sighele were among the most prominent supporters of Nordic Aryanism in Italy. In *La mala vita a Roma*, which was dedicated to Cesare Lombroso, they insist on the need to understand what they present as the Italian masses' abject behaviors through a bioracial lens. They explain eagerly that segments of the "popolino," a term also used by Fabbri, had not yet gone through all the stages of cultural evolution and were stuck in a condition of quasi-feral instinctiveness. In line with Lombroso's criminology, they attribute this delay to the racial divide imagined to be running through the nation. Whereas the white Aryan stock prevalent in the North had progressed to rational behavior and moderation, those of Mediterranean ethnicity had been spoiled by the sun and centuries of contact with Africa and the East, with Hamitic and Semitic blood. Niceforo and Sighele, who like Lombroso were socialists, argued that it was urgent to civilize these other Italians, to heal the problems that their laziness and vice had brought upon the country. Otherwise, Italy would remain "unified but not united" and decay even further.

To resolve the uneven development that kept Italians apart from one another, *La mala vita a Roma* did not plead for structural investments that would ameliorate the living and working conditions of the masses. It did not ask for opportunities or schools to reduce crime; it did not support a redistribution of wealth. It instead entreated the Italian state to ramp up its medical-penal apparatus and create institutions where Italy's natural-born criminals could be either reformed or contained until their deaths—until they changed or vanished, as the book's ending dramatically puts it. Unlike hard-core Aryanist theories, Italian racial science under liberalism recognized the possibility of relative improvement even in individuals from presumed inferior breeds, such as southerners or Semites, on the condition that they assimilated the Italian spirit.

I pause on *La mala vita a Roma* because this intervention—juxtaposing the Risorgimento call to unify the people and Lombroso's racist science—challenges the "color-blindness" through which prefascist Italian political history has been written and showcases the central place occupied by race in the postunification project to remake Italians that I have already touched on. As Miguel Mellino, among others, reconstruct, Italian state racism did not start in 1938, with Fascism's racial laws.[19] It had already been implicated in the process of so-called national rebirth carried out by the House of Savoy and hegemonic ruling blocs. In aligning cinema with the elites' ideology, in branding the cinema as a Risorgimental media weapon, Fabbri could not help but embrace the racial capitalist project and "civilizing mission" discourse upon which Italian unification was undergirded. On the one hand, *Al Cinematografo* medicalizes delinquency and connects it with a specific genus of people: the race that remains, the remnants of a time and a world past that, whenever possible, need to be redressed to grant them the great opportunity of contributing to modern Italian life. On the other hand, the novella remediates the cinema as an apparatus that, similar to the medico-penal institutions of *La mala vita a Roma,* could save some of this stock from their natural unruliness and harvest them as labor: if it had been possible to turn the "negroes" from the Black continent into bodies in service of white pursuits, why couldn't the same result be achieved with Italy's own quasi-Black savages?

Describing the workings of biopower under racial capitalism, Ann Laura Stoler emphasizes the stratified operations of governance characterizing the capitalist-colonial order.[20] White bourgeois individuals are trained to reproduce the social order, while the underclass—racialized as backward—is disciplined to produce economic wealth. *Al Cinematografo* ends with a similar class-, race-, and gender-specific conversion.

Outside the cinema, the dysgenic "genìa" that Fedi kicked out of the theater tries to take their revenge. The un-Italian group has organized Olga's kidnapping and rape. In a dark alley, the underdeveloped breed of Italians attempts to neutralize Fedi and Giusti to have Olga for themselves. Fedi fights back with his knuckleduster and then draws the pistol he always carries for protection, given the armies of thugs endangering modern Italy. He is about to shoot when another weapon intervenes to exorcise the specter of race mixing and miscegenation: a young man comes out of the cinema and commands the gang to leave. He is their former leader, who has had a change of heart thanks to the movies. *The Poor Mother* made such an impression on him that he could not go on with the same existence; he had to become a different person. Now, he can finally emerge from the underworld and leave behind his primitive customs. The cinema has imparted on the young thug the idea that the way forward in life is work rather than crime: the cinematographic apparatus has brought him "from bad to good living" (63), and an honest job will allow him to evolve from undeveloped lowlife to national resource. It is a process of whitening through work that Fabbri articulates.

But film has also made Fedi renounce his own rogue living in favor of marriage to Olga and fathering a family. These two men from distinct socio-economic backgrounds and with very different racial profiles were stuck in unproductive, abject lifestyles, but thanks to the movies, they embrace healthy forms of existence. Those whom the cinema cannot reform or cure, those whom the cinema cannot reclaim or civilize, end up embroiled with the other great modern apparatuses of normalization and social control. From Professor Giusti we learn that the gang members will end up in jail or committed to a mental ward under the care of a good phrenologist. For their kind, there is not much hope. But for the people who are moved by cinema, for the folks who can live good, proper lives, it is time to go to discuss the details of the wedding and dowry at Giusti's house. The Italian dreams of a peaceful home and homeland are coming true, thanks to cinema's power to change people.

One of the last films viewed by this nice Italian family before they go home is *Trains of America,* a documentary feature about the U.S. railroad system. In *Trains of America,* we see modernity, we see speed, we see the majesty of the trains, these mechanical snakes running at full speed and "huge huge huge" (67) on the metallic tracks. We also see elegant, comfortable interiors and perfected class/race relations. Earlier, Fabbri had voiced a great deal of appreciation for the zeal with which thirty Black men served the white explorer on his African hunting trips. Now, *Al Cinematografo* marvels at the industry showcased by the Black servant on the train who cares for the refined white travelers.

> Every five minutes, the adorable *moretto* [dark-haired boy], making less noise than a mouse, comes and offers passengers candies, perfumes, books, newspaper, cigars, drops, photographs, maps, fruit, knick-knacks, and so forth. He leaves them there for you, on the ample, comfortable red-velvet couch without proffering a word. If one wants to buy something, that's good; otherwise, he collects his stuff, without insisting, always silent, and goodnight! He goes away, to come back in a bit, of course. (69)

Gramsci famously characterized liberal rule in Italy as a case of internal colonialism, where the lower classes were racialized as inferior, infantilized, and maintained in a condition of quasi-forced labor to serve the demands of a capitalist bloc that was ramping up its colonial ambitions.[21] It is thus unsurprising that the segregated United States—the land of technological progress, opulence, and strict color lines—is hailed as a model of civility in *Al Cinematografo*. In the United States, Fedi and Giusti recognize not only the type of nation Italy ought to become—modern, efficient, and rich— but also the kind of workers the homeland needed to achieve such an aspirational whiteness: affable, meek, and silent, creatures that, like *moretti* and mice, can be disposed of when their presence becomes a nuisance.

BARBARIC INVASIONS: PIRANDELLO'S
QUADERNI DI SERAFINO GUBBIO OPERATORE (1915)

Whereas 1907's *Al Cinematografo* branded the movie theater as a kind of heterotopia, a space where the normal flow of existence is suspended and healthier national bodies are styled, nearly a decade later in *Quaderni di Serafino Gubbio operatore* there are no substantial differences between the forms of life that the motion pictures elicit and the degraded existences that people already endure. Fabbri built up film as a security apparatus to be deployed in the battle to control, redress, and put to work both the elites (Fedi) and the unevolved Italian *genia* (those who dressed and behaved like members of the "primitive" Bula tribe). Pirandello instead approaches the camera—"macchina da presa" in Italian, that is, the machine that captures—as a synecdoche conjuring the ruined state in which industrial capitalism under liberal rule has trapped the people. Historian Philip Cannistraro posits that Italian liberalism and Italian cinema underwent simultaneous crises in the 1910s.[22] Pirandello's fictional notebooks of a resentful cameraman evoke the entanglement of these two crises, raising the alarm about the "stench" permeating the liberal nation and taking stock of a film industry whose melodramatic scenarios and operatic affectations did nothing but accelerate the disintegration of a people that had never really come together.[23] Pirandello's scathing take on liberal Italy and its (film) culture was not an isolated case.

Italy's economic growth at the beginning of the twentieth century had allowed the ruling parties to temporally reconcile the opposing interests of various social factions, fostering a situation of relative national peace after the turn-of-the-century turmoil. However, the slowing down of the economy in the 1910s and Italy's entrance into World War I put a definitive end to Prime Minister Giovanni Giolitti's aspiration to broker a peace between capital and labor, or—according to the liberal racial order—between the white elites and the darker masses. The sense of a lack of cohesion and purpose in national life intensified. The *mala vita*—which in Niceforo and Sighele's 1897 study appeared confined to bigger Italian cities—was perceived as a pandemic fifteen years later. However, unlike before, Italy's ruination was not considered the population's fault; it was the state's failure to properly govern Italians that had led to this. Giolitti was dubbed the "ministro della *mala vita*" (the minister of bad living, of the underworld) by socialist politicians, and liberal governance was faulted for failing to impress a clear direction on national life, leaving it at the mercy of a tardy second industrial revolution and doing nothing to remedy the social fragmentation brought about by it.[24]

In this context of antiliberal resentment, a form of "antiracist racism" —as Fabrizio De Donno aptly calls it—took hold of public imagination.[25] This new racial paradigm did not contest the fact that there were two species of humans dwelling in Italy, but it inverted the traditional and hegemonic hierarchies between these distinct stocks. Giuseppe Sergi was the most authoritative voice in the protest against liberalism's racialized geopolitics and the assumption that white people, Italian elites included, were better than darker and southern folks. Bringing together skeletal morphology with paleology and archaeology, in foundational texts from the end of the nineteenth century like *Origine e diffusione della stirpe mediterranea* (*The Mediterranean Race: A Study of the Origin of European Peoples*) or *Arii e Italici* (*Aryans and Italics*), Sergi advanced the argument that Western civilization and culture were not birthed in the North by Aryans but in the Mediterranean by "olive" races like the Italic stock (*stirpe*).[26] Simultaneously anti-Black, anti-white, and anti-Asian, Sergi was careful to specify that this olive race did not originate from a mixing of the inferior Black, white, and Eastern races but was a pure and original racial aggregate. Moreover, he pontificated that science proved that before having been civilized by Rome and before contact with Mediterranean culture, the white North was a land of barbarians living in semiferal conditions—so a space that was not much different from Black Africa.

But if this were true, in light of the racial superiority exhibited by non-white, non-Black Mediterranean nations and the Italic lineage especially, how did one account for the current ruination that afflicted the olive-skinned stock? Why, Sergi asked, was the finest race that has appeared in Europe experiencing such decline in the present, to the point that, after millennia of glory and beauty, it was compared to Africa and ruled by the descendants of the barbarians who had invaded the peninsula in the Early Middle Ages? Sergi's answer was that while Aryans (like pack animals) are naturally disposed to order and discipline, there is something excessive in the Mediterranean race—an energy, a creativity, a spontaneity, an individualism, a taste for freedom and for experimentation—that was a blessing but also could become a curse. When this natural excessiveness is not mitigated and held in check, as it was not in liberal Italy, it favors chaos and anarchy instead of revolutions in the arts, sciences, and culture. Industrialization acted as a sort of catalyst for the natural unruliness that characterized Italians. Thus, Sergi advised, it was urgent to restrain them through racially appropriate cultural forms and policy interventions, before the sort of autoimmune logic governing the Mediterranean specimens brought the Italian breed to self-extinction.

Can we find resonances with Sergi's racialized antiliberalism and his ideas on race-making in Pirandello's *Quaderni di Serafino Gubbio operatore*? Doesn't this early film novel articulate cinema as an apparatus that could restrain the excesses of Italian humanity and hence contribute to the reordering of national life that Sergi, among many others, advised to be so crucial and critical?

Quaderni has been discussed at length. Scholarship has reviewed in depth and with precision the resonances between its take on mechanical reproduction and the stances on the apparatus later elaborated by Benjamin, Zavattini, Bazin, Baudry, Dziga Vertov, and Siegfried Kracauer.[27] Most discussions, however, overlook the situation out of which his fictional notebooks grew and thus miss the implicit political reverberations of Pirandello's intervention. In this regard, Fiora Bassanese highlights the three-fold dimension of *Quaderni*: it is at once an exemplary tale of the destructive mechanization of modern life, a depiction of an Italian cinema and its odd denizens in crisis, and a nostalgic take on preindustrial Italy.[28] Building upon this analysis, I consider how the different textual layers of this film novel interface, so as to relate its intertwined expectations for new cinematic forms and new forms of Italian living with concurrent phantasies of racial rebirth that challenged liberal rule and paved the way for the fascist putsch.

The protagonist and narrator of *Quaderni* is Serafino Gubbio, a troubled man and the most highly skilled cameraman at Kosmograph, a big production house in Rome. Growing up, Gubbio wanted to study humanities and philosophy. However, his family pushed him toward technical studies and thus he moved to Liège, Belgium, to become better acquainted "with all the machines invented by man for his own happiness" (32). This move is not the beginning of a process of enrichment for Gubbio. On the contrary, in line with antimodern and anti-Nordic sentiments, the sojourn in one of the centers of the European industrial apparatus has devastating effects on Gubbio, to the point that he eventually loses contact with reality and the people around him. Back in the southern Italy of his origin, Gubbio squanders an inheritance and then drifts to Rome. There, Gubbio begrudgingly finds a job but still has no stable attachments or relationships. Gubbio insists he does not mind this solitude, which he paints as a choice. But it is clear even from the beginning of *Quaderni* that Gubbio hails from a position of disappointment, resentment, and frustration—deluding himself that his isolation is a blessing in disguise, a refuge keeping him safe from further disappointments, especially with women. Unable to admit his own unhappiness, Gubbio gloats about how his disinterest in worldly things has trained him to become a master of mechanical reproduction.

Gubbio's impassibility—we learn from his diaries—has allowed him to dominate the cinematographic apparatus to the point that he can accurately modulate the shutter speed of his camera to match the pace at which a scene unfolds before him. Alas, such a remarkable talent is wasted at Kosmograph. The films he is forced to shoot to make a living, Gubbio laments, follow the blueprint that made the fortune of silent Italian cinema: exotic settings, lavish productions, operatic passions, unrealistic plotlines, stylized characters, a penchant for melodrama, and overblown rhetoric. But Gubbio's reservations about film production in liberal Italy are not exclusively a matter of style.

In Gubbio's eyes, the aesthetic and narrative features of current national cinema are actually contributing to Italy's disaggregation by feeding the public's addiction to cheap attractions. Aroused by films and the other attractions of modern times, people move frantically and relentlessly from one activity to the next, from one distraction to another. The excessive and unbound character of the Italian people that Sergi warned about appears in *Quaderni* to be out of control, unleashed by the power of industrialization to melt all traditional cultural forms and social norms into air. The consequence of "the mechanical framework of the life which keeps us clamorously and dizzily occupied" (4) is a constant, trancelike state wherein one is always preoccupied by what one can do next, by the latest new experience to enjoy. Using a category from Sianne Ngai, one could say that the affect characterizing Pirandello's representation of Italian life under liberal capitalism is zaniness: the unrelenting and destructive desire of nonstop acting and doing that disregards the unsustainability of this ethos of living.[29]

In *Quaderni,* Italians are manic but exhausted, hyperactive but dull, hysterical but apathetic. The situation is not yet as dramatic as it is in the United States, where, Gubbio warns, citizens drop dead while carrying on their everyday business, but Italy is getting there quickly. We notice again here a reversal of values vis-à-vis the terms of Fabbri's *Al Cinematografo.* The United States and the "North" more broadly no longer represent a model but rather a token of the future of death and disaggregation that the nation will experience if the body politic does not reform its ways. The machines in *Quaderni* are not native to Italy but come from the United States, Germany, and France to corrupt the population, putting a whole nation out of joint. Even language is under threat. Gubbio grouses that Italians don't speak Italian anymore, and one is surrounded everywhere by foreign words. Creativity has been replaced by the passive internalization of foreign life patterns that merely reflect the urgencies of the cycles of production and consumption. The invasion of foreignness in the text coincides with a return to barbarism. *Quaderni* characterizes this becoming-modern as a regression that has led Italy to drift away from its history and catapulted the people into a different time-space, a dystopic future with no gods, no poets, no ideals, no language of Dante, only mechanical monsters and vain idols. Gubbio laments:

> Man who first of all, as a poet, deified his own feelings and worshipped them, now having flung aside every feeling, as an encumbrance not only useless but positively harmful, and having become clever and industrious, has set to work to fashion out of iron and steel his new deities, and has become a servant and a slave to them. (7)

The tempos of the present production-consumption cycle rob individuals of the opportunity to disconnect—to enjoy blocks of free time when they can pause and consider what they are doing with their lives. Given their lack of opportunities for self-reflection, men and women keep making the same mistakes; they keep looking for happiness in the wrong places and, disappointed by the outcomes of their decisions, make even worse choices. People keep rearranging their lives, but all their efforts "hardly fail to reveal themselves sooner or later as illusion or vanities" (11). The machines they have built in the hope of satisfying their needs and desires do not offer them peace. It is as if all these new technologies, cinema included, are gimmicks—to use another of Ngai's categories—that have caught the nation in their spell, generating incoherent existences that are not worth living, lives that are wasted away serving and servicing the machines that were supposed to make our lives better.[30] For Gubbio, these unrestrained lives everyone is living cannot but lead to unhappiness, dissatisfaction, and ultimately rage.

> I look at the women in the street, note how they are dressed, how they walk, the hats they wear on their heads; at the men, and the airs they have or give themselves; I listen to their talk, their plans; and at times it seems to me so impossible to believe in the reality of all that I see and hear, that being incapable, on the other hand, of believing that they are all doing it as a joke, I ask myself whether really all this clamorous and dizzy machinery of life, which from day to day seems to become more complicated and to move with greater speed, has not reduced the human race to such a condition of insanity that presently we must break out in fury and overthrow and destroy everything. (4–5)

Gubbio insists that cinema could prevent such an explosion of violence. Notwithstanding his disdain for the way his production company writes the world (*Kosmograph* = *cosmos* + *graphein*), the operator eyes mechanical reproducibility as a means to heal Italian behavior and bring back some law and order in the country. Considering how unhinged everyone has become, considering the risk of an explosion of rage and violence, the film industry should embrace the medium's specificity and deploy the technology of cinema to document a "life that is not life anymore." By stopping the flow of lies and fictions, the apparatus would give men and women the opportunity to become aware of a reality on the brink. It would give them a chance to reconsider all their rushed decisions and infantile cravings. The camera operator sighs again: "Ah, if my profession were destined to this end only! If it had the sole object of presenting to men the ridiculous spectacle of their heedless actions, an immediate view of their passions, of their life as it is" (151).

Gubbio's opportunity to capture on film the tragic consequences of modern living comes during the shooting of the grand finale of a silent film titled *The Woman and the Tiger*. An English lady is traveling through the savage Indies, fending off a host of suitors and mishaps. In the heart of the jungle, her convoy is attacked by a tiger. The wild animal is about to maul the noblewoman, but a hunter shoots the tiger and saves the woman's life. As Gubbio explains: "India will be a sham, the jungle will be a sham, the travels will be a sham, with a sham *Miss* and sham admirers, only the death of this poor beast will not be a sham" (92). In fact, Kosmograph has acquired from the Rome Zoo a tiger unfit for life in captivity. She is too wild to live on, but her death will not be in vain, Gubbio muses, as she will be fed to the movie camera.

Aldo Nuti will play the part of the hunter saving the English Miss from the beast. He is the former lover of the Russian diva Varia Nestoroff, who in the film plays the part of a seductive Indian woman, in brownface. To shoot the film's spectacular ending, Kosmograph will put Nuti, the tiger, and Gubbio in the same cage: Gubbio will film the scene while Nuti puts the tiger down with a real rifle.

Lights, camera, action. Nuti takes aim at the tiger, the tiger approaches, and Gubbio starts filming. Nuti turns around; instead of aiming at the tiger, he aims at Nestoroff, who is on set as everyone else to check out the realization of this incredible cinematic attraction. Nuti shoots and kills Nestoroff just seconds before being fatally attacked by the tiger. Gubbio goes on filming. Impassible, he records the macabre spectacle of modern life, composing a brutal reminder of men and women's life expectancy in zany liberal Italy. In fact, bringing misogyny and xenophobia together, Nestoroff in *Quaderni* stands for the threat that is compromising the Italian body politic. This "razza di donna"— breed of woman—liberal in her sexuality and willful in her desires, has the same effects on men that liberal modernity and liberal cinema have: she unleashes their excessive nature, their insatiable wants. Thus she needs to die, in a sort of apotropaic gesture against all the ills she is made to embody.

By shooting Nuti's murder-suicide, Gubbio hopes to create a graphic memento that will make an impact on the public. Crowds do flock to the cinemas to catch Gubbio's footage, but nothing and no one changes in Italy. The Italian public does not receive Gubbio's filmed reality as a warning; it does not take advantage of the occasion to make amends. Italians are neither healed nor redeemed by cinema. Gubbio abandons the movie camera forever and returns to his notebooks, becoming hospitalized in a mental institution and committed to an obstinate silence. The cameraman appears stunned by his failure to change things, to remake the people. However, having established that the human race is destined to fare poorly in this world insofar as it cannot liberate itself from fictions and illusions, why did Gubbio even hope to make a difference?

Consider Gubbio's reflections on animal contentment and the unhappiness of men (the original text uses the gendered term *gli uomini* to refer to humanity). The very separation from nature that propels man into history also condemns us to an existence marked by disappointment and frustration. Whereas animals live in blessed communion with their environment and can satisfy their primary needs instinctively, human beings do not enjoy such a fusion with their reality. In *Quaderni*—and in Pirandello's writings in general—men have the same characteristics as Sergi's Mediterranean specimens: we are excessive beings who bask in the superfluous, who always want more and cannot be satisfied with what we have. We have more than we need, but never enough. An insatiable desire distinguishes men from animals, making contentment impossible. This feature is something endemic to the human race, a marker whose negative effects can be curbed, as in the times of the gods and poets, but are running rampant in the current age of steel and iron. While animals are content in their small dens and nests, in Pirandello's works men leave behind their homes, women, and families for better homes, women, and families—which, unsatisfied, they leave behind as well. They keep chasing false needs and phantom desires.

Benjamin pointed to *Quaderni* as one of the first works to deal with the alienation produced in the epoch of technological reproducibility. Yet Gubbio's notebooks cannot be squarely read as a critique of capitalist alienation, as Robert Dombroski also proposes.[31] This is the case because the text's disdain for the zany affects and destructive gimmicks that dominate life under industrial capitalism is not couched in a structural analysis of capitalism itself. What the text raises concerns about is not an integrated system of production and consumption but the excessive behaviors it generates. What the text wants is for people to behave differently, to interact with the present differently, to be more intentional in how they go about their lives and interface with modern novelties, because the way they are currently carrying themselves is compromising the survival of a phantasmatic traditional Italian way of life and a series of systems of privilege engrained into it. *Quaderni* does not show any consideration for the bodies that were most maimed in serving the modern economy.

The lives of Italy's colonial subjects and of the Italian proletariat are beyond the scope of *Quaderni*; the Italian masses are not featured at all in the text, and Africa is mentioned only once, presented as the location of harmless geographical exploration rather than as the site of colonial violence. For *Quaderni,* servitude and slavery do not appear to be problems in themselves. It is only the loss of status and privileges of middle-class men, their transformation into metaphorical servants and slaves, that matters for Pirandello. The film novel thus labors to trigger resentment not against capitalism per se but against the ruling liberal block that did nothing to protect the poor Italian men from the upheaval that modernity supposedly brought about. Using "man" as a metonymy for humanity, however, *Quaderni* harnesses the feeling that by doing harm to individual Italian men, one is also harming human life in itself, that the crisis of Italian masculinity here staged was also a global crisis that concerns everyone. Plights of the particular are reframed as the revelatory tale of more generalized looming catastrophe.

Additionally, Pirandello cannot simply criticize capitalist alienation because for him alienation is the inalienable human condition; it is the tragically ironic destiny of the human race.[32] The condition of displacement and homelessness that one experiences under liberal modernity is only superficially a matter of political economy, being more fundamentally a racial question. Modern-day alienation and commodity fetishism, for Pirandello, grow precisely out of our race-determined incapacity to know reality and ourselves, to create good lives and good homes for ourselves. What are the machines, apparatuses, and devices that the characters in *Quaderni* have attached their lives and bodies to if not a host of failed experiments at racial self-realization? What are they if not prosthetic organs, as Bernard Stiegler would call them, through which the human race has tried in vain to construct happy lifeworlds and happy selves?[33]

Given what he knows of animals and men, Gubbio deluded himself that he could save the nation just by projecting on the big screen the insanity and degradation of Italian life under liberal rule. Throughout his notebooks, Gubbio passes judgment on the naiveté of the people around him, on how pointless and misinformed everyone else's life decisions are. Yet, at the end, he is the one in the wrong. The effort to deploy mechanical reproducibility to raise awareness and reverse the effects of technology on the Italian body politic is just another futile attempt to rely on machines to order collective life rather than on the past remedies of poetry or art or religion. Gubbio's failure, then, removes the cameraman from the position of authority often granted him and remarks on the separation between author and protagonist that the novel had more subtly established throughout. Pirandello himself makes a cameo in the diegetic universe of *Quaderni*: many have recognized the double of the author in the man who is "delicate, pale, with thin, fair hair; keen, blue eyes; a pointed, yellowish beard" (6) and who predicts, in notebook 1, that Gubbio will become obsolete soon.

Here, Pirandello's stand-in alludes to the fact that one day Gubbio will be expendable: once cameras can regulate their shutter speed automatically, no one will need Gubbio's talents and he will be "suppressed, replaced" by some mechanism. But he is also useless because the cameraman's attempted weaponization of the apparatus to redeem the human race, or Italians at least, is misinformed. As Michael Syrimis cogently points out, although Serafino is the name of an angel—that is, of a messenger—we should not take Gubbio's call for documentary realism seriously.[34] Treating this disgruntled man, an incel *avant la lettre*, as an enlightened film theorist, as many have done, would contradict not only Pirandello's worldview but also Gubbio's own assessment of our race's inability to become aware of itself, achieve self-consciousness, and change.

The joke has always been on Gubbio, and on those who took seriously the cameraman's considerations on the redemptive dimension of immediacy and technological reproducibility. Notwithstanding his posturing, Gubbio's speculations are far from being objective and on point: they are additional symptoms of the human incapacity to reckon with the real and to live well, of the profound sickness afflicting the human race and contemporary Italian men especially. At every turn of a page in the operator's notebook, it is easy to perceive the breaking apart of a fragile masculinity in crisis and poisoned by entitlement, self-importance, and resentment; by the fantasy of being someone other than who he is; by all the small and large delusions of a man who feels victimized but is unable to read his own affects and those of the people around him. Gubbio himself is an unhinged body compromised by contact with European modernity (his sojourn in Belgium first, then his obsession with Varia Nestoroff), and the snuff film he shoots is nothing but the apotheosis of a long filmic tradition composed of melodramatic, Orientalizing attractions. A southern Italian man killing a Russian diva for revenge and then being mauled by a tiger, while everyone watches: spectators cannot wait for this spectacle; it matches the sensibility of the times.

Through quick changes of scale, perspective, and pace, through flash-backs, pans, and abrupt cuts, through a style that indeed has a cinematic feel, Pirandello's stylistically more modernist work does not just stage an Italy that is decentered, frantic, erratic, and without restraint—an unchecked nation suffering from a profound identity crisis. The convoluted and wind-ing prose of the novel also conjures its protagonist's distraught mental state, amplifying, in all their inarticulacy, broader social fears and hopes about the impact of industrialization on traditional forms of relationality and life. The well-ordered Italy and the well-meaning cinema of Fabbri's *Al Cinematografo* never came to fruition. And in the confused pathos of *Quaderni*—even in its morbid murder-suicide—we can perceive a frustra-tion with the present, a misplaced nostalgia for a phantasmatic traditional Italy, and a commitment toward a future that can no longer be addressed by Italian liberalism and its film forms. This is the case because the appara-tuses of liberal Italy, including the cinematic apparatus, can only reproduce a "condition of insanity" (5)—they can only further foreign lifestyles, just as other imported machines are doing.

Yet this does not mean that all hope is lost—quite the contrary. As I mentioned, Sergi had insisted on the urgency of developing racially appro-priate cultural forms that could discipline what he considered the excessive and self-destructive nature of the Italian people, to shepherd this breed of humans toward greatness once again. *Quaderni* promotes a similar feel-ing of urgency, by foregrounding the trope of insubordinate life in desper-ate need of healing and saving (the plethora of references to Christian eschatology is also important in this regard). Gubbio's failure, his inability to deploy the *macchina da presa* for the presumed greater good, does not quash but rather further incites the hope that someone might eventually figure out how to weaponize film forms to capture the nation in a more proper ordering. Thus, on the one hand, following Alberto Asor Rosa, one should recognize in *Quaderni* the effort to demystify the liberal elites' mythic account of progress and industrial modernity. On the other hand, with Giuseppe Panella, one ought to consider how Pirandello's own de-mystification circulates an account of the human race and Italian reality that implicitly establishes its own mythologies.[35]

If the human race is so misguided, if the malaise of liberal Italy is so serious, if the threats looming over its men are so frightening, then the remedies that could save the authentic Italian people from going extinct cannot help but acquire a mythical dimension. In *Quaderni*, we have the myth of the cinema as the device of the century; but we also see the mythology of the new man behind the movie camera, a healer-artist who can transform film forms and thereby mitigate, reclaim, or remake Italian life. *Quaderni*—like Sergi's *Arii e Italici*—is an apocalyptic text indeed, one that dwells in the time of waiting and cultivates both absolute discontent with the present and extraordinary hope for a different future. Pirandello's textual machine functions as a powerful erotic-phobic apparatus, amplifying resentment against liberal modernity and its cinema while simultaneously harvesting the millenarian desire for alternative forms of government, film, and life. But how does one get to this alternative Italian future?

Given that people are incapable by nature of finding their way through life, there is no point in just showing the public the decay of Italy under liberal rule. A phenomenological realism similar to the kind that Bazin will praise in the postwar period will not work. To have an effect, to become a political weapon, cinema needs to do something different from reproducing reality "as is" and Italian lives as they are. It also needs to acquire a normative dimension and impose upon the public what this reality and these lives ought to become in order for happy endings to become possible. *Quaderni* emphasizes that the human race lives in illusions and that people's cravings are influenced by the fictions they consume at the movies. Hence, the way to a better Italian future would be to project better Italian lives onto the big screen, even and especially if such lives do not yet exist. What Italy ultimately needed were better fictions and healthier illusions. As a mere operator, Gubbio cannot bring them about. A brilliant author could, but he would have to be supported by an appropriate productive system and backed up by a forward-looking director. In 1915, when *Quaderni* was published in its original serial format, it was difficult to imagine anyone who could lead the film industry in the "right" direction and allow it to amplify the lives that Italians presumably had to live for their own good and for the good of the nation. In 1925, when the novel was rereleased in book form and with its definitive title, Italians—Pirandello included—had found the *dux* they desperately felt they needed to be directed by.

Both Italian and Anglophone scholarship tend to dissociate Pirandello's support of Fascism from his poetics, insisting that there is not anything intrinsically fascist in the Nobel laureate's art.[36] Yet this conclusion is belied by the damning opinion piece Pirandello authored for the one-year anniversary of the fascist March on Rome: "La vita creata" (The created life,

1923) manifests in this regard how the step from Serafino Gubbio to Mussolini might be as short as the one that, according to Kracauer, separates Dr. Caligari from Adolf Hitler.[37] Allow me to translate a long passage from "La vita creata," as if to let Pirandello speak for himself.

> Mussolini can only receive blessings from someone who has always felt the immanent tragedy of life, which, in order to acquire consistency, requires a form; but then senses death in whichever form it consists in. Since life is subject to relentless change and motion, it feels imprisoned by form: it rages and storms and pounds until finally is able to escape. Mussolini has shown himself to be well aware of this double and tragic law of movement and form, with so much force that he wants to reconcile the two. Movement must be restrained in an ordered form, and the form cannot become empty, a vain idol. Form must welcome life, pulsating and quivering. In this way, life would be constantly recreated and not resist the act that imposes a form on itself and on others. The revolutionary movement inaugurated by Mussolini with the March on Rome and the methods of his new government seem to me to be, in politics, the necessary and authentic realization of my own conception of life.

To my knowledge, no one has ever mentioned Fascism in regard to *Quaderni di Serafino Gubbio operatore*. "La vita creata," however, conjures a much more profound connection between Pirandello's fictions and his political choices; between the discourse on life, that is, the biology, that emerges in his celebrated works of art, and the reasons why he blessed Mussolini's coming. Indeed, there are some lines in "La vita creata" that are almost literal repetitions of passages from his works of fiction. The lamentation over modern forms of relationality as vain idols, the need for a revolution in how the body politic moves, the affected pathos over a life that is disordered and thus must be restrained at all costs: these would not be out of place in *Quaderni*, nor in Sergi's racial anthropology. *Quaderni*, "La vita creata," and Sergi's work share what I would characterize as a sort of *cruel vitalism*. While these interventions recognize the force of life and desire to defy all social norms and traditions, they also betray an absolute distrust in the power of the people to govern their own bodies and drives. This vitalism is thus cruel because the notice of the power of the living is not liberatory (as in Baruch Spinoza, Nietzsche, or Deleuze) but, by marking bare life as intrinsically guilty and culpable, enables both the repression of individual freedoms and the biopolitical remaking of collective life. As the work of Étienne Balibar also suggests, in terms of political practices and projects, in the end it might not matter much whether one writes about a life to be created, a race to be restrained, a stock to be reclaimed, a nation to be healed, a populace to be disciplined, or a people still to be made.[38] Using different signifiers and through different frameworks, one can be amplifying the same fear-mongering panic in regard to human beings' ability to form good lives for themselves without external tutelage. This biological anxiety about human autonomy and agency, "La vita creata" shows, has direct biopolitical bearings; it comes with its own sets of inarticulate, but not inconsequential, commitments and allegiances.

In light of the perfect alignment, so emphatically professed by Pirandello, between his own conception of life and Fascism's methods of government, it is not surprising that the Duce insisted on enlisting the Nobel laureate when the regime—in preparation for its imperial acceleration—decided to look beyond documentary cinema and started to invest in fictions to restrain the nation's biological body while exploiting its vital force.

2 Workers Entering the Military-Industrial Complex

Pirandello's and Ruttman's Acciaio

Workers Leaving the Factory in Eleven Decades (1995) is a thirty-seven-minute multiscreen installation by Harun Farocki. In it, the Turkish German scholar and artist compiled scenes from one hundred years of cinema history to stage film's reticence to figure work. Farocki's installation proposes that cinema was born at the factory gates, and since the Lumière brothers' 1895 film depicting humble men and women clocking out, moving images have remained averse to accessing the workplace. Farocki explains in an accompanying essay that the specificities of the capitalist mode of production—the division of labor, the mechanization of behaviors, etc.—render it difficult to adapt modern work life for a feature film and to tell an entertaining story about it. Narrative cinema takes up the existence of individuals, in opposition to how the "work structure synchronizes the workers, the factory gates group them, and this process of compression produces the image of a work force."[1] Traditionally, feature films do not know what to do with the image of compact community assembled at and through work. It is for this very reason, Farocki concludes, that the cinematographic apparatus rarely crosses the factory gates or stages labor more broadly. When it does, one must thus take notice and address the reasons for such an anomaly.

Alessandro Blasetti's *Sole!* (*Sun*, 1929), *Terra madre* (*Mother Land*, 1931), and *Vecchia guardia* (*Old Guard*, 1935); Mario Camerini's *Rotaie* (*Rails*, 1929) and *Gli uomini che mascalzoni . . .* (*What Scoundrels Men Are!*, 1932); Walter Ruttmann's *Acciaio* (*Steel*, 1933): Italian cinema, between the end of the 1920s and the beginning of the 1930s, was reborn through a series of films revolving around the realities of labor under Fascism. Why was this the case?

Why was there this anomalous interest, precisely at the juncture when the film industry got back to work? What did national film achieve by featuring—within the context of Fascism's totalitarian and imperial acceleration—the ordered, productive, disciplined mass of people that work supposedly elicits?

In the previous chapter, I traced how Gualtiero Fabbri and Luigi Pirandello remediated the cinematographic apparatus into a weapon that, by manipulating the people's affects and emotions, could amend collective behavior. The next three chapters explore how the deployment of film into a tool to make a properly Italian racial assemblage concretized under Mussolini. It is the relationship between labor as a film subject and the subjectification of Italian labor to Fascism that I unpack in this cluster. While I focus on Camerini and Blasetti in chapters 3 and 4, here I look at Ruttmann's *Acciaio* and the Pirandello scenario upon which it was based, *Gioca, Pietro!* (Peter, play!), to begin considering the forms of affects and audiovisual forms through which national cinema, with its captures of Italians doing their jobs, sought to get an Italian race to work for the regime.

As discussed in chapter 1, in "La vita creata," Pirandello motivated his support for Mussolini by explaining that Fascism was necessary.[2] In his declaration of faith to Mussolini, Pirandello explained that human life, to find happiness, ought to be restrained in proper forms, and that Fascism would create appropriate structures of living for the Italian people since they had proved unable to fashion good lives for themselves. Presenting Mussolini as a formidable maker of life ("artifice di vita"), Pirandello cultivated codependency between Italy and Fascism: the people needed the regime, for they needed a form, a style, a home—they needed to be ordered and disciplined after liberalism had allowed the body politic to run amok. Ten years after such an enthusiastic blessing of Fascism, *Gioca, Pietro!* and *Acciaio* conjure a similarly disempowering imaginary, using the factory and the workshop to achieve a series of results: to inspire public awe in the might of the regime's life-making power, to showcase the good lives that Fascism made for the people, and to stage the labor that the cinematographic apparatus needed to take up in support of the ongoing biopolitical remake of the body politic.

PIRANDELLO FROM ANTILIBERALISM TO STATE CAPITALISM

The city of Terni, in the central Italian region of Umbria, has a long history. Founded in the seventh century BCE, it was conquered by the Romans four hundred years later, and under their rule it became an important commercial hub—thanks to its strategic position on the Via Flaminia. Terni lost prominence with the barbarian invasions of Italy in the early Middle Ages, only to flourish again after it was incorporated into the Papal States during the Renaissance. The small city became renowned for metallurgy at the end of the sixteenth century, when its ironworks was founded to process the raw materials mined in the Monteleone caves seventy miles to the northeast.

Annexed to the Kingdom of Italy through a unanimous referendum in 1860, Terni—a painters' favorite spot in the Grand Tour—became a paramount component of the young nation's military-industrial complex due to the abundance of both cast iron and water sources that could generate the hydropower required to feed plants and factories. The Royal Arms Factory was established in 1875, and less than ten years later, thanks to a combination of public capital and investments from larger private financial institutions, the Terni *acciaierie* (steelworks) were born. The great manufacturing plant powered by the nearby Marmore Falls was primarily meant to provide Italian factories with the cast iron necessary for armoring battleships—a crucial asset for protecting the nation's independence but also a fundamental weapon to fulfill Italy's ambition to become a modern European nation-state and thus acquire colonial possessions. Yet the liquidity crisis that followed the 1929 global economic depression put the industrial complex, and with it many other Italian factories and businesses, on the brink of closure. Loans and investments from the private sector were simply not enough to keep the mill's gates open. To prevent Italy from losing an invaluable resource for its national security and expansionist aspirations, in the early 1930s the Italian state—by then fully controlled by the Fascist Party—became the majority stakeholder in the company.[3] Mussolini determined that the nationalization of the plant, as an emblem of the grandeur of Italy's state capitalism, had to be celebrated with a film. He demanded that someone with an international reputation be involved in the project. Considering his outspoken support for the regime but also his long-standing engagement with the cinema, Pirandello—who would win a Nobel Prize in 1934—was the obvious choice. Pressed by the president of LUCE, Giacomo Paulucci de' Calboli, Pirandello agreed to write, in collaboration with his son Stefano, the treatment for a feature film on Terni's steelworks to be produced by Cines.[4]

Cines was Italy's most prestigious and consequential production company. It was founded in 1908 and achieved success in the 1910s with silent classics such as Enrico Guazzoni's *Quo Vadis?* (1913) or Nino Oxilia's *Rapsodia satanica (Satan's Rhapsody,* 1915). But Cines, and Italian cinema more broadly, had great difficulties navigating the economic crisis brought about by World War I and adapting to the changing consumption and production patterns conjured by sonorization. The company suspended activities until 1929, when its equipment and facilities were bought out by the dynamic film exhibitor Stefano Pittaluga, who already controlled about one hundred theaters throughout the country. With the purchase of Cines, Pittaluga vertically integrated production and distribution, securing a monopolistic position in the national market. In 1930, Cines released Italy's first sound film—the sentimental comedy *La canzone dell'amore (Love's Song)* by Gennaro Righelli—but not even such a milestone, or the fact that it was practically the only company producing movies in Italy at the time, was enough to make the operation viable. Even with some financial support from the state, the national market was just too small and the production costs too high to make cinema a financially sustainable business. When Pittaluga died in 1931, Cines was on the cusp of bankruptcy. By then, the regime had realized both that fiction film could become a weapon of government and that Italian cinema could not exist without the state's logistical and economic support. Similar to the fate of the Terni steelworks and a host of industries deemed essential to Italy's status and prestige, Cines was nationalized to prevent it from closing.[5]

Under Pittaluga, Cines had started to explore how the cinematographic apparatus might sustain government. This interest became more urgent as the fascist state involved itself more directly in the company's activities. Cines's direct connection with the regime propelled it to become an aesthetico-political laboratory for trying new technologies of sight and sound and for delivering on the new responsibilities with which the regime had charged sound film. While cinema unquestionably had to work for Fascism, it was still to be determined whether particular film forms were more suited to be deployed as biopolitical arms. Propaganda and creativity were thus not mutually exclusive, and this brought about the situation of aesthetic pluralism that Marla Stone reviews so precisely in *The Patron State*: indeed, the regime's relative openness to a variety of art and film forms was less a matter of actual pluralism than a manifestation of what—through historian Emilio Gentile—we could describe as the experimental nature of fascist totalitarianism.[6]

The years 1932 and 1933 were particularly important for Cines. In conjunction with the tenth anniversary of Fascism's rise to power, under the artistic direction of the pundit and literary critic Emilio Cecchi, the company developed prototypical film forms that aspired to have a decisive impact on Italian film language and Italian history. As Vincenzo Buccheri traces, although Cecchi never turned his back on genre fiction, he sought to move away from purely escapist cinema and instead have domestic production tackle national life. By involving artists and intellectuals in the film industry, the plan was to develop model films that would reconcile art, politics, and entertainment. There was a special investment in realism, as the register was considered the most effective for projecting how different Italian localities and constituencies fitted together in the larger scheme of things. The first years of Italian sound cinema at Cines were, Gian Piero Brunetta points out, characterized by an effort to forge a shared experience of national identity that mediated Italy as a united organism while at the same time respecting the regional and positional differences that characterized the country.[7] It was the labor of articulation between the local and the national as well as between the different socioeconomic blocks that the production company had prominently taken up.

Pirandello was very familiar with Cines. Its studios had inspired the depiction of Kosmograph in *Quaderni di Serafino Gubbio operatore*.[8] *La canzone dell'amore*—which Pirandello loathed—was a loose adaptation of one of his short stories. Yet Cecchi's Cines was no longer the Cines that Pirandello used to know. It was a direct extension of the fascist state apparatus; it was the company that, as we will see in chapters 3 and 4, with Blasetti's *Terra madre* and Camerini's *Gli uomini che mascalzoni . . .*, revolutionized Italian sound cinema and showed how realism could bring together entertainment and race-making. In *Quaderni,* the Cines film studios had provided Pirandello with the ideal location to stage Italy's decay under liberal modernity and stoke resentment against the ruling elites and their dissolute film culture. Now, in the 1930s, this collaboration with the Rome-based company gave the playwright the opportunity to tweak his earlier assessment of industrialization and celebrate the good that comes from serving and servicing the nationalized machines. The same venues and technologies that before, under Giolitti, Pirandello had presented as responsible for Italy's *mala vita,* under a different political economy were cast in a new light, and their redeeming qualities were amplified. *Gioca, Pietro!* is in fact a hymn to the perfect symbiosis established between living and dead labor under fascist rule, which seeks to remediate how the people felt about both industrialization and state power. Pirandello had begun *Quaderni* with a bleak account of mechanized living. *Gioca, Pietro!* opens instead with a more reassuring and inspiring techno-human ensemble.

We are at the factory gates. It is early morning and the workshop is still sleeping. As the machines awaken and pick up speed, they sound like living, breathing creatures, their hearts pumping rhythmically.[9] Human voices join the machinic riffs rising from the plant, and the laborers hum a song that builds on the tunes and cadences of the factory in motion. A perfect synchronicity is achieved between people and technology, and it is this very collaboration of steel and flesh that assures Terni's vitality. Without work, without the steelworks, Terni would be a desolate, dead place, *Gioca, Pietro!* implies. Instead, thanks to the metallurgic complex and the massive workforce gathered there, the town's existence is punctuated by a lively playfulness, mediated in Pirandello's treatment by an allegro musical score.

Gioca, Pietro! does not overlook the brutal working conditions in the steel mills yet emphasizes that only in and through strenuous labor can men realize themselves. Filippo is a dignified foreman who, after giving forty years to steelmaking, can no longer keep up with the pace of the factory. He has no regrets and feels proud of what he has made of himself, but it is time to retire. Although Filippo will soon be awarded the coveted star of merit for labor, to him the biggest reward would be to see his son take up his leadership position in the plant. Giovanni is a brilliant young man who has not found his place in life yet and is wasting his acute intelligence. Filippo tries to convey to Giovanni that a man can only fulfill his truest potential by embracing rather than resisting hard work: it is on the factory floor that one learns discipline, esprit de corps, and moral sense; it is in the workshop that real men are made.

Notwithstanding social and familial pressures, Giovanni cannot relinquish his fantasies of independence and commit to the assembly line. He does not want to sacrifice his freedom, insofar as he fears that any definitive life choice will eventually feel like a prison. It is precisely this lack of direction in life that makes him restless. It is easy to recognize in Giovanni's insatiable desire that constant hunger, that unhealthy frenzy for more that *Quaderni* had warned against and Giuseppe Sergi had recognized as an essential feature of the Italian race. Giovanni, in Pirandello's scenario, functions as a powerful manifestation of the assumption that without rules, without guidance, individuals drift away from the common good. Pietro, Giovanni's best friend, is the opposite. He has no complicated desires and is perfectly satisfied with the life he has: Terni, steelmaking, hopefully Chiara.

The day of the town fair, the plant workers rest to honor Filippo's service. After a parade of Blackshirts and a speech delivered by a high-ranking member of the Fascist Party, Giovanni finds himself withdrawing from the festive crowd. What a man his father is! Staring at the mill's gate, Giovanni reconsiders his priorities. A community, a job, a home, a family, and children one day: what more does a man need to be happy in this world? He understands, too, that he has always been in love with Chiara; he rushes off to her house to serenade and propose to her. But Pietro is already there, about to do the same. The two friends begin to argue. Since life is just a game, let's play, Giovanni suggests: let's both propose to Chiara and see what happens. Chiara is enraged by these childish antics and quickly dismisses both suitors. The next day at work, Pietro and Giovanni show off their masculinity, skills, and force, in a battle to prove to each other and to the factory at large who is the best mate for Chiara—the one who is more productive and thus more worthy to reproduce, to *fare razza*. A moment of distraction is enough to provoke a tragic accident: a white-hot ingot falls onto Giovanni, leaving him paralyzed from the waist down.

Giovanni's disability and impotence do not compromise his lightheartedness. When Pietro comes to visit him in dismay, he offers a single piece of advice: Pietro should play, because he still can. Pietro picks up on his friend's implicit blessing and proposes to Chiara. They talk and, the scenario specifies, they become one as they walk away toward their new life. Giovanni cannot move, but he is still going places. At the end of *Gioca, Pietro!*, the young man is content. His eyes twinkling with hope and faith, Giovanni is working on a small mechanical apparatus. He has had this idea for a new device in his mind for a while, and now that he can no longer trifle away his life through play, he has the opportunity to focus, to put his innate Italian ingenuity to good use. The sound of his metal file fades out and is subsumed by the music of the steel mill at work. Since he cannot birth a family anymore, since his impotence prevents him from biologically contributing to the making of an Italian race, he will produce new machines to support his country and his people. Maimed but happy, paralyzed in his wheelchair, Giovanni has embraced his lot in life.

With such an evident juxtaposition between physical/inauthentic and spiritual/authentic liberty, the finale of *Gioca, Pietro!* is far from subtle.

Once his ability to move is compromised, the man who would have sacrificed everything to preserve his own social mobility accepts that true self-fulfillment can only come from a stable and industrious life, from discipline and compliance. He comes to terms with the fact that a community can overcome tensions and divisions, and thus prosper, only when its men become part of a larger assemblage, when—as Sergi's advised—they restrain their individualism to concentrate their energy and ingenuity on something other than erratic cravings and desires.

To bring this romanticization of labor to the screens, Pirandello had approached Sergei Eisenstein: the script's Stakhanovism seemed to resonate with the rhetoric of Stalinist U.S.S.R, and—besides—the director of *Battleship Potemkin* and *Strike* (both 1925) had many admirers in Italy, even within the regime. Such a fascist appreciation of Soviet film is less surprising than one might think.[10] Given Fascism's commitment to winning over the working class, it somehow made sense to take communist cinema as a model. Notwithstanding his respect for Pirandello, Eisenstein declined to be involved in the project after becoming aware of the film's entanglement with the fascist war machine. Hitler's power was on the rise in Germany, and fascist hierarchs had already started eyeing the first feature film sponsored by the regime as an opportunity to forge a cinematic axis between Rome and Berlin. Pressured by the fascist hierarchy, Cecchi connected with Walter Ruttmann. The subject of the film seemed like a perfect fit for the director of *Berlin: Symphony of a Great City* (1927), who had also worked as director of photography for Fritz Lang's *Metropolis* (1927) before going on to make public hygiene documentaries for the Weimar Republic, including *Enemy in the Blood* (1931).[11]

Yet Cecchi and other key players at Cines feared that Ruttmann's preference for avant-garde formalism and elaborate montage would be too foreign to Italy's taste and sensibility. Consequently, they assigned novelist Mario Soldati to assist the director as a sort of native informant who could facilitate the translation of Ruttmann's film language for national audiences. Soldati had just come back from a long stay in the United States, and his familiarity with American film was considered a great asset in light of Italian audiences' fondness for Hollywood. The collaboration between Ruttmann and Soldati resulted in *Acciaio*. Buccheri cogently characterizes the film as an endeavor to find a fascist approach to sound cinema by juxtaposing two great traditions of European modernist film—formalism and documentary—in a sort of "abstract realism" in which the meaning of reality is

conveyed through 1920s avant-garde techniques, insofar as these very techniques were considered the most appropriate to break through to the popular masses.[12]

In his 1929 think-piece "Se il film parlante abolirà il teatro?" (Will talkies
abolish theater?), Pirandello insisted that, for the good of the nation, Italian sound *cinematografia* should avoid relying too heavily on narration and
dialogue and instead become *cine-melo-grafia*: a language of "pure vision
and pure music" that would move people's hearts and make the strongest
impression on their subconscious.[13] In line with these insights, Ruttmann
and Soldati reduce the narrative of *Gioca, Pietro!* to a minimum, disregard
character development, and emphasize the spectacular rendition of Terni's
optical and aural grandeur. Siegfried Kracauer held that Ruttmann's commitment to arranging audiovisual attractions for the spectators was the
mark of a shallow cinematic intelligence. For Kracauer, Ruttmann—unlike
Dziga Vertov—did not have anything meaningful to say about the real, and
so was satisfied with transforming the landscapes his camera captured into
a sublime show of sights and sounds.[14] However, in *Acciaio* the transformation of the industrial present into a mighty audiovisual spectacle appears
to be a conscious aesthetic decision that is the direct consequence of a
precise political operation. In filming Pirandello's treatment, Ruttmann
focuses on capturing the forms, noises, and rhythms emerging from Terni
as they are direct expressions of the powers commanding this Italian location, and thus the country more broadly. While on-location shooting and
nonprofessional extras nestle fascist state capitalism in traditional Italian life,
the film's abstract style and editing techniques conjure the higher authority responsible for giving form to Italian reality. Realism and formalism
coexist because the film is about both Terni's material reality and the forces
giving form to it. *Acciaio* is saturated with extras watching and listening in
the background, signaling to the film's viewers that they should pay attention (Figure 3).

Ultimately, the film's public is made to occupy the same position as the
spectators of the track cycle race and the visitors to the steel mill in the
early scenes of the film: a sublime "eye-opening" audiovisual attraction is
about to be exhibited before them.

MADE IN FASCIST ITALY

The plot and overall tone of *Acciaio* differ from *Gioca, Pietro!* in significant
ways. Mario (Pietro Pastore) has just finished his military service. While in

FIGURE 3. Factory visitors exhibit glee and fascination as they watch the steelmaking processes in *Acciaio* (Walter Ruttmann, 1933).

the army, he indulged in the company of sex workers, but now he is ready to settle down and marry the young laundress Gina (Isa Pola). Although his military fatigues are gone, the time to serve is not over: he will start wearing the "civilian uniform" and fulfill his duties to the nation in a manner appropriate to his new status, as a worker and a father. However, Mario's homecoming to Terni does not goes as planned: Gina is now with Pietro (Vittorio Bellaccini). Mario tries to let it go. Mario, Gina, and Pietro spend a night at the fair, enjoying the rides in sequences nodding to Jean Epstein's *Faithful Heart* (1923). But when a local politician, and with him all Terni, thanks Mario for all his service, Gina finds herself gazing at him with desire, gratitude, and admiration: serving Fascism is sexy, it appears. The two dance the night away, causing an enraged Pietro to attack Mario. The ensuing fight—the film audiovisually establishes—tears Terni apart: whereas the beginning of *Acciaio* was characterized by choral captures of the town assembled together and moving in unison to the same beat on either the factory or dance floor, after the fight we see individuals struggling against each other and hear a cacophony of screams, insults, and opinions. Shot-reverse-shot patterns take over long takes, and this stylistic shift emphasizes the feeling of a fractured community. The ominous consequences of this fragmentation and disaggregation manifest themselves the morning after. As dawn approaches, the sound of the machines waking up first inter-cuts with and eventually silences the commotion coming from town. The urgencies of labor are making themselves heard, to the characters but also to the spectators. The factory siren demands Terni's undivided attention and warns the people that the temporality of production dominates the town's landscape. Reminded of their duties and of the temporal rules norm-ing their lives, the workforce heads to the factory gates. But Pietro and Mario persist in their divisions even on the factory floor: instead of work-ing together, they exchange angry looks and provocations, until Pietro gets so distracted by the dispute that he gets crushed by an ingot and dies on the job.

As was the case for *Gioca, Pietro!*, in *Acciaio* the dangers of factory work are simultaneously acknowledged and affectively foreclosed. Ruttmann's expressionistic lightscape, Michael Cowan argues, silhouettes the blast fur-naces, transforming them into giant monsters threatening the workers with fire, molten metal tongues, and mechanical arms (Figure 4).[15] At the same time, the film insists that there is nothing structurally wrong with the safety protocols adopted in a fascist-owned factory. At fault are the indi-viduals who infect the sanctity of the workplace with personal trifles and distractions, undermining the smooth functioning of the state's military-industrial apparatus and putting national security at risk—ultimately thus compromising the future of the Italian ethno-nation.

Toward the beginning of *Acciaio*, the famous ten-minute "factory sym-phony" sequence dramatizing the steelmaking process comes to a sudden halt due to a workplace incident that silences the machines: a momentary distraction on the part of a laborer has almost cost him his life, but even more importantly, it has halted production. Coworkers use the racialized term *macaco* (ape, monkey) to shame the distracted laborer, and they blame the incident on his lack of work ethic. Adding injury to insult, they also call on the boss to give him a good beating to teach this irresponsible man not to come to work with girls on his mind. This insistence on the culpability of living labor and the innocence of the state and its mechanisms achieves two goals. On the one hand, it disallows imaginaries of class awareness and workers' solidarity; on the other, by stressing authority's capacity to

FIGURE 4. Men hard at work at the beginning of *Acciaio* (Walter Ruttmann, 1933).

redress what are projected as self-destructive behaviors, *Acciaio* metonymically builds up the necessity of the fascist state's restraining presence in people's lives. The boss who righteously disciplines the worker is in fact an employee of the fascist state, given that the plant has been nationalized.

Pietro's death constitutes another powerful, and disempowering, memento of what happens to individual bodies and the body politic alike when individuals drift away from heteronormativity and state-sanctioned codes of conduct. If Pietro loses his life, Mario and Gina are sentenced by Terni to social death. Set designer Gastone Medin does an incredible job of turning the film's background into a chorus condemning the outcast laundress and welder, turning the public against them. We catch glimpses of graffiti insulting Mario; we feel the eyes of a reunited community (played by local nonprofessional extras) on Gina as she walks through Terni; we hear the weight of the town's moral condemnation in the comments whispered on the factory floor and on the streets. Children simulate a stoning by throwing rocks and dirt on Gina's dress, which is hanging to dry in her courtyard.

Mario wastes time in the bar; he has lost interest in Terni, Gina, the future, everything. He sees a picture of racing cyclists in the newspaper and wishes that he had never returned to this "inferno." The picture of the bicycle race comes to life, and Mario is now part of the action. He has climbed on his bike and is sprinting to catch up with the racers, leaving Terni farther and farther behind. But Mario cannot keep up with the group, and he gives up, dwarfed by the hydroelectric basin that powers both Terni and the *acciaierie* (Figure 5).

Alone, Mario catches a glimpse of the workforce biking into town. He follows with his eyes the ordered and poised journey of this perfectly harmonious and synchronized assemblage of Italian workers to the factory gates. The sounds of the steelworks make themselves heard again; they are summoning Mario, who cannot but respond to their call. No longer dreaming of being different, he will comply; through the toll of labor, he will atone. Gina, who is watching alone from a distance, is relieved that Mario has reckoned with his place in society. Mario races to the mill and crosses its threshold as the gates close behind him. At the end of the film, Mario—focused, serious, isolated, contained, dedicated, in a sort of grayscale rendition of a Kazimir Malevich painting—is working in a crane that, as it moves away from the camera, assumes the semblance of a suspended cage. *Acciaio* closes with a shot of the Marmore Falls' powerful jets filling the screen with white. The purity of the laborious life has been restored.

FIGURE 5. A defeated Mario in front of the hydroelectric basin powering Terni in *Acciaio* (Walter Ruttmann, 1933).

Rossano Vittori writes that *Acciaio* betrayed both the spirit and the substance of Pirandello's treatment.[16] The betrayal here is not political: both film and scenario project an Italy without classes or class struggle, foreclose a structural gaze on labor issues, promote the same models of the good life, and flag personal aspirations as destructive and self-destructive desires. In both cases, what creates tensions and conflicts is resistance to the gendered behaviors required by state apparatuses and social institutions to work. Society is itself depicted as a human-machinic assemblage whose nexuses and automatisms should not be challenged. However, *Gioca, Pietro!* and *Acciaio* do strike different chords, deploy different affective registers, and rely on different imaginaries, in order to favor sociopolitical docility and boost (re)productivity.

Gioca, Pietro! projected the assimilation and subsumption of individuals within the collective as sacrifices worth making, insofar as they are the precondition for collective happiness and personal enrichment. Pirandello's scenario does not instruct Italians to renounce what they are but to adapt; it does not prompt them to fuse with the military-industrial complex and submit to it but to collaborate with Fascism's technologies for the greater good. The promise that *Gioca, Pietro!* makes to Italians is that if they re-modulate their lives and synchronize them with the needs of the nation-alized machines, they will thrive. However, given the *genio e sregolatezza,* genius and unruliness, proper to the Italian race, the fact that national sub-jects are pushed off the right track by naughty desires is not something that outrages Pirandello. Mediterranean men—we know this from Sergi—are exuberant beings by nature, and this unavoidable racial feature is what makes Italian men powerful and weak at the same time. Giovanni in *Gioca, Pietro!* is an improper state subject, yes, but he is also an inventor whose ingenuity will contribute to Italy's fortunes after he is able to rein in his immoderate vitality. This forgiving attitude vis-à-vis what are presented as the excesses of Italian masculinity allows *Gioca, Pietro!* to close in a reassur-ing way, with a double happy ending.

Acciaio, by contrast, establishes that any violation of the status quo and of the normal ordering of things is a great offense to the powers that be, an outrageous provocation that will lead to a terrible reprisal. In Ruttmann's and Soldati's hands, Pirandello's trivial moral parable turns into a brutalist cautionary tale about what is expected of national bodies under fascist state capitalism. The film demands that Italian subjects sacrifice everything—especially their own individuality and personhood. But this absolute sur-render does not even come with the promise of a better life. Surrender only assures a body's enhanced survival as an anonymous component of the workforce. No whitening is in sight. No one is happy in Terni's hell: everyone is doing their job covered in sweat and soot. Appropriately, the sound score composed by Gian Francesco Malipiero for *Acciaio* lacks the allegro and cheerful movements that Pirandello originally suggested and is instead marked by a tragic aria and the deafening sounds of the factory and the falls calling the ethno-nation to its duties. In line with his earlier comments on Fascism, with *Gioca, Pietro!* Pirandello portrays the regime as a life-shaping authority, a saving power able to reconcile factory produc-tivity, social reproductivity, and individual happiness—enabling in this way the fantasy of a good capitalism that, without changing property relations, could still eradicate the very social tensions and alienated behaviors that Pirandello had flagged in *Quaderni.* Ruttmann, conversely, implants into Italian reality and history a merciless conflict between private desires and the public interest, mediating the urgency to annihilate one's own self in order to avoid retribution.

Acciaio was released in Germany with the ominous title *Arbeit macht glücklich* (Work makes one happy). However, the only instance of contentment one encounters in the film is that of the fascist industrial apparatus. There is nothing liberating about the final sequence of Mario's surrender and his solitary confinement in a factory crane. Moreover, even if Pietro's father appears to forgive Mario and Gina for what happened to his son, there is no indication that they will be welcomed back into the community or form a family. The fact that after Pietro's death we always see them isolated, neither as a couple nor in a group setting, attests that their downfall in the film's diegetic universe is irreversible: by isolating, by singling them out, *Acciaio* judges and bans them; Mario and Gina have proven unfit to reproduce and unworthy of being members of the community, and thus they can only belong to Italy as fungible bodies, in the guise of disposable labor power. Gina, marked by the indelible stigma of guilt, will keep toiling as a laundress, while Mario commits himself to the *acciaierie*. In retrospect, then, *Acciaio* might appear as a somber foreshadowing of the sort of happiness and freedom that working for Nazi Fascism entails. With the German title in mind, it is impossible not to think of the *Arbeit macht frei* sign looming over the entrance of Auschwitz when—over Malipiero's musical *contrapunto*—the factory gates close behind Pietro. As Piero Garofalo notes, Ruttmann's representation of Italian men and women at work is anything but consoling: whether through their sweat or through their blood, the workers ought to "keep the machinery of state capitalism running."[17]

However, Garofalo is still able to find some harmony and lyricism in *Acciaio,* especially in the descriptive sequences capturing Terni's surroundings and the Marmore Falls, which were probably shot by Soldati. To me, the depiction of nature and water in *Acciaio* feels very different from, say, that of *Piccolo mondo antico* (*Small Ancient World*), Soldati's 1941 directorial debut. Drawing upon a long literary and pictorial tradition eulogizing Italy as a land blessed by nature, in *Piccolo mondo antico* Soldati stages the country's environment as a model of harmony, and the calm lake waters at the beginning and end of the film signal that Italians can overcome divisions and find unity only by reconnecting with the law of their land. Soldati's lifeworld is small and ancient: it is *a misura d'uomo,* "on a human scale."

Such a lyrical celebration of perfect harmony between human beings and their environment appears absent from *Acciaio.* Something to keep in

mind is that the Marmore Falls are not even natural but an artificial product of state intervention: they were created by the Romans in 271 BCE,
when they diverted the Velino River toward the Marmore cliff in order to
reclaim the malarious swamplands plaguing the city of Rieti. The water
we see in *Acciaio* is therefore not a natural treasure but a danger to human
life that state power alone (first the Roman Senate, now the fascist state)
could redeem and transform into a resource for sustaining collective living. Without the salvific intervention of state authority, there would be no
natural harmony or lyricism in Terni or elsewhere. Not only is it individuals' nature to lose themselves and turn against each other when left alone
by state power; nature itself would be a threat to human life were it not
reclaimed by the state.

To evoke the presence of the higher force looming over Terni and its
people, and by extension over the Italian nation as a whole, Ruttmann
deploys different audiovisual strategies. High-angle shots of Gina, Mario,
and the whole town dwarfed by the waterfalls and their hydroelectric basin;
the rhythmic alternation between horizontal pans on living beings and
vertical pans on the falls' dam and the metallurgic hub; the frenetic inter-
cutting of the subdued existences that people live in Terni with deafening
scenes capturing the steelmaking process and the Marmore Falls' imposing gorges: through these compositions, Ruttmann conjures the sense of a
sublime imbalance of power. *Acciaio* is all about Terni's material reality, yet
such a reality owes its existence to the falls and to the factory, and above all
to the state that owns them both.

Initially, through parallel editing, *Acciaio* highlights the similarities
between Terni's mundane reality and what happens in the falls-powered
and state-run factory. For instance, we first see children playing with a
press in a yard, and then we are transported to the steelworks floor, where
a machine that looks like "a human limb with augmented power" is beating on an incandescent block of metal.[18] The analogical relation between
these two spheres—the private and the national(ized), the home and the
workplace—is soon turned into a hierarchy. By means of sonic-photo montage, Ruttmann chases the forces giving form to private existences and
guides the public from the concrete to the abstract, from the specific to the
general, from the town to the factory to the falls and beyond—affectively
mediating the state-industrial apparatus as an awe-inspiring power before
which the people can only bow. Beyond the power of water and steel,
the sublime authority of the fascist state looms large. Within the fires of

steelmaking, it is Fascism that shines. The ultimate attraction is the regime itself. The cult of the machine paves the way for the fetish of the state and of its worldmaking power, which is simultaneously a power to harvest energy (water, labor) and weld forms (steel, identities). What the film therefore ultimately mythologizes is Fascism's irresistible and terrible power to mass produce not only Italian goods but also a good Italian race. This is the mighty force with which Ruttmann's film confronts the spectator, the power that shall break individuals' will and assemble a collaborative collectivity. The terrible power to subject the living is a power that the cinematic apparatus also tries to wield.

Toward the end of *Acciaio*, in the sequence depicting Mario's epiphany, we see the shadows of Terni's men biking to work projected on the waterfalls and swallowed by the jets, and then, in the next scene, we see them reemerge in a single, synchronized, poised cluster as they are sucked in by the *acciaierie* (Figure 6). This is no longer a group of workers entering the factory on bikes but rather an alloy of flesh, metal, and Fascism, what Kracauer might define as a "mass ornament," the artificial social

FIGURE 6. Workers are sucked in by the factory at the end of *Acciaio* (Walter Ruttmann, 1933).

machine created by stripping men and women of their very humanity (their desires, sexuality, sensuality) and dehumanizing them to the status of mere means. Since capitalist production is not natural, Kracauer explains, capitalism must destroy individual human beings and transform them into tiny parts, so that they can "effortlessly clamber up charts and service machines."[19]

Thus, the scene in which the Italian workforce coalesces into a mass ornament devoured by the factory, intercut with shots of Mario alone and destroyed by his short-lived decision to hold on to his individual identity, does more than merely project the need to comply and conform. This moment pressures one to renounce everything to become a state asset. The film is an epic story whose hero is not a character but rather the state that shapes and puts to work even the most resistant matter. It is for this reason that throughout the film, the public is made to identify with dead labor, with the needs of a state-run factory, rather than sympathizing with the living laborers that struggle through Terni. In fact, in *Acciaio,* spectatorial pleasure comes from experiencing Mario's transformation from feeling superior to and exempt from the toils of work, to accepting his subalternity relative to them and submitting to the demands of the state, these transcendental, sublime powers giving form to reality. Even Gina is ecstatic to see Mario succumb. We pity the wreckage of his life, but at the same time, experiencing his wreckage offers the public a feeling of relief and security. We are not him; we will not put ourselves in his situation. We have seen and heard and felt what he could not, and now we know the dreadful consequences of defiance and noncompliance.

Acciaio was highly appreciated in Germany, and an impressed Joseph Goebbels was especially eager to employ Ruttmann to advance Nazism's steely romanticism and reactionary modernism.[20] Ruttmann was commissioned to direct the opening montage sequence for Leni Riefenstahl's *The Triumph of the Will* (1935) and then hired to shoot propaganda documentaries on Nazi industry. Ruttmann died in 1941 as a result of the injuries he suffered on the front, working for the Third Reich. In Italy, Ruttmann's last feature film flopped; its performance at the box office was underwhelming, to say the least. Trying to make sense of the failure of *Acciaio,* a film critic commented in 1933:

> *Acciaio* is a work which ought to have been better understood by the Italian public. . . . The epic character of the life in the workshop is shown with

fascinating and mysterious symbols. Can it be that our public is so insensi-
tive as not to feel the dominating power of machines with their monstrous
and inexplicable vitality? The tongues of fire which Ruttmann sees shooting
out in every direction through the smoky darkness as the workers toil belong
to a new mythology.[21]

Possibly, the public could not connect with *Acciaio* because the generic conventions, dreadful mythology, and terrifying symbolism Ruttmann deployed
in the service of "fascinating Fascism," to use Susan Sontag's expression, was
too foreign, too new, to Italy.[22] It is true, in fact, as Pirandello suggested,
that the film ended up assembling a reality that felt quite different from the
quaint national real conjured by so many concurrent Italian movies. *Acciaio*
was indeed much closer to Weimar Republic films—*Metropolis* comes immediately to mind—than to the imaginary articulated by the Italian cinema
of the era: the coeval *Treno popolare* (*Tourist Train*, 1933) captures the same
localities featured in *Acciaio*, and yet the picturesque Terni countryside
from Raffaello Matarazzo's film feels likes a totally different reality vis-à-
vis the one Ruttmann stages. James Hay comments that *Acciaio* emanates
the "kind of sacred and mystical aura traditionally associated with ritual
caves" (Figure 7).[23] It might then be that the film's lack of impact in Italy
was determined by Ruttmann's attempt to lionize Fascism by means of a
sensibility and cultural tropes that were more German than Italian.

Furio Jesi, a cultural critic active in Italy in the 1970s, suggests in this
regard that Nazism and Fascism appealed to very different genres of racial
imaginaries and affective registers. According to Jesi, Nazism's inception
and success were connected with the fantasy of a "secret Germany," with
immemorial folk tales about dark forces to which the Teutonic peoples owed
their existence.[24] The monsters haunting the German cinema of the 1920s
and early 1930s express precisely the perverse longing to connect with these
mysterious powers and fuse with them, almost in an orgiastic fashion, to
transmute into a new species of being: a race of masters and supermen.
The Nazi state apparatus, Kracauer implies in *From Caligari to Hitler*, came
to be perceived as the incarnation of a dreary higher power that the ethno-
community should simultaneously fear and venerate, and to which it owed
anything and everything. In order to really understand what's going on in
Acciaio, one would want to consider what Philippe Lacoue-Labarthe and
Jean-Luc Nancy dub the "Nazi myth": the phantasmagoria of the state as
a ruthless creature that can be appeased only through self-sacrifice and the

FIGURE 7. Workers labor on the factory floor, the flames behind them making them appear almost as if in a ritual cave in *Acciaio* (Walter Ruttmann, 1933).

sacrifice of the unworthy, a creature that—as Hitler threatened with the Nero Decree—can even order the total destruction of the very race it was ruling over when the people proved themselves unfit to be remade into *Übermenschen*.[25] Except for liminal figures, such Massimo Scaligero or Julius Evola, Italian culture, and with it fascist racism, was generally insensible, if not averse, to this sublime mystique of fright and ecstatic transaction with prehistoric and superhuman forces.

Expanding on Gramsci's interpretation of Fascism as the expression of petit bourgeois aspirations and fears, Jesi argues that the only quasi-mythology that the regime could rely on was that of the *domus,* the peace provided by a home and a family. "Home" is not a mere metaphor in fascist discourse, Jesi insists. It constitutes the Italian foundation of Mussolini's myths of rebirth, healing, and security. Underlying pompous fascist rhetoric about empires and colonies, about destiny and *Romanitas,* about making the Mediterranean a mare nostrum again, Jesi highlights the securitarian fixation with constructing a microcosm in which social and property relations "reveal the presence of extremely solid walls: those of the home, the family-run company, the city."[26] For Jesi, Fascism presented itself as a collective endeavor that sprouted in an almost organic fashion from Italian land and history and captivated the population by promising a home and domestic peace at a juncture when Italians' lives—as we saw in *Quaderni di Serafino Gubbio operatore*—were being destabilized by the transnational flow of goods, bodies, imaginaries, demands, desires, and forms of intimacy. Obviously, for the country to become a true homeland to its people after the liberal catastrophe and within the context of the Red Scare, sacrifices had to be made, people had to restrained, and violence had to be deployed. Yet, even in the infamous slogan *Me ne frego* ("I really don't care," as on Melania Trump's notorious jacket), Jesi detects a promise of human happiness—a very specific form of happiness, no doubt—that was missing from Nazism's inhuman mysticism. Under its benevolent totalitarian rule, the regime vowed, people would fare better, and the precondition of that betterment would be the ability to comply.

This precise promise is what disposed many Italians, including Pirandello, to embrace Fascism and to submit to its demands: the sense of a titanic contest between the state and the people that *Acciaio* materializes through its overbearing film forms was not central in the fascist imaginary. Fascism was not fighting the Italian race; it was fighting for and with them. Its war was a simpler one: a war for home, a war for safety and security, a war to make better persons, rather than one leading to orgies of feelings or to incredible transmutations of the living. If we think about it, the new Italian men and women that the regime promised to make were quite normal people after all; they were fathers and mothers, workers and caregivers, community members ready to serve. To make such a banal race, to contribute to Fascism's race war efforts, one didn't really need heavy editing and sublime overtones; pretty movies might have been enough to do the job. As I begin explaining in the next chapter, independent of the regime's direct control but staying truer to the colors of Blackshirt racism, Blassetti and Camerini had since the end of the 1920s been relying on a much simpler cinematic language to promote fascist living as the trivial, banal solution to the big and small problems afflicting Italy. It is by considering the affects generated by the real that films like theirs staged, and not—as a journalist instead argues—the reality that Fascism created, that we can perhaps rationalize how and why Italy fell for Mussolini.[27]

3 White, Red, Blackshirt

Blasetti's Ecofascist Realism

> The screens are awaiting a new cinema which would be
> the expression of a new race.
>
> —Alessandro Blasetti, "Lettera aperta ai
> banchieri italiani"

A long-held fantasy in Italian historiography and popular imagination posits that racism is something that the regime turned to in the 1930s as a result of Nazi influence. Yet xenophobic sentiments and racialized tropes of national identity were engrained in Fascism's project from its very inception. Consider in this regard the speech Mussolini gave in Milan in October 1922, three short weeks before the March on Rome.[1]

We are at war, Mussolini said; we are surrounded, he suggested, and in such a time of danger and crisis one ought to be ruthless against the enemies within. These enemies are not only the communist thugs who spread the germs of insurrection, profiting from the socioeconomic crisis that emerged in the aftermath of World War I. The liberal state is perhaps even a bigger threat to national security than the red virus. On the basis of a "false conception of life"—Mussolini explained, using an expression that could well have been from Luigi Pirandello—the ruling liberal elites gave the population choices and freedom rather than norms and restraints. It is precisely the state's absence from the people's existences that enabled national life to become so undisciplined. Confused and lacking discipline, some Italians embraced the reckless hedonism that characterized northern European societies, with their rotten democracies. Others had started to look at barbaric Russia for ways to address the discord between labor and capital, workers and owners. Egoism and materialism were causing some Italians to drift away from their history and traditions—to forget who they were and what their country was.

There are those who know that Italy, "from the Alps to Sicily," is a country characterized by a fundamental unity of custom, language, religion, and habits. And there are those who grumble about irremediable divides tearing apart the social fabric. There are the healthy, normal, upright folks who entrust themselves to Fascism, and the infected segments of the bourgeoisie and proletariat who need to be healed or neutralized. There are the hardworking Italians, and those who are unwilling to make sacrifices for the common good. There is the nation that eagerly awaits Fascism's coming, and the country's enemies who have been seduced by absurd and criminal Asiatic doctrines. But the time for the final fight over Italy's "color," to use a term from Mussolini's speech, had come. Eulogizing the righteous violence deployed by fascist armed squads to eradicate egoism, slave morality, and communist delinquency, Mussolini urged all true Italians to join the battle against the improper lifestyles preventing the nation from realizing its full potential.

Even if Mussolini's call to arms did not explicitly mention race, his incendiary speech negotiated key points of concurrent racial science to evoke an ongoing clash of civilizations and build up the fascist takeover of Italy, confirming that—as Alexander Weheliye argues—the operations of nationalism do not differ constitutively from those of ethnic or biological racism.[2]

As far as Italian bodies were concerned, Mussolini dropped the geographical and phenotypical North-South/White-Dark divisions that—as we saw in chapter 1—characterized Aryanist criminal anthropology (Lombroso, Niceforo) as well as, to a certain extent, Sergi's Mediterraneanist raceology. From Sergi, Mussolini adopted the anti-Asian stance but also the resentment against weak democratic governance and the idea that the ruling elites had spoiled national life by embracing way too liberal mores and letting the people go wild. From the Lombrosian school, he inherited the pathologization and biologization of class conflict: communists are degenerate subjects whose discontent is fomented by foreign abject doctrines and who are spreading a dangerous illness.

Through these tactical appropriations, Fascism overcomes the divisive racism from the liberal era and involves the reunified ethno-nation in a new race war, a spiritual-biological war against the infectious ideologies that are contaminating the body politic. Once Italians are no longer divided into two conflicting breeds and pitted against each other according to their nature (geographical origin, skin color, skull morphology, or social extraction), they can in fact deploy as "one single force" against two equally ethnically foreign existential threats: liberalism's dissolute capitalism, traditionally racialized as northern European white; and the red, degenerate Bolshevism coming from "Asia." Aryans and Mediterraneans vanish from Italy, which now becomes populated by three new species of people: communists, liberals, and true Italians, those who will join the Blackshirt fight in defense of authentic national life. According to this order of discourse, being antifascist means being a deviant Italian. National bodies are now identified, profiled, or "colored" on the basis of their styles of existence and political commitments rather than on the basis of epidermal schema or hereditary traits. In this way, the country is re-racialized along three nonphenotypical color lines: communist red, liberal white, and fascist black.

In this regard, echoing Ruth Wilson Gilmore's *Golden Gulag,* it is important to stress that racism is not ultimately a question of epidermic schemata or skeletal morphology, blood or skull. Racial categories and racialized interpellations are biopolitical operators that seek to enforce specific modes of embodiment. Hence, to draw again upon Weheliye and Rhiannon Welch, one needs to recognize that the point of racism is the production and exploitation of race; that in racism, the need to police life, to manage desires, to control what bodies can and will do is more fundamental than skin color or physiognomy. This is precisely why "race" is the key device for and in Western modernity: as Foucault's genealogies of biopolitical rule imply, racism's power to affect how people behave has been a crucial resource for the subjection of life to capital within and without the borders of Europe.[3]

The fact that racialized imaginaries subject and subjectify according to the urgencies of the colonial-capitalistic order is also evident in Mussolini's speech. In a juncture of sociopolitical volatility, in the context of the red biennium and proto-revolutionary agitation, the point of organizing hate campaigns against nonnative, un-Italian red communists and white elites was to pressure new subjects—fascist subjects, individuals subjected to Mussolini's authority and ready to take part in the race war for a stronger and greater Italy that Fascism was launching. The recoloring of the body politic that Fascism advanced by means of Mussolini thus had the function of involving the nation in the Blackshirt way to white supremacy. But with whiteness being the structural by-product of white supremacy, the subjects Fascism aspired to create, notwithstanding its anti-elite stances, were unmarked white lives, bodies that behaved as white bodies do while remaining color-blind to their own racial identity. The Blackshirt people were in all effects a white race, even if they never consented or recognized themselves as such.

This chapter surveys Alessandro Blasetti's cinema from the "years of consensus"—the phase of fascist history from the great land-reclamation campaign of the late 1920s to the occupation of the Ethiopian soil in the mid-1930s. It scrutinizes how the director's "ecofascist" figurations of a national environment at the mercy of white and red Italians supported the production of a Blackshirt army of white lives and its mobilization for Fascism's old and new colonial battles.

DRAINING THE SWAMP

Alessandro Blasetti was born in Rome in 1900, and at age seventeen he completed his first feature film, *La crociata degli innocenti* (*The Crusade of the Innocents*), a lost historical drama based on a script by Gabriele D'Annunzio. Blasetti then turned to film criticism, denouncing in his columns the disarray into which the Italian film industry had fallen and exposing the lack of vision of top producers and administrators as the cause of foreign dominance of the national market.[4] By the end of the 1920s, 80 percent of the features distributed in Italy were produced in the United States, and Blasetti was concerned about the impact of imported films not only on Italian cinema but also on Italian life. Did both face extinction due to such a formidable invasion? Would American film annihilate domestic production and then go on to impose on the national public foreign models of sociality and belonging?

To counter the threat of Americanization, Blasetti initially pursued a sort of independent, low-budget political cinema, as he was convinced that national film could not improve its market position or do anything to keep Italy Italian until the apparatus was controlled by either private investors or state-appointed administrators. For Blasetti, cinema, like all the arts, had to be funded by the state and supported by private patrons but also had to retain its freedom from both politics and the economy. Paradoxically, only by remaining independent would cinema generate financial and political gains. Writing against what in today's critical landscape we would dub "auteurism," Blasetti insisted that film was a collective endeavor—for two reasons. First, to make good movies, a collective of professionals and talents had to work together freely and collaboratively. Second, good movies were movies that simultaneously entertained *and* bettered the collectivity. As Stephen Gundle and Michela Zegna argue, Blasetti articulated the synergy between cinema, spectacle, industry, and politics earlier and more consciously than anyone else—including the hierarch Luigi Freddi, who had participated in the March on Rome and is most often credited for the rebirth of national film as fascist cinema.[5]

Although Blasetti held the LUCE Institute in high esteem, he considered the separation between entertainment and useful cinema to a large extent artificial and forced. For him, fiction films could be deployed in defense of authentic national life more effectively than documentaries or newsreels. The Americans, the Germans, the French, and so on: every race ("razza") had expressed its own cinema and was in turn expressed by cinema—except for the Italians. It was thus time to move forth with a new cinema that would manifest the Italian race, that would amplify the core features of a race that film, and with it the world, had so far disregarded.[6] Blasetti's stance was that this new race that showed itself onscreen would acquire consistency offscreen, and the ethno-nation Fascism was talking about would then be made into something effective and concrete, something relevant and that mattered: not just a fantasy or a discourse or a possibility but as a real historical force.

Blasetti's position on cinematic representation anticipates the insights on the *reality effect* articulated by Fredric Jameson in his cryptically titled 1992 essay "The Existence of Italy." Juxtaposing Marxist historiography and a Heideggerian appreciation of art's worldmaking power, Jameson suggests that the historical function of realism under capitalist modernity is to concoct representations of reality that elicit the novel forms of subjectivity needed for such a reality to actually come into being.[7] Something similar happens in Blasetti: in the director's semiotics of cinema, the referent of cinematic representation (the new Italian race) is not something that exists already but something that film allows to happen. Cinema for him was, in a certain sense, an apparatus presenting Italy's racial future.

There were, however, two major obstacles preventing this cinematic reveal of the Italian race, which would eventually lead to a different Italian real. For starters, Italy lacked the production companies willing to contribute to the cinematic production of new Italians and a new Italy. Second, since it was still barely in its infancy, the Italian race could not yet express itself cinematically, being deficient in autochthonous talents and professionals.

To deal with the second issue and teach young Italians film language, at the end of the 1920s Blasetti set up the first filmmaking courses in Italy at the public conservatory of Santa Cecilia. Having burned bridges with most of the key players in Italian film for his scathing criticism of the industry, and with the regime still officially unconvinced of fiction cinema's biopolitical affordances, to address the first issue Blasetti created his own production company to finally be able to feature the Italian race on the big screen. He raised some money from wealthy fascist sympathizers and forward-thinking hierarchs, but the majority of the budget was "crowdfunded." From the pages of *Cinematografo,* Blasetti issued a plea that each reader contribute what would amount to $100 today for a new Italian cinema. Three hundred of them responded to the call, and in 1929, the film cooperative Augustus released its one and only movie before going bankrupt.

Sole! (*Sun,* 1929), one of the last silent films shot in Italy, swiftly elevated Blasetti's status. Only the first reel remains, but even from the eleven minutes (256 meters) conserved at the Cineteca di Stato it is clear why this film was hailed as a revolution. Without money for fancy sets or stars but with a crew of young talent supporting his vision (Aldo Vergano, Goffredo Alessandrini, Gastone Medin), Blasetti had no choice but to bring the camera outside and shoot mainly on location, relying on B-list actors for the lead roles and employing locals as extras. Liberated from the norms and practices of the studio system, Blasetti's camera ventures through the Lazio marshes, pastures, and encampments to raise enthusiasm around what Mussolini dubbed "the war that we prefer": the settler-colonial reclamation of the Pontine Marshes near Rome, which was just getting started.

In popular culture and public opinion, Rome was the gateway to a darker Italy and bleaker Italians. Indeed, the city was still associated with tropes of criminality, decay, and racial degeneration. We might recall the racist depiction of the Roman underground—primitive, backward, quasi-African—from Alfredo Niceforo and Scipio Sighele's *La mala vita a Roma* as well as the stench and chaos that permeated the city in Pirandello's *Quaderni di Serafino Gubbio operatore.*[8] Mussolini was committed to enhancing Rome's standing, so that the capital of the soon-to-be fascist empire would be a worthy successor of Julius Caesar's Rome and the Rome of the popes. Rome was gutted, and large-scale projects transformed its center. Via dell'Impero—today Via dei Fori Imperiali—was to connect Piazza Venezia, the location of Mussolini's office, and Altare della Patria, the monument celebrating modern Italy's liberation and unification, to the Colosseum, to establish a link between the nation's glorious past and its present. Yet this was not quite enough. Mussolini wanted to build a brand-new fascist Rome whose white marbles would outshine ancient Rome's ruins and the Cupola of St. Peter's Basilica. He identified the almost depopulated areas that now constitute the city's southern outskirts as the perfect site for the regime's urban development ambitions. This is where Fascism would build its monumental cinema-city, Cinecittà, and later the EUR neighborhood with its iconic Square Colosseum.[9]

Even farther south was the swampland that neither ancient Rome nor the Church had been able to reclaim. As Steen Bo Frandsen suggests, the sanitizing of this wild territory was connected to the urban development plan for a "Great Rome," on the one hand, and with Fascism's logic of coloniality on the other.[10] The reclamation of the Pontine Marshes was in fact promoted as the first battle in the regime's endeavor to civilize southern peoples and save them from the ruinous conditions into which they had fallen after centuries of exploitative government by wicked national elites or foreign rulers.

The Mussolini Law of 1928, as Suzanne Stewart-Steinberg traces, called for an ambitious *bonifica* (sanitation, reclamation) of thousands of acres of land, in both southern Italy and Africa, in order to transform what were painted as empty spaces and retrograde human stocks into integral components of a fascist empire. With the ten-year anniversary of the March on Rome nearing, "special significance was given to the three hundred and ten square miles of marshland" south of the nation's capital.[11] The region was infested by malaria-carrying mosquitos and had to be drained and sanitized, but something also had to be done with the decayed bodies stranded there. There were few permanent settlements in the region, and its inhabitants (no more than two thousand people, mainly shepherds, woodcutters, and their families) were suffering the consequences of an unhealthy environment, living—the regime insisted—in a heinous state of moral and physical abjection. Accordingly, more than 100,000 settlers were relocated to the swamps, both forcibly and voluntarily, in order to transform this toxic environment and its degraded stock into a morally and physically healthier species of Italians: the homesteaders were mostly World War I veterans and peasant farmers from the "industrious" Veneto. Stewart-Steinberg writes:

> Their orders were to settle the lands and actively contribute to the regime's various battles: the autarchic "battle of wheat" and other products geared to

self-sufficiency, the demographic battle of births, and finally also the defense of the Italic race, for the latter was supported by the idea that population transfer and therefore cross-breeding between the variously imagined "Italic" stocks (*stirpi*) would, just like the reclamation of lands, produce a vigorous new people capable and strong enough for further colonial ventures.[12]

The reclamation of the Pontine Marshes was really built up as a monument to the regime's capacity to bring light even to the darkest of lands and to enlighten even the most backward of peoples. As Federico Caprotti suggests in his work on fascist ideal cities, the faux medieval burgs and rationalist architecture in white marble emerging from the swampland were to be a sort of shiny model landscape showcasing the brighter world that Mussolini was fighting to build in dark Italy but also in Black Africa. There was, Mia Fuller's research confirms, a clear and direct entanglement between Fascism's internal and external colonial ambitions, and in the regime's dreams, Asmara and Addis Ababa were to be remade to resemble the EUR, Sabaudia, or Littoria.[13] But also the white people emerging from the marsh were to be models. Out of the reclaimed southern fields, Blackshirt whiteness would spring: in fact, the new stock breed there would be modern and civilized, proving that southern Italians were not Black, but they would not be elite white either, given their work ethic, grittiness, non-bourgeois attitudes, and readiness to sacrifice. This sort of race would serve as a perfect model for the kind of subjects that even darker bodies, Black bodies, could aspire to become.

To affectively authorize Fascism's coloniality as a civilizing and world-making enterprise, Blasetti starts *Sole!* with a closed gate. The camera confronts the marshes, and the opening title card presents this wrecked landscape as the field of eternal strife between evolution and degeneration. As the gate opens, the exploration of this dark, gloomy borderland and its people begins. A series of cross-fades moves the viewer across the deadly spaces of the malarious land: there are men toiling in the mud, skulls and rotting carcasses of large animals, herds of wild buffalo stomping on people and destroying everything in their way, a toxic territory and an environment in ruin. Yet the "march of progress," as the title card dubs it, can finally begin: the *bonificatori*—the "reclaimers," that is, the colonists in charge of reclaiming this devastated milieu—have arrived and will soon get to work. To force on the public a propagandistic experience of the sanitation efforts, Blasetti makes the spectators embrace the perspective of the reclamation teams venturing into this wild Italian south. First, he positions the camera on a raft surveying the marshes. Then, he moves it to a train running on a newly inaugurated railroad and hauling the materials and the labor force that will be needed to complete the civilizing mission. The spectators, in this case, do not merely see the marshes through the settlers' point of view. They are also made to share the regime's perspective on the work that will be done there. The verticality that Blasetti articulates by elevating the camera from the level of the mud and the water to the train's locomotive sanctions Fascism's colonization efforts as something naturally springing forth from the landscapes that they intervene on: *Sole!* solicits the regime's intervention as necessary given the very nature of the places, but also the faces, about to be targeted.

Piero Garofalo writes about the influence of Soviet cinema on the film's aesthetic and imaginary, but its references also include ethnographic documentary, which introduced the ways of "primitive" peoples to "modern" publics, and above all the Western, with its mythology of the frontier and of the pioneers fighting bandits and winning over, or suppressing, defiant darker-skinned natives. The colonists do, in fact, teach the marsh people hard work and modern techniques, and—in an impressive dolly shot— the camera moves around an industrious settlement, documenting with its dynamism the incredible progress made once the locals interiorize the true Italian ingenuity and work ethic. This is an important scene not only for its technical complexity and affective import but also because it will serve as a blueprint for how to mediate the encounter between progressed fascist settlers and backward native bodies in the father lands that Fascism set out to reclaim. As Ruth Ben-Ghiat shows, both LUCE newsreels and narrative films downplayed the violence of Italian colonialism and manifested Italy's presence in Africa as a beacon of civility, modernity, and morality.[14] In *Sole!*, Fascism is conveyed in the same manner: bearing not destruction but culture.

In an interview from the 1960s, Blasetti remarked that the work of Enrico Ferri was a crucial reference for him while writing and shooting this film. Ferri was a Fascist Party senator who insisted that racial degeneration was the result of a combination of natural predispositions and environmental conditions. Ferri's influence on the project comes through in the insistence with which the film connects the fascist conquest of a degraded landscape with the moral enlightenment of the people living there, who need to be cultivated, reclaimed exactly as the barren, underdeveloped environment in which they are embedded.[15] Even the lighting in *Sole!* contributes to advancing its ecofascism. The dramatic chiaroscuro set design, curated by Medin, effectively expands on the film's title and brings the point home: where there was darkness and blackness, now there are glimmers of sun and light.

However, this work of enlightenment does not proceed unbothered. The Mussolini-led march toward brighter times comes to an abrupt end due to the swamp people's resistance. To mediate such a standstill of progress and change, Blasetti's camera—which had been very mobile and forward-moving until then—halts and becomes still. A group of hunters has gathered in assembly to question the homesteaders' intentions, concerned about the changes that they bring about: will drinking, for instance, be banned? Through a series of close-ups, Blasetti captures the signs of moral vice and biological decay in these men's faces: huge earrings, buboes, sores, scars, rotten teeth. A young man, Silvestro (Vittorio Vaser), is especially distrustful. After examining the order to vacate their dwellings so that the sanitation process can continue, Silvestro turns dramatically to the camera, inciting his mates to oppose the invaders and defend their land and way of life. He then rushes to the house of the community leader, Marco (Vasco Creti), in order to summon him to the uprising, but Marco is not there.

Silvestro takes this opportunity to corner Marco's virginal daughter Giovanna (Dria Paola), and this assault is another way in which Blasetti conveys that antifascism is a dangerous form of degeneration, that it is abject desire motivating the stock of Italians who foment conflict and challenge the regime's campaigns. Through Giovanna's point of view, the public sees Silvestro menacingly advancing forward—emotionless eyes, a sinister grin, black hat, a dark shadow cast on his face and with total blackness in the background. The frame composition, a frontal medium close-up, and the black backdrop make Silvestro look like one of the portraits from Lombroso's criminal anthropology studies. But there is also a resonance with the closing shot from Edwin S. Porter's *The Great Train Robbery* (1903) that visually conveys what the plot narrates: those who oppose Fascism are violent criminals and pathological subjects (Figure 8).

Silvestro is profiled, identified as a deviant by the cinematographic apparatus here, and Blasetti again uses the camera to discriminate between who is a racially appropriate Italian and who is not.[16] When in fact earlier *Sole!* had featured the engineer head of the development team, Dr. Rinaldi (Marcello Spada), it captured him well lit, in a lateral close-up as he is busy advancing the reclamation works. He is not a mugshot; he is not a threat.

FIGURE 8. Silvestro, the bandit-deviant, smirks at the camera in *Sole!* (Alessandro Blasetti, 1929).

Dr. Rinaldi, like the other colonists, emanates an aura of enlightenment, uprightness, health, and morality that is paramount for the film's operation: to remediate the swamp into a battlefield between the Italian race that remains and the one to come. This clash between the racial past and future of Italy follows the expected chromatic pattern: darkness on one side, light on the other—with a ray of sun shining on Rinaldi's forehead and rendering him luminescent. The last fifty minutes of the film are lost, so we do not get to see how this confrontation plays out. But it is possible to reconstruct what might have happened after Silvestro's heinous attempt on Giovanna from the screenplay by Vergano as well as from film stills and reviews published in magazines from the time.[17]

    Giovanna's father gets home just in time to prevent her from being raped by the depraved agitator, exorcising the threat of miscegenation. Father and daughter then rush to meet Dr. Rinaldi to figure out what is going on, if the homesteaders' concerns are on point. Rinaldi convinces Marco and Giovanna that no abuse is taking place: it is in everyone's interest for the swamp to be drained. Rinaldi and Giovanna are falling in love. Silvestro, resentful at having to give up his land and the woman he covets to an outsider, organizes an assassination attempt against Rinaldi with the collaboration of a crass woman who is the antithesis of the pure and chaste Giovanna. But at the last minute, Silvestro recognizes Dr. Rinaldi: they fought side by side during the Great War and Rinaldi even saved Silvestro's life. Silvestro finally understands that there are not two separate groups or factions. Natives and developers are one: they are Italians; they are hard workers; they are one race. The clashes between locals and *bonificatori*, colonized and colonizers, end: Rinaldi and Giovanna will start a family; and the savage natives finally step into the light, step into Blackshirt whiteness, evolving from hunter-gatherers into rural workers.

Sole! was highly appreciated by the press and by the young film enthusiasts gravitating around the Cine-GUFS, the university film clubs created by Fascism in the early 1930s. When Blasetti claimed that not only Italian cinema but also neorealism came out of the swamps, he was not completely delusional.[18] The experience of *Sole!,* with its decision to sidestep the studio system and create a direct connection between the apparatus and the soil, would be incredibly influential not only for the development of fascist realism and of imperial cinema but also for the new realist wave of the 1940s and 1950s. The mark of Blasetti can be felt distinctly, especially in Luchino Visconti's, Roberto Rossellini's, and Giuseppe De Santis's own postfascist "eco-cinemas"—I am thinking not only of the melodramatic capture of the marshes in *Ossessione (Obsession,* 1943) and *Riso amaro (Bitter Rice,* 1949), or of the camera that flows with the wind and the river in *Paisà (Paisan,* 1946), but also of the politicized landscapes from *La terra trema (The Earth Trembles,* 1948), *Stromboli* (1949), or *Non c'è pace tra gli ulivi (No Peace under the Olive Tree,* 1950).

Notwithstanding the praise it garnered, Blasetti's independent film could not secure adequate distribution. Augustus closed down, and Blasetti, having been poached by Cines, finally agreed to shoot talkies. Like many others, he had initially branded these a foreign genre and too radical a deviation from traditional Italian cinema, which as we know had blossomed during the silent era. Blasetti ended up directing fifteen sound films under the regime, experimenting with different registers and alternating between purely commercial productions and films that, like *Terra madre (Mother Land,* 1931) and *Vecchia guardia (Old Guard,* 1935), supported Fascism's endeavor to make a race that would get to work for the regime. What is notable about these films (besides their artistic merits) is that in order to mobilize the people and stage Fascism's redemptive power, they resort to racialized tropes and racializing moves that are incredibly similar to those that characterize contemporary right-wing populisms. In fact, *Terra madre* and *Vecchia guardia* populistically stoke resentment against "white" elites and blame them for the country's ruination—even for the spread of the red threat and the birth of antifa thugs. With the marshes drained, Blasetti singles out another kind of swamp as responsible for endangering the nation.

ESCHEWING THE ELITES

Terra madre picks up where *Sole!* ended: there is still a lot to do for the fascist utopia to come into full bloom. A somber chant rises from the titular "mother land" bordering the swamp, and with it the noises of rural labor. This is one of Blasetti's first sound films, and the use of diegetic sound, as Lara Pucci notes, is impressive. Pickaxes hitting the earth, the thudding hooves of charging cattle, and the footsteps of the peasants working the soil resonate with the surrounding landscape to aurally mediate "the physical and symbolic solidity of this place and the connectedness of its inhabitants to it."[19] There is a materiality, a weight, to this location that makes it feel real but also right. The humble peasants—men and women, young and old—are a sturdy, gritty stock. Hardworking, dedicated to the fields, they toil until dusk, relentless, resolute, to prepare the soil for the crops. Labor is both naturalized as an integral feature of the Italian landscape and a defining trait of the people's identity. Yet there is a problem: the farmstead lacks modern machines, and thus the peasants cannot work as efficiently and productively as they would want to. In light of the identitarian features of *Terra madre*, this also means that these peasants, by not working as effectively as they could, fall short of attaining their true selves.

Eating their supper in a modest hut, catching some warmth from the fireplace, the peasants complain about the lack of investment and attention from the young aristocrat who owns the farm. Unlike his late father, he wastes most of his time in the city and does not seem to understand that the estate needs someone who can command, someone who will provide the workers with the guidance and resources they need to do their jobs. In a virtuoso two-minute sequence combining pans and lateral tracking shots, Blasetti moves the camera through the gloomy room, capturing the natural commitment of these rural Italians to labor but also a growing suspicion toward the new *padrone* (master, boss). Is he the guide that the land needs? The Duke (Sandro Salvini) is about to inspect the estate, and the farm laborers are looking forward to discussing with him what comes next.

A motorcade now invades the tranquil countryside, exciting the stock and the people. The Duke is not alone. He came from the city with his friends, who look like a different breed from the Italians working in the fields. They are fashionable, pale, cosmopolitan, fake, artificial; we are a few miles away from Rome, but to them this is a completely foreign land. The city crowd cannot respect the sanctity of the place. The Duke's latest girlfriend, Daisy (Isa Pola), cannot stand farm life. Skinny, bougie, vain, she sleeps in, and—smothered in white linen beddings, laces, and perfumes—treats the locals as servants, incessantly ringing the bell she keeps on her nightstand to demand their services. In the film, Daisy functions as the embodiment of the *donna-crisi,* or "crisis-woman"—in the fascist imagination a dangerous type of well-to-do modern woman with "an extremely thin and consequently sterile body that purportedly confirmed her cosmopolitan, non-domestic, non-maternal, and non-fascist interest."[20] How could someone like this, and with such a strange name for a good Italian woman, fit in and belong amid the fields and the workers that feed a nation?

Unlike his girlfriend, the Duke is happy. In rural Italy, he feels at home and among his people. During one of his long horse rides surveying and reconnecting with his land and stock, the Duke hears a prayer in the distance and slowly makes his way to what looks like a mobile tabernacle where a country priest is officiating mass. Following the Duke, the camera moves discreetly so as not to profane the sacred space. A dolly shot captures the devotion of the peasants as they invoke the Virgin Mary for protection and forgiveness. The Duke dismounts his high horse, putting himself at the level of his workers and joining them in their prayers. Through a scale progression from close-up to medium shots to full shots, Blasetti moves the camera away from the religious gathering, closing the sequence with a pan over this pious assemblage. The Duke is on the margins, but for the first time we see him in a choral scene gathering with his own workers. He takes particular interest in a young, voluptuous, but pious peasant, who in the next scene pretends not to know who he is and flirtatiously questions his intentions. Emilia (Leda Gloria) is the daughter of the estate manager, and since her mother died, she has been taking care of her younger siblings when not working in the fields. Throughout the film, shot-reverse-shot

FIGURE 9. Above, Daisy, the "crisis-woman," and below, Emilia, the "peasant woman," in *Terra madre* (Alessandro Blasetti, 1931).

patterns establish that Emilia is the total opposite of Daisy (Figure 9): already her name showcases her organic connection with the Italian land—Emilia Romagna is the region where the Duce was born.

In a medium shot framing Emilia and the Duke holding hands and whispering to each other as lovers would do, the young woman complains that their master has abandoned them. Everything is going to ruin without him: the swamps are advancing again; workers' morale is hitting new lows and their dissatisfaction is ever growing. The Duke resents the charges, but Emilia does not back down: "If the master were an intelligent man, with the right vision, if he belonged to our race [razza] and had something in his heart, he would agree with me." The Duke sighs and replies: "So it appears your master does not belong to the same race [razza] as you." Emilia, maternal, reassures him: since the padrone was born here, it will only take a few steps on this land to remind him of who he is, where, and with whom he belongs (Figure 10). The southern fields are presented here

FIGURE 10. The Duke rekindling the connection with his race in *Terra madre* (Alessandro Blasetti, 1931).

as a space where Italian men will reclaim their white patriarchal masculinity, and with it their authentic racial affiliations. As Fascism moved from internal to external colonialism, films such as Blasetti's *Aldebaran* (1935), Camerini's *Il grande appello* (*The Great Appeal,* 1935), Augusto Genina's *Lo squadrone bianco* (*White Squadron,* 1936), or Alessandrini's *Luciano Serra, pilota* (*Luciano Serra, Pilot,* 1938) began attributing the same restorative function to other Souths—the African colonies—and to other fields: the warfront.

Blasetti insisted that his decision to shoot on location, outdoors as much as possible, and to eschew stars in favor of what I would call "native performers" as extras was meant to rehabilitate Italian film practices and challenge the market dominance of manufactured sentimental comedies and melodramas. When one of the city dwellers in *Terra madre* dares to suggest that the estate could be turned into a movie set, Blasetti is trying to establish a distance between his own intervention and the sort of fictions the public was familiar with. The argument was the same as that made by Pirandello in *Quaderni* and by Ada Negri in the 1928 short story "Cinematografo": current cinema, with its operatic passions and fantasy travels in foreign worlds, was compromising the Italian moral fiber, making the most naive and impressionable spectators fall for foreign pleasures, desires, and lifestyles that could only lead to ruin or death.[21] In the face of an attack against the Italian spirit, film had to do its part. Italian society was as usual under siege, and thus, as usual, had to be defended.

Nevertheless, despite the textual and paratextual outrage against genre fiction and commercial cinema, Blasetti's ecofascist realism does not actually shun generic conventions (the same would hold true for Pirandello and Negri, but also neorealism). On the one hand, Blasetti is committed to remediate *Terra madre* as a different kind of cinema: not a fiction, but something serious, concrete, relevant, and "real." On the other hand, he politicizes the romantic and melodramatic register in order to mediate— through the love story between the Duca and Emilia—a quasi-erotic attachment between the Duce and rural Italy.

The fact that the Duke connects with Emilia during a Mass is important. After the reconciliation with the Church sanctioned in 1929 by the Lateran Treaty, Fascism could embrace Catholic traditionalism as a fundamental building block of its racialized identity politics. Italy was a fascist *and* a Christian nation, with the Catholic Church and the Fascist Party collaboratively caring for the spiritual and physical health of the body politic. But the signing of the Lateran Treaty also cast a new light on the

Catholic peasant masses and the lifeworld associated with them. The South, and rural Italy more broadly, was no longer what it still was in *Sole!*; it was no longer the backward "Other within" that had to be civilized and whose retrograde superstitions had to be redressed. On the contrary, peasant men and women, rural fertile mothers and unsophisticated fathers— hardworking, faithful, committed, observant, their skin marked by the grit and many hours in the fields—were hailed by the regime as an emblem of racial virtue and a stronghold of Italian tradition, an antidote to the depraved modernity enjoyed by the elites, whose pale skin was so rarely kissed by the sun. Rural Italians, an embarrassment for the ruling blocs under liberalism and branded as darker bodies, became a state-sanctioned treasure and were celebrated as a source of pride. In order to appeal to rural masses, Fascism gave dignity and importance to identities and subjectivities that liberal capitalism disdained; it proposed, Gaia Giuliani writes, a project of race-nation-empire in which even underclass Italians could feel included, valued, and recognized. Not only did the regime develop a socioeconomic order where "warfare, industrial production, and urban and infrastructural development went together with traditional family life and agricultural production."[22] It also conveyed that to move forward, the Italian race needed to look backward—and hence, in a key move to understand the success of its populism, elected as authentic Italians those who were earlier chastised for their lagging behind. The drag was, in a sense, the future for the Italian race.

In such a context, Giuliani continues, the *contadina* (peasant woman)— with her patriarchal values, maternal instincts, and bursting reproductive sexuality—became a particularly important trope in fascist discourse. This mode of life was eroticized as the embodiment of a racially appropriate Italian femininity, an antidote to liberal, foreign, northern European toxic womanhood that was key to generating the healthy, strong, dynamic, ordered, and disciplined stock that the homeland needed. The body of the woman was a fundamental battlefield for Fascism because through it passed the spiritual and biological destiny of the ethno-nation.

Thus, the rural mass scene from *Terra madre*, one of the first cinematic implantations of Christianity in the Italian landscape and the beginning of the love story between the peasant world and a duke, is important for two reasons. First, it celebrates the recent reconciliation between Roman Catholicism and the Italian state. Second, and conversely, it sets up a strife between two very different kinds of Italian people, giving the Duca/Duce the opportunity to show everyone, the public especially, his true allegiances. In fact, he must decide which nation, which men and women, which *razza* —to use the film's own terminology—to embrace and support. Will he side with Emilia and her rural breed or Daisy and her city crowd?

Following a chromatic strategy that is in line with Fascism's bid on the "darker Italy," with its antimodern, "grittier" iteration of white supremacy appealing to the subaltern masses, in *Terra madre* high bright white and ivory brand improper behaviors, while darker tones and more "rustic" textures of white are associated with the lifestyles that ought to be prized. The contrast between Emilia and Daisy is especially apparent: the first, brunette and olive skinned, is usually featured garbed in black garments or traditional religious clothing and captured through sober and somber lighting, giving her a distinct material depth; and the second—blonde, pale, blue eyes—is depicted as always draped in satin, furs, and often through high key lighting, which flattens her out. As James Hay suggests, smooth, silky whiteness and monochromatic luminescent lighting often functioned in Italian film under the regime as markers of privilege.[23] In *Terra madre,* they are used to flag predatory subject positions, behaviors, and environments, which were those traditionally associated with urban cosmopolitan elites who had self-identified as northern European white.

In his overview of whiteness in film history, Richard Dyer notes that in contemporary horror cinema, white characters are often the bringers of death. Dyer connects this trope with Karl Marx's appropriation of vampire mythology: the unproductive upper classes are vampires that need to suck the life out of the working people in order to live on.[24] The elites in *Terra madre* are characterized by a similar nefariousness, and they are even pictured through visual strategies that anticipate the stylistic choices of contemporary Marxian horrors. We can think, for instance, of the blinding whiteness that Daisy from Blasetti's film and Rose (Allison Williams) from Jordan Peele's *Get Out* (2017) share (Figure 11).

However, in Peele's comedy horror, but also in films such as Brian Yuzna's *Society* (1989), George Romero's *Land of the Dead* (2005), or Bong Joon-ho's *Parasite* (2019), elites are condemned within the context of a larger take on the economic and power structures responsible for creating a class of bloodsuckers and an exploited underclass of workers. In *Terra madre,* on the contrary, there is no structural critique of white privilege, only moralistic outrage against privileged elites. It is for this very reason that Blasetti's film, a sort of hillbilly elegy in its own right, has nothing progressive about

FIGURE 11. Rose's blinding whiteness in *Get Out* (Jordan Peele, 2017), as her face is illuminated by the glow of her computer monitor and she coolly sips a glass of milk.

it; it serves instead as a weapon foreclosing class struggle and to sustain Blackshirt supremacy in national life. Hardworking Italians do not need to take up arms and transform the system: they just need to find someone of their own breed to whom they can entrust themselves for protection. They need a Duce, or to stay with the film's metaphor, a *duca*. Ultimately, then, Blasetti's representation of peasants' work ethic, moral fiber, and lifestyle serves to salvage the very structures responsible for the alienation and exploitation of subaltern Italy by the haute bourgeoise and state power. *Terra madre* not only directs the public to take pride in hard work and sacrifice, elevating them into a blessing in disguise; it also harnesses a sense of precariousness and insecurity that calls for a savior.

We know that biopolitics and state racism entail a shift in how rulers are perceived by the people they seek to control. In order for the state to assume the pastoral function previously fulfilled by the Church, the sovereign ought to be accepted as a benevolent authority who knows the land and the people, has their best interests in mind, and is thus able to care for them in the face of any and all threats. So the people need to feel imperiled but also to believe that those in charge will lead them to safety and do them good. In the fascist pastoral of *Terra madre*, Blasetti affectively conveys that the Duce is precisely the guide that the true Italian race needs in order to prosper, by showing off the Duke's skills as a master cowboy ("bovaro"), drawing from the popular LUCE iconography of Mussolini working in the fields.

Gathered around the corral where the cowherds have mustered the cattle to be measured and branded, elite and subaltern Italians meet. The "white" people look with superiority and repugnance at the "primitive" way in which the stock is handled and the branding conducted. The Duke does not approve of this attitude and mingles with the dark-skinned peasants, who, in contrast, are celebrating such a crucial event in the life of a farmstead. The influence of the Western and the association between the American and Italian frontiers are again evident. The Duke sits on the fence with a glowing Emilia. Excited, as if to reclaim his own masculinity and mastery, he jumps into the pen and tackles a buffalo, grabbing the powerful animal by the horns and wrestling it to the ground, so that its body can be marked and claimed. Blasetti immerses the viewer in the ring and enmeshes us in this intense fight. Lateral tracking shots moving in antithetical directions capture the opposite reactions of the two Italian breeds present at the scene. The workers are excited, proud, supportive, and enthusiastic; the elites are disgusted and baffled. Now that he has shown his capacity to harness the power of the land, the peasants—addressing the camera directly—beg the Duke to stay and take care of them: as the stock, as the public, they have been claimed. Still, the Duke decides to leave the somber folk meals of the Italian countryside for the well-lit but sterile poker tables, the lies and affairs that the rich—and childless—enjoy in the city (Figure 12).

But his race needs him. The Duca had decided to sell the property to his friends. What he does not know is that they have no intention of supporting the farmstead: they are involved in a shady development plan to evict the peasants, demolish their shantytown, create a road connecting the estate to the highway, and turn the farm into a retreat of sorts. To speed up the eviction of the peasants and the renovations, the buyers set the estate ablaze. Emilia reaches the Duke on the phone; he rushes back from the city and saves rural Italy from the city elites, and with it a child who is trapped in a burning stable. He renounces urban life forever and returns where and with whom he belongs. Finally, he is back in charge—we even see him adopting Mussolini's infamous stance, hands on his hips and his gaze toward the future: the Duca/Duce has straightened up his allegiances; nothing can go wrong now.

At the end of the film, we are back where we started, where everything starts: on the fields, at work. Emilia and Marco (she is now on a first-name basis with the Duke) toil together, always surrounded by children. Marco

FIGURE 12. Two tables: ritzy card-playing and peasant chatter in *Terra madre* (Alessandro Blasetti, 1931).

does not want her to work the land anymore; now that he and the machines are around, women need to stay home and provide a different kind of labor to the community. Emilia playfully protests: she wants to keep working. Marco insists that one day he will get the strong-willed *contadina* to say yes to him. Emilia blushes and runs away, only to turn around after a few meters to invite the Duke to come along. As Emilia and Marco run toward the horizon together, the camera pans left, showcasing an Italian countryside in full bloom and assembling a picture-perfect homage to heteronormativity and reproductive futurity. The swamp has been drained; the "white threat" is neutralized. Pickaxes and shovels break through the soil: thanks to everyone's hard work, thanks to the recognition of peasants and owners that they are part of the same race that shares the same values and priorities, the motherland is being plowed and will soon bear fruit. Emilia, the maternal woman, will too. The future of the race is safe and bright.

REOPENING ITALY

To model the gendered workforce that the regime needed for its efforts, *Terra madre* romanticized the prosperous destiny seeded by the collaboration between good bosses and productive masses. With *Vecchia guardia*, Blasetti continues to weaponize the apparatus to simultaneously make and mobilize an Italian race. Yet in this case, he changes registers—shifting from romance to epic—to tell a cautionary tale of what happens to a place when the racial unity of capital and labor is compromised, leading to an eruption of class conflict. In this film from 1935, Blasetti travels back in time to 1922 to paint a brutalist picture of Italy under the yoke of careless liberal rulers who allowed the red threat to spread across Italy and shut down the country. From the metaphor of the swamp in *Terra madre* to the insistence in *Vecchia guardia* that there can be no future or history beyond the horizon of labor, and that being closed for business is both a disgrace and a betrayal of national identity, the tropes and imaginaries from 1930s Italian Fascism continue to resonate with those from twenty-first-century America.

Vecchia guardia takes place in the days leading up to the March on Rome. We are again in southern rural Lazio, around Frosinone, and everything has come to a halt. The communist thugs have infiltrated the quaint village where the young boy Mario (Franco Brambilla) lives with his family. His father, Dottor Cardini (Gianfranco Giachetti), is the head physician at the local psychiatric hospital, and his older brother Roberto (Mino Doro), a veteran, is now a high school teacher still waiting for an assignment. Schools have been ordered to stay closed for safety reasons in light of the explosive sociopolitical situation, but Roberto is not idle. He is a militiaman, head of a combat team of proud Italian boys who gear up every day and go out to hunt down the rebels—rich and poor united against the common enemy. Mario idolizes his big brother and is eager to join Roberto's *squadraccia* (militia squad) in their punitive expeditions. Mario always wears the Balilla uniform, a clear sign that being a Blackshirt is more than a political choice; it is an identitarian feature—the core of authentic Italianity. With the Christian cross and war memorabilia in the background, he promises Roberto that he will do his part to get Italy going again. For the film, Communism is not merely an economic or political danger; it is a biological threat to the very existence of an Italian race. Everything has stopped due to the spread of the red virus—not just the production of material goods but also the reproduction of the nation's body. Roberto would like to start a family, but how can he plan a life under these conditions? And he's not the only one suffering: with the whole of the public sector shut down, unemployment is through the roof. The good Italian people are hurting. Futurity is being sabotaged. For Blasetti, an inoperative environment is a ruined space, and the slow times of the film's beginning effectively convey the sense that Communism inevitably leads to the bankruptcy of history.

Things take a turn for the worse when the male nurses from the psychiatric ward decide to go on strike, after months of waiting for Rome to respond to their demands. They are not bad people, just frustrated and disappointed. Dottor Cardini sees this—sees them—and tries to mediate. He calls *il ministero* (the ministry), but no one answers. He makes the rounds of the local politicians, but to no avail. The apparatuses of liberal Italy are unable or uninterested in protecting national life from the looming catastrophe. The mayor is attending to his estate, where he exploits the workers and does not allow the peasants' children to taste even a single grape. The school principal dedicates more time to pursuing his students sexually than to taking the steps necessary for the schools to reopen. No one in charge registers that the situation is deteriorating and that the people are about to explode. Without an efficient government and without leaders who care, the town goes mad. The patients escape the psychiatric ward. Meanwhile, the Reds are getting stronger and have almost taken over the town. Blasetti works hard here to demonize demands for socioeconomic justice and to paint a positive picture of fascist repression.

Roberto's militia squad is presented as the one and only force opposing the thugs who are keeping the town hostage. Even the police are useless and prefer not to intervene. One day, Roberto and his men conclude that children cannot be kept out of class anymore: they will reopen the local school, even if protesters and rebels have already assembled to fight back against this decision. A violent clash between communist thugs and Blackshirt heroes erupts. Finally, after a scene of street violence reminiscent of the infamous Ku Klux Klan sequence in D. W. Griffith's *Birth of a Nation* (1915), Roberto's *squadraccia* is able to momentarily prevail. With the collaboration of the teachers, they get the kids back into the classroom, standing at the school's gate and defending the right of young Italians to learn and grow. The presence of Roberto's unit is enough to disperse the crowd of rebels who were planning to break into the school and impose a new shutdown. But when night falls, the threat returns. When the saboteurs reach the power plant, the town is left completely in the dark. A small-scale civil war erupts. Things cannot go on like this any longer. Analogously to *Sole!* and *Terra madre, Vecchia guardia* asks the public to pick sides, to decide on which side of the political color line to stand: with the Blackshirts who reopen Italy or the Reds, these "enemies of the people" who compromise Italian futurity.

Mario decides that it is time he joined the righteous battle to restore order, and he is killed in action. Blasetti's camera is surprisingly still through the first hour of *Vecchia guardia,* so when the camera starts moving after Mario's death, its motions become charged with incredible meaning. Blasetti, in total control of film language and technique, sets up a great moment of cinematic emotional manipulation: pulling in twice on Mario's corpse, he forces the public to face the sacrifice of this little Italian patriot and confront what it means for the collectivity (Figure 13).

Mario is brought home with all honors, and the town falls into absolute silence. Even the Communists back off. This is too much: the life of a child is sacred, we are reminded by a nun in tears. Through long descriptive pans of Mario's room, Blasetti conjures the eerie emptiness that his death has left behind. But Mario has not departed. After his death, Blasetti incorporates a POV shot from the perspective of Mario's body lying in rest in his fascist youth uniform, as the town pays him homage, affirming Mario's

FIGURE 13. The dead Mario rests in peace, dressed in his fascist youth uniform in *Vecchia guardia* (Alessandro Blasetti, 1935).

continued presence and articulating the sense of a communion between living and dead; between past, present, and future. Mario is still with us, the film establishes; he remains as part of a larger history that the living will be proud to fight for and build in his name.

At Mario's funeral, the wind makes the cypresses weep, producing the impression that the landscape itself is partaking in fascist mourning and, by extension, naturalizing Fascism as something embedded in Italy's very nature. But this environmental sorrow is soon muted by the Blackshirts' belligerent invocations of Mario's name as they perform the fascist roll call: "Mario Cardini—presente, presente, presente." Mario is present as a memory, an example, a warning, and a call to arms. The trajectory initiated by his sacrifice cannot stop. The film's rhythm intensifies, and the camera movements track how Mario's sacrifice is transforming the town's political and human environment. There are no opposing factions anymore; the protagonist of *Vecchia guardia* now becomes the collectivity, the one Italian race united against its common enemies. The whole community now dresses in black, and fascist anthems are heard on every corner. Accompanied by the ghost of his dead son, who is inciting him, "Forza papà, forza papà" (Courage dad, courage), even Dottor Cardini joins the convoy launching the assault against those who endanger the biological survival of the true Italian people. It is time to storm Rome; it is time to take back Italy. The film's closing card reads: "together with the living marched the dead who were born again at Mussolini's call."

In presenting the days leading up to the March on Rome as a *vigilia* (eve)—a term that Italian speakers mainly use to refer to the night before Christmas—the opening title card of *Vecchia guardia* immediately begins memorializing the fascist insurgency as a miraculous event. The closing card completes this canonization of Fascism by casting Mussolini in the role of lifesaver and even metaphorical redeemer of dead children, that is, of the aborted possibilities of life, of futurity. In this way, Blasetti turns fascist history into a wondrous happening the public should be proud to be part of, something in which it would want to participate.

But why use so much heavy-handedness in characterizing fascist power as a saving grace? What was the point of remarking so emphatically that Fascism had saved the nation from the white swamp and red virus? Why put in so much effort to make the people identify with Blackshirt armed squads and violence?

When *Vecchia guardia* came out in 1935, Fascism had quashed even the last glimmers of opposition. With Gramsci on his deathbed and Palmiro Togliatti in Moscow, Mussolini was stronger than ever. If we remain at the level of representation—what the film shows and tells—it is difficult then to understand Blasetti's operation. But if we consider the affects and subject positions this filmic device triggers with its ecofascist representation of Italian environments under siege, then things might make more sense. This film—and the same could be said about Blasetti's other historical reenactments, most notably *1860* (1934) and *Ettore Fieramosca* (1938)—is more about Italy's future wars than its past battles. With Fascism about to accelerate from nation- to empire-building, the country had to commit to even more heroic endeavors. The Italian people's allegiance to the regime had to be more unwavering than ever, given what was lying ahead.

The ethno-nation that rose up in 1922 thanks to Mussolini had to get out of its workwear and don the uniform—to assure Italy's survival, keep other children alive, liberate other peoples from wicked rulers, bring light and prosperity to other dark localities, and fight the red virus at its root. The Old Guard had fulfilled its duty; now it was time for the New Guard to do its part. Franco Brambilla, the child actor who played Mario in *Vecchia guardia*, was born in Rome the year of the great fascist march on Italy's capital and died at twenty fighting for Fascism on the Eastern Front. This was the new race that Fascism made and Blasetti's new cinema so insistently expressed on the screens. Fredric Jameson is right: the fictional lives that realism concocts do not always remain mere fictions.[25]

4 The Shame of Escapism

Camerini's Anthropological Machines

While the 1920s were years of profound crisis for Italian film, the debate on how to effect its comeback was vibrant and energetic. The scene was divided into factions, each with its own project of cinema and idea of what had to happen for domestic production to become sustainable. Toward the end of the decade, two groups decided to take matters into their own hands and escalate the "culture war" (*agitazione culturale*) for a new Italian cinema to actual moviemaking.[1] There were the crowdfunded pioneers led by Alessandro Blasetti, but there was also the more poised contingent that came together around Mario Camerini.

Camerini's films about city life and Blasetti's coeval movies set in the Italian countryside are commonly read in opposition. On the basis of the *stracittà–strapaese* rift, they are often presented as harnessing incompatible imaginaries that are expressions of, respectively, Fascism's urbanist and rural- ist models of economic development. Indeed, in a variation of the North–South racialized axiology, the *strapaese* movement defended as properly Italian the traditional values and religious zeal that supposedly were embed- ded in rural locations whereas the *stracittà* proponents insisted that the authentic Italy was the one found in the nation's industrialized cityscapes.[2] Yet in order to succeed, the regime had to appeal to town *and* country alike—swaying its way the salaried masses working in factories and in the service industries but also the rural petty bourgeoisie and subaltern peasants who were to support the growth of the ethno-nation's biological body through produce and progeny. The fact that the regime could get behind a multiplicity of imaginaries and projects of being-together is thus not nec- essarily a sign of the presence of "competing fascisms" within Fascism, as

Mark Antliff argues. The reliance on complementary discourses, styles, and registers can be seen as an attestation of the regime's anti-ideological and nonconsensual approach to governing—of the *trasformismo* or, to use a more elegant category, "polyvalent mobility" through which Fascism commanded Italian labor.[3]

Throughout the 1920s, Gramsci had strategized about the necessity of unifying rural and urban workers into a class that could effectively challenge the capitalist block. In order to safeguard Italian capitalism and support its colonial ambitions, the regime had to transform Italian laborers from threats into resources, to evolve a conflictual multitude of subject positions into a race that would fight for and with Fascism. For this to happen, contrary to what consent-based explanations of state power posit, the regime didn't necessarily have to impose one single common *Weltanschauung* upon the people. What mattered was that Fascism supplemented the repressive workings of violence with biopolitical weapons—including discursive apparatuses and filmic machines—that would enable the variegated forms of identities, the different kinds of authentic Italian men and women, necessary for the existence of a colonial, capitalist Italy. With this context in mind, in this chapter I approach Camerini's depictions of urban underclasses tempted by deviant desires as part of the same race war as Blasetti's ecofascist cinema, a war that sought to fashion national subjects amenable to fulfill the localized responsibilities Italy assigned them.

Although Camerini's and Blasetti's films might have been moved by analogous political urgencies, the way each functioned is quite different. Blasetti puts viewers in the position of the Blackshirt stock toiling to birth a better future for its motherland: it is by having the public experience the pride earned from participating in fascist worlding that Blasetti captures life in specific imposed courses of action. Camerini, instead, resorts to shame to make race.

A crucial theorization of shame's impact on behaviors and identity formations was proposed by the French Jewish thinker Emmanuel Levinas coevally with Camerini's imposition in the Italian mediascape. In *On Escape*, written in 1935 in the wake of Hitler's takeover of Germany, Levinas connects the feeling of shame with the experience of being riveted to oneself. What is oppressive in shame for Levinas are the constraints of embodiment; what causes shame for him is the perception of being the body that one is and the impossibility of becoming a body of a different kind. It is for this reason that Eve Kosofsky Sedgwick assigns shame a central role in her politics of emotions, insisting that this profoundly intimate affect is the "place where the question of identity arises most originally and most relationally." The deeply personal and intensely social dimension of shame was also emphasized in *Being and Nothingness*, in which Jean-Paul Sartre characterizes shame as a process involving a noncognitive, embodied, emotional recognition of what one is: in shame, I am ashamed of what I am, writes Sartre, specifying, however, that for shame to cut us to the quick, we must be in the presence of others.[4] The fact that shame, unlike guilt, is an affect that requires the exposition of the self to others, that is, a system of gazes, transpires already in the example invoked by Levinas: Charlie Chaplin, who has swallowed a whistle that betrays his identity every time he breathes, in *City Lights* (1931). Not only is the tramp unable to hide from himself, but he is also unable to hide from the judgmental looks of upright citizens— meaning that in shame we are revealed both privately *and* publicly, to ourselves and society, as the embodied self that we cannot escape being.

In this regard, feminist philosopher Lisa Guenther has highlighted important resonances between, on the one hand, Levinas's account of shame as an affect blocking the self into a limited set of life possibilities, and, on the other, his concurrent description of antisemitism and racism as biopolitical devices that suppress futurity by turning one's identity into a destiny. Shame and racism both pin lives down. Guenther explains: to impose on human bodies an inviolable nature, a firm biological identity, is to chain them to their self in a way that suppresses their capacity to change. Reading together Levinas's *On Escape* and his "Reflections on the Philosophy of Hitlerism" (1934), Guenther allows us to take notice of the fact that shame— insofar as it fixes one's sense of self and silences the aspiration to take flight—can be redeployed as an apparatus of racialization; it can be weaponized to overwrite people's sense of what is appropriate and possible for the species of bodies they are made to feel to be. Shame imposes burdens and borders on life, as Frantz Fanon perfectly explains in *Black Skin, White Masks* when recounting the nauseating experience of being glanced at and called a "negro" by a white child on a train, while only wanting to enjoy being a human among other humans. At the mercy of the white gaze, Fanon feels to have been imprisoned, *fixed*—"in the sense in which a chemical solution is fixed by a dye."[5] Recognizing the impossibility of sharing the same space, the same world, with the white man, Fanon writes that he subjected himself to an objective examination that turned his body into an overdetermined racial legacy: "I discovered my blackness, my ethnic characteristics;

and I was battered down by tom-toms, cannibalism, intellectual deficiency, fetishism, racial defects, slave-ships, and above all else, above all: 'Sho' good eatin'.'"[6]

Drawing upon these phenomenologies of shaming, in the following pages I show how Camerini exploits shame so as to have the Italian body politic discover and assume the responsibilities connected to its own supposed ethnic identity. Even when apparently politically indifferent, Camerini's films under Mussolini—this is my argument here—consistently work as devices of racial subjugation and subjectification that "fix" the population and neutralize the risk of class indiscipline.

ITALY IN AFRICA

From a wealthy and well-connected family, Camerini turned to filmmaking in the early 1920s, after fighting in World War I. In 1927, he leveraged the relative success of his *Maciste contro lo sceicco* (*Maciste against the Sheik*, 1926) to start the Attori e Direttori Italiani Associati (ADIA) consortium and produce the last big Italian colonial film of the silent era: *Kif Tebbi* (1928).

Set during the Italo-Turkish war of 1911–12 and shot mostly on location in Tripoli and the Libyan desert, *Kif Tebbi* features a Tripolitanian notable who, having traveled to Europe and discovered civilization there, can no longer tolerate the backward, violent, sexist Ottoman rule. In one of the most evocative sequences of the film, beautifully described by Alberto Farassino, Ismail (Marcello Spada) gazes meditatively at the desert, "and the stretches of sand transform into sea, which is crossed by boats that, through mental associations and montage, transform into construction sites, cranes, factories, trains, and tracks."[7]

In the wake of this fantasy of colonial progress, the news arrives that the Italians have landed in Tripolitania, and Ismail is called to his duties. Instead of leading the resistance against the invaders, Ismail focuses on protecting his love interest, the young subaltern woman Mne (Donatella Neri), from the violent advances of Turkish soldiers and local notables. The Turks take notice and, growing suspicious of his pro-European and proto-feminist stances, sentence Ismail to death. The final sequences of *Kif Tebbi* are lost, but the Cineteca di Bologna, which curated the film's restoration, pieced together its ending on the basis of reviews and plot summaries from the time of the film's release. Ismail escapes prison just in time to reunite with Mne and celebrate the Italian flag waving over the Libyan desert. The Ottoman monsters have been defeated; women will be finally treated humanely; civilization can eventually be exported to Africa and make it less bleak, less Black.

Notwithstanding the plethora of Orientalist, anti-southern, anti-African, and anti-Muslim tropes, through its femonationalism *Kif Tebbi* makes a point to discriminate between those ethnicities that can be righted and those that are beyond saving. There is a sort of *differential racism* at work in this film that distinguishes a backward Hamitic South to be reclaimed from a monstrous Semitic East to be annihilated. Marcello Spada plays Ismail in blackface, but his character's complexion is fair and his features are Mediterranean, signaling a biosomatic proximity with the West that the Turks—depicted with dark faces, hooked noses, frizzy hair, and beady eyes—cannot even aspire to. The Turk in *Kif Tebbi* is more than the enemy in the struggle over Libya: he is the embodiment of all that Italy shall not be.[8] Yet *Kif Tebbi* is not preoccupied with projecting what Italy itself is or should be.

In the film's eagerness to separate and hierarchize nonwhite peoples, Camerini neglects to differentiate between Italy's racial character and northern European whiteness. Does being Italian coincide with smoking and wearing fancy suits, as Ismail does after coming back from his European escapades? The very fact that Ismail does not discriminate between European locations and that he holds souvenirs and women from all his foreign travels equally dear is an attestation of the film's cosmopolitan attitude that is somehow at odds with the logic of fascist identity biopolitics. *Kif Tebbi* was made for the international market and in a moment when the regime was gearing up for its own colonial raids. In recounting the 1912 Italian invasion of Libya, the film sells Italian colonialism to the world by presenting it as a European phenomenon. However, in aligning Italy with European colonial modernity and characterizing it as a modern European "white" force, *Kif Tebbi* fails to articulate a discourse on national identity that could contribute to the effort of making real Italians, of making a Blackshirt race.

When Camerini returned to the colonies in 1935, this time to Eritrea to film *Il grande appello* (*The Great Appeal*), he corrected this stance, working hard to impose on the public a specific racial imaginary about Italy and Italians. In fact, the film, a celebration of the recent invasion of Ethiopia and of the birth of Italian Africa financed by the fascist war apparatus, strives to border the features of proper Italian masculinity by documenting the conversion of Giovanni Bertani / Jean Bertanì (Camillo Pilotto) from dissolute race traitor fraternizing with English, Spanish, Black, and anti-Fascist bodies in Djibouti to national hero. It is his son's look of contempt that summons Giovanni to his responsibilities and shames him into embarking on a process of personal growth that will lead him to reconsider his priorities in life, eventually turning him into a patriot ready to kill and die for the imperial expansion of the homeland. With this tale of personal conversion and colonial deployment, *Il grande appello* bears witness to the structural complicity between Fascism's biopolitics and its racism: the point of reclaiming an improper body is to create expendable subjects that will subdue human beings that are categorized as inferior. Living a good life, being an authentic Italian body, and reuniting with one's race means, in Camerini's diegetic universe, suppressing Black bodies while exposing oneself to the risk of early death.[9]

While the workings of racializing biopolitics are apparent in *Il grande appello* given the blatantly racist and colonial imaginaries it amplifies, they are no less significant in the seemingly apolitical films by Camerini, those that contribute to Blackshirt rule in more subtle and possibly more nefarious ways. Indeed, even in works that are not explicitly concerned with Italy's racial identity or territorial expansion and that do not contain explicit political preoccupations, under the pretense of objectively capturing national reality, Camerini was still serving the regime's logic of coloniality.[10] For instance, films like *Come le foglie* (*Like the Leaves*, 1935), *Darò un milione* (*I'll Give a Million*, 1935, based on a scenario by Zavattini), and *Ma non è una cosa seria* (*But It's Nothing Serious*, 1936, based on Pirandello's play) are patronizing eulogies that idealize work ethic and resilience to hardships by staging spoiled elites that venture in the underclasses' simple lifeworlds and learn from these "poveri ma belli" (poor but beautiful) Italians. Yet Camerini's most unforgettable and impactful films under the regime are those that travel in the opposite direction, those that—with irony and a light touch—document the humiliating misadventures of humble Italian men and women breaching class lines that are racially transcribed and behaving as people they are not.

BREACHES

A proletarian couple losing themselves in a casino (*Rotaie* [*Rails*, 1930]); a chauffeur posing as a car owner and a young salesgirl dreaming of living like the women she serves (*Gli uomini che mascalzoni . . .* [*What Scoundrels Men Are!*, 1932]); a news agent posing as a count and a nanny mingling with the haute bourgeoisie (*Il signor Max* [*Mr. Max*, 1937]); a young woman stealing commodities she cannot afford and a delivery boy living beyond his means (*I grandi magazzini* [*Department Store,* 1939]): the films from Camerini's celebrated working-class tetralogy follow the same plotline. They are stories of common Italians who, according to the films' value system, have fallen for vain fantasies of socioeconomic betterment and pretend to live lives that are not theirs to live in the first place. Building upon Judith Butler's assertion that identities are produced iteratively, the repetitiveness of these films by Camerini should not be understood as redundancy but rather as a crucial feature of their race-making performances. By means of repetition and difference, this series of films rivets the spectatorial body to very precise commitments and obligations.[11]

Gian Piero Brunetta notes that the success of these films by Camerini was in great part due to the director's creation of relatable characters with whom the urban masses could easily identify.[12] Maurizio D'Ancora and Käthe von Nagy (*Rotaie*), Vittorio De Sica and Lia Franca (*Gli uomini che mascalzoni . . .*), and then De Sica and Assia Noris (*Il signor Max* and *I grandi magazzini*) play the part of young underclass Italians enticed by the goods, lifestyles, and experiences made possible by workers' toil under capitalism, only to be reminded that those things are not for them—even if it is people like them who are making all of modernity's wonders possible. For the success of what is, ultimately, a defense of a political economy based on intersectional class / gender exploitation, the fact that the national public identified with Camerini's simple, troubled Italians is key. With thrilling montage techniques derived from the cinema of attraction, traveling sequences immersing us in the characters' reality, point-of-view (POV) shots showing us reality from their perspective, and close-ups zooming in on their emotions, Camerini's escapism makes the public experience what his protagonists are feeling—the jouissance ignited by evading their naturalized subject positions, the shame making them aware of the inviolable laws governing their embodied existence, the humbling that derives from being caught in their attempted escapes, and the positive reinforcement that ensues from getting involved in less-extravagant desires and pleasures. But by identifying with them, spectators themselves feel the shaming pressure to live heteronormative lives; they themselves are summoned to stop dreaming about a different existence and commit to a destiny of productive and reproductive labor.

Camerini's cinematic devices might be considered examples of what Giorgio Agamben has dubbed "anthropological machines"—apparatuses that individuate specific forms of human embodiment and subjectivity by warning individuals about who they are not and should never become. As Sylvia Wynter argued in "Beyond the Word of Man," human beings carry themselves in the world according to regulatory representations of that which constitutes the optimal model of the subject and of that which constitutes the Abject. For Wynter and Agamben, the production of Man—the ideal self—is an oppositional process, one that implies the degradation of certain forms of life into tropes of impropriety.[13] After Charles Darwin, such an impropriety, originally framed as a question of original sin and thus deployed religiously, was translated in racial and/or biological terms: the Abject is the dysgenic Other. Wynter explains that this otherness is primarily embodied, outside Europe, by the native populations of Africa and the Americas with their nonwhite skin, while within the West it is the abnormal—the biologically compromised individual who yielded to different forms of sickness (from mental illness to communism to poverty to, in a certain sense, Jewishness)—who is cast as a fallen creature. The Black, the Native American, but also the poor, the queer, the rebel, the Jew, the Muslim: these are just some of the abject living beings that Western modernity has woven into existence to produce Man.

To produce a Blackshirt humanity, that is, properly Italian men and women who would do their part at home and in the colonies, Camerini, a scion of the high bourgeoisie who partook in the dolce vita of Via Veneto, instead abjectifies white elites. Through processes of othering, internalization, and shaming, he then incites the public to reject the hedonism presented as the mark of bourgeois whiteness. In populistically raising resentment against unproductive people rather than a whole mode of production, against the excesses of consumerism rather than commodity fetishism, this type of intervention ends up eliciting social compliance and pushing the body politic to work for Fascism's corporatist, conflict-free version of reality. In the final instance, Camerini's films amplify the feeling that challenging the subject position one occupies and evading the life one leads is both impossible and unappealing.

It is impossible because class differences are not merely a question of money: elites are a different species of people. In *Gli uomini che mascalzoni . . .* and *Il signor Max*, set designer Gastone Medin underscores this difference chromatically and through decor. Thanks to an inheritance, Gianni (De Sica) in *Il signor Max* might have temporarily been able to pass for a count and breach into the "first-class" world, with its swan hats, fancy silks, cream-colored tablecloths, and shining white drapes. However, by the end he must admit that he still lacks some "sfumature" (shades), to become like the "signori di nascita" (gentlemen by birth). As his uncle warns Gianni—with Mussolini memorabilia in the background—those men, and especially those women, are not for him; people like him have nothing to do with that lifeworld and that lifestyle. By featuring a winding white road breaking through the Italian landscape and the tag line "a dangerous turn in a bachelor's life," the film's poster already signaled that elite whiteness is not for everyone. It is thus not surprising that in the film Gianni ends up looking ridiculous while attempting to do "white people stuff": he falls into the water while horseback riding; he is hit by his new friends' tennis balls while playing tennis in an immaculate ivory outfit.

The work of Silvan Tomkins becomes relevant here, as it clarifies how shame emerges after an interest or enjoyment has been activated, and operates by inhibiting those engagements, directing individuals toward behaviors socially constructed as more suitable.[14] Similar to Fanon's experience during his train ride with white people, Gianni is eventually shamed into recognizing where, and with whom, he belongs. He is no sir, no mister, no Max, just a regular, humble Gianni. Hence, the right fit for him is a family-oriented nanny, not a high-society lady who dresses as scantily as the women in the movies. Gianni's places in life are the *lavoro* and *dopo-lavoro*, work and the after-work clubs created by Fascism to keep the salaried city masses entertained in a healthy and monitored environment.[15] It is important to pick up the presence of Blackness in a space where Italian labor belongs.

In the *dopo-lavoro* enjoyed by Gianni's family, the Blackshirts have created a jazz orchestra. A Black man with exaggerated facial features is depicted on the drum set (Figure 14). Through this racist portrait, Camerini and Medin draw a visual connection between the workers living in fascist Italy and the formerly enslaved African Americans living in the segregated United States, racially profiling Italian labor and imposing upon them the same lower nature that Blackness has been burdened with. This passage could be considered an instance of "return of the repressed"—a moment when the true colors of fascist Italy are projected on the screen. The Black man represented on the drum set functions to all effects as a humbling memento of the fact that subaltern Italians will never whiten themselves enough to belong in upper-class spaces and to enjoy life.

But changing one's position in society in Camerini's films is not only impossible; it is also unappealing because the rich are presented—similarly

FIGURE 14. A Blackshirt jazz orchestra playing in a workers' club with a racist caricature of an African American man on the drum set in *Il signor Max* (Mario Camerini, 1937).

to the visual rhetoric articulated in *Terra madre* (*Mother Land,* 1931)—as dissolute, vacuous, sick. By depicting them in extravagant staged interiors and under obvious studio lighting, Camerini emphasizes the artificiality and sterility of their existences as well as their detachment from, and thus lack of concern for, real Italians. Camerini's films are replete with examples of higher classes' disregard for lower folks. In *Il signor Max,* the teenaged tantrum-throwing countess treats her babysitter (Noris) like a home servant; in *I grandi magazzini,* a store manager tries to frame Lauretta (Noris) for the burglary ring he himself is running while simultaneously blackmailing her for sex; in *Gli uomini che mascalzoni . . . ,* a count and then an industrialist try to seduce lower-class salesgirls by means of expensive dinners and empty promises. However, Camerini does not blame the elites for their toxic behaviors, lies, and machinations. At fault are the naive Italians who should know better than to mix with people of that sort. In *Il signor Max,* for example, Gianni's uncle mocks him for having wasted so much time and money unsuccessfully pursuing a high-society woman. Why would one even aspire to live a different life and become white, so to speak, when one has the opportunity to respond to Fascism's great appeal and be a hardworking, childbearing Blackshirt Italian? That the "probleme global" of Camerini's cinema is class/gender compliance is evident as early as his *Rotaie,* the film that marked the passage of Italian cinema from silence to sound: the film was distributed as a silent film in 1930 and then rereleased sonorized in 1931.[16]

GAMBLING LIFE AWAY

A young couple. A shady hotel in a buzzing Italian city. Penniless, overwhelmed by preoccupations, shunned by their families, isolated and alienated, Giorgio (D'Ancora) and Maria (von Nagy) contemplate suicide in *Rotaie.* But a train passing by and then the shining lights emerging from the cityscape bear witness to the material wealth and adventures that the present has to offer. Giorgio and Maria reconsider their decision and flee the hotel, ending up in a train station. There, advertisements for beautiful locations to explore fuel their desire to leave everything behind and start afresh. Felicitously, Giorgio and Maria find a wallet full of cash and use this windfall to purchase first-class tickets to elsewhere: only a sort of miracle would allow a radical change in socioeconomic status. On the train, they meet the Marquis Mercier (Daniele Crespi), who seduces them into joining him at the grand hotel and indulging in a foreign life consisting of gambling, drinks, dancing, sports, and lax morals. It is important to notice that Camerini has a cameo as one of the habitués of this world, in a sort of metacinematic attestation of the position he and his cinema occupy— where they speak from and with whom they are affiliated.

After a few days of pure jouissance, the problems begin. Giorgio loses everything at the roulette table. Humiliated, defeated, with his head in his hands, he needs to reveal who he really is. The only way for the broke man to pay his gaming debts and hotel bill is for Maria to give in to the marquis's indecent proposal. Close-ups on Maria and the Frenchman effectively communicate the nobleman's abject inhumanity and Maria's humiliation at being exchanged and exploited: But what can she do? Isn't this what being a woman comes down to for *Rotaie* (Figure 15)? Giorgio, alone in his room, peeks into a nearby apartment complex and sees the lives of honest working people. The alternative is clear, and Camerini will reiterate the point throughout the film and in his later works: the shameful underclass bodies can be either put to work or violated. Giorgio rushes to the marquis's room to stop Maria from giving herself up, and together they withdraw from a world where they don't belong. Giorgio cleans his face in a public fountain, as if to wash away from his subaltern skin the elite mask he had put on. With the little money they have left, Maria and Giorgio buy a ticket to return home.

In the third-class train car in which they travel, they are reminded once again of the life course that is right for people like them. First, they feel humiliated to be among the poor, but slowly their attitude changes. Through Maria's and Giorgio's POV shots, Camerini offers us sympathetic portraits of the industrious Italian proletariat: the signs of hard work mark the dark faces of the humble travelers, yet they maintain a dignified demeanor.[17] This is the perfect Italian humanity. After the temptation of social mobility and class flight, after the shame of having invested their bodies in racially inappropriate pleasures, in behaviors that are okay in France perhaps, Camerini foregrounds production and reproduction as the only possible routes to happiness. Maria and Giorgio are sitting with a family of four. They are

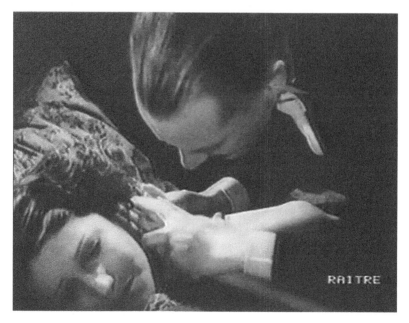

FIGURE 15. Working-class shame and elite abjection in *Rotaie* (Mario Camerini, 1929).

poor but comfortable; the parents' lifetime of hard labor has paid off. They have enough to feed themselves and their two children. The oldest, perhaps five or six, is munching on a piece of fruit; he offers some food to Maria and Giorgio, who look at him with hungry eyes. The youngest is breastfeeding. Maria leans forward and gazes at the mother nursing her baby. Eventually Maria smiles: she turns to Giorgio with a knowing look and is overjoyed when she is given the baby to cuddle (Figure 16). Life is back on track. The real pleasures of life are not to be found elsewhere; they are easily attainable by Maria and Giorgio as long as they stay in line, as long as they stay true to their working-class nature.

A series of fades move the film from the train car to the railroad, then to a factory's gates—and the roar of the train's engine is subsumed by the sounds of the industrial apparatus. An impressive traveling shot immerses the public in the factory's interiors and then takes us back to Giorgio, who—his face covered in soot—is attending to the machines with pride. It's hard work, but the reward is priceless: Giorgio's shift is over and, in a scene reminiscent of a Lumière brothers film, he joins the crowd of workers leaving the factory; he has become part of something bigger than he is, and his acceptance of his lot in life has earned him the right to joy and futurity. *Rotaie* documents a journey similar to the one Walter Ruttmann recounts in *Acciaio* (*Steel*, 1933), but for Camerini the acceptance of work and factory life feels totally different, as it is accompanied by promises of belonging. While *Acciaio* reduces living to working, and thus accordingly ends with the protagonist caught by the industrial apparatus, in *Rotaie* work is the way out, the exit strategy that defeats the alienation and isolation that Giorgio and Maria were experiencing at the beginning of the film. At the end of the movie, Maria is waiting for Giorgio at the gates, like many other wives waiting for their husbands. While he eats the snack she has brought him, she knits—perhaps a romper for a baby on the way? They walk home and smile, with labor in the backdrop and a family in their horizon (Figure 16).

Set to be produced by Blasetti's Augustus before the company went belly-up, *Rotaie* represents, with *Sole!* (*Sun*, 1929), a seminal moment for the remediation of realism into a crucial device for making and managing subjects in Italy. The very structure of the film contributes to projecting realism as an eminently biopolitical register. *Rotaie* is divided into three sections, each characterized by a different aesthetic, and with each aesthetics attributed a specific function.[18] Maria and Giorgio's existential crisis is

FIGURE 16. Gendered figurations of labor in *Rotaie* (Mario Camerini, 1929).

represented through visuals indebted to German expressionism with its dark contrasts, accented shadows, and dramatic camera angles. The section in the casino and grand hotel, with its glossy interiors, sensual camera movements, and escape into dream worlds, is modeled after the French and American comedies of the 1920s. Finally, the train and factory sequences, through which Camerini renounces escapist cinema and wields the apparatus to show Italians who they really are, to show them the way home, are characterized by a quasi-documentarian gaze. In the film, expressionist aesthetics is highlighted as a means to produce anguish in the spectatorship, comedy as a genre that distracts and brings off-track, and realism as the cinema that leads back to the racially appropriate life path.

ON SCOUNDRELS AND MANNEQUINS

Camerini's effort to remediate realism as a racializing apparatus extends beyond *Rotaie* and continues throughout the 1930s, reaching its artistic peak at the ten-year mark from the March on Rome, with *Gli uomini che mascalzoni . . . (What Scoundrels Men Are!*, 1932) possibly the most accomplished fascist movie from Mussolini's Italy.[19] A sensation when it came out, the film contributed to launching the talkies in Italy and constituted Vittorio De Sica's breakthrough performance as a screen actor. It was produced by fascist-controlled Cines and written by Aldo De Benedetti, the prolific Italian screenwriter of Jewish descent who, under the gradual institutionalization of antisemitism, would be forced to work uncredited and at bargain prices to make ends meet.[20]

Vis-à-vis *Rotaie*, *Gli uomini che mascalzoni . . .* drops any reference to the alienation and isolation experienced by Italian labor, and with it the reference to German expressionism, as if to scrub away any stain marring the fascist real. By resorting to a binary narratological and stylistic structure, the film is able to impose on the public a Manichean opposition between proper and improper, sane and abject, modes of Italianity. Camerini's film was advertised as a story featuring love and labor: the taglines accompanying its release note that its romantic plot takes place within a "context of joyful labor" and that "the most meaningful and complex manifestation of labor" will function as the background to the romance. The film's promotion thus effectively verbalizes and manifests the very performance of Camerini's filmic machine: to romanticize work.

Gli uomini che mascalzoni . . . starts with a shot in many aspects analogous to the one at the beginning of Blasetti's *Sole!* In that case, we saw a

wooden gate opening onto the Pontine Marshes; in this case a metal shutter rolls up and reveals Milan's Piazza del Duomo in all its beauty. If Blasetti invited the public on a journey through the malarious swamplands
about to be reclaimed, Camerini's journey takes us to Milan. As critic
Filippo Sacchi noted in a 1932 review of the film, this was the first time that
Milan was featured on the screen, and "who could imagine that it could be
so photogenic?"[21] The apparent preoccupation of *Gli uomini che mascalzoni* . . . is then to promote what Milan stands for, that is, "vital operosity,"
to stay with Sacchi, and thus also sell to the spectatorship the industrious
Blackshirt way of life that keeps Italian cities going day and night. From
beginning to end, the film's rhythm is incredibly quick; it is a sound film
that unfolds with the gait of a silent one, Francesco Savio argues.[22] There
are no dull moments or descriptive sequences, and the fast pace as well as
the dynamic tracking shots mediate Milan's energy and entice the public
to join in and contribute to its vitality.

It is dawn, and people are waking up. There are, however, people who
have been up all night. Tadino (Cesare Zoppetti) is a taxi driver who has
just clocked out. Before heading home to catch some sleep, he stops by a
bar to pick up some milk and enjoy a well-deserved grappa. At the store,
he crosses paths with an older couple consuming a leisurely breakfast. He
taps on the man's tuba hat and, in a thick Milanese accent, jokingly tells
the other customers that these are the people who are taking away everyone else's bread—but it is unclear who these people are: are they hoboes
or elite? At the end, it does not really matter, since the populist stab at
unproductive subjects who benefit from common Italians' sacrifices—if we
think about it—works even better in this way: elites and hoboes are the
same; they are interchangeable in the joke because they are both cast as
parasitic subjects.

At home, still covered in filth, Tadino wakes up his daughter Mariuccia
(Franca). It is just the two of them; Tadino is a widower and has done his
best as a single parent. Mariuccia borders, however, on spoiled and materi-
alistic. "Rise and work," Tadino lovingly encourages his little loafer as he
heats up her milk, but she takes her time. Mariuccia's immaculate white
bedding, ivory nightgown, and cream leather slippers are in stark contrast
with the dirt that covers Tadino's existence. The shining white things we
encounter in her room might attest, like so many Lacanian *objets petit a,*
to Mariuccia's unattainable desires—investments that are out of place given
the subject she is and the family she belongs to. Their shoes especially reveal

the different paths that Tadino and Mariuccia tread in life. Tadino's worn-out leather boots bespeak a lifeworld very similar to that brought forth by Vincent Van Gogh's *A Pair of Shoes* (1886): a reality made up of toilsome treading, tenacity, grit, and fear of not having enough. Mariuccia's ivory high-heeled slippers, with their almost immaterial smoothness, are used by Camerini and set designer Medin to both introduce and denigrate the young woman's dreams, her aspiration to live as the characters of the photonovels she is so fond of, or as the fancy women shopping in the exclusive perfume and jewelry store where she works.

This store is one of the few settings in *Gli uomini che mascalzoni . . .* that was reconstructed in the studio, and Medin does not do anything to hide the artificiality of this environment. On the contrary, by emphasizing its fakeness by means of decor and lighting (everything is spotless, glossy, immaculate, well lit, but also flat), *Gli uomini che mascalzoni . . .* signals the dangerousness of the place. Like other white spaces appearing in Camerini's cinema and mapped so precisely by James Hay (such as the grand hotel in *Rotaie,* the cruise ship in *Il signor Max,* and the mall in *I grandi magazzini,* to name a few), the store where Mariuccia works is a zone of contact, where people from different classes meet and interact.[23] While unavoidable, this intercourse between workers and consumers, poor and rich, can also cause contagion: the risk is that workers themselves will buy into the commodities, services, and lifestyles they are selling, and thus develop fantasies that might compromise the strict but unspoken class hierarchies along which Italian society ought to be organized.

The governmental quandary staged here by Camerini is not so dissimilar from the challenge European powers faced in the colonies: white people and their subaltern subjects could not be kept separate, and yet each had to persist as a segregated form of life to maintain the hierarchical stratification that made their exploitation possible. This led, Ben-Ghiat shows, to Italian cinema shifting its representation of the relations between colonized and colonizers to avoid enabling interracial intimacies and engagements through exotic portrayals of Black women. It also provoked a debate in fascist circles and in the press—I will return to this in chapter 7—on which kinds of films colonized Black people should be allowed to see.[24] Races had to meet and yet could not mix; classes had to do the same to assure the stability of the capitalist mode of production under fascist rule. Camerini does not take away from the Italian public the escapist pleasure and distraction that characterize the genre that, with its decor and lighting style marking chic lifestyles, was known first as "white cinema" and then "white telephone cinema." Yet in contrast to films such as Goffredo Alessandrini's *La segretaria privata* (*The Private Secretary*, 1931), in which a humble private secretary marries into the ivory world of the elite, in Camerini the pleasure principle does not prevail; fantasies are followed by stern reality checks calling the public to order. Escapism is both denounced and redeployed in the service of Blackshirt supremacy on national life.

On her way to work, Mariuccia runs into Bruno (De Sica), who is captivated by her simple beauty. Bruno's accent and features hint at the fact that he is not originally from Milan: might he be one of those southerner scoundrels who relocated from the countryside to cities in the great internal migration of the 1920s? (De Sica was born in southern Lazio, while Franca and Zoppetti were from northern Italy.) In lively sequences taking the spectator on a journey through Milan, Bruno follows Mariuccia on his bicycle, first as she walks to the bus stop and then on the bus to work. Mariuccia is intrigued but cannot help disdaining him as a lower kind of Italian vis-à-vis the men she might aspire to. As her friends comment when Bruno unsuccessfully tries to strike up a conversation with her, "We don't like men on bikes." Humbled but not defeated, Bruno promises he will need to buy a car then: he cannot admit to being poor; he cannot admit he is a worker. A salaried driver but also a bit of a rascal, Bruno borrows a car from his boss without asking, shows up when Mariuccia gets off work, pretends to be a wealthy man, and talks her into taking a ride with him. The POV shot from the car's cabin, coupled with quick cuts and fast motion, communicates the jouissance of this evasion—a moment of de-subjugation and de-subjectification in which the two workers are able to transcend their positionality. On the Lago Maggiore, Mariuccia and Bruno enjoy a boat ride, a meal, some wine, and then they dance to the tune of "Parlami d'amore Mariù" (Little Mary, talk to me about love), a song written for the film that would soon become a hit as sung by De Sica himself, making the young performer a multimedia star.

The escapist fantasy, however, comes to an abrupt end when reality strikes back. Bruno is spotted by his boss and hurries back to work, abandoning Mariuccia at the lake. Humiliated and stranded, Mariuccia regrets this day off from real life. Bruno is fired and must find another occupation. He is hired as a personal chauffeur by a pale nobleman who has some peculiar demands: his car, Conte Piazzi explains, is the color of café latte, so the car's driver needs to be café latte colored as well. Bruno is thus taken to a store and dressed in a mocha livery, turning him—much to the salesgirls' amusement—into a perfect replica of the tanned mannequin they have on display (Figure 17). But there might be another layer to the joke the film plays on Bruno. When Piazzi states that he wants his driver to be the color of café latte, is he only referring to the color of the livery Bruno is given, or also his skin tone?

In the next scene, we discover that Conte Piazzi is courting Mariuccia. With his luxurious car and brand-new chauffeur, he is waiting for the young woman outside the *profumeria* (perfumery). Bruno tries to hide from her gaze: he does not want Mariuccia to find out he is of humble origins, since he is still convinced that she is a material girl who likes other kinds of men. Among the posters behind him, we see an ad featuring a smiling Black man (Figure 17). I want to pay attention to this background of Blackness looming over Bruno—considering that this is not the only time that Camerini deploys racist imaginaries of Black men in association with representations of working-class Italians. Moreover, De Sica's own face in this sequence is made to appear particularly dark (Figure 17). Is Camerini again using the medium to profile, classify, "fix"—in the sense Fanon used the term in *Black Skin, White Masks*—Italian workers?

Stuart Hall famously commented that race is the way in which class is lived.[25] I do wonder whether *Gli uomini che mascalzoni . . .* might be mocking as self-delusional Bruno attempts to conceal who he really is, conveying that—no matter how hard they try—simple Italians cannot hide their true colors: they are dark-skinned *mascalzoni*, plebs who are the color of café latte. As such, they can smile and work, live in the fashion of the "good" Black man from the poster, or try to evade their identity, but things will end badly for them as they will fall into the hands of more exploitative masters who treat them how darker-skinned scoundrels are treated. Bruno decides to walk away from his new *padrone* (master), revealing himself to Mariuccia as he dramatically takes off his livery. "Ah, servants," Conte Piazzi sighs to the young woman he is trying to seduce. But now that she knows who Bruno is, Mariuccia is eager to rekindle their connection—with the condition he accepts his working-class destiny.

Mariuccia finds Bruno a job at the Milan Fair but then goes out with the industrialist who gave him the job—to further secure Bruno's position but possibly also to have some fun. The film's implicit sexism becomes explicit at this point. After humbling Bruno for his attempts to evade his working-class status, to escape the foreclosed destiny that has been implanted in

FIGURE 17. The color of the Italian working class in *Gli uomini che mascalzoni . . .* (Mario Camerini, 1932). *Opposite above*: Count Piazzi stresses to amused salesgirls that he likes his chauffeurs to be the same color as his car, mocha; *opposite below*: Bruno at work in his mocha livery, a poster of a smiling Black man in the background establishing a visual connection between the worker's identity and Blackness; *above*: Camerini completes the racial profiling of the Italian working class by accenting the quasi-Blackness of Bruno's phenotype.

his dark skin, the film now "slut shames" Mariuccia. Bruno, who is himself out on a date, sees Mariuccia with the industrialist and berates her for enjoying his attentions. "Women are all the same," Bruno comments, urging not just Mariuccia but also the women in the audience to engage in more appropriate pleasures. Similar to the scene from *City Lights* that Levinas cites to explain the workings of shame, Mariuccia tries and fails to hide (Figure 18). Bruno's contemptuous gaze fixes her status as a sexed body that can either be enjoyed in exchange for favors or loved. The second scenario is clearly the superior one, insofar as it enables her to build a family and contribute to birthing Italy's future. Filled with shame for compromising what Gayle Rubin has dubbed the "political economy of sex" that naturalizes women into the role of caretakers (wives and mothers) of labor power, Mariuccia runs away in tears from the temptation of being too modern and liberal, and it is precisely her contrition that makes Bruno want to marry her.[26] Seeing her weep and discovering that she has given him the greatest gift in life, a good job, Bruno decides that Mariuccia is not like all other women; she is a "good girl" after all, and thus worthy of his commitment.

Continuing in this conventionally sexist vein, Bruno half-jokingly lays down his conditions for marrying Mariuccia: she will no longer work; she will always be home, making risotto. Tadino, who has witnessed this reconciliation between Bruno and his daughter unobserved, takes them out for a quick celebratory toast and declares that it is time to get to work. He sends his daughter home, foreshadowing her future of domesticity and household labor, and brings Bruno with him in the cab to teach his future son-in-law the ropes. As they drive away in the night, the darkness that now absorbs Bruno marks the beginning of a brighter future, of an ordered heteronormative existence sheltered from the temptations of escape.

FIGURE 18. Bruno "slut shaming" Mariuccia in *Gli uomini che mascalzoni . . .* (Mario Camerini, 1932).

And yet the ending of *Gli uomini che mascalzoni* . . . feels anticlimactic and almost bleak compared to the pleasure and lightness that characterize the moments when Mariuccia and Bruno temporarily escape their destinies as workers. If escapism is shameful and ruinous, compliance reduces life to an already written narrative in which lives become facts and bodies have no room for action: no autonomy, agency, or freedom whatsoever. Whenever Camerini's characters choose labor over enjoyment, as they always do, their lifeworld shrinks, their bodies stiffen, their existences become repetitive, and they themselves start appearing almost like things. In *Gli uomini che mascalzoni* . . . , not only is Bruno restyled on the model of a mannequin; when he commits to work, his personhood becomes engrafted with technology and turns into a sort of mechanical apparatus busy performing the tasks assigned to it. It is as if, in deploying cinema as a technology of the self affectively coding into bodies strict commitments and obligations, Camerini cannot but turn these bodies into fascist technologies.

There is indeed very little vitality left in the operose modes of existence that Camerini's cinema shames Italian men and women into embracing. This is the case because by imposing models upon the body politic, one ultimately produces mannequins, dolls, simulacra—as Camerini's last major hit under Mussolini, *I grandi magazzini*, admits. The film is once again a tale of impropriety that naturalizes specific property relationships and the relations of power on which they are grounded. Lauretta (Nonis) and Bruno (De Sica) meet in the department store where they work and fall in love. Tempted by a femme fatale, Bruno buys into consumerism and neglects Lauretta, who is then tempted to steal commodities from work to match Bruno's lavish new lifestyle. Accused of crimes she didn't commit, Lauretta falls into despair, only to be saved by Bruno: the two stop messing around and eventually commit to a simple good life. Taking place almost exclusively within a grand department store, *I grandi magazzini* conjures a hyperstaged reality and features Italy's transformation into a controlled environment, a supervised setting where everything is regulated and people are mere copies and duplicates. Although it abandons plein-air shooting for the brand-new sound stages of Cinecittà, in a sense *I grandi magazzini* might be Camerini's most brutally honest and "realistic" work. Fascist modernity—to follow Ben-Ghiat—entailed a mass production not only of goods but also of existences.[27] And through the pervasive presence of mannequins throughout the film, Camerini evokes precisely the unoriginal dimension of Fascism's "created life," to circle back to an expression by Pirandello.

The film's opening titles run over a carousel of stylized mannequins that look like its characters. To avoid being caught stealing, Lauretta poses as a mannequin close to a mannequin modeled upon herself (Figure 19). But there are several apparitions of mannequins resembling De Sica throughout *I grandi magazzini,* and in an amusing scene Bruno feels uncanny in recognizing himself in one of them (Figure 19). Finally, at the end of the movie, accompanied by some friends, Lauretta and Bruno contemplate the future in a display window: they look at baby dolls slowly turning on a lazy Susan, but in the reverse shot they are the ones gazed at through the glass, made to look like mannequins on showcase. As Barbara Spackman brilliantly suggests, *I grandi magazzini* can be approached as a telling projection of the biopolitical fantasy—both Fascism's and Camerini's—of transforming a scoundrel people (as subaltern Italians had always been profiled to be) into a race of heteronormalized bodies completing tasks without any hesitations or second thoughts.[28] But bodies that are all the same, bodies that lack vitality and the capacity to change, turn into bodies that do not matter. They are fungible bodies that can be disposed of as one wants, since they are not really alive and are easily replaceable. In this regard, there is a fleeting image from *I grandi magazzini* that is stuck in my mind: the dismembered body of the mannequin dressed like Bruno being discarded. What this *corps morcellé* manifests is nothing but the expendability of life under (fascist) capitalism.

We are far beyond the promises of nation building and reassurances of belonging that marked the years of the consensus. *I grandi magazzini* premiered at the 1939 Venice Film Festival with an enthusiastic Joseph Goebbels in the audience; Italy's racial laws had been promulged the year before, and the fascist ethno-nation was preparing to enter World War II, in order to take the world after having occupied Ethiopia. The great Italian race had finally been made, and now it was time for it to make Italy greater. A transitional film, *I grandi magazzini* groomed the body politic for the work ahead. Men had to be ready to serve and protect, as attested by Bruno's transformation in the film from roguish delivery boy into a brave, proud, black-coated guardian of the department store's precious assets, a man eager to do whatever it takes to protect Italian goods and Italian women. As Karen Pinkus traces in *Bodily Regimes,* rubber trench coats in the fashion of the one Bruno is wearing in *I grandi magazzini* were introduced in the national market in the late 1920s by the Pirelli Tire Company in Milan, one's of Italy's key suppliers of arms and other material to the fascist war

FIGURE 19. The indistinguishability of organic and inorganic bodies in *I grandi magazzini* (Mario Camerini, 1939).

apparatus. They were designed for the harsh weather of northern Italy and advertised as a sort of peacetime armor that would protect Italian bodies from the elements. This very way of promoting them evoked the proximity between peace and war and affectively prepared men for the perspective of harsher environments and harsher work assignments.[29] But women had to do their part as well. Learning from Lauretta's mistakes, they needed to consume wisely and autarkically, support "made in Italy" products, avoid despair, and become model employees until it was time to become model housewives who create more and more model lives for Fascism's initiatives—little Italians who, similar to the dolls in the display window at the end of the film, are just puppets to play with.

5 The White Italian Mediterranean

De Robertis, Rossellini, and Fascism's Melodramatic Imperialism

Please, I cannot breathe.

—George Floyd, May 25, 2020

We're all victims. Everybody here. All these thousands of people here tonight. They're all victims. Every one of you.

—Donald Trump, December 5, 2020

The siege on the U.S. Capitol on January 6, 2021, had been long in the making.

While at the onset of the Trump phenomenon, politicians and pundits hastily dismissed the appeal of the New York real estate speculator as a fleeting and superficial anomaly, his election and what his presidency unleashed in the country made most reconsider. Only something running deep in the United States could have led to an attempted coup. What might have triggered such an explosion of political violence? Taking her cue from the infamous "You will not replace us" chant that underscored the Trump years, Olga Khazan's answer is *white fear*—the fear of extinction that has seized so many men and women who identify as white Americans. As Jacques Derrida commented in the aftermath of 9/11, there is a might in performances of weakness, and the political benefits connected with claiming the role of righteous victim are precisely what Khazan takes into consideration in order to address recent American history.[1]

Building upon the work of sociologist Mitch Berbier, Khazan traces how, in the early 1990s, the alt-right and the Republican Party began decoupling white identity from claims of white superiority, embracing instead a victim mentality. Until the Ronald Reagan era, white supremacy in the United States was predicated upon the biased assumption that Americans with a European heritage were racially superior to other ethnic groups. As U.S. society became more diverse and a multicultural ethos developed, the trope of white subalternity acquired prominence in the nation's mediascape. The brewing sensation was that white people's prerogative to be who they were and behave as they did was under attack by "minorities," and thus that whiteness itself was at stake. As Ku Klux Klan leader Tom Robb maintained in 1992, "even if we were nothing but a race of cavemen, we still have a right to preserve our heritage and culture and give that to our children. Nobody has the right to deny that from us. And that is the attempt that's being done today."[2] Who is the real victim here? This is the question that the new strategies of white supremacy amplified, so that it could infiltrate the collective imagination and go mainstream.

Feelings of subjugation and subalternity do appear laughable coming from white Americans, considering the structural privileges undergirding their lives. They are, after all, as Khazan writes in her *Atlantic* piece, "the most powerful group of people in the world." However, the experience of white fragility and precariousness should be taken seriously rather than merely mocked because it has become the foundation of today's power structures and color lines. Fredric Jameson describes conspiracy theories as "the poor man's cognitive mapping."[3] In a similar vein, discourses enabling white paranoia and fright should be regarded as devices of affective mediation that gaslight demands for socioeconomic justice by making everything about an imaginary community of innocent, righteous, and victimized "us." Ultimately, white victimhood functions as a powerful weapon of entitlement and discrimination, since it establishes an unspoken but clear hierarchy between the pain that counts and that which can be disregarded. In projecting the feeling that the only real suffering is white suffering, one is indeed also promoting the sense that white Americans are the only human beings who really matter—the ones who, being exposed to such grave existential dangers, are truly deserving of sympathy, care, and protection.

In this regard, Elisabeth Anker provides an especially generative framework for reckoning with how the orgy of melodramatic feelings that has taken over American public discourse has implanted into collective sensibility the projection of a white America in pain and at risk; of a tranquil ethno-community being killed by the swamp, antifa thugs, rioters, elites, queers, globalization, nasty women, foreigners, critical race theory, and so on. In order to confront the ongoing risk of American Fascism, one needs to dissect how, when it is Black men and boys and people of color of all genders who are treated as disposable bodies and shot or choked to death on U.S. streets, white people came to feel like the protagonists of a national "mega-melodrama," where their own lives and way of life are on the line.[4]

It is true that ugly feelings—as Sianne Ngai might dub them—are persistent, key governmental devices under Western modernity: the informing thesis of this book is that racially charged anxieties about collective living are constitutive for the production and reproduction of subjects who would perform the capitalist-colonial order.[5] Yet it is also true that the inflammatory rhetoric against enemies, both within and without, threatening society escalates in tandem with the escalation of requests made to the "authentic" national community in the name of the greater good. It is precisely this uglification of affects and media accompanying the radicalization of the work that subjects are summoned to take up in order to protect "their people" that I discuss in this chapter, through examples from early 1940s Italian film. In this way, I hope to contribute to challenging the myopic presentism that—as Angelica Pesarini posits—characterizes mainstream analysis of the current ethno-nationalist resurgence and highlight common strategies of affective mediation that fascisms, old and new, deploy to establish their grip over the living.[6]

Through Blasetti and Camerini, in the previous chapters I speculated on how cinema's assurances of belonging, betterment, and happiness might have contributed to fascist rule in the phase of Blackshirt history that goes from the end of the 1920s to the invasion of Ethiopia. Here I document how, as the Regime prepared to enter World War II, national film embraced a brutal vision—to use Karl Schoonover's expression—and came to rely on ugly sensations to keep the nation working for Fascism. Recent interventions by Claudio Fogu and Valerie McGuire emphasize the Mediterranean Sea's paramount importance in fascist geopolitics and fascist rhetoric about the need to wage war against the world.[7] In this light, I focus on Francesco De Robertis's *Uomini sul fondo* (*S.O.S. Submarine*, 1940) and De Robertis and Roberto Rossellini's *La nave bianca* (*The White Ship*, 1941) to show how national film opened a wound of aquatic vulnerability that could only be sutured shut by the forceful and righteous belligerence of the fascist state. Reviewing these films in the context of their times, I argue that their gruesome depictions of maimed and suffocating Italian sailors amplified Fascism's claims of an unprotected body politic, of an exposed people that ought to go to war to neutralize the threats coming from the sea that was once theirs.

In postwar scholarship, *Uomini sul fondo* and *La nave bianca* have been commended for their dry, objective, realist capture of a people in distress. Bazin, for instance, describes them as antispectacular and uncompromising in regard to the regime. In contrast, I characterize them as racial melodramas and insist on the ways these films wielded affects to highlight Italian pain and project Italy's involvement in World War II as a humanitarian intervention in defense of an innocent nation on the brink of extinction. Rhythmic montage, highlighted parallelisms, overlong spectacles of pain and sacrifice, dramatic scores, an ecstatic ending of deferred and sublimated pleasures: the formal excessiveness that characterizes *La nave bianca* and *Uomini sul fondo* attests that these filmic devices are not informed by the impulse to capture reality "as is" but rather by the urgency to capture the spectatorial bodies in mobilizing regimes of feeling. Similarly to the effects of sentimental drama, porn, and horror as per Linda Williams's analysis, paramount in De Robertis's and Rossellini's racial melodramas is the fact that the "body of the spectator is caught up in an almost involuntary mimicry of the emotion or sensation of the body on the screen."[8]

Yet, in the bodily genres Williams discusses, affective excesses are figured on female bodies and thus—insofar as the public is made to embody women weeping, orgasming, or dying—male spectatorial pleasure is tied to a breakdown of the gender divide. Conversely, *Uomini sul fondo* and *La nave bianca* promote the public's identification with Italian soldiers risking their lives and the women making sacrifices for them, so as to allow the fascist people to cross the racial divide sanctioned by the 1938 racist laws and vicariously enjoy the experience of persecuted lives under colonial modernity. The pleasurable *racial affect* that De Robertis and Rossellini's *reality effects* elicit is in fact the fantasy of a victimized good Italian race under attack from the water. This precise way of feeling about the nation and the sea, I show in the coda to this chapter through Rossellini's *Un pilota ritorna* (*A Pilot Returns*, 1942) and *L'uomo dalla croce* (*The Man with the Cross*, 1943), was crucial to redeem in the public imagination not only the attempted reclamation of the Mediterranean but also the regime's meddling in even not-remotely Italian "elements," like the Greek skies and the Russian earth.

The Italian ethno-nation had waged war against the South, antifascist living, and nonconforming bodies; it discriminated against Italian Jews, invaded Ethiopia and gassed its people; it stormed and bombed Greece and Albania; it traveled all the way to the Don River, to assist Nazi Germany in the plan to conquer the western Soviet Union. And yet the real victims—the ones who could not breathe, who were imprisoned, encircled, held down, who carried the world's weight on their shoulders—were Italians. Would we have done what we did, would we have continued collaborating with the worst, would we have performed crimes against humanity, if we did not feel somehow like good people at risk and thus in the right to do what we did? Aren't the sentiments of white vulnerability and innocence, as Ida Danewid suggests through James Baldwin's *The Fire Next Time,* exactly what trigger the crime?[9]

Vladimir Lenin used the expression "ragamuffin imperialism" to accent Italian colonialism as ineffectual, underfunded, and irrelevant. This is a problematic way of naming Italy's expansionism since the phrase underplays its brutality and seriousness.[10] Considering the victimhood fueling fascist governance and expansionistic efforts, melodramatic imperialism might work better as a name for our violence.

BARELY ALIVE

The importance of the seas for European totalitarianisms usually goes unacknowledged, possibly because the recognition of water as the fundamental element for Nazi Fascism would also require recognizing colonialism as a driving force of modern history. As philosopher Carl Schmitt explains in his 1942 *Land and Sea*—a world history in the form of a tale written for his eleven-year-old daughter—World War II can be interpreted in many regards as the culmination of the conflicts over colonial territories and resources that had started with the European settling of the Americas five hundred years earlier.[11] Dominating the world's waters meant not only controlling global trade but also regulating access to the colonies with their raw materials and expendable labor power: this is why Hitler and Mussolini were invested in the seas and shared the aspiration of turning their countries into naval superpowers. As far as Italian totalitarianism was concerned, the regime's project was to challenge the British hegemony over the Mediterranean and the Red Sea, taking over Gibraltar, the Suez Canal, and the Bab al-Mandab Strait in East Africa to control the routes connecting Europe to the Pacific Ocean and the Americas as well as to the Indian Ocean and Asia.

Significantly, these plans for marine dominance were severed from the long tradition of European extractive and settler colonialism to which they belonged and were instead sensationalized as a matter of life and death. Foucault famously commented that under biopolitics, wars are waged "on behalf of the existence of everyone; entire populations are mobilized for the purpose of wholesale slaughter in the name of life."[12] Fascism's wars are no exception. Italy's anticommunist repression, the coup, the invasion of Ethiopia, and then the entrance into the war were mediated not as acts of violence but rather as struggles for survival—as the efforts of real Italian people to secure for themselves and for other threatened races the resources they needed to live on. The fight against improper national bodies who spoiled Italy's spiritual and physical welfare with their foreign dispositions was already underway; now was the time to wage war against the United Kingdom, the great sea monster that could easily starve the nation's biological body by means of maritime blockades and economic chokeholds. As David Rodogno argues, the expansionistic impetus of 1930s Fascism was a direct emanation of the regime's original political biology.[13] The regime's melodramatic imperialism and its racial health concerns were structurally and chiasmatically intertangled—one had to dominate the world to allow the Italian race to be great again, and one had to make the Italian race great again so to allow it to dominate the world. This entanglement of victimhood and imperialism is the centerpiece of the speech that Mussolini gave to the Grand Council of Fascism in 1939.[14]

In this highly affected intervention, Mussolini emphasized that only countries that could sail unbothered around the world were truly free. Italy was thus imprisoned, not only because it lacked access to the oceans but also because the fascist nation was surrounded by virtual enemies such as Malta, Cyprus, and Greece, which were ready to form a "chain" with England and suffocate Italy. Given the imminent calamity emerging from the Mediterranean Sea, the nation had no alternative but to strike back and reclaim what ancient Romans had dubbed Mare Nostrum: a march toward the oceans was the natural extension of the fight in defense of Italian life that Fascism had launched with the March on Rome. Yet Mussolini was aware that the nation was very skeptical about the viability of a war. Thus in his speech to the Grand Council, he also reassured the hierarchs that he had already directed the propaganda machine to emphasize how vital a conflict against Great Britain was for Italy's very survival. And Italian cinema did indeed stir the waters, supporting the projection that it was the British presence in the waters that surrounded the Blackshirt ethno-nation—not Fascism—that was endangering Italians.

Luigi Pensuti's *Dr. ChurKill* (1941), a six-minute animated newsreel inspired by *The Strange Case of Dr. Jekyll and Mr. Hyde*, is possibly the most obvious and ugly manifestation of the self-exonerating rhetoric that Fascism relied on to emotionally manipulate Italians into war making. In 1941, *Süss the Jew* was released in Italy, and *Dr. ChurKill* relies on similar antisemitic tropes to portray England as the puppet master of a global conspiracy against humanity. In Pensuti's cartoon, whose title strikingly resonates with the infamous "Killary" Clinton moniker of yesterday's United States, the Bank of England is depicted as a great spider with gigantic tentacles that extend to faraway seas, and Winston Churchill is represented as a monstrous shape-shifting creature with thick dark skin, a sinister grin, clawed hands, and an avarice for gold. This monster conceals its true colors by transforming itself into a white progressive democrat and pretending to help people in need. The modern-day golem travels from place to place—from factories to the Suez Canal to oil fields—scavenging for profit and exploiting "other races' hard work," to use the voice-over's own terms. But its time has come: Blackshirt squads have exposed the creature and are hunting it down. *Dr. ChurKill* ends with bombs over London, a triumph of doves taking over the frame, and English flags disappearing from the Mediterranean Basin, the Middle East, and Africa. As the voice-over concludes, twinning biology and politics, only when the heinous emblem of exploitation is eradicated will life on earth bloom again.

Dr. ChurKill was produced by the Industria Cortometraggi Milano (INCOM, Industry for Short Films Milan)—an entity created in 1938 with the function of exploring new ways of engaging with the public since the LUCE newsreel model was getting worn out. While Pensuti's cartoon blended political satire with national-racial exaggeration to make an impact on the spectators, a more subtle take on aquatic domination characterizes another INCOM production: Rossellini's directorial debut *Fantasia sottomarina* (*Underwater Fantasy*, 1940). In this short film, Rossellini mixes sequences from Roberto Omegna's naturalist documentary *Uno sguardo al fondo marino* (*Gaze on the Seafloor*, 1936) with original footage shot in his home aquarium to tell a story akin to *Finding Nemo*. A young porgy ventures away from his den to meet up with his love interest, but he is attacked by an octopus. Two morays come to the assistance of this small fish in the big ocean, yet they cannot do much against the long, strong arms of the predator. The porgy mobilizes an army of allies in the fight against the predator, and this multispecies water community, united, is able to defeat the common enemy.

The camera, from behind the aquarium glass, mimics the flow of life at sea, which can go from tranquil to hectic in a matter of seconds. The score punctuates the action, and montage is used both to anthropomorphize the animals and to heighten the affective import of the film. *Fantasia sottomarina* also has an important haptic and immersive quality: when the octopus attacks his prey, he pins it to the aquarium's walls—pushing it toward the camera's lens and taking over the frame with his tentacles. Moving toward the camera, the octopus is also moving in the direction of the spectator, who is made to occupy the position of the prey. As we see the octopus coming at us through water that the fight has made murky and viscous, we can almost feel its tentacles extending from the screen to the skin, smothering us (Figure 20).

To film this short, Rossellini filled dead fish with lead and manipulated them with strings, like puppets. For the battle scenes, he threw live

FIGURE 20. An octopus smothering the spectatorial body in *Fantasia sottomarina* (Roberto Rossellini, 1940).

octopuses, morays, lobsters, and fish in the small tank—turning their struggle for their lives into a macabre spectacle for the human public. Approached through the lens of ecocriticism and posthumanism, *Fantasia sottomarina* is in all regards a snuff film. More than a love for the ocean and for nature, more than an appreciation for the precarity of life or an interest in alterity, what moves Rossellini in his debut is the will to experiment: experiment with what he can make a body do for the camera but also— as Giuliana Minghelli argues—to experiment with how film forms can be used to move spectators' bodies.[15] Whereas directors such as Omegna and Jean Painlevé were committed to the cinematographic apparatus as a means of exploring the mesmerizing beauty of underwater life, Rossellini—closer to Walt Disney, as Luca Caminati aptly concludes—was more interested in exploiting nature and film techniques to construct captivating moral parables.[16] In the final instance, then, what is the moral of the story being told by *Fantasia sottomarina*?

It is the story of the ominous creatures in our waters and of the violence they are capable of; it is the story of a peaceful and diverse community that is victimized by a terrible monster but that comes together to defeat it. One must agree with Enrique Seknadje-Askénazi that this story, although not manifestly political, does not exist in an ideological vacuum. As Jameson reminds us, we must always historicize. Thus Rossellini's short cannot and should not be abstracted from the larger historical context of war, empire building, and anti-British fearmongering in which it is couched.[17] The very fact that Rossellini's debut short was produced by the same entity that delivered *Dr. ChurKill* suggests that *Fantasia sottomarina* also constituted an effort to find new ways to mobilize the people—to eschew LUCE's explicit geopolitical lessons and move the population by triggering inarticulate bad feelings in regard to the sea, feelings that stuck with the viewers much like the suckers of an octopus's tentacles.

A similar attempt to incorporate anxiety in the Mediterranean seascape and use embodied sensations to stir up the people to war also characterizes Navy captain Francesco De Robertis's first feature film, *Uomini sul fondo,* for the newly established Centro Cinematografico del Ministero della Marina (Navy Ministry Film Center). This film not only manifests a decisive shift in the aesthetic and affective registers deployed by Italian feature film in support of Fascism but also showcases most clearly cinema's power to contribute to political history and governmental processes through seemingly apolitical chronicles of human lives in distress. Realism has been praised in film theory (I am thinking especially of Bazin and Roland Barthes) for its capacity to punctuate our consciousness, to make us feel for the fragile bodies and lives that the camera exposes to our gaze. *Uomini sul fondo* is an important cautionary tale of how feelings like love and empathy, once they are enmeshed with existential fear, can turn ugly and be easily weaponized for the worst.

In an article from 1948, renowned film journalist Guido Aristarco criticized De Robertis's war cinema for its incapacity to bring into focus the enemy against which Italy was fighting. De Robertis responded that that the enemy was the sea itself. This response should not be dismissed, as it bears witness to the director's project to depoliticize and naturalize the war, to turn Fascism's belligerency into something that has to do with the elements, the environment, and bare life rather than with geopolitics and the appropriation of resources.[18] Leaving global history and politics off-frame, *Uomini sul fondo* scales back the field of vision and zooms in on fragile Italian bodies, so as to convey the atmosphere for a body politic on the brink without having to also explicitly embrace a political project or ideology. The film's visual and narrative focus on Italian soldiers running out of air effectively harnesses what Peter Sloterdijk dubs "atmo-terror": the sensation that our very environment—the air, water, and soil, the very conditions necessary for the bare survival of organic life—is under attack.[19] One of the first times atmo-terrorism manifested itself in human history was in 1935, when Italian planes launched gas attacks against Ethiopian soldiers and civilians (including women and children) to annihilate the country's obstinate resistance to the fascist invasion. With this in mind, it is especially exploitative that *Uomini sul fondo*—which De Robertis consciously planned as a *film d'atmosfera,* an "atmospheric film"—appropriates the experience of airlessness to mediate bodily excesses that obfuscate the truths of fascist history and start giving Italians and the regime a new body, a new identity.[20]

Uomini sul fondo features the A103, an Italian submarine involved in a pre-war exercise. Submarines were already used as prime offensive and defensive weapons in World War I, and their strategic importance in the new conflict increased radically, given their increased autonomy and their ability to trespass into territorial waters undetected. The drill depicted in the film requires spending as much time as possible submerged, to put the structural solidity of the boats to the test but also to allow the sailors—and the public with them—to develop resilience to the pressures that are coming. The A103 is pushing things to the limit.

The camera moves through the restricted environment, and a long lateral pan reviews the crew. We notice class differences between soldiers of different ranks but also the differences in their accents, facial features, skin tones, and body types. Yet, bringing together these different Italians through editing and camera movements, *Uomini sul fondo* connects all the people on board and conveys the feeling of a diverse but compact racial totality. De Robertis's *uomini* (men) are not *mascalzoni* (scoundrels); they are not excessive beings, they are not to be formed or re-formed. The way that they are framed conveys the sense of bodies that fit in perfectly. And it is particularly important in this regard that these bodies are not even "fictional": the cast is composed exclusively of real Navy operatives playing themselves. What we see projected on the big screen are thus the disciplined lives that fascist totalitarianism has supposedly made: suffering in silence but proud of their social roles and subject positions. De Robertis showcases the perfect synchronism between flesh and technology, organic matter and steel, focusing especially on the militarized bodies' capacity to interact and communicate with the submarine's apparatuses.[21] But these bodies are also fragile and exposed to the elements, notwithstanding the iron cocoon enframing them and the technologies augmenting their abilities. Close-ups and medium shots convey the stress that these men are experiencing: the fatigue and the hunger are obvious in their dull eyes and furrowed brow; the absolute silence on board—broken only by the crew's sighs and moans, the shrill metallic noise of the submarine's fuselage under pressure, and white noise coming from the radio—is haunting.

All the submarines have returned to the base; only the A103 is still out there. After sixty hours, the captain finally gives the order to surface. The men are starved and air is so scarce that the sailors are experiencing early signs of paralysis and blindness: a POV shot makes the public experience the sailors' loss of vision through their eyes. As it is preparing to surface, the A103 is hit by a steamer and sinks to the seabed, turning its operatives into the titular "uomini sul fondo" (men on the bottom). Water, food, and air are already scarce—and the impact has damaged some internal circuits, such that fluoride gas is pouring into the submarine's compartments, transforming the machine from a protective shell into a gas chamber and death casket. The heat is unbearable. The sailors take off their uniforms to get some relief (Figure 21). By stripping these bodies down and staging them as bare lives, De Robertis turns fascist soldiers into mere human beings. But these lives in danger, these men on the bottom we are made to care for and identify with, are not simply men. As Alexander Weheliye reminds in his scathing critique of Agamben's work as color-blind and hence implicitly discriminatory, bare lives do not exist under racial capitalism; there are only and always specific forms of living that are gendered and raced according to the urgencies of the capitalist-colonial order.[22] Thus the naked bodies from De Robertis's film ought to be recognized as the bearers of a violent history and an imperial enterprise that *Uomini sul fondo,* through its surplus of pathos and embodied sensations, works hard to exorcise and keep off scene—implicitly recognizing them as obscene.

The Italian Navy promptly comes to the rescue of the submarine and of the brave Italian seamen who now, pinned on the sea floor, cannot breathe. All the rescue efforts are futile. The lever that is stuck can only be released from inside a chamber totally saturated with toxic gasses. The courageous stoker Leandri—who had almost lost the use of his hand during the drill due to carbon monoxide poisoning—sacrifices his life for the greater good. After having secured the survival of his crewmates and of the precious war machine, he collapses.

FIGURE 21. Bare lives in *Uomini sul fondo* (Francesco De Robertis, 1940).

A POV shot lets the viewers experience Leandri's last moments. Before drawing his last breath, he catches a glimpse of a sign attached to the submarine's wall that reads, "I am proud of you." Leandri finds consolation in this message of approval, whose "I" is implicitly but obviously Mussolini, and can die content in knowing that he is making the Dux but also his people proud by sacrificing his life. After living through the breathless and exhilarating experience of being on the bottom, the public, too, can enjoy a much-awaited climactic rise. The rhythmic alternation between Leandri dying and the submarine being ejected to the surface, emerging into the open through a cloud of white foam, welcomed by the jubilation of the men and boats involved in the rescue operation, allows the spectatorial body to partake in the dual pleasures of being a national hero and of being saved.

The viewers travel from the water to the land, from the submarine to the base, from the maritime abyss to the surface, and then to the humble dinner tables where families are holding their breath for the sailors and the churches where prayers are said for them. By means of montage, De Robertis not only indissolubly links the sea to the nation's soil, staging the Mediterranean as an integral part of Italy. In assembling civilian and military spaces so tightly together, he also erases the boundaries between war and peace. The opening intertitle of *Uomini sul fondo* announces that the privilege experienced by "gli uomini dei sottomarini" (literally, the submarines' men) consists in the fact that U-boat crews cannot distinguish between "life in peace" and "life at war." But in putting us in their position, by making us feel what it is like to be in a sunken submarine—running out of air, dying from the heat, at the mercy of an unforgiving environment, unwavering, ready to do whatever it takes to protect one's country and one's people—the film grants the public the same privilege. It is Italy as a whole, as one nation and one body politic, as one united race, that is pinned on the bottom and gasping for air. De Robertis's cinema works metonymically. The suffocating bodies that *Uomini sul fondo* features are not metaphors for a country strangled by economic tariffs. They belong to the same organic totality as the viewers, to an organism that is lacking the breathing space it needs to survive. Their vulnerability is thus our vulnerability, because the sea that is causing their death is also causing our death— given the enemies circling the peninsula and infesting our waters. Instead of showing war, De Robertis evokes for the viewers what is like to be in it. Because the actors are actual Navy operatives, viewers at the time of the film's release knew that these bodies pretending to suffer and to die were bodies now at war to ensure everyone's safety; they were bodies that might have experienced in reality what they were pretending to experience in the film. Some of them might never come back home, might be forever stuck at the bottom of the sea it was so vital to police, patrol, and control to guarantee a bright future for the fascist ethno-nation. As the song chanted by the sailors in distress makes explicit: on the bottom of the sea one dreams, but one can also die.

Uomini sul fondo features extensive use of Guglielmo Marconi's radio towers and Antonio Meucci's telephone buoys, and in one scene an Italian mother is able to use a radio-telephone bridge to talk with her son, who is stranded in the submarine. In featuring the role that these new Italian technologies have in connecting lives, connecting localities, De Robertis positions his own cinema in the same genealogy of technologized nation building. Through editing, *Uomini sul fondo* builds a shared national experience characterized by the fear of subalternity and death—thus it shapes a victimized "us." It also maps the spaces that need to fall under Italian rule in order for us to stop being at the bottom and without resources to live on. In the film's final sequence, the A103 submarine finally cruises away, with an Italian flag raised at half-mast on its fin, accompanied by an army of battleships paying tribute to it. Once its silhouette has exited the frame, exposing the calm, open sea to our gaze, a message appears from the luminous horizon: "To the memory of the men who never resurfaced from the depths of the SEA in order for it to be OURS." As all the other words fade, we are left to read "MARE NOSTRO," our sea, superimposed over the Italian flag.

It is Gabriele D'Annunzio who popularized the expression used by the ancient Romans to name the Mediterranean Sea, turning it into a watchword for Italy's colonial ambitions. The infamous motto is featured in the "proemio" of his *La nave* (*The Ship,* 1908), a tragic play set in 552 CE that celebrates Venice's rise as a united imperial power.[23] The beginning of *La nave* is actually a flash-forward. From the ship where a common homeland for all Venetians is established, an order is given: "Arm the prow and set sail toward the world." A prayer is then raised: May God bless the sailors who drowned and protect those crossing the seas; may the Lord "turn all the Oceans into the Mare Nostro." *Uomini sul fondo* appropriates the prayer but represses the connection between the urgency to appropriate the globe's seas and Italy's project of world domination. In this way, in sync with Fascism's melodramatic imperialism, De Robertis can redeploy the reclamation of the Mediterranean as a matter of self-preservation. Let us not forget that *Uomini sul fondo* went into production a few months after Mussolini's address to the Grand Council of Fascism, where the Duce emphasized the need to persuade the nation of the vital necessity of turning the Mediterranean into an Italian sea, to make it belong to us again.

But "us" who? Who is the "us" of which Mussolini speaks? Who are these Italians to whom the Mediterranean would belong?

SEASCAPES OF RACIAL EXCEPTIONALISM

At first sight and against phenotypical evidence, the "Manifesto della razza" of 1938 unequivocally affirmed that Italians were Aryan, that is, white.[24] In reality, this intervention, which was authored by Italian scientists and paved the way for the promulgation of the Racial Laws, is fraught with all sorts of tensions in regard to Italy's relation to whiteness. At play in the "Manifesto" is a sort of racial exceptionalism that simultaneously grafts fascist Italy onto white Europe and severs the two. The distinction between "big races and small races"—more general ("maggiori," major) and more specific ("minori," minor) ways of taxonomizing human masses—in fact allows the document to posit that although Italians are indeed Aryans in a generic sense, it would be more precise to identify them as Mediterraneans. As Claudio Fogu argues, through the authorizing category of "Aryanism," the "Manifesto" biologically elevated Italians to the rank of white people, drawing Italy closer to Germany and establishing uncrossable race lines separating them from both Jewish Italians and Black colonial subjects.[25] But through the reference to the Mediterranean, the document distinguished Italian whiteness from *majoritarian* European whiteness and reconnected Italians with the history of *minoritized* peoples from the Global South—a history that was first one of civilization and culture and then became a history of subalternity, exploitation, suffering, and subjection. Notwithstanding the regime's embrace of Aryanism in the aftermath of the alliance with Hitler, Giuseppe Sergi's thesis on Mediterranean supremacy in world history remained the racial horizon proper to fascist Italy. In the regime's imaginary, the Roman Mediterranean was the cradle of Western civilization, and the crises that the West was experiencing were the result of the very race that had birthed Europe being put down and held back. Superior insofar as biologically Aryan but historically minoritized as nonwhite races were, Italy could pose as the liberator of all oppressed peoples and claim a hegemonic position in the Mediterranean region and beyond—to once again show humanity the way forward.

The corpo-realism in *Uomini sul fondo* was praised in postwar criticism for its apolitical, objective, uncompromising, immediate representation of the human element of war—a notable anticipation of neorealist aesthetics and ethics. Scholars as distant as Bazin and Brunetta, among others, not only overlook the film's heavy formalism and overblown pathos.[26] They also miss how its melodramatic focus on bodies in danger, on bodies to be saved, overwhelms geopolitical history and gives substance to the fantasy of Italy's racial exceptionalism. Whereas the Italian technology and ingenuity showcased in the film attest to the nation's intellectual primacy—its "white" mind—the character displayed by its people bears witness to Italy's big, warm, pacific, southern heart. Mussolini's large chest and imperial jawline are perspicuously absent from *Uomini sul fondo,* which is instead populated by the caring gazes and reassuring features of an ordinary Italy concerned with the destiny of its sons, of real officers contemplating the destiny of their men, and of real sailors reflecting on the destiny of the puppy they have on board. In humanizing Italy and Fascism's war machine, De Robertis ultimately reracializes the fascist nation into a good people who are not gearing up to take over the world but are just trying to survive.

La nave bianca, De Robertis and Rossellini's 1941 film for the Navy Ministry Film Center, expands on this operation and deploys color to further embody the presumed difference between a predatory, parasitic, violent whiteness (the major whiteness of the North and of the world's colonial superpowers) and Italy's whiteness (the minor Mediterranean whiteness that was the exclusive prerogative of Italians). De Robertis's solo feature had stripped its soldiers down to hide the continuity between the regime's ambition to appropriate the Mediterranean, on the one hand, and Europe's colonial history, on the other. *La nave bianca* instead dresses the fascist war machine in a blinding white, and through its army of white-clothed doctors, nurses, and injured soldiers, it identifies Italian whiteness as the whiteness of victims and caregivers. With this film, Italian masculinity especially changes its skin.

Italian men are no longer the master race that, in splendid desert whites, proves its superiority by killing Black lives, as in Augusto Genina's *Lo squadrone bianco* (*The White Squadron,* 1936) or Goffredo Alessandrini's *Luciano Serra, pilota* (*Luciano Serra, Pilot,* 1938, with Rossellini as assistant director). Italians are now a victim race that might soon see its coastline violated. Samuel Agbamu rightly points out that the status of the Mediterranean shifts in the fascist imaginary as Italy's involvement in the war develops.[27] The Mediterranean ceases to be a space to be traversed to reach the much-coveted colonial realm, as it was, for instance, in Blasetti's *Alderbaran* from 1935. It instead becomes an unsecured boundary through which Italy's mortal enemies are creeping into the ethno-nation. *La nave bianca* feeds into Fascism's victim mentality and supports its melodramatic imperialism by featuring a crossed Mediterranean instead of Mediterranean crossings.

As with *Uomini sul fondo, La nave bianca* opens with an intertitle assuring viewers that all the characters in the film are real people playing themselves and captured in the reality of their daily occupations, emotions, and humanity. Here, however, the people featured are both men and women. As Maria Antonietta Macciocchi suggests in her groundbreaking 1970s research on women under Blackshirt rule, the film's commitment to a more diverse representation of Italians doing their jobs is not informed by a desire for realism or inclusivity.[28] In order to reproduce itself, Fascism relied on toxic forms of masculinity *and* femininity. Thus, by prominently featuring women, *La nave bianca* specifies the work that the two genders had to take up within the new context of war and naturalizes caregiving as women's destiny. In this regard, the romantic subplot in the film might be read in connection with its effort to engage with women, as a more diverse range of emotions and sensations is deployed here to appeal to a diverse audience. Among the different body genres discussed by Williams, the sentimental drama—"the weepie"—is as a matter of fact the guilty pleasure traditionally associated with women's cinematic consumption.

We are at war, but the sailors aboard the Italian Navy's majestic battle-ship can enjoy some well-deserved time off. They write to their *madrine di guerra,* young women serving the country as soldiers' pen pals, to keep their spirits high. Some letters, the sailors hint, border on erotica. The stoker Augusto Basso's letters to Elena Fondi, an elementary school teacher, are different. They are in love and will meet soon in Taranto, where Basso's ship is deployed. Elena will recognize her *marinaretto* (little sailor) thanks to the white carnation—a symbol of pure love—he will be wearing. Just as Basso is about to disembark, duty calls. Renzo Rossellini's score changes from romantic to bellicose. Enemy ships have been spotted in Italian waters, terribly close to the Adriatic coastline, and need to be pushed back. Elena is at the port when Basso's ships sails off to combat. She sobs and she salutes. She understands that the homeland is at risk and that Italian men's job is to keep national soil free from foreign bodies.

During the clashes—reproduced by mixing original reenactments, news-reel footage, and sequences from the Navy training film *I gas di guerra sul mare* (*War Gases on the Sea*, 1934)—many sailors are maimed. Bloody gashes, broken arms, bandages, burn marks: *La nave bianca* morbidly emphasizes the effects of war on the flesh of our boys, who at the beginning of the film were introduced as so lovable and affable. Basso is in especially bad shape. He has been blinded by a gush of toxic gasses and needs to undergo emergency surgery. By cross-cutting between combat scenes and the medical intervention on Basso, *La nave bianca* conjures a synergy between war and medicine, warriors and doctors: in both cases, it is a matter of curing a *vulnus*—of healing an open wound. Through binoculars, we see looming on the horizon the British ships infesting our sea, paralyzing our traffic, compromising our ability to move, and preventing us access to what we need to assure our bare survival. They are the geopolitical *vulnus* that is causing so much pain, and in the same ways that our soldiers' injuries need to be sutured, the Mediterranean ought to be sealed, because it is only

FIGURE 22. Basso is evacuated in a boat, swathed in a white shroud, in *La nave bianca* (Francesco De Robertis and Roberto Rossellini, 1941).

when this vulnerable body of water is secured that Italian bodies and the Italian body politic will stop hurting. The mighty weaponry of the Italian Navy does its job: the enemies withdraw behind smoke screens. The doctors' hard work pays off as well: the intervention on Basso is successful. He is safe but still in bad shape: his innocent body wrapped in white shroud, Basso is evacuated to a hospital vessel—the eponymous white ship—to fully recover (Figure 22).

On the *Arno,* he finds his injured crewmates but also some Nazi soldiers, who are jolly good fellows as well. In a choral scene that speaks to the film's connection with the racial laws' efforts to bring Nazism and Fascism closer together, we see Italian and German war operatives on the ship's deck, singing the same tune, each in their native tongue, and recovering together under the warm Mediterranean sun. Taking care of them is an army of volunteer nurses from the Red Cross—among whom is Elena, who has taken a leave of absence from her job as a teacher to serve Italy and its sons in a manner befitting the country's national emergency. The woman recognizes Basso by the medal he is still wearing but decides not to reveal her identity. Elena did not play favorites with her pupils; now that she is a *crocerossina* (Red Cross nurse), she cannot afford to love any man in a special way. It is notable that in a film that works so hard to suppress the aspirations informing the fascist investment in the Mediterranean, characters hide their identities and desires as well—as if to emphasize the necessity of repression for the greater good. After recovering his sight, Basso recognizes Elena as well but accepts that this is not the time for romance. While sentimental dramas are characterized by the temporality of the "too late," this racial melodrama mobilizes the time of the "not now, not yet." National security comes first, and romantic love needs to be deferred to an unspecified time to come. The patriotic love to which romance must be subordinated, however, comes with its own form of enjoyment.

At the end of *La nave bianca,* Basso's warship returns to port from the combat zone after successfully warding off the enemies. Basso rises from his sickbed and is joined by Elena, who supports and embraces him. Together, they passionately gaze at the battleship's homecoming. In a medium shot, the camera frames their ecstatic faces, literally illuminated by the appearance in the sickbay's porthole of the majestic Italian battleship and its phallic arsenal (Figure 23). Sexual enjoyment gives way to the ecstasy of patriotism, as tears of fascist jouissance mark Basso's and Elena's patriotic eyes.

FIGURE 23. Elena's and Basso's patriotic gazes looking out toward the horizon at the end of *La nave bianca* (Francesco De Robertis and Roberto Rossellini, 1941).

The camera then moves forward, into a close-up on the red cross on Elena's white uniform, voiding the screen, as Ben-Ghiat notes, "of all reference to surrounding reality."[29] A cross-fade leads to the film's final dedication: "To the stoic sufferings and to the resolute faith of the wounded of all armed forces. To the silent abnegation of those who soften their suffering and nurture their faith." Not only does this homage confirm the essential woundedness of the Italian body politic and the gendered division of labor that *La nave bianca* so prominently features; it has an additional performative value. The film reminds the public of their options ahead: either assume the position of men and fight; or adopt women's quiet support for the armed forces' efforts, taking care of the fragile, precious bodies of those who risk their lives for the survival of the Italian race.

After Mussolini's downfall, Rossellini downplayed his involvement in *La nave bianca* by pointing out that he did not figure in the credits of the film. Neither does De Robertis: both *Uomini sul fondo* and *La nave bianca* are presented as developed and directed by the Navy Ministry Film Center. On other occasions, he would blame the regime for having altered and softened his brutal gaze on war by introducing the romantic subplot between Basso and Elena.[30] Against the grain of such self-excusing forgetfulness, it is now well documented that Rossellini was well aware of the romantic subplot of *La nave bianca,* since it was an integral part of De Robertis's original treatment. Moreover, it is precisely in the second half of the film—in the "romantic" segment—that Rossellini's touch becomes evident. Ben-Ghiat argues: "Elena, a carrier of rectitude and charity as well as a love interest, is a prototype for characters in later Rossellini films."[31] And in many regards, *La nave bianca* truly constitutes a prototypical film for Rossellini: this work is rife with themes and stylistic choices Rossellini returned to throughout his career. The presence of pain in the world, the importance of care, the tension between private love and public urgencies—these motives are all constant in Rossellini's oeuvre. Additionally, the graphic representation of suffering bodies and the admiration for the people attending to them are common features in Rossellini: the stylistic and ideological distance between *La nave bianca* and Rossellini's "democratic" films might then be shorter than is usually acknowledged. In Rossellini, it is always the presence of evil in the world that makes painful deaths unavoidable facts of life. The specificity of *La nave bianca* lies in its representation of evil as a transgression of a nation's natural borders and the borders themselves as extending, nearly infinitely, past the horizon of the mare nostrum. It is important in this regard that the film's British ships withdraw from sight but are not gone. They are there, behind smoke screens, threatening with their invasive presence the very existence of Italy and of Italians. Thus, with fright being turned into an integral element of the national environment, the racial geopolitical anxiety harnessed by the film asks, "How far is far enough?": how far will the British ships have to be pushed back, but also how far will the fascist war machine have to go—literally and metaphorically—for the Italian race to be really safe? It is this experience of the Italian sea and of what lurks on the horizon for the country that allows *La nave bianca* to spin Italian expansionism as a righteous act of self-defense, to stop the hurting. Ben-Ghiat reads the film's general iconography as a manifestation of that Christian humanism, that empathy for human suffering, which will also be the mark of Rossellini's celebrated postwar works. Yet humanism is precisely the alibi that makes the film's affective justification of fascist war-waging so effective.

The problem with Rossellini's humanism here and elsewhere, a problem that the field of film studies has been unwilling to acknowledge, is that the director's emphatic appreciation of the vulnerability and sanctity of life is not as innocent as it presents itself to be. Since it is only specific lives, bodies, and identities that are actually depicted as being in danger and thus in need of protection and care, Rossellini's humanistic stance makes matter only certain lives, which are staged as tokens of human life in itself: the enemies of a particular historical form of life are in this way mediated as threats to human life itself. But this is a more general problem with how Western humanism works: on the one hand, it purports to care for the interests of humanity as a whole; on the other, it cannot but establish that some are more human and humane than others, and thus that one needs to do whatever it takes to protect this exemplary humanity from what Naoki Sakai has dubbed "the Rest."³² In the case of *La nave bianca*, the ideal humanity mediated as being under attack and in need of protection is fascist humanity, and this leads De Robertis and Rossellini to implicitly demonize fascist Italy's enemies as enemies of humanity and to explicitly romanticize the regime as the life force whose exclusive preoccupation is humanity's well-being. How can humanity live on if the *most* human of the human races, the race that birthed civility and Western humanity, dies out? In consideration of the discriminatory thrust of white humanism, Aimé Césaire famously concluded that the "West has never been further from being able to live a true humanism—a humanism made to the measure of the world."³³ The humanism in *La nave bianca* does not live up to the world either.

The entanglement between humanism, racism, and imperialism in *La nave bianca*, and its effort to humanize the fascist state and its war machine, is especially evident in an earlier scene from the film that deploys a camera movement very similar to that which, later on, elevates Elena into an emblem of Christian charity. The leadership of the *Arno* is holding a meeting to plan the next rescue mission. Gathered around the table are the military commanding officers but also the head physician and the head nurse. In the background, we see pictures of Mussolini and of Italy's king, Victor Emanuel III (Figure 24). The captain explains that the injured soldiers picked up in the colonies will disembark, so as to make room for the many Italians maimed during the recent battles in defense of territorial waters. As he reassures the others that he has readied the surgery rooms and facilities necessary to take care of an army of injured soldiers, the camera moves in on him—relegating both the king and the Duce out of the

FIGURE 24. Whitening Italian Fascism as Mussolini's portrait looms overhead in
La nave bianca (Francesco De Robertis and Roberto Rossellini, 1941).

frame. This empathetic, caring, and authoritative captain, in his immaculate
white Navy uniform, surrounded by the medical personnel donning their
white uniforms, is now made to serve as the voice and face of the fascist
ethno-nation fighting to survive.

Renzo Rossellini's score kicks in and the elegiac music is used as a sound
bridge as the film jumps from the meeting to a surgery room where a team
of physicians, in their white coats, has successfully saved a maimed soldier.
Colonialism is mentioned, yet the focus on Italian pain immediately forecloses the possibility of feeling the pain of others—Black pain, the suffering
that Italians have caused. In this way, notwithstanding the crimes against
humanity the good people had perpetrated in Ethiopia a few short years
earlier, notwithstanding the rising discrimination against Jewish Italians,
the film can project Italians as the only truly suffering race: the race at risk
and in need of saving is us, not the peoples the West had brutalized for
so long. Rather than pervaded by a consolatory ideology, *La nave bianca*
appears driven by the urgency to excuse, trigger, and mobilize.

The manifest goal of De Robertis and Rossellini's textual machine is in fact *to whiten*: whiten Fascism, whiten Italian colonialism, whiten the bodies performing totalitarianism, whiten the regime's claims over the world's seas, and whiten the Blackshirt history in which the film is trying to involve the public. But in this apparent operation of whitewashing, the Mediterranean also changes color. The *Arno* sails on to save more lives, and the dark sea—replete with threats, replete with death—that the *nave bianca* is traversing is made white by the wake of the Italian hospital boat. Thanks to Fascism, the Mediterranean is not a bleak border zone anymore. It has finally reverted to a white Italian space.

In presenting the sea as a reclaimed mare nostrum, what *La nave bianca* conceals is the Mediterranean's Blackness. The expression "Black Mediterranean" has been mobilized by authors working at the intersection of Italian studies and critical race theory, such as Alessandra Di Maio, SA Smythe, Angelica Pesarini, and Camilla Hawthorne, among many others, to flag the Middle Sea's pluri-centennial history as a site of violence and terror, slavery, and the exploitation of Black lives. In a book from 2022, the Black Mediterranean Collective explains: "scholars of the Black Mediterranean challenge the romanticization of the Mediterranean as a space of convivial exchange and unfettered hybridity, pointing to oft-overlooked histories of racial violence and their contemporary reverberations."[34] In making invisible through its orgy of self-pity the true color of the mare nostrum, *La nave bianca*—which was funded by two brothers who had made a fortune by building roads in the fascist empire—amplifies a way of feeling about Italians and the Italian milieu that has deep reverberations in past and present national history. It is only insofar as we recognize how the Mediterranean has been racialized as a white Italian space and Italians as a victimized good race that we can come to terms with the power of current proto-fascist securitarian discourses regarding an African invasion of Italian soil.[35] But, as I show in the next section, by keeping close to Rossellini's fascist corpus, this racial melodrama whitening the regime and the Mediterranean also served as a powerful foundation upon which to build in order to defend Italy's deployment well beyond its sea.

HUMANE WARRIORS, HUMANITARIAN WARS

After *La nave bianca*, De Robertis and Rossellini parted ways. De Robertis kept working for the Navy Ministry Film Center, insisting with *Alpha Tau!*

(1942) on the need to take over the Mediterranean in order to keep Italy free and Italians alive. By featuring five Navy operatives visiting their respective hometowns on a two-day leave, *Alpha Tau!* stages an Italy maimed by bombs—dropped by planes stationed on the aircraft carriers bearing down on the Italian coastline. De Robertis then followed Mussolini to Salò and, in 1945, directed for the puppet state the unconvincing *La vita semplice* (*The Simple Life*), a eulogy of unpretentious living that, with its critique of financial speculators, borders on antisemitism. In the postwar period, De Robertis gained attention especially for his anti-Black *Il mulatto* (*Angelo*, 1950), possibly the earliest cinematic rejection of *jus soli* (birthright citizenship) in national cultural history. Using as its backdrop the charming sights and sounds of the Mediterranean Sea, this film amplifies the message that mixed-raced children, even those born in Italy, belong elsewhere.[36]

Rossellini's postfascist cinema is of course incredibly well known, while his films from the Blackshirt Ventennio have long remained unaccounted for. This is somewhat expected, given the traditional lack of engagement with realist cinema under the regime. But this specific suppressed memory has a particular weight to it. By avoiding Rossellini's work for Fascism, scholars have failed to reconsider the mythic status of the director and, with it, of neorealism itself. *La nave bianca* is in fact part of a trilogy in which Rossellini anticipates audiovisual strategies that have defined the neorealist supposed ethico-aesthetical revolution—the use of nonprofessional actors, long takes, outdoor shooting, elliptical narration, voyage form, and consciousness of clichés, just to name a few—to cast a positive light on the various arms of the Italian war apparatus as the fascist ethno-nation marched east. After featuring the Navy and the Mediterranean in the film codirected with De Robertis, Rossellini moved on to the Air Force and the invasion of Greece in *Un pilota ritorna* and the Army and the Russian campaign in *L'uomo dalla croce*. The category of "male melodrama," as elaborated by Catherine O'Rawe and Dana Renga on the heels of Williams's discussion of "male weepies," is particularly fruitful for thinking about these films.[37] Through their focus on brutalized Italian men who experience pain and trauma and yet remain empathetic in the face of other people's suffering, these works compel their viewers to feel pity for those performing fascist imperialism—a pity that the national public can turn onto itself. Who are the sympathetic perpetrators so movingly featured on screen, these men with so much weight to carry on their shoulders, if not the

Blackshirt race itself? In obscuring the real cause of the painful reality they put on display, *Un pilota ritorna* and *L'uomo dalla croce* continue to mediate convenient alibis for a whole nation as the time of reckoning came ever closer.

Un pilota ritorna is based on a scenario by Vittorio Mussolini, the Duce's son, and centers on the first deployment of Gino Rossati (Massimo Girotti) in the Royal Italian Air Force.

> Interior. Middle-class house. An older woman is giving a piano lesson to a young girl. There are a few pictures on the piano: pictures of a child at different ages, a picture of a young man in a military uniform. The girl asks her teacher if the man is her child, and she replies that he is her son, her only son, who is now a soldier. Cross-fade.

Rossati, one of Italy's many sons serving their nation, arrives at his air base. He meets his colleagues and then goes out with them for a night in town. The soldiers chitchat with some women who read for them a newspaper article waxing poetic about the winged heroes who cross the skies, these modern knights who serve their nation in order for tomorrow to be, finally . . . Rossati, the rookie, is enjoying being treated as a hero, but the commanding officer, Trisotti (Gaetano Masier), silences their praise: "Do not bother us with this stuff," he instructs the women, who stop reading the newspaper article. Through this early scene, the film verbalizes its own intervention: do not bother the public with the official and worn-out rhetoric of state propaganda. As Peter Brunette argues, a fundamental accomplishment of Rossellini's first solo feature film is to challenge the glorification of combat and soldiers.[38] Daily life at the air base is mediated as trivial and dull, with soldiers complaining about their shifts and assignments before complying with the work with which they have been tasked—in the end, they are only following orders. But war-waging itself is presented as something mundane, uninteresting, and utterly non-epic: a job among others. To conjure the banality of war, Rossellini relies on a combination of ellipses and repetitions. The elliptical style through which he narrates the combat operations has the function of stripping war of any and all grandeur. By recycling the same footage to recount Rossati's different missions, the director mediates it as something cliché and repetitive.

Mission 1. Rossati's squad flies over the Mediterranean and bombs Greece.
Some targets are destroyed. Mission 2. Rossati's squad crosses the Mediterranean again and bombs Greece again: some other targets are destroyed, but
Trisotti dies in the air battle that ensues. Mission 3. Another day, another
Mediterranean crossing, another bombing mission, another fight with enemy
forces: Rossati's plane is downed and the young pilot becomes a prisoner
of war.

In the camp, Italian immigrants who had settled in Greece and Italian
soldiers who had invaded it await their destiny alongside Greek refugees.
Fallen from grace, fallen from the sky, Rossati is now part of a homeless
multitude yearning for safety and traversing a maimed landscape marred
by bombs, blood, and tears. Rossati's change of status and perspective is
accompanied by a dramatic change in the film's audiovisual profile. As the
Germans advance and the Greek–British army withdraws, the prisoners and
refugees are transferred from location to location, and Rossellini follows
their plight through long panoramic shots—including a very effective and
immersive 360-degree pan—lodging the desperate mass of human beings
in the ruined environment that surrounds them.

By now, Rossellini has renounced the "aerial view," the distanced disinterest with regard to the destructiveness of war that, as Noa Steimatsky
maps, characterized not only earlier aviator films but also Marinetti's and
the futurists' take on war.[39] "Long silences with a grandiose rhythm made
of almost nothing, full of dazed gazes"—this is how Renzo Rossellini, who
curated the film's score, describes the second part of *Un pilota ritorna*. In
this regard, Mino Argentieri emphasizes Rossellini's work as an important step in the development of an antinarrative stance and analytic gaze
that will then lead to neorealism's characteristic slow pace.[40] In fact, in the
segments of *Un pilota ritorna* that take place in Greece (which were actually shot close to Rome), narration gives way to description, and action-
cinema—to use Deleuzian categories—gives way to a cinema committed
to registering the suffering brought about by war. This commitment is,
however, partial and interested. It is partial because the only pain that matters in the film is Italian pain—they are the ones suffering in camps; they
are the innocent victims of war. We don't get to experience the suffering of Greek women forced into prostitution in exchange for food by the
Italian soldiers, or the random executions that the Royal Army carried
out to terrorize the population, effecting a governance by fear as it had

done in Ethiopia.[41] The commitment is interested because by embedding wounded Italian bodies into a wounded landscape, Rossellini naturalizes Italian pain, turning—again—a suffering Italian humanity into a synecdoche for the whole of humanity and consequently remediating the violence done against Italians as something unnatural. What is remarkable is that for the film, those performing crimes against nature and humanity are not only the Brits. The Germans are also cast in the role of monsters.

A child is sick but there are no medicines to cure him or food to nourish him: the Brits have destroyed everything. A German Stuka bomber attacks the Brits who are shepherding the column of displaced people through the ruined lands of Europe without any regard for the civilians in the convoy. In both cases, shot-reverse-shot patterns confirm the sense of clear distinction between victims and tormenters, between the kind of people that Italians are and the folks from northern Europe. This war is not between Greece and Italy anymore: Greeks and Italians are part of a battle they are not waging; they are the targets, the collateral damage of an inhumane conflict scorching the earth. An Italian soldier needs to have his leg amputated. Performing the surgery is an Italian doctor who resettled in Greece. The doctor asks: "Chi vuole assistere?"—who wants to assist, to help with the procedure, but also who wants to attend, to bear witness? Rossati volunteers, and by following him in his performance as assistant nurse, the public occupies the praiseworthy position of the compassionate witness. A Greek soldier is also there, surveying the intervention from afar. He can hardly hold back his tears when he hears the screams of the Italian soldier undergoing surgery without anesthesia. How can Italians be bad if even the enemy feels for them? Moreover, given that the Greek enemy feels for Italians, Greeks cannot be the real enemy. Through the flash of sympathy felt by the Greek soldier toward an Italian one, *Un pilota ritorna* overturns existing geopolitical allegiances and unifies colonized and colonizer as part of a compassionate, suffering Mediterranean humanity from which the heartless Germans and Brits are excluded. This is why the film, notwithstanding its tear-jerking representation of war, cannot be understood as an anti-imperial film. By means of an orgy of pity and self-pity, thanks to its abjectification of northern European whiteness, through its sympathetic representation of Italian soldiers doing their jobs, through Girotti's moving performance, *Un pilota ritorna* represses the possibility of acknowledging Italians in their role of "architects of the tragedy" in which Rossellini's realism immerses the public.[42] But the film also attempts to bear witness to the righteousness of fascist imperialism: since Greeks and Italians share the same humanity, since they are *una faccia una razza*—"one face, one race," as the fascist aggressors promised the aggrieved Greek population and the film confirms by means of casting choices—they belong together; they ought to be part of the same sociopolitical formation.

And yet, by putting so much emphasis on Italian goodness—on the fact that war is something that Italians do but that does not compromise the integrity or the humanity of Italy's sons, daughters, mothers, and fathers— the film leaves crucial questions unanswered: Why would a good race get involved with all this? Why would the smiling and happy child that we know Rossati to be from his family pictures subject himself to so much pain and violence? Why, after having fled captivity and making it back to his homeland at the end of the film, should he go back to war making? How can he be at peace with himself after all that he has seen and heard, after having experienced what the war does to peoples and places on the ground—not through the newspaper cutouts Rossellini uses to recount the progress of Greece's occupation? If war is only a job, as the film's visual strategies establish, why would Italians pick up such an occupation? Just to bring together Greeks and Italians?

When *Un pilota ritorna* went into production, the illusion of a quick and easy war of expansion had already evaporated. People were starting to ask questions—and Rossellini's solo debut attests to this climate of doubt. In order to affectively authorize the war, to get the population through more sacrifices, to keep them obeying orders, to keep them bombing, killing, destroying, invading, and fighting, a larger-than-life enemy had to be looming over Italy. New existential threats were needed, crueler and even more dangerous than England. Twenty years after the March on Rome, Rossellini's *L'uomo dalla croce* brings fascist cinema to a close by returning to its original public enemy: the barbaric and depraved communists who are represented, unsurprisingly, as bearing the stigmata of racial degeneration with their broad faces, high foreheads, sunken eyes, and protuberant noses. In working with set designer Gastone Medin and embracing the stylization of Communism as a biospiritual illness that Medin had already articulated in Blasetti's *Sole!* (*Sun*, 1929), with *L'uomo dalla croce* Rossellini answers the questions that *Un pilota ritorna* and the nation raised, ultimately blessing Fascism's war by reframing it as a Christian crusade against the degenerate red infidel race.[43]

For the last film of his fascist trilogy, Rossellini worked with another key player in the regime's apparatus. After collaborating with the Duce's son on *Un pilota ritorna*, for *L'uomo dalla croce* it was the pundit Asvero Gravelli. With the periodical he edited, *Antieuropa*, Gravelli launched a campaign of hate against liberals, Americans, Jews, feminists, queers, and Communists—whom he singled out as the carriers of a contagious disease that was provoking the agony of the Italian race and that would ultimately lead to the cancellation of Western civilization—while lauding a blend of Fascism and Catholicism as the only possible antidote to the global pandemic afflicting humanity.[44] *L'uomo dalla croce* projects the redemptive force of fascist Christianity by recounting the story of an Italian chaplain (Alberto Tavazzi) caught up in the Russian campaign. The film's lead character was inspired by Father Reginaldo Giuliani, who, as part of the *squadristi cattolici* (Catholic paramilitary squads), followed D'Annunzio in the Fiume expedition of 1919, then marched on Rome with Mussolini in 1922, and finally died in East Africa while giving comfort to the Italian colonial army brutalizing Ethiopia. By means of its titular character, this work reimagines the Italian army as a group of compassionate men who are not invading a foreign nation but liberating its people from godless oppressors.

By means of parallel editing, *L'uomo dalla croce* tells two stories at the same time: the grand narrative of Fascism's reclamation of the Communist desolate land; and the microhistory of the chaplain, who teaches the native population how to pray, baptizes a newborn, and even converts two Communist leaders to Catholicism. The religious microhistory of which the chaplain is the protagonist is precisely what gives meaning to the larger political history featured in the film and what affectively justifies the war and more sacrifices. With his words and actions, the chaplain shows what Italians are made of but also why they are doing what they are doing: they are here on another humanitarian mission, to bring back to life people who, having fallen victim to an evil lie, are dead inside. The enemy that Fascism confronts is death, and the regime is waging war for life, to prevent the deadly virus of Communism from spreading further and condemning even more souls to eternal damnation. This is the responsibility the regime has taken up—that we need to take up—and this weight is conveyed in the film through a powerful scene in which we see the chaplain bringing to safety an injured man, carrying him on his shoulders, just as Rossatti had done with the amputee soldier in *Un pilota ritorna* (Figure 25).

FIGURE 25. The burdens shouldered by Italian masculinity in Roberto Rossellini's *Un pilota ritorna* (1942) and *L'uomo della croce* (1943).

The last sequence of *L'uomo dalla croce* makes its effort to "spiritualize" the regime's war making so as to redeem Fascism and fascists especially apparent. As the Italian liberators close in on a village occupied by the evil enemy, the chaplain sees a wounded Communist leader agonizing on the battlefield. Under heavy crossfire, the army chaplain crawls to Fyodor and teaches the hardcore atheist the word of God: "Our Father, who art in heaven, hallowed be thy Name . . . ," they recite together. Fyodor dies redeemed, but the chaplain is fatally shot. Lying in the mud, about to breathe his last breath, the chaplain raises his head to see what is going on around him. Micro- and macrohistories meet again, but now it is political history that provides meaning to personal stories. Through a 360-degree pan from the POV of the dying chaplain, *L'uomo dalla croce* makes the spectator identify with him while also embedding his sacrifice in the larger movement of the fascist redemptive crusade.

The chaplain sees the Italian army winning the battle and liberating the village. He can die in peace, surrounded by the sights and sounds of the fascist war apparatus advancing and continuing its reclamation of corrupted peoples and contaminated environments. The chaplain lets himself collapse. The camera tilts down to match the movement of his lifeless head falling to the ground. It then closes in on the red cross badge on his uniform, similarly to what had happened at the end of *La nave bianca*. As if the point was not clear enough, an intertitle guides the spectators' interpretation of the film's ending: "This film is dedicated to the memory of all the military chaplains fallen in the crusade against the godless, in defense of the homeland and to bring the light of truth and justice even in the land of the barbaric enemy." According to Brunette, against the grain of such an intertitle, the final images and sounds of the film offer their own counter-rhetoric. He writes: "the forlorn music and the sad, sweeping movement of the camera over the smoking remains of the village signal an obvious world-weariness at the horror and destruction of war."[45] There is no doubt that Rossellini is not interested in romanticizing or glorifying war. Yet in blaming the racialized other for the destruction taking place around us, in creating a Manichean opposition between good and evil, in pitching a pious Fascism against a degenerate Communism, in conjuring the horizon of race wars, *L'uomo dalla croce* affectively outlines a clear divide between just and unjust peoples, just and unjust violence, exactly at a moment when opposition to the regime was growing stronger.

It is true that *L'uomo dalla croce* conjures the dream of a united humanity that has overcome divisions.[46] But the way it advances this dream confirms racialized hierarchies and caesuras within the human realm. The unification it proposes can in fact only happen on the condition that the inhuman part of humanity, the not-quite-humans who are sick and need to be healed, change their way of life and accept the truths brandished by those who are enlightened. The similar visual rhetoric employed to portray the chaplain's approach to Fyodor and the forward movement of the Italian troops confirms that, for the film, there is perfect harmony between the colonizer and the converter, between the Church's pastoral mission and that taken up by the fascist state. One can of course argue that *L'uomo dalla croce* is a betrayal of the Christian humanism that Rossellini gets right in other films. Yet another interpretation is perhaps that Rossellini's film is manifesting the structural entanglement between Catholic proselytism and the long tradition of colonial racialization and otherizing that promotes the most brutal conquests under the banner of civilizing missions.

Any form of civilizing campaign relies on the pretense that those who are carrying out the violence are not the true enemies. This is also how *L'uomo dalla croce* justifies the Christian–fascist crusade: "I am not the enemy," promises the chaplain to a Bolshevik leader. The barrage of images of the barbaric and immoral, repulsive and degenerate communist horde does not leave any doubt regarding who the real monster and the real hero are in the brutal race war projected on the big screen. On the one hand, as Marla Stone shows, Rossellini's film triggers the greatest possible anxiety as to what might accompany the red race's victory in the war.[47] On the other hand, it delivers once again, as Italian realism had been busy doing since *Sole!*, the national body politic to the regime by means of racialized feelings and racialized landscapes. In projecting the real as a stage of an epochal race war, *L'uomo della croce* cannot but amplify the feeling that Fascism and fascist living are the only chance of salvation for an endangered Italian humanity.

However, what if Italy's existential threat was not constituted by phantomatic "them" but by us? What if there was no saving grace in Mussolini nor in the race that the regime, and with it national cinema, had been trying so insistently to make? In the next two chapters, I look at how Vittorio De Sica and Luchino Visconti occupied cinema in order to favor patterns of affects that might release the people from the fascist state's deadly grip.

6 De Sica's Genre Trouble

Laughing Fascism Away?

> Many advise me to write something more important. I have
> never been able to understand the meaning of this advice. In
> my view, what I write is of the utmost importance.
>
> —Aldo De Benedetti, "Scusatemi, ma le commedie
> so scriverle soltanto così . . ."

> In the life of humans . . . the only important thing is to find
> an escape route.
>
> —Giorgio Agamben, *Pulcinella*

A monstrously giant sovereign, whose torso is made up of a multitude of
tiny individual bodies, watches over a citadel: the frontispiece of Thomas
Hobbes's *Leviathan* is possibly the most iconic emblem in the history of
political theory. Discussed at length since the book's release in 1651, the
illustration has been interpreted as a powerful visualization of the modern state's demand to incorporate the individual bodies of its subjects,
with the goal of assembling a compact, united, and productive body politic. But—besides the sovereign's torso—there are further details in the
famous frontispiece worth noticing.[1] For instance: the sovereign, standing
beyond the city's territory, is emerging from the sea; the place he is attending to is deserted except for armed guards and plague doctors with their
distinctive birdlike beak masks; the heads of the individual bodies consti-
tuting the political body, the social macro-machine, are turned toward the
sovereign.

   The sovereign emerging from the sea illustrates the connection between
Western history and water. As we have seen, water can be thought of as

racial modernity's primal element because, in the wake of the conquista-
dores' explorations, oceans became the battlefield on which peoples' life
or death, freedom or subalternity, depended: nations needed to control
the seas to protect themselves from the monstrous dangers that are supposedly creeping into the mainland and threatening the community's biological life, but they also sought to dominate the seas to ensure access to
the labor power and raw materials of the colonial realm. The fact that in
the frontispiece the only visible inhabitants of the city are soldiers and doctors is a detail that attests to the securitarian and sanitary logics dominating modern state power, the governmental obsession with policing bodies
to the point of emptying out social life and turning everyone into servants
of the existing order and of collective health. Finally and fundamentally:
the subjects' heads oriented toward the king conjure how sovereignty is in
the final instance, Giorgio Agamben argues, an "optical illusion" founded
on a system of gazes, on a way of looking at the sovereign but also at reality.[2] In order for the population to submit to the state's authority, in order
for it to be subject to the iterations of subjectivity that state power proposes
and propagates, the community needs to feel in danger but also needs to
regard the sovereign as the saving force to which it turns for protection
against the imaginary foes endangering the community.

It is in light of this appreciation of sovereign power as a mode of gazing
and a system of mediation that we can understand Agamben's investment in comedy as a genre that could oppose the operations of biopolitics.
Tricksters, toons, Pinocchio, Pulcinella: comedic characters are for Agamben inspiring role models, the heralds of a coming community, because
they refuse to live according to sovereignty's optics—because instead of
subjecting themselves to the blackmail of ruling authority, they shun heteronormativity and heteronomy in the name of autonomy and freedom.
As Agamben traces, comedy in ancient Greece functioned as an antidote
to tragic stances on life and defeatist tendencies.[3] In times of danger especially, comedies instructed the community that living beings can construct
a happy future for themselves by using their bodies differently from how
they are pressured to do. For this reason, the best comedies—those that
stay true to the genre's origins—are the ones that cultivate sociopolitical
indocility in the body politic.

So far in *Cinema Is the Strongest Weapon*, I have dwelled on how film
under Mussolini staged an Italy under the threat of internal or external
enemies, amplifying an experience of national life that secured the regime's

race-making efforts. Now I consider the tactical counterdeployment of the cinema from weapon of sovereignty into an apparatus that could render inoperative the racializing gaze of fascist realism and thus ultimately contribute to unmaking the compact, policed, and sanitized collectivity the regime had strived to realize. In the next chapter, I show how Luchino Visconti and the *Cinema* media activists mobilized the high-contrast lighting of melodrama to convey simultaneously the bleakness of Blackshirt living and the allure of sexuo-political queerness. Here, I speculate on the ways in which Vittorio De Sica's understudied films from the early 1940s sustained a quasi-anarchist conception of virtue—one where, as happens in exemplary forms of comedy per Jewish philosophers such as Henri Bergson and Walter Benjamin, virtuous behaviors are not those marked by deference and compliance but those characterized by the utmost disregard for the authorities and mechanisms ruling over the present.

BEFORE NEOREALISM

Although so many insightful pages have been dedicated to Vittorio De Sica, his directorial activity before the partnership with Cesare Zavattini has seldom been the focus of attentive critical scrutiny, possibly in part because the movies he directed under Fascism do not fit with hegemonic accounts of what important cinema looks like. *Rose scarlatte* (*Red Roses*, 1940), *Maddalena zero in condotta* (*Maddalena Zero for Conduct*, 1940), *Teresa Venerdì* (*Doctor, Beware*, 1941), and *Un garibaldino al convento* (*A Garibaldian in the Convent*, 1942) are indeed narratively, stylistically, and tonally very different from De Sica's most renowned and celebrated realist works.

As early as his first big collaboration with Zavattini, *I bambini ci guardano* (*The Children Are Watching Us*, 1943), De Sica captures the dread characterizing contemporary Italian life, and even after Italy's transition to democracy, from *Sciuscià* (*Shoeshine*, 1946) to *Umberto D.* (1952), the award-winning director continued to advance a critique of Italian society focusing on the systemic barriers preventing common people from living well, from living lives that do not end in tragedy. It is precisely in light of the tragic dimension of Zavattini and De Sica's realism that André Bazin juxtaposes their poetics and Franz Kafka's.[4] In both cases, Bazin explains, it is a matter of allegorizing how the socioeconomic structures of modern society push people toward behaviors that are necessarily marked by guilt and shame. The unhappiness to which De Sica's and Kafka's characters are consigned is but the consequence of the unhappy lifeworlds that they inhabit, and thus—Bazin concludes—the pessimism of works such as *Ladri di biciclette* (*Bicycle Thieves*, 1948) or *The Trial* (1915) constitutes a stern protest against a real that cannot fulfill its promises and is only able to set up the people for failure. There is nothing Kafkaesque or tragic in De Sica's pre-Zavattini and pre-neorealist films—romantic comedies that instead of following men in crisis and at the mercy of state institutions feature young women pursuing transgressive desires and grappling with the apparatuses seeking to contain, to appropriate, their vital energy.

These incredibly successful films sprout from the collaboration between De Sica and a changing team of artists, which included talents occupying minoritized subject positions: two women and a Jewish Italian man. Maria Stephan is credited as assistant director for *Maddalena zero in condotta,* and Margherita Maglione shares credit for the screenplays of *Teresa Venerdì* and *Un garibaldino al convento.* I was not able to find any additional information about these women, who—in a case that is more unique than rare—broke the fascist film industry's glass ceiling and were employed in jobs that were typically the prerogative of men. But the most crucial collaborator for De Sica in these films, as David Bruni proves through invaluable archival research, was the Italian Jewish playwright Aldo De Benedetti—whose first big hit at the movies was Mario Camerini's *Gli uomini che mascalzoni . . . (What Scoundrels Men Are!,* 1932), the very film that turned De Sica into a multimedia star.[5]

Although De Benedetti was the main writer for *Rose scarlatte, Maddalena zero in condotta,* and *Teresa Venerdì* and revised the screenplay and dialogues for *Un garibaldino al convento,* he could be credited only in *Rose scarlatte*—which reached movie theaters in spring 1940. Italy's entrance into World War II in June 1940 coincided with an exacerbation of the discrimination against Italian Jews.[6] Blamed for spoiling the authentic ethno-community with their pernicious influence and wicked blood, in the aftermath of the racist laws from 1938, Italians of Jewish descent were banned from working in law enforcement and in the public sector as teachers, doctors, professors, or lawyers. The new discrimination policies also forbade them from being employed in state-managed companies in the cultural industry (music, cinema, radio, theater, etc.). In 1940, this ban was extended to private production companies as well; hence De Benedetti could only write films uncredited—and he wrote many between 1940 and 1945. But someone noticed and publicly complained about this challenge to the autarkic effort of keeping Italian cinema Italian, that is, free from voices and views

that were considered foreign to the national heritage. In 1943, the journalist Giorgio Almirante, who in 1946 would become the first leader of the
neofascist Movimento Sociale Italiano, denounced directors including De
Sica, Mario Mattòli, Giuseppe Amato, and Carlo Ludovico Bragaglia for
paying "a Jew" under the table to write their films while assisting him in
finding other jobs.[7] For Almirante, this was unacceptable. De Benedetti was
not to be pitied or sympathized with: he was speculating on his position to
get paid more than "Aryan writers" without even paying taxes on his exor-
bitant profits.

Obviously, De Benedetti's condition was far from being the advantageous
one painted by Almirante in his antisemitic rant, putting the man's very
livelihood in danger. Bruni has reconstructed with precision the exploitative working terms De Benedetti often had to accept to make ends meet
as well as to make himself valuable enough to be shielded from more violent iterations of racial discrimination. Yet with De Sica, the working relationship appears to have been different: the correspondence and contracts
I was able to consult at the De Benedetti Private Archive suggest that De
Sica treated the playwright with respect, dignity, and fairness, as a peer rather
than an exploitable and expendable body. The different relational modality
led to some of the most unforgettable films from fascist Italy. Since, however, the rom-coms De Sica directed under Mussolini with De Benedetti as
a key author were largely forgotten postwar, it might be useful to briefly
summarize their main plot points.

Rose scarlatte, De Sica's debut behind the movie camera, is the adaptation of *Due dozzine di rose scarlatte* (*Two Dozen Red Roses*)—one of the most
frequently staged Italian plays of all time, which De Benedetti wrote in
1935 for De Sica's theater company.[8] In the film, Marina (Renée Saint-Cyr)
is bored with her conjugal life. In search of new emotions and wanting to
enjoy the taste of freedom, she is getting ready to go on a vacation alone.
Marina's husband, Alberto (De Sica), is looking forward to her departure,
since it will give him the opportunity to court other women. As a matter
of fact, he has already started to do so: he just sent two dozen red roses
to a countess, signing the accompanying card using the nom-de-plume
Mystery. By mistake, Marina is the one who receives the roses, and she
believes a secret admirer sent her the flowers. Alberto discovers the mix-
up but continues to send Marina roses, to see how far her new desires will
take her. In love with Mystery and the unknown, Marina decides to divorce
Alberto—until she discovers that her mysterious lover and her husband

are the same person. In the end, Alberto and Marina forgive each other and leave together for Venice, committed to travel away from their ways and lives.

Maddalena zero in condotta and *Teresa Venerdì* are remakes of Hungarian films also derived from stage plays. *Maddalena zero in condotta* features Elisa Malgari (Vera Bergman), a professor of business correspondence at an all-girls' school. To find relief from her boredom and loneliness, from a life that is so dull that it is barely worth living, she writes love letters to Mr. Hartman, the fictional receiver of the business letters that she teaches her students to write. A Mr. Hartman (De Sica), though, actually exists: he is the heir of an Italian family, the Armanis, who relocated to Austria and Germanized their surname. In a lucky turn of events, he receives one of Elisa's letters and immediately travels from Vienna to Rome to find the author of such an endearing piece of writing. After a series of misunderstandings and gags, the rambunctious student Maddalena (Carla Del Poggio) sets up Hartman with Malgari, while at the same time seducing Hartman's cousin, Stefano (Roberto Villa). Tired of waiting for a move from this nice guy wanting to behave properly, in a memorable scene Maddalena puts on lipstick and kisses Stefano in a shamelessly inappropriate public display of affection.

Teresa Venerdì is the story of an orphan (Adriana Benetti) who falls in love with Pietro Vignali (De Sica), the young doctor who works at the institution where she resides. Another orphan, jealous of Teresa, writes a fake love letter to the doctor, signs Teresa's name, and makes sure the nuns in charge of the orphanage read it. The nuns—alarmed by the letter and wary about how the young woman gazes at the doctor (Figure 26)—decide to send Teresa, who has turned eighteen, to work for a crass butcher. Teresa is forced to flee and finds refuge at the doctor's house. There, she discovers that Dr. Vignali is in a dire economic situation and thus strikes a deal with the father of the doctor's current fiancé: she will leave him alone if all his debts are paid off. She also writes a goodbye letter to the doctor, announcing with plenty of pathos what she has done for him (Teresa comes from a family of performers, after all) and proving all her worth. Vignali falls for Teresa, deciding to marry her and start a new life with her elsewhere.

Un garibaldino al convento is the only one of these films by De Sica that is based on an original scenario. A long flashback takes us from current Italy to the time of the Risorgimento wars. Caterinetta (Del Poggio) is a

FIGURE 26. Teresa gazes with longing for Dottor Pietro in *Teresa Venerdì* (Vittorio De Sica, 1941).

troublemaker who is sent by her family to a convent where nuns run a boarding school. There she finds her archenemy Mariella (Maria Mercader). Mariella has a secret relationship with Franco (Leonardo Cortese), a Garibaldian fighting to liberate Italy from foreign domination. Before leaving to join the war, Franco gives Mariella *Le ultime lettere di Jacopo Ortis* (*The Last Letters of Jacopo Ortis*), Ugo Foscolo's heartbreaking 1802 epistolary fiction, as a token of his love. Wounded in battle, Franco hides in the convent where Caterinetta and Mariella are boarded. But the Bourbons are on his trail and assault the convent to capture him. With incredible courage, Caterinetta steals a horse and escapes from the siege and the Bourbons, intercepting the Italian army and leading the charge to save the freedom fighter.

On the basis of an understanding of the labor of cinematic representation still grounded in the Aristotelian notion of *catharsis,* De Sica's entertaining rom-coms have been quickly dismissed in postwar criticism as juvenile concessions to Fascism's distraction industry. As David Forgacs suggests in

"Sex in the Cinema," the traditional Italian view on fascist media posits that Mussolini's rule benefited from escapist films allowing the public to take a break from the dreariness of life under the regime.[9] But perhaps there is more to De Sica's and De Benedetti's iteration of escapism than scholars—blinded by postwar hegemonic pro-realist prejudices conflating seriousness, progressiveness, and importance—were able to see. Perhaps the anti-tragic and anti-Kafkaesque stance of these pre-neorealist works by De Sica is not the mark of their complicity with power but rather the very key to accessing their oppositional thrust.

In this regard, it is important to point out that De Sica's pre-neorealist films were positively reviewed when they came out by the antifascist film critic and screenwriter Giuseppe De Santis, who was quite severe with Roberto Rossellini's engaged and serious realism. De Santis, who I discuss further in the next chapter, especially praised De Sica's films for the kind of Italian humanity they featured, for the dreamlike Italy they projected on screen, and for the way they ironized situations that one would usually consider the most earnest.[10] I choose, thus, to dwell on the humor, the Italians, and the Italian real from De Sica's films under Fascism to question the intuitive assessment of their politics. I ask: might these overlooked and dismissed films cowritten by an overlooked and dismissed Jewish playwright making art under the conditions of racial discrimination alert us to how laughter can be deployed against racism, sexism, and heteronormative arrangements in collective life, that is, to undo the machinations of biopolitics?

But before getting to De Sica's progressive laughter, allow me a detour to outline a different kind of laughter that has often been confused with resistance. This is the humor that seems, on the surface, to leverage an attack on the powers that be, all the while jovially concealing its own solidarity with the rule of the present.

S/M HUMOR

With his 2011 "The Phenomenology of the *Cinepanettone*," Alan O'Leary effectively challenged Italian film criticism's inclination to consider politically and ethically worthy only the works that capture the real with an uncompromising gloomy gaze. However, his poignant intervention almost ended up sanctioning an opposite and equally problematic scholarly tendency: the tendency to consider as intrinsically liberatory the antics and jouissance that the comedic mode affords. This position is problematic because, as Lauren Berlant and Sianne Ngai signal in a 2017 special issue of *Critical Inquiry* dedicated to laughter and humor, "comedy has issues" as well.[11] At a time when the worst of Western history is coming back, in the guise not of tragedy but of farce, it is then even more paramount to emphasize that laughter per se is not necessarily a progressive affect—even when one is laughing at power or at powerful figures. Mockery and trolling have been key building blocks of Donald Trump's and Matteo Salvini's rhetorical strategies, but many former comedians have used the tools of their trade to acquire power and prominence in countries like Brazil, Italy, and—more recently—France. The case of Beppe Grillo, satirist turned political guru of a populist movement not immune to xenophobic and neofascist tendencies, is the perfect case in point to highlight the connection between the current global reactionary cycle and what Arpad Szakolczai dubs the "commedification" of the public sphere.[12]

Grillo acquired new relevance in Italian public life in the late 2000s, after organizing events and manifestations whose point was to flip off political institutions and ridicule their members for their vices and shortcomings. The outrage against degraded politics and wicked politicians that the 2007 "Vaffanculo Day" (literally, "Fuck-Off Day") unleashed was instrumental for Grillo in setting up his own political organization. Grillo's performances of abjection solidified a community of resentful and grandstanding individuals who believed themselves victims of all sorts of conspiracies, considered themselves morally and intellectually superior to everyone else, and thus felt in the right to reclaim power. I mention this example as it confirms how a certain laugh, while apparently disruptive, does not upset but rather reaffirms, but in a dejected form, the status quo. There is a wit that effectively bothers the forces and imaginaries ruling over the present, and a second type of humor that plays the game of the established order. Grillo's humor neatly falls into the latter category, given how it delegitimized institutional figures to foster not structural change but merely a change of the people in charge. Italian Fascism had its own examples of such problematic parodies and satires that, by reducing systemic problems into matters of lax morals or gross ineptitude, foreclosed deeper and more transformative experiences of the present.

Whereas the Turkish magazine *Akbaba* used a scathing dark irony to indict Mussolini's regime as a continuation of European racial capitalism and colonial violence, one could find more superficial jabs at Fascism in the Western international press, including, for instance, vignettes ridiculing the Duce as a lap dog at Hitler's service or portraying him as a leader more interested in sexual positions than in military maneuvers.[13] National press, especially the satirical journal *Marc'Aurelio,* featured unflattering takes on Mussolini and other top hierarchs, but like those appearing in Western media, these targeted not the larger historical dynamics but individual behaviors—as if the problem at stake were not the country Fascism had assembled but how certain fascists carried themselves. Camerini's *Il cappello a tre punte* (*The Three-Cornered Hat,* 1935) is a perfect illustration of how ridiculing fascists or people in power is not necessarily a challenge to Fascism or to power.

The historical comedy is set in seventeenth-century Naples under Spanish domination. The city is tired of the constant abuse, and a rebellion is imminent. The governor (Eduardo De Filippo) is disinterested in making things right and spends more time pursuing Carmela (Leda Gloria) than governing his city. He tries everything he can to seduce the beautiful miller, yet all is in vain. Frustrated, the governor jails Carmela's husband, Luca (Peppino De Filippo, Eduardo's brother): since the governor and Luca look alike, the governor's plan is to pass as Luca and trick Carmela into sleeping with him. But Luca escapes from prison and starts posing as the governor— triggering all sorts of misadventures and humiliations for the lecherous ruler. Luca even gets close to bedding the governor's spouse. Confronted by the consequences of his mischief, emasculated, and ridiculed by his people and his own wife, the governor repents and commits to taking the necessary steps to regain trust and authority; he even goes as far as improving the way his subjects are treated.

The fact that Camerini's farcical historical reenactment constituted a caricature of Mussolini was not lost on the public. The Duce's son Vittorio, who was establishing himself as a key figure in fascist cinema, took to the press to defend his father's honor. From the pages of a fascist youth journal, the livid Mussolini heir called for Camerini's exile: his film was simply too anti-Italian and antifascist for the director to remain unpunished. Camerini's reaction? He basically told Vittorio Mussolini to be quiet, suggesting he was a brat who hadn't sacrificed anything for the nation.[14] Camerini flaunted that, in contrast, he had fought in World War I to create a greater Italy, implying that by risking his life for the homeland he had earned the right to speak up and talk back. The proud reference to the war, a crucial moment for Italian nationalism and colonialism, attests how *Il cappello a tre punte* did not intend to contest the imaginaries, affects, dynamics, and forms of subjectivity upon which Fascism was founded. In the tradition of Machiavelli's theater, it was instead a matter of using caricature and farcical exaggeration to warn the people in power of behaviors that could put their command at risk, while also deluding the public that the sovereign could indeed become someone that the collectivity could rely on.

At the end of *Il cappello a tre punte,* the governor's wife orders him to put his real clothes back on and to become worthy of them. I want to take notice of this admonition, as it expresses the fundamental operation of Camerini's filmic device: redress constituted authority and functioned to make power appear worthy of itself because—as Agamben posits through the frontispiece of *Leviathan*—the constitution of a stable sociopolitical assemblage depends precisely on the way the sovereign is regarded. The final reconciliation in *Il cappello a tre punte* between sovereign and people, coupled with the benevolent portrayal of the governor's misconduct, confirm that this film was not using laughter to upset Fascism but rather to reinforce its grip on the population.

It is true that spectatorial pleasure in the film is connected with the experience of what we might dub sovereign schadenfreude, that is, the enjoyment derived from watching the pain, downfall, or humiliation of the powerful. Because the misfortunes that the film turns into amusement belong to the governor, one could agree with Carlo Celli that *Il cappello a tre punte* triggers a sadistic relationship to power, a desire to see it harmed that would lead to anti-statist stances in real life.[15] Yet the film crucially pins the possibility of a "happy ending" to the end of the carnivalesque inversion of roles: the abjectification of the governor into a common citizen can only be momentary because, for the miller and her husband to be reunited, the governor needs to regain his position. The appeal of heteronormativity is here mobilized to sanction sociopolitical hierarchies that split the collectivity into rulers and subalterns. Hence, if initially *Il cappello a tre punte* makes the public laugh sadistically at the sovereign, it ultimately concocts desires that lean toward masochism—the desire to see the governor back in his place, the desire for being properly governed, the desire for everything to return to how it was. The church bells accompanying Luca and Carmela as they travel back home at the end of the film are the aural cues of the blessing that constitutes the return to normality. In the final instance, *Il cappello a tre punte* uses humor as an instrument to preach morality and reinstate order. For this reason, Camerini's laughs are not antifascist challenges but tools of government; they are, as Mino Argentieri says, "risate di regime," regime's laughs.[16]

Is the laughter elicited by De Sica's rom-coms marked by a different temporality and politics vis-à-vis the ones discussed in this section? I argue that this is the case. On the one hand, De Sica's sentimental comedies push the people to modify their own ways of living rather than promoting the resented self-complacency and sense of superiority that, as I suggested in the example of Beppe Grillo, is a prominent feature of contemporary populisms and para-fascist movements. On the other hand, De Sica's films are committed to turning upside down—in a sort of situationist *detournement*— the very formula and forms of Camerini's cinema. It is almost as if De Sica as director hijacks the very same talents that had made Camerini's fortune (De Benedetti but also Medin) to put his own actorial body at the service of an entirely opposite wager. For Camerini, it is always a matter of weaponizing irony to foster political stability and socioeconomic reproductivity. We have seen it already with Camerini's films starring De Sica: his films are stories of normalization and return to order that weaponize shame to naturalize racialized subject positions and state-sanctioned codes of behavior. De Sica's directed films take leave from the power-complicit humor that characterizes Camerini's cinema and instead contest the very foundations of fascist biopolitics and race-making. Accordingly, De Sica's films mobilize a different kind of spectatorial pleasure, relying on a different form of laughter. In order to explain the features of this humor, I start from the pages Bergson dedicated to the experience of the comic—especially noteworthy because, when reviewing De Sica's comedies in 1942, De Santis noticed a Bergsonian quality to them.

VITAL OPTIMISM

Bergson's *Laughter* dates back to 1900.[17] What is most relevant in this context about the French Jewish philosopher's influential reflections on the comic mode is the connection he draws between laughter and the experience of an excessive rigidity of individual and collective behaviors. As emerges with even more clarity in his later works, especially *Creative Evolution*, for Bergson the main traits of human life are dynamism and the capacity to re-form itself. Yet despite creative energy being the fundamental feature of human life, individuals and societies can fall prey to traditions and become ossified. If we neglect cultivating our creativity and agency, human life can betray its core nature and acquire characteristics that are distinctive to machines and inorganic matter—that is, rigidity, fixity, stiffness, and predictability. In Bergson, Emily Herring sums up, history itself is the result of the dialectic between creative energy and normalizing tendencies, at the level of both individual bodies and the body politic.[18] And the experience of the comical is, for Bergson, the social device that flags those instances where the vital force has lost so much power that it has given way to automatized customs and mechanized behaviors. Laughter, therefore, is an affect that manifests and warns at the same time. What it warns about is the "automatic regulation of society" and what it manifests is the need for human beings to reclaim their creative energy, their power to remake themselves and their lifeworlds.

Through his discussion of laughter as a warning affect signaling the excessive standardization of existence and of the comic as a challenge to the depotentiation of human beings' vital agency, Bergson specifies the theory of incongruity. According to the theory of incongruity, laughter is the reaction to a perceived radical difference between how things or people should be ideally, and how they actually are, that is, between expectations and experience.[19] For Bergson, the ideal world is a world ruled by change and creativity, and it is for this very reason that his reflections on laughter imply a structural relation between the comic and the dimension of futurity. By pointing out the absurdity of a hyper-regulated real, of mechanized forms of life, of existences that are dulled and petrified by all sorts of interiorized automatisms, a certain kind of humor does in fact interrupt the ruling order of things to reactivate the drive to evolve and experiment in the human body. In a certain sense for Bergson, those who experience laughter are sent into the future; they are consigned to the dimension of virtuality. De Sica's comedies conjure a similar kind of laughter, one that lifts living beings from the weight of an overdetermined reality and conveys them to the unexplored potentialities that the future might hold. Because a *deliverance* is in play, it is appropriate that De Sica's rom-coms all feature letters as key elements of their narratives.

Mystery's notes to Marina in *Rose scarlatte* (Figure 27), the love letters in *Maddalena zero in condotta* and *Teresa Venerdì*, and the gift of *Le ultime lettere di Jacopo Ortis* in *Un garibaldino al convento*: by staging the effects of these pieces of writing on the bodies, desires, and lives of those who send and those who receive them, De Sica allegorizes the power of writing and fiction in general, and cinematographic writing and fiction specifically, to ridicule the normalized lives people live in the present and hence favor

different ways of being an Italian body. We are very far from the weaponization of cinema as an apparatus used to naturalize identities and subject positions. De Sica's investment in film does not appear connected with
the medium's power to capture life, to contain and put to work bodies'
vital energies. Rather, he seems more concerned with cinema's capacity to
enable a rejection of the interiorized norms of behavior that dominated
the fascist present. The camera in his films does not judge but empowers;
it does not condemn the will to escape but rather spotlights the appeal of
noncompliance. What is at play in his works is not so much what the fascist race ought to be but the very fact that Italians can become different—
thanks to writing, thanks to fiction, thanks to laughter, and thanks to cinema
and the affordances of freedom, leisure, and liberality that escapism allows.
For this reason, the settings of these comedies are also quite significant.

De Sica's films take place in what we would consider disciplinary and
disciplined spaces: the home (*Rose scarlatte*), the school (*Maddalena zero
in condotta*), the orphanage (*Teresa Venerdì*), and the boarding school (*Un
garibaldino al convento*). However, their rules and codes, that is, the writing

FIGURE 27. Marina reading and dreaming of Mystery in *Rose scarlatte* (Vittorio
De Sica, 1940).

systems that norm their functioning, are shown as "always-already" disrupted by the clash with the writings of desire. By setting his narratives in Italy rather than abroad—as was often the case for escapist works—De Sica figures a national real that is less controlled than the regime might want to concede. Within these disciplined but disrupted spaces, De Sica represents the conflict between types of writing—fictions versus regulations, love letters versus grade books and bills, and so on. In so doing, he stages the different functions that writing can perform. There are forms of writing that are technologies of the self that both subject and subjectify, discipline and punish, engender and racialize; and there are writing gestures whose wager is the destabilization of reality and identity formations.

Already in Maria Montessori's 1910s theory of education, and then in the post-1960s French feminist tradition, the act of writing has been featured as a performance that can lead to unexpected materialities of the self and of others.[20] De Sica deploys genre cinema as a technology that writes difference through a two-fold Bergsonian laughter. He makes the audience laugh at those who are stuck within traditional rules and defer to the established order, but he also makes the public smile along with the courageous young women who shun hegemonic societal expectations for how they should behave and how they should use their bodies. Ultimately, De Sica's rom-coms conjure an Italian real on the brink between immobilism and change, order and indiscipline. Granted, this is also the situation in Camerini's comedies in which De Sica starred. However, in a film such as *Gli uomini che mascalzoni* . . . , spectatorial pleasure hinges on the reaffirmation of the gendered and racialized boundaries of fascist biopolitics. Through shaming, Camerini put everyone back in their place and contributed to annihilating what Levinas, as we saw in chapter 4, dubbed the capacity of escaping oneself. It is also for this reason that his films have a circular form. In De Sica's escapism, instead, we experience a romanticization of the effort to break free from the identitarian interpellations that rule society, an authorization of human beings' uncontainable vitalism and vitality. Unlike Pirandello's and Sergi's, this vitalism is not cruel. There is a vital optimism at play here since living beings are portrayed as perfectly able to fashion good lives for themselves, without being restrained or disciplined by state apparatuses.

In fact, in De Sica's cinematic worlds, bodies are not destined to certain naturalized roles or subject positions: there is no pre-lapsarian "before" to which the camera urges characters, and spectators with them, to return.

But there is also no urgency or emergency, no exceptional existential threat or race war that would require subjects to make obligatory choices and commit to prescribed ways of living—to even endure minoritization and embrace fungibility, as women or Jewish people often had to do to survive Mussolini's Italy. The Italy that manifests itself in these romantic comedies is a radically anti-tragic space where bodies do not expose themselves to danger or retribution when they dare to pursue the pleasure principle and, akin to Herman Melville's Bartleby, prefer not to become cogs of the social machine, with all its rules and regulations.

It is precisely because there is nothing holding these human beings back, nothing disallowing characters from pursuing desires that bring them away from work, duties, and sacrifices, that De Sica's affective landscapes bear no trace of shame or guilt. There is nothing wrong with the fact that Marina from *Rose scarlatte* just wants to enjoy herself and even decides to leave her husband to pursue, literally, the unknown. There is nothing inappropriate in the gaze through which Teresa reveals her desire for the young doctor Pietro in *Teresa Venerdì*. It is not a problem at all if, in *Un garibaldino al convento,* young women read prohibited books that make them long and yearn instead of submitting to the rules of virtue and moderation Catholic school tries to implant in their bodies (Figure 28). Maddalena, in *Maddalena zero in condotta,* wants to eat pastries and make out with the man she is trying to seduce rather than learn how to be a skilled secretary and behave like a "good girl," and the film articulates a nonjudgmental space wherein she and the public can indulge these transgressive appetites (Figure 29).

Considering that De Sica's unapologetic women arrived at the movies when the quality of Italian life was becoming even more grim, why shouldn't his rom-coms be interpreted as release valves at a historical juncture characterized by war, violence, pain, and sacrifice? One could argue, for instance, that the shameless women protagonists from De Sica's films were characters male spectators could fantasize about, finding relief from real women and the real world. Were this true, these works would include a sexualization of the female body along with the representation of epicurean behaviors. Instead, despite the allusion to a freer sexuality not necessarily connected with the realms of reproduction (social or sexual), De Sica does not give in to the male gaze.

Mouths, legs, smiles, and cleavage captured in soft focus through close-ups or sensuous camera movements are nowhere to be found in his comedies; there are no sexual fetishes to be stared at and neatly framed by the

FIGURE 28. Vain attempts to discipline female bodies in *Un garibaldino al convento* (Vittorio De Sica, 1942).

FIGURE 29. Maddalena getting ready to satisfy her appetites in *Maddalena zero in condotta* (Vittorio De Sica, 1940).

camera. Instead of turning the young women he features into passive objects to be looked at, De Sica stages them as active subjects to be looked up to. Marina, Maddalena, Teresa, Mariella, and Caterinetta are inspiring agents of change and progress in his films, and their agency is figured by the director through a hard-to-frame mobility and energy. De Sica's young women are in perpetual motion: they go in and out of the frame constantly, bringing an element of disorder into the picture that mirrors the generative disorder they bring into the ridicule and regulated lifeworlds in which they dwell but to which they do not belong. It is thus a new gaze on traditionally minoritized subjects that is here a matter of sustaining. It is a nonmale gaze on Italy and Italians that is being subtly conjured in these rom-coms.

The male gaze itself is exhibited and ridiculed in one of the most amusing sequences from *Maddalena zero in condotta*, as Ramsey McGlazer unpacks in a brilliant essay.[21] Hartman and his cousin visit the school where Malgari teaches and where Maddalena is a student to try to identify who wrote the mysterious love letter. Their plan—not the brightest, to be sure—is to observe the students, hoping to catch some kind of tell that would betray the letter's author. The school custodian accompanies them through the halls, where they review the students' bodies as the girls rush to class. What is crucial about this scene is what De Sica frames to be gazed at: not the female students but the male gazers themselves. The students go through the halls, too fast to even be identified, and while being observed (in vain), they audaciously stare back at their observers (the school is named Audax, after all, McGlazer notes) and run off scene. They do not fall prey to the male gaze and they do not allow the gaze of the men to capture them. The men, instead, stand still with glassy eyes, staring at bodies that inevitably flee away from them. The janitor, having noticed Hartman's wonderstruck stare, asks him to stop looking—so to avoid making a "brutta figura," a poor figure (Figure 30). But it is the film as a whole that, as the janitor does in this scene, works to disfigure the male gaze, challenging the cinematic vision that finds pleasure in fetishizing and objectifying female bodies. Throughout *Maddalena*, the male gaze is constantly cited and renounced.

The film does offer several glimpses of disciplined female bodies, for instance in class or at the gym, but these choral and beautiful images of mechanical order, and the pleasure that one could derive from their consumption, are invariably upset. In the gym scenes, the camera (by pulling

FIGURE 30. Disfiguring the white male gaze in *Maddalena zero in condotta* (Vittorio De Sica, 1940).

back in one case, and through a lateral pan in the other) immediately redirects the public's attention away from the disciplined assembly of young women, spotlighting instead the broken-down body of the elderly gym teacher. The amusing object of the gaze here is "the leader [who] cannot lead," a man who keeps going with his routine with ridiculous results, not the tamed bodies that he is supposedly in charge of.[22] Analogously, in sequences taking place in the classroom, the cinematographic apparatus captures momentary instances when the students behave in an orderly and controlled fashion, for example when the girls sit still and are terrorized, subjected to the gaze of the male chemistry teacher. Yet this stiffness, this dullness, brings the viewer no satisfaction. In De Sica's universe, indiscipline, playfulness, and the interruption of the normal order of things are what lead to joy. It is only when the superficially tamed collectivity erupts, when order is disrupted by Maddalena's and her allies' antics, that the public rejoices.

In an essay from 2001, Celli recognizes in the chemistry teacher a stand-in for Giovanni Gentile—the philosopher responsible for Fascism's reform of the school system who would be executed by the partisans in 1944 for his collaboration with the Salò puppet state.[23] In light of Celli's identification, it is particularly important that *Maddalena* casts such a dark shadow on this disciplinarian professor and the ways he treats the students: the camera does not shy away from pointing out his violence as he selects a subject to examine, and by underscoring this sadism, the apparatus abjures the workings of authority and discipline. Unlike in other important "schoolgirl films"—for instance the initiator of this subgenre, Goffredo Alessandrini's *Seconda B (Second B,* 1934)—the public does not identify with he who lays down the law but with she who has no regard for it. Alessandrini's film foregrounded the dangerous desires that dwell in young women's bodies and lead them to inappropriate behaviors, inside and outside the classroom—making the spectatorship sympathize with the males in power who are victims of the girls' mischief. As Marcia Landy comments, *Seconda B* depicts female students in an unsympathetic manner bordering on misogyny.[24] In De Sica, it is the opposite. The role models are precisely those who do not sit still and who refuse to be assimilated into the system, those whose bodies do not conform. The role model is Maddalena, who constantly looks for opportunities to create havoc and shows the utmost disrespect for constituted authorities and social norms. It is her gaze on the world that the public is made to embrace, because her creative energy is irresistible—not even the chemistry teacher can do anything to counter it. After having been hit by a storm of paper balls, the Gentile look-alike appears incredulous at the latest of Maddalena's mischief (Figure 31). What is happening? Coats are moving around the classroom by themselves, appearing to greet each other with empty sleeves? Speechless, perplexed, afraid, the professor takes off his glasses and stares with his eyes wide open—visual cues of a gaze in crisis and a compromised authority.

Yet it is not merely the authority of the male gaze that is mocked in *Maddalena.* The authority, the power of the men embodying a certain way of looking, undergoes a similar challenge. These men, for *Maddalena,* are white men—the male gaze in the film is a white men's thing, it is a white male gaze. Thus, in featuring a powerless male gaze, is not the film also somehow deconstructing the authority of whiteness? Allow me to circle back to the scene of Hartman inappropriately gazing at the students because it brings up—in a quite subtle way—the issue of race and racism.

The school custodian, we remember, had urged Hartman to stop looking, yet the admonition comes too late: the gazing man is caught red-handed

FIGURE 31. Visions of disbelief: authority in crisis, from *Maddalena zero in condotta* (Vittorio De Sica, 1940).

by the school headmistress. In the next scene, in line with the nonlinear and fragmentary narrative style of De Sica's comedies, *Maddalena* does not feature the confrontation between the headmistresses and Hartman but cuts back into the classroom. The geography teacher, *professoressa* Varzi, is speaking with passion of the anthropological characteristics of the Georgian people, who—she says—at times are considered the "ideal prototype of the white race." After making sure that the students are taking notes—they aren't; they are working on the next prank—she continues to preach about Georgian men, who "with their majestic build, but at the same time slender, dark, and handsome features, endowed with a certain uncommon physical force, remind more of mythical heroes rather than people of our time." The school bell rings, and she stops abruptly: the zeal with which Varzi was venerating white people is just her job, a job that she was not doing particularly well given the students' lack of engagement and interest.

As the *professoressa* exits the room, we enter into the office of the headmistress, who wants to understand what Hartman and his cousin are doing in her female high school, exchanging such looks with teenagers. She questions the two men, who clumsily try to explain their presence. Is this what white men are? Is this the master race for which Italians had to go to war, colonize, enslave, die, and kill, the race for which someone like De Benedetti was being persecuted and discriminated? Are these the descendants of the glorious white people we just heard about in class and that Fascism wanted kids to believe in? On the one hand, *Maddalena* ridicules coeval racial science by mediating it as a discourse that is both overblown and underwhelming. On the other hand, the film introduces a humorous discrepancy between what Italian men—insofar as they are white people— are promised to be and what they actually are: not the protagonists of a mythic destiny and of epic feats but characters of ridicule who look at things and people in the wrong way.[25] If we think about it, this is a constant throughout De Sica's comedies from the Ventennio: Italian men are put on display and then mocked. Overall, national masculinity does not come off particularly well in these films.

In *Maddalena,* Hartman is a playboy of sorts; his cousin borders on incompetent; the gym teacher is falling apart; the chemistry professor is an outdated disciplinarian; and the janitor is a sexist wimp who thinks that "chicks" can do without math and history but not without lipstick and powder—thus his wife, who does not wear makeup, is not a real woman in his eyes. In *Rose scarlatte,* Marina's husband seems a bit sadistic and his side-kick is inept. The doctor from *Teresa Venerdì* is another good-for-nothing, and then there is the crass and violent butcher Teresa is sent off to. The father figures from *Un garibaldino al convento* are not impressive either: they are stuck in worn-out formalities, upholding an outdated idea of culture and the arts, spending their time in meaningless squabbles. There are a couple of notable exceptions to this derision of Italian masculinity—which is, *Maddalena* established, the toxic masculinity of white people. Both are from *Un garibaldino al convento*: there is the estate's keeper Tiepolo (Fausto Guerzoni), an offbeat man who disobeys the no-animal rule at the convent and lives with a cloud of singing blackbirds; and there are the heroic Garibaldians, the most radical and revolutionary subjects among the Risorgimento fighters, since they were fighting not only to liberate Italy from foreign occupation but also to build a democratic, progressive, and secular country. Yet even in these cases, the representation of Italian men is not immune from critique. Both Tiepolo and the Garibaldians look down at Caterinetta and treat her like a *ragazzina,* a little girl. One of the freedom fighters dares even to spank Caterinetta to put her in her place. But she speaks up against this violent and sexist infantilization, demanding to be treated with dignity and respect. "I am not a kid; I am one of you," she says to De Sica, playing the part of a perplexed-looking Nino Bixio. And De Sica, as director, concedes to Caterinetta's demands.[26] In fact, later in the film, we see her riding at the head of the squadron of red-shirted Garibaldians, leading the charge to rescue their comrade. A woman who is also a freedom fighter: there are not many of them throughout Italian cinema, with the overbearing gaze equating womanhood to wifehood and motherhood precluding the possibility of imagining a plurality of ways of "being women"—to quote the title of Cecilia Mangini's documentary ending with a woman with a rifle on her shoulder and walking away toward her fight.

But if it is true that De Sica's rom-coms use Bergsonian humor to make fun of interiorized norms and mechanized living, if they subtly mock racism and sexism, if truly these genre films deconstruct the white male gaze's authority and the authority of the gazing white males, do they construct and authorize any particular alternative gaze? What kind of nation do they want the public to believe in? What affective experience of the national space-time do they sustain?

With their fragmentary and episodic structure, thanks to fast-paced narratives that continuously alternate between the establishment of order and order's disruption and where the characters' actions never come to a halt, De Sica's comedies assemble a world that is immersed in becoming, a reality that is striated by norms and desires that are irreconcilable with each other and whose clashes generate precarious arrangements of sociality that are always on the brink. These blockbusters mediate an exuberant body politic that has constantly been made, unmade, and remade: not a homogeneous, compact, serious totality but a playful constellation of plural ways of living in the country. The effort that appears to dominate De Sica's early films is to sustain an experience of Italy marked by a *Spielraum* that is actually greater than what one would expect in a totalitarian state.

Spielraum—field of action or room for play—is a concept I borrow from Benjamin's "The Work of Art in the Age of Its Technological Reproducibility."[27] In an early version of the famous essay written in response to Nazi Fascism's aestheticization of politics, Benjamin considers different uses of technology, distinguishing between capitalist technologies that subject individuals to the drudgery of productive living and an alternative deployment of technology that can instead expand the horizons of human

existence. Cinema for the German Jewish philosopher is the key apparatus
in this second use of technology, insofar as the machine has the ability to
expose how alienated and exploited are the lives that people live in service
of the assembly line. Quite unexpectedly, as Miriam Hansen shows, in Benjamin's viewpoint, the genre that could most productively carry out this
revelation of alienation was comedy. Entering into an implicit dialogue with
Bergson, Benjamin suggests that characters' actions in comedies showcase
the possibility of playing with the order of things—triggering in the public the invigorating and liberating awareness that there is no overdetermined destiny or tragic fate holding human beings captive to hegemonic
lifestyles or sociopolitical formations.[28] In De Sica's comedies, the "things"
characters play with and act upon are the family, the school, the home—
that is, apparatuses responsible for the production of racialized and gendered Italian bodies. By featuring affective challenges to these biopolitical
devices that sought to make proper Italians, the director is thereby able to
reenchant the gaze through which the nation is looked at, conveying that
Italy is not a country dominated by inviolable codes of behavior but rather
a territory with plenty of room for action and enough space for effective
identity maneuvering.[29]

The most glaring manifestation of this effort to reenchant Italy is from
Rose scarlatte. In a scene bordering on magic realism, Marina, in a spectacular white fur coat, is watching an outdoor ballet performance, with Mystery whispering in her ears about the allure of embracing the unknown;
the magic of what might be and what might happen if one is brave enough
to believe in the future is felt distinctively in this sequence (Figure 32). The
real danger De Sica's characters face is not constituted authority: in the
end, the fascist apparatuses' grip on Italian life is shown time and again
to be too ridiculous and ineffective to be taken seriously. The real danger,
as it was for Bergson, lies in defeatism and habituation. As professor Elisa
Malgari suggests in *Maddalena zero in condotta,* the problem is that people
adapt to living in the real world, so they give up on their dreams. To protest this situation, Malgari behaves in the fashion of a "killjoy," as defined
by Sara Ahmed.[30] She does not smile, pretending all is well; she gets in the
way of other people's enjoyment by pointing out with aloofness that the
present world, the world of work and domestic labor, is grim and that only
in a different world could authentic joy be gained. And De Sica himself,
in Hartman's role, sustains Malgari's protest against disenchantment: he
explains that there is no logic in no longer living one's dreams, in giving in

to disillusion, because sometimes dreams and reality coincide, and reality is often even better than dreams. But since this is the case, then the best way to live reality is to keep dreaming. Appropriately, the most inspiring quality De Sica's characters share is that they do not give in to life as it is or concede to factual reality; rather, they use imagination, creativity, and ingenuity in the pursuit of happiness and to explore new possibilities of life.

Teresa Venerdì reflects explicitly on the regenerative and salvific function of imagination in a reality where violence and discipline are presented as the solution to any problem. In an emblematic scene, Teresa reads lines from *Romeo and Juliet* with a friend, finding a way to escape the sad reality of the orphanage but also articulating desires she still does not know how to handle. Theater is a serious matter because it teaches how to live, says Teresa to the person who is trying to shame her for having played out a love scene. And in fact the orphan will use fiction to survive her difficult reality. As Jacqueline Reich notes, Teresa masquerades often and plays different roles until she becomes the persona she needs to be for the doctor to choose her over the other two women with whom he is involved: a talentless poet (Irasema Dilián) and a vaudeville actor (Anna Magnani).

FIGURE 32. Reenchanted Italy from *Rose scarlatte* (Vittorio De Sica, 1940).

Landy has observed that Dr. Vignali chooses the best performer for his companion. However, Reich, through Butler, specifies that the performance in the film is life itself: performance is a means to achieve one's goals and dreams, Reich concludes in "Reading, Writing, and Rebellion."[31] Yet it is also true that the goals and dreams entertained by the protagonists of De Sica's comedies are not so transgressive or revolutionary after all.

Contrasting *Maddalena zero in condotta* and Jean Vigo's *Zero for Conduct* (1933), McGlazer points out in this regard that while the formal structure of Vigo's featurette builds up to the final rebellion during which the students occupy the school, in De Sica's film, despite the nods to indocility and anti-authoritarianism, "all roads lead to the living room, where utopia is closed off."[32] Toward the film's end, in fact, Hartman, Malgari, Maddalena, and her sweetheart convene in Maddalena's parlor, where misunderstandings are resolved and marriage plans are laid out under the watchful eye of Maddalena's father. The killjoy and the trickster eventually become docile subjects that belong at home.

The ruse of De Sica's cinematic reason coalesces around this: to let the spectators indulge in a fantasy of freedom, in the illusion that there is enough room and magic in the world for anyone to be able to fulfill their dreams and desires, while simultaneously teaching that the nuclear family, and by extension sociopolitical reproduction, is the ultimate dream. The scene where Hartman teaches Malgari how to dance is a particularly revealing one for McGlazer, as De Sica in this instance would be performing the same operation the film itself is carrying out: teaching uncooperative bodies how to move appropriately while pretending to release them from the societal impositions and gendered interpellations that burden their lives.

There is no doubt that in mocking the outdatedness and inefficacy of traditional apparatuses and strategies of government, De Sica is also building up the cinematographic apparatus's soft power—its power to intervene in collective life and impact the nation's bodies without resorting to violence. Such remediation especially comes through in *Teresa Venerdì*, in which De Sica plays the part of the young doctor replacing the old crone whose go-to medicine for all the girls' problems was castor oil—the remedy also used by Fascism to treat political opponents.[33] Although this textual reference confirms De Sica's interest in remediating the role that cinema could play in national health at a crucial historical juncture, I am less sure than McGlazer that the audiovisual forms concocted by the director work according to the logic of "repressive tolerance" and toward a postdisciplinary disciplining of the body politic. Even De Sica's anti-utopic endings maintain a remarkable heterotopic valence insofar as they formally sustain the desire to travel elsewhere, to evade reality as is—to look for ways out of a ruined present.

In this regard, Reich notes that the heteronormative idea of the good life that materializes in Italian schoolgirl comedies' happy endings is often a negotiation with the laws of genre fiction, a concession to the cultural industry, which, however, is not able to foreclose the utopic imaginaries that these films' rhetorical structures unleash. The boundaries and limitations to agency, autonomy, mobility, and rebellion that some films' narrative arcs evoke are in fact for Reich ephemeral and subject to rupture given the power of the dreams of pleasure and horizons of freedom previously mobilized.[34] This holds true for De Sica's commercial fictions as well, to the point that their endings are themselves ruptures and ruptured. The very form of his early films affords an openness to the dimension of futurity that seems to me in stark contrast with other forms of escapism, for instance—as I have argued—Camerini's.

In *Rose scarlatte,* Marina and Alberto reconcile, but they also decide to leave for Venice together—in a sequence that resembles the ending of Federico Fellini's *I vitelloni (The Bullocks,* 1953). The last shot of the film is a POV shot of the couple that, from the train, look out from the window and leave behind Rome and the life that they know: are they really saying goodbye to mystery and the unknown, or does this finale feature a journey toward a new life?

Analogously, *Teresa Venerdì* does not end with a return but with a departure. In contrast to the Hungarian play on which it was based, De Sica's film does not come to a close inside a home but on the run: Teresa is taken away from the orphanage by Dr. Pietro; they will get married, but they will also relocate to a different city and move on to a different reality. Film forms redundantly accentuate this twofold redemptive flight from a compromised here and now. In the final moments of the movie, we see Teresa and her doctor walking away and exiting the frame not once but twice: the first time when they leave the orphanage, and the second when they leave the post office from where Dr. Vignali has communicated to his father the decision to start afresh somewhere else. The first case is particularly audiovisually rich when reviewed today, as it anticipates the security camera aesthetics embraced, for instance, in Michael Haneke's *Hidden* (2015). Teresa and Pietro are captured from the point of view of the orphanage's director, who from her office on the second floor is tracking the couple's movement. By framing them through a high-angle shot that is also the POV of authority, De Sica turns Teresa and Pietro's departure from the orphanage into an allegorical withdrawal from the oppressive reach of control and discipline (Figure 33). The children's choir we hear in the background sets the tone for the scene and romanticizes the couple's flight out of sight.

The last sequence in *Maddalena* cuts away from the living room, where marriage plans are discussed, to the classroom. The headmistress is teaching business correspondence until the school finds a substitute for Professor Malgari. After the havoc caused by the letter that reached Mr. Hartman, the headmistress has decided that it is safer to come up with a new fictional addressee: the students will now write to Mr. Carlos Eredia from Barcelona. Yet a student stands up and interrupts the headmistresses: are we sure, she jokes, making everyone laugh, that Carlos does not exist either? Notable in this finale are two things. The first is that both Malgari and Maddalena have deserted the fascist school apparatus: the embrace of their bodily desires has brought them elsewhere, to a place that remains a mystery. But it is also important that the film leaves the last words to a student who might

FIGURE 33. Teresa and Pietro evading the gaze of control at the end of *Teresa Venerdì* (Vittorio De Sica, 1941).

take Maddalena's place as troublemaker and has already given herself the right to talk back to power, questioning—through her humorous parrhesia and the laughter it provokes—the distinction between truth and fiction, real and imaginary, possible and impossible.[35]

Finally, *Un garibaldino al convento* does not even build up to a traditional happy ending. After the long flashback to the Risorgimento epoch, the film returns to the present, where we discover that Mariella's Garibaldian soldier died in combat and the young woman was never able to forget him. So more than the end result, more than how and where the story finishes, what is key in this comedy is the emphasis on the urgency of living the life one wants to live no matter what—even if such a life does not align with the life deemed natural, normal, and appropriate by ruling authorities and traditions, even if such a life veers away from the horizons of reproductive futurity.

We should not forget that De Sica's rom-coms were produced at a moment when the state was tasking Italian men and women with abject assignments in the name of their race's survival, subjecting the population to progressively direr sacrifices, and imposing more severe restrictions on Italian bodies' autonomy and freedom. We also need to remember that these comedies about women resisting capture and grappling with heteronormativity were cowritten by a Jewish man facing discrimination. By keeping these details in mind, the critical thrust of De Sica's cinematic authorization of the fight against societal impositions and to reclaim control over one's own body might become even more readable. When power becomes so prominently interested in how people live, resistance to power becomes a matter of living differently. "Resistance," hence, is a quality of De Sica's escapist works insofar as they promote the feeling that a good life is the life that evades the tragic dictates of work, duties, and sacrifice, an easy, playful, entertaining life that transgresses the boundaries of what was allowed and afforded to the early 1940s Italian body politic. Although they do not articulate an explicit critique of the fascist real, through laughs and smiles, *Rose scarlatte, Maddalena zero in condotta, Teresa Venerdì,* and *Un garibaldino al convento* write into public imagination the invigorating sensation that escaping the gendered and racialized impositions of fascist biopolitics is not only possible and right; it is the fun thing to do. Aren't these films, then—to quote De Benedetti—of the "utmost importance"?[36]

7 Queer Antifascism

Visconti's Ossessione *and the* Cinema
Conspiracy against Ethno-Nationalism

With *Queer Cinema in the World,* Karl Schoonover and Rosalind Galt expanded the boundaries of queer film, mapping intertwined oppositional figurations of desire and community, the intimate and the public, across a number of contemporary global locations. Operating from the feminist perspective that the personal is (bio)political, the authors of this important book from 2016 identify a film's queerness in its power to effect modes of embodiment that destabilize dominant orientations and arrange, through daring formal choices, dissident horizons "of affiliation, affection, [and] affect."[1] In this chapter, I extend Schoonover and Galt's framework from cinema's geography to its history—not in order to draft a linear evolution of LGBTQ+ filmmaking but to contribute, with my take on Luchino Visconti's *Ossessione* (*Obsession,* 1943), to establishing a diachronic counterarchive of queer cinematic resistance.

David Forgacs insists that the sociosexual imaginary from Visconti's debut is rife with "reactionary elements" and that there is "nothing intrinsically anti-fascist" about the film's narrative.[2] While it is true that *Ossessione* shares some narrative and tonal components with other works from late fascist Italy, it is difficult to ignore how such an adaptation of James M. Cain's *The Postman Always Rings Twice* also inverts the blueprint of cinema under the regime. Films like Ferdinando Maria Poggioli's *Addio, giovinezza!* (*Goodbye Youth!,* 1940) or Alessandro Blasetti's *Quattro passi fra le nuvole* (*Four Steps in the Clouds,* 1942) depict transgression but only to stage the return to the norms of tradition as the best route ahead for a race under threat. *Ossessione,* on the other hand, associates the pursuit of happiness with the constitution of a nonconforming body politic. Hence, in the following pages, I reconstruct how the hybrid transnational aesthetics mobilized in the film knock off-kilter the gendered and classed borders of the ethnonation, advancing the adoption of "foreign" lifestyles as the only chance to move beyond Fascism's ruinous race-making endeavors.

Yet in order to fully appreciate the originality of *Ossessione* and to substantiate an antifascist reading of its transgressive system of figuration, it is crucial to first linger on the context of struggle wherein the film emerged. *Ossessione* was not merely the brilliant debut of a great auteur; nor, contrary to what Bazin's genealogy of neorealism might suggest, did it sprout spontaneously and organically from the rotting corpse of Italian totalitarianism.[3] No other Italian film "was more calculated, more conceptualized, more prepared and consequently less spontaneous."[4] *Ossessione* was a highly mediated intervention that constituted the final operation of the so-called *Cinema* cell—the communist formation that had infiltrated the eponymous journal and that had been involved in a conspiracy against Mussolini's dictatorship since 1941, initially waging its opposition through a series of film theory essays advocating for a new Italian realism. At the time, it was easy for readers to hear the distant sound of a battle in the call for a paradigmatic shift in the way Italian reality was captured on film and disseminated on screens. However, the political import of the critical pieces that build up to *Ossessione* remains underexplored.

For the most part, Italian and anglophone scholarship frames the realism elaborated in *Cinema,* and to some extent *Ossessione* itself, as an anticipation of what Millicent Marcus describes as "neorealism proper." Keeping in mind Tom Gunning's warnings against the normative tendency to treat previous moments in media history as preparatory periods for later "classical" styles and practices, I ask: What can we learn about "resistance" once we stop reviewing the film style strategized in *Cinema* and then deployed in *Ossessione* in light of postwar neorealism? Rather than reading the *Cinema* intervention in Italy's mediascape as a transitional step toward a proper, and properly Italian, national cinema to come, I approach it as an aesthetic-political disruption that attests the political malleability of realism well beyond the Bazin–Baudry "divide." Important essays by William Van Watson and Giuliana Minghelli have traced the exceptionality of *Ossessione* vis-à-vis the mediascape of the time. However, by overlooking the film's complex genealogy, these scholars might have overlooked how the *Cinema* provocation, by addressing sex and class, also contests racism.[5]

The first section of this chapter investigates how the cell's theorization of realism opposed the exploitation of cinema as a race-making technology. In this case, I distinguish the racist weaponization of the cinema proposed in *Cinema* by Maurizio Rava (the former governor of Somalia) and Vittorio Mussolini (the Duce's son) from the remediation strategized by Visconti, Mario Alicata, and Giuseppe De Santis. In the second section, I focus on the display of queer living in *Ossessione* as the most viable alternative to Fascism, tracing how the film's forms reflect the earlier elaboration of an alternative experience of the Italian real. In the journal, the cell had posited that a cinema that aspired to authenticity could not shy away from showcasing Italy's potential to become other. The complex metonymic structures of *Ossessione* give audiovisual substance to such a horizon of change, staging transnational encounters and unconventional attachments as occasions for revolutionary modes of being together and in the world. A film about desire, as Jonathan Mullins has cogently characterized it, *Ossessione* showcases how certain forms of love could challenge the reproduction of the fascist race.[6]

FROM RACE TO LANDSCAPE, FROM DESTINY TO HISTORY

The revitalization of Italian film in the 1930s coincided with the burgeoning of a lively paratextual debate in magazines and technical journals that strived to formalize a properly Italian way to sound cinema. Such deep reflection on film style, forms, techniques, and technologies constituted an effort to reckon with the medium's specificity but also an attempt to articulate how cinema might best serve the regime's plans for social normalization and territorial expansion.[7] The recognition of film's bearing on national life came, in fact, with a heightened degree of anxiety: given cinema's impact on the collectivity, one had to make sure that only those movies that promoted racially appropriate behaviors reached the movie halls. In light of these biopolitical concerns over mediation practices and film forms, it is fitting that Maurizio Rava, the vice governor of Tripolitania and former governor of Somalia, penned the very first article in *Cinema*, the authoritative journal founded in 1936 with the aim of honing the cinematographic apparatus in fascist Italy.[8]

In "I popoli africani dinanzi allo schermo" (The African peoples before the screen), Rava establishes a definitive connection between cinema and white supremacy, insisting that film has a crucial bearing on racial hierarchies and race relations, especially in a colonial setting. Preoccupied by the increased contact between Italian colonists and their Black subjects in the expanding fascist empire, Rava singles out miscegenation as the most serious problem of the present. Fascism's settler colonialism and its project of world domination required armies of bodies—hence Mussolini's "battle for births." Yet it was crucial that these newly mass-produced lives were of the right color and make. Given these related concerns over racial identity and sexual behavior, Rava proposes to ban from the colonies films that could trigger improper longings in the public. It was not simply a question of blocking the release of films that, with their exotic and sensual representation of Black women, might push Italian men to trespass the color line and thus endanger the purity as well as the future of the ethno-nation. It was also a matter of controlling which image of white people ("bianchi") reached Africa, so to govern how Black people gazed at Italian men and women.[9]

Consider, Rava intimates, cinema's influence on children, how it models their way of speaking and walking but also their aspirations, dispositions, and desires. Then consider the potentially catastrophic effect that portrayals of imperfect white men and sexually available white women could have on populations that are as impressionable as children. By projecting films that cast a negative light on whiteness in places like Somalia, Libya, or Ethiopia, one would risk tainting the natives' judgment of the white master race, and thus also their attitude in regard to white supremacy itself. To ensure the prestige of the Italian race—a fundamental component of imperial dominion and colonial apartheid, according to Rava—colonial administrators should then block the release in Italian Africa of works that might compromise the fearful deference that local populations harbored for Italian masters and their women. What is notable about the very first article published in *Cinema* is the precision with which it connects the exercise of white supremacy with the realms of media and sexual reproduction. As Ann Laura Stoler highlights, the modern anxiety over sex (What are acceptable forms of sexual intercourse? How does one properly represent desire?) cannot be dissociated from the trajectories of state racism and biopolitics: policing sex is a way to police social reproduction, and thus a means to control the future.[10] As Rava's essay makes clear, the way bodies are represented at the movies ought to be severely policed, lest the prestige, integrity, supremacy, and whiteness of the Italian people be compromised both at the heart and at the margins of the empire. At stake at the movies was the very existence of the Blackshirt race.

A similar concern with correctly reproducing the Italian race also characterizes the interventions in *Cinema* by Vittorio Mussolini, who had become
the journal's editor in chief in 1939 and was one of the most vocal proponents of weaponizing film in support of imperial expansion and internal governance. While Rava focused on what cinema shouldn't be doing,
Mussolini gave detailed instructions on the route that national film ought
to follow to become an effective biopolitical apparatus. In the editorial
"Ordine e disciplina" (Order and discipline), Mussolini pressures producers, directors, and screenwriters to docilely accept Fascism's "attentive scrutiny" and "friendly assistance." In "Razza italiana e cinema italiano" (Italian
race and Italian cinema), an essay penned after the promulgation of the
Racial Laws in 1938, the Duce's son further specifies how this medium can
assist fascist race-making.[11] Mussolini first laments the lack of realism in
current Italian cinema, then affirms that for national cinema to be realistic,
it must capture Italian racial unity onscreen. More specifically, Mussolini
presses Cinecittà to follow Hollywood in its treatment of moving images
as natural emanations of the body politic. Filmic representations convey
the nation; therefore, Mussolini urges, directors should cast only actors and
actresses whose bodies affirmed the Italian race in all its glorious beauty
and physical prowess. In fact, no matter how diverse Italians might look,
they must be recognized as sharing one race and one destiny based on their
shared biological and historical heritage. Rural yet modern, poor yet courageous, provincial but urban; heroic, young, lively, self-confident, exuberant,
and audacious—such was the Italian race that a proper national cinema
had to capture and broadcast. By making the core features of the Italian
people more recognizable and reputable abroad, cinema would contribute
to the affirmation of the fascist lifestyle on the world stage. Moreover, in a
time of transnational expansion of the homeland, a precise representation
of the Italian race would make the people proud of their identity and thus
inspire them to docilely and enthusiastically fulfill their biologically determined destiny.[12]

Ernesto Laclau was one of the first to highlight that racial imagination is a central engine for social reproduction under fascist populism.[13]
But whereas for Laclau racism functions as an apparatus of ideological
justification, for Vittorio Mussolini the frame of race is key because of its
affective affordances. For Mussolini, cinema did not need to convince the
people that they were a race, so as to have them consent to the regime
or legitimize the existence of Fascism. Rather, cinema ought to inspire the

people to *perform* racism, to ensure the survival of a white Blackshirt Italy even after the Duce's death. There are two distinct ways in which the reference to race is a resource for policing collective existence. By engrafting Italian identity on an overdetermined biohistorical patrimony, it naturalizes history and disseminates the sense of a foreclosed futurity. At the same time, by recoding the dissimilarities within the country as merely somatic and happenstance variables of the same archetypical matrix, the reference to race neutralizes difference and mediates a pacifying feeling of community and co-belonging. A true Italian cinema was a cinema that would effectively involve the people in Fascism's projects and practices.

Despite the efforts and demands to transform film into a powerful weapon for making race, for governing the nation and expanding the empire, from the early 1940s onward film became a battlefield for the regime. The entry into World War II, intended to catapult the Italian people to the world stage, had turned out to be a catastrophe. After years of relative political consensus, the brutal realities of war struck a great blow to the fascist state's capacity to keep Italy and its film industry in check. Even directors sympathetic to the regime now were reluctant to deploy film forms in support of Blackshirt rule. In 1941, Camerini directed *I promessi sposi* (*The Betrothed*), and the film's long, brutal panoramic shots over a Milan tormented by the plague conveys the angst of a nation in disarray. Fascism was in such crisis that even Blasetti was changing registers and moving away from an outright apology for the present. In 1942, he adapted for the screen Sam Benelli's *La cena delle beffe* (*The Jester's Supper*), a farce that denounced the downward spiral of violence in Medicean Florence and somehow anticipated the looming civil war. The regime's suspicion of cinema was so high that in 1942 Benito Mussolini personally ordered movie theaters to pull Goffredo Alessandrini's adaptation of Ayn Rand's *We the Living,* detecting an antitotalitarian subtext in the film's condemnation of communist Russia. The defeats in Albania, Africa, and Russia were sinking Italians' confidence in the regime but also Fascism's confidence in its own people and apparatuses of government.

In regard to cinema, the regime's preoccupations were directed especially toward the Centro Sperimentale di Cinematografia, which—under the direction of Umberto Barbaro and Luigi Chiarini—had become "the foreign legion of anti-fascist intelligentsia."[14] With the Centro, Fascism had created a state-of-the-art facility that formed skilled screenwriters, cinematographers, and directors. This very training made it possible for film practitioners to navigate the intricate censorship system, experiment with film norms, and elaborate alternative deployment of the apparatus. Ironically, it was Vittorio Mussolini himself who introduced Luchino Visconti to this cohort of what today we might describe as media activists.

Mussolini's heir was a passionate admirer of Jean Renoir, and in 1939 he brought the French director to Rome to adapt *Tosca*. Renoir fled the country when Italy declared war on France, leaving his young assistant Luchino behind to complete the project. Mussolini introduced Visconti to the editors at *Cinema*, a journal that under his tenure had become a think tank for students from the Centro Sperimentale, whose impatience with the regime was growing. The thirty-three-year-old Visconti—whose homosexuality was an open secret—immediately bonded with the nonconformist editorial office of *Cinema*, especially Giuseppe De Santis and Mario Alicata. Both in their twenties and members of the banned Communist Party, De Santis and Alicata had started pondering ways to intertwine art and political activism in the same fashion as Renoir had done in the France of the Popular Front. In Visconti, they recognized someone who—because of his experience, connections, and wealth—could help in their efforts. At that point, the *Cinema* cell was established. Besides Visconti, future Academy Award–winner De Santis, and the future cultural leader of the Italian Communist Party, Alicata, the group included soon-to-be directors Antonio Pietrangeli and Carlo Lizzani, Gianni and Dario Puccini, novelist Alberto Moravia (who was of Jewish descent), and Pietro Ingrao, who in 1976 would become the first Communist to chair the Italian Chamber of Deputies. Among the members of the cell, Alicata and the Puccini brothers already had files in the political registry of antifascist activities, but the whole group was under surveillance.[15]

The merits of a "politicization of aesthetics" that would challenge Nazi Fascism's "aestheticization of politics" were being assessed not only in Germany and Vichy France but also in Italy. In contrast to Nazi Germany, Italy still boasted venues where dissent from official cultural politics could be voiced. It was not out of mere liberality or pluralism that Fascism allowed these spaces to persist, but rather to promote that artistic creativity without which the regime believed that a politically effective fascist art would not materialize. The strategy dictated by the underground Communist Party was to cautiously occupy these free-speech zones to challenge state-sanctioned cultural forms, experiment with new discursive regimes, and make contact with other freedom fighters. The strategy might appear as an iteration of what Antonio Gramsci calls a "war of position": a struggle that takes place within the realm of collective fantasy, with the goal of shaping an alternative popular culture that would pave the way to armed revolt.[16] In the case of the *Cinema* cell, the entry point to this cultural war was the debate on filmic realism.

From the interwar period onward and all the way to Vittorio Mussolini, the debate on realism was a site of power–knowledge struggle between conflicting accounts of the Italian real with radically different ideological implications.[17] "Realism" constituted a fraught term in Italian culture, functioning as a sort of empty signifier that different groups wielded to advance their varying political ontologies. De Santis, Alicata, and Visconti did the same: they took a stance on the issue of realism in film in order to elaborate a perspective on collective identity, a political project, and an articulation of the medium that were incompatible with those expressed under fascist racism. The antifascist and antiracist thrust of their new realism emerges for the first time in De Santis's "Per un paesaggio italiano" ("For an Italian Landscape," 1941).[18]

De Santis begins this programmatic manifesto—the "per" (for) in the title should not be overlooked—by repeating the claims that Vittorio Mussolini and others had made repeatedly in *Cinema*: Italian reality and real Italian people were missing from the movie theaters; realism had not yet been achieved; Italian film needed to achieve realism. Yet the brilliant student at the Centro Sperimentale swerves away from clichéd positions and instead questions the necessity of holding on to the master trope of "race" as the definitive truth about the nation. In "Razza italiana e cinema italiano," Vittorio Mussolini demanded that cinema capture Italians as one race and one people. Parroting his father, he insisted that

> the somatic differences among Italians, the differences which distinguish the blond from the brown, differences of skin color and skull shape, do not prevent us from agreeing with illustrious scientists and asserting the existence of one Italian race that includes all Italians, from the Alps to Sicily.[19]

De Santis obliquely signals that Mussolini's magic formula for achieving realism in film was ill-conceived. How could Mussolini steer the film industry toward realism when he had completely misunderstood the core features of Italian reality and identity? Italians not only looked different from one another but *were* different, insofar as their fundamental imprint came from their relationship to their surroundings and not from a common spiritual–biological patrimony:

> We are surely saying nothing new by claiming that the landscape [*paesaggio*] in which each of us was born and has lived contributed to making us different from one another. And herein lies God's mark, which we are unfortunately accustomed to seeing profaned to such an extent that a peasant from Sicily can appear identical to one living in the Julian Alps.[20]

Although De Santis never mentions race, it is the main focus of his article: by regrounding Italian identity in exteriority, he renounces the frame of racism altogether. From this perspective, "Per un paesaggio italiano" can be described as an exploration of the irrelevance of race when it comes to understanding, and thus representing, a lifeworld. As De Santis reiterates in the sensuous prose of "Il linguaggio dei rapporti" (The language of relations), what human beings hold within themselves, "they have stolen . . . from their elements, from their relations, from their peculiar ways of being in communion with others, from the tree that grows in their gardens or from the passerby they have briefly encountered in the streets."[21] A person does not live in the world as a silkworm enclosed in its shell: she is, De Santis underscores, surrounded by comrades, animals, gardens, streets, mountains, the sky, a sea, and life. For this reason, filmmakers interested in witnessing Italy had no other option than narrating the diverse environments constitutive of the country, situating their plots against the backdrop of actual landscapes. Otherwise, Italian cinema would confine itself to staged depictions of Italy, visualizations that bear no trace of the radical differences between Sicilians and people from the Alps, for instance. De Santis does approvingly comment upon the coeval efforts to achieve realism in Italian cinema (Blasetti, De Robertis, Rossellini); yet, to all effects his proposal for a new national cinema overcomes realism's way of gazing at Italy and Italians.

Two important consequences follow from De Santis's argument that are at odds with the tenets of fascist realism:

1. Notwithstanding Fascism's presumed reclamation of the country, a unified national reality did not exist: Italy was radically diverse.
2. The Italian nation that cinema ought to propagate was not a united race-people but rather a fragmented territory inhabited by a constellation of different forms of life.

With the *paesaggio* as a backdrop, the *paese* (the country) not only appeared diverse but also felt precarious. If identity was detached from race, Fascism's claim of a predetermined fate for the population collapsed: there is a strong sense of agency that emerges from De Santis's manifesto. Noa Steimatsky pointedly describes De Santis's piece on realism as a review of how Italian localisms upset the spatial mythology of a centralized ethno-community. I would add that the *Cinema* cell's emphasis on Italian landscape also challenges the temporal order of racial determinism, conjuring a different experience of history, a contingent temporality at odds with the idea of a spiritual–biological destiny.[22] Indeed, what happens to our attitude toward history when we are reminded that the landscape—the force informing who we are, according to De Santis—is partially of our own making? If the form that life acquires is the result of a nondeterministic interaction between group and environment, then by acting on the environment a community also acts upon itself. This means that identities and peoples are always in a state of becoming, open to negotiation; it means that the future of the nation belongs to those who dwell on its soil; it means that futurity is the very horizon of belonging. Consequently, for De Santis, an authentically new Italian cinema would need to convey this fundamentally transformative dialogue in which people engage with one another and with their surroundings.

The protagonist of Mussolini's realism was a homogenous people captive to an overdetermined racial fate. In contrast, De Santis figures a landscape with an open-ended history. With an ecocritical sensibility derived from his peasant origins, De Santis painted the nation as a changing microcosm, a contingent and unstable assemblage crawling with life, passions, energies, possibilities, and futurities. In so doing, he also devised an audiovisual regime that, as Derek Duncan argues, instead of contributing to fascist governmentality would upset the very racial order of truth in which the regime was couched.[23] In reality, Italians were not a race and did not have a destiny; in reality, there was no fixed Italian identity for Fascism to police, defend, and secure in the first place. What defined Italy as a place and a people was difference and becoming, which also meant that, by trying to unify Italy and by showing a unified, overdetermined Italy, Fascism and fascist cinema were doing violence to the Italian real.

"Per un paesaggio italiano" was only the inception of the *Cinema* cell's attack against dominating mediations of Italian reality. The group soon took aim at the "calligraphic" mode in national cinema in a way that resonates with the French New Wave's 1960s rejection of quality cinema, which was mockingly referred to as "cinéma du papa," dad cinema. Their positions also echo Roman Jakobson's considerations on how revolutionary forms of art establish their status in dialectical opposition to previous works, which are denounced as insufficient in terms of both form and content.[24] The *Cinema* cell's problem with domestic production was that it blindly reduced the search for a proper film style to a question of technique and forms, neglecting to consider larger issues of the politics of representation. Obsessed with technical perfection, directors such as Mario Soldati and Renato Castellani had failed to feature the Italian lives that mattered the most. In their 1941 "Verità e poesia: Verga e il cinema italiano" ("Truth and Poetry: Verga and Italian Cinema"), Alicata and De Santis ridicule the staged, superficial, sterile, provincial, polished pictorialism of recent Italian films, all of which busily monumentalize the most trivial details of national life.[25] Yet somehow, surprisingly given the unmediated dimension one usually associates with neorealism, Alicata and De Santis state that significant preparation is necessary to eschew trite audiovisual paradigms. Taking a stance, as Umberto Barbaro had done earlier, against the mystical trust in the movie camera's capacity to capture the real by means of technical reproduction alone, Alicata and De Santis point out that filmmakers had to open their horizons and expand their frames of reference before scouting ports, fields, and factories. Before even thinking of taking their cameras to the streets, film practitioners had to read southern writer Giovanni Verga.[26]

The approving reference to Verga's tales about Sicily had apparently contentious overtones. In the concurrent social imaginary, Sicily still represented a space and a time incompatible with the desired image of a "modern, imperially ambitious fascist Italy as it was entering the war."[27] This *paese* was at the margins of the nation not only geographically but also linguistically, culturally, politically, and historically: with his novellas, Verga contributed to the image of Sicily as something different, a remnant of otherness impossible to assimilate. Whereas for centralized state power radical difference was an unresolved problem, for the *Cinema* cell it constituted an answer, a resource to excite the collective imagination. In fact, for them, the people memorialized by Verga approximated prerevolutionary subjects fighting for freedom and happiness. His novellas featuring Sicilian workers (fishermen, peasants, miners) limned suffering yet combative social groups who were bravely engaged in changing their lifeworlds, bearing witness to a reality that was resilient to the reclamation plans concocted by the regime.[28] In essence, the *Cinema* cell believed that Verga's subaltern people were the protagonists of a history that had nothing to do with the singular racial destiny that, according to the fascist establishment, cinema had to manifest. Verga's Sicilians were the heroes that Italian popular culture lacked; they were fighters but not cut from a Blackshirt cloth.[29] Ultimately, the *Cinema* cell hoped that Verga would open filmmakers' eyes to this other history taking place at the nation's margins, causing them to reorient their cameras away from model citizens and toward antagonistic Italians, and forcing them to take notice of overlooked fractures, frictions, and tensions within the country. Alicata and De Santis admit that Sicily will mean nothing to those interested in cinematic awards or technical perfection. Yet to those "who believe in an art which above all creates truth," Verga indicates the one historically valid urgency: "the urgency of a revolutionary art inspired by a humanity that suffers and hopes."[30]

The proposal for a new cinema committed to representing the lives and struggles of these other Italians, a realism that would develop a new truth regime and have spectators experience the nation differently, did not go unnoticed. A few weeks after the publication of Alicata and De Santis's first article on Verga and Italian film, a vitriolic intervention in *Cinema* protested that film was a medium of immediacy and that literature had no place at the movies.[31] There was no deeper truth to be discovered beneath the fascist ordering of things—no struggle, no tension, no violence, no underground conflicts; no explosive hopes, aspirations, or potentialities to be explored. Accordingly, there was no need for directors to re-view Italy through Verga; the Italian real was immediately available to anyone who cared to record it.

It comes as no surprise that Alicata and De Santis's intervention caused such an outrage. "Verità e poesia" denounced that what passed for Italian reality on the screen was a fiction; it held that cinema still failed to convey the nation, despite its self-proclaimed authenticity. In one swift provocation, *Cinema* questioned national cinema and, therefore, given the complicity of media and power since the early 1930s, Fascism itself. If films that featured a suffering yet pugnacious humanity were considered more authentic, important, and inspiring than state-sanctioned movies promoting the united, happy, active, disciplined Italian race, then Mussolini's grip on the nation suddenly seemed compromised. How could the Duce effectively govern the people if he did not even know who they were? As Luchino Visconti soon reiterated, an authentic outlook on the Italian people and the nation's possibilities could only be accessed via Sicily's mediation.

In his earlier essay "Cadaveri" (Corpses), Visconti had extended the polemic initiated by De Santis in "Per un paesaggio italiano," denouncing the comatose state of Italian cinema and the nefarious consequences of state control over film production. The industry, Visconti warned, was in the hands of corpses who, unaware of being dead, insisted on writing screenplays.[32] In "Tradizione e invenzione" (Tradition and invention), Visconti singles out Verga as the author who could steer the industry past the "banality and . . . misery typical of current scenarios."[33] Visconti emphatically recalls that it was by reading Verga that he started sensing that Italy was much more than he had previously understood. The Sicily one could read about in *I Malavoglia* (*The House by the Medlar Tree,* 1890) was physically and symbolically alien to the Italy usually exhibited in the cinemas. It was a wild landscape inhabited by a people that had nothing in common with the ordered nation concocted by Fascism. Verga's land of passions and conflicts functioned metonymically as an alternative reality through which Visconti could see that, beyond the domesticated lives so often represented in the movies, there were other bodies and other lives waiting to be discovered. Visconti essentially pointed to Sicily as a way to escape the hollow promises and premises of fascist modernity, a return to the "core feature of human life," as he puts it.

In letters sent from prison after being arrested for his antifascist activities, Alicata raised doubts about Visconti's fascination with Sicily: he was afraid that Visconti might be indulging in primitivist phantasies similar to those informing F. W. Murnau's *Tabu: A Story of the South Seas* (1931). Dispelling charges of what today we would call essentialism and antihistoricism, in his "Cinema antropomorfico" ("Anthropomorphic Cinema")—an essay promoting the imminent release of *Ossessione*—Visconti clarifies that a cinema that captures humanity's essential characteristics is a cinema that features life's potential to change.[34] The core of human life, Visconti specifies, is to be found not in an atemporal essence but rather in the "mystical discovery" that one is not well but could do better: no matter how corrupt individuals are, they still have a chance to repent and transform their lives. This empowering sense of agency is precisely what *Ossessione* mustered for Visconti. However, the film did not merely project that Italians could change their situation and be different, that social life was not overdetermined by tradition or race but instead coincided with an openness toward the future that Italians had, for their own sake, to pursue. By means of its disruptive system of figuration, the final act of the *Cinema* conspiracy against Fascism charted more clearly the "lines of flight" on which the people might want to embark in order to travel beyond the destructive normality harnessed by the regime. Since Italians were not a race, who could they be?

WHAT A BODY POLITIC CAN DO

By the spring of 1943, the tide had turned against the regime. While Stalin's Red Army pushed back on the Eastern Front, the Allies had taken Tunisia, putting them just a few short miles south of Sicily. The worker strikes in Turin and Milan were unmistakable signs of an expanding unrest in the North. Fascism was under siege. Mussolini was losing control of his country, his people, and his party. It is at this historic juncture that *Ossessione* was released.

Barbaro was enthusiastic, coining the term *neorealism* to describe the film's effort to manifest a new national real. He was among the few that praised *Ossessione*. The Minister of Popular Culture denounced the *Cinema* operation as "reeking of latrines," and critics condemned it as a crass representation of Italian life—a deplorable imitation of what they saw as the coarse cinema of Marcel Carné and Jean Renoir. In the midst of this unprecedented smear campaign, the police so discouraged theater managers from screening the film that very few people could actually see it. Vittorio Mussolini did catch the work that had originated in his editorial office; he did not like it one bit.[35] "This is not Italy! This in not Italy! This is not Italy!" he allegedly protested, storming out of his private premiere.

Mussolini was right in not recognizing his nation in the country that the film projected. *Ossessione* was truly anti-Italian, and not merely from a formal point of view, given its endeavor to conjure a hybrid style that would bring together Verga, American noir, and French naturalism. *Ossessione* was an anti-Italian work because the people it portrayed were radically other from the Italian race that Fascism sought to produce and demanded that cinema reproduce. If, as the film maintained, twenty years after Mussolini's rise to power the nation remained a swamp dominated by toxic affects, then perhaps the problem was not simply the Duce or fascist rule. The problem might lie instead in the faith that a race war reactivating "traditional values" would shelter the people from disaster. In this sense, *Ossessione* did far more than denounce the degradation of the nation's health, blame Mussolini for it, and advocate for a change in leadership. The *Cinema* cell indicted Fascism as the culmination of a longer trajectory of racialized traditionalism and suggested that a good life could only be found in the desertion of hegemonic arrangements of intimate and social life.

Gino (Massimo Girotti) is a drifter. Homeless and jobless, he arrives at a roadside inn owned by the aging Bragana (Juan de Landa) and his young wife, Giovanna (Clara Calamai). During the hobo's work-stay at the inn, Gino and Giovanna fall for each other. Giovanna, who has had enough of her husband, is seeking a partner for her murderous plan: kill Bragana, pocket his life insurance, take over the inn, and start a new home and family. Gino hesitates between going back to his unattached existence on the road and embracing the home life with which Giovanna entices him. The outsiders Spagnolo (Elio Marcuzzo) and Anita (Dhia Cristiani) give Gino refuge in the cities of Ancona and Ferrara, urging him not to give in to the lure of domesticity and mainstream notions of sex, gender, and family. But in the end, Gino cannot resist Giovanna. He murders Bragana, only to get himself arrested and Giovanna killed.

The *Cinema* effort to project the darker side of the Italian present is foreshadowed from the opening sequence of *Ossessione*, which also stages the film's dialectical relation vis-à-vis coeval Italian realism through its intertextual reference. Over a melodramatic soundscape and through the frame of a truck windshield, the viewer is exposed to a grim and desolate Po Valley, nothing like the enchanted countryside seen and heard in the opening of Blasetti's *Quattro passi fra le nuvole*. The people who inhabit the Italian countryside are as desolate as their landscape: a couple with no children and out of love; an ex-soldier turned Blackshirt turned abusive husband, inept business owner, and animal abuser; a former sex worker who orchestrates the death of the man who rescued her from the streets and then relegated her to the status of housemaid; a drifter with no reservations about sleeping with a married woman and killing her husband. Peter Brooks famously argued that the cinematic removal of housetops and the representation of the sad family existences playing out beneath them is a typical gesture of any narrative that strives to establish itself as realistic.[36] Within the context of Fascism, the *Cinema* reappraisal of domestic life acquires a particular valence. Keeping in mind the normalizing pressures dominating Italy under the regime, the film's brutal vision of family life emerges as a provocative challenge to state-enforced attachments and investments in heteronormativity. What is, in fact, this longed-for home? What is this place for which one should sacrifice everything? For *Ossessione,* it is the time-space of melodrama.

In *Visconti: Insights into Flesh and Blood,* Alexander García Düttmann argues that Visconti's films are characterized by a melodramatic aesthetic of excess that shatters the stable identity of the viewers and pushes them to feel another possible life pulsing beyond the lives that are assembled in the here and now—a life, as Jonathan Goldberg puts it, "beyond the legal, the social, the rules of existence." In a 2017 lecture delivered in Berlin, Düttmann returned to the topic, lingering on the weird bursts of laughter in Visconti's later films, most notably *Morte a Venezia* (*Death in Venice,* 1971). For Düttmann, these outbursts showcase how the melodramatic imagination entails a charged emotional register culminating in a queer jouissance, where any fixed arrangement of subjectivity is compromised.[37]

Ossessione, an example of "melodramatic realism" for Henry Bacon, bears no trace of the liberating pathos that Düttmann and Goldberg, in an almost Bataillean fashion, deem central to Visconti's queer utopianism.[38] By using melodrama to read Italian history and by capturing the melodramatic dimension of current national reality, *Ossessione* resorts to the system of light, color, sound, and music typical of the register to achieve two goals. On the one hand, through this affected aesthetic, Visconti evokes the powerful hold of the Italian investment in domesticity: we might think of the overwrought camera movements and emphatic soundscape that pull Gino toward Giovanna and the home-space at the beginning of the film. On the other hand, the melodramatic chronotopes of an immutable world in which individuals are hostage to pathological passions and victims of an irreversible temporality are mobilized to show how the compulsion toward normality and tradition entails an affective blockage, a compromised system of attachment, a rush of longing and yearning that immunizes history from becoming.

Alicata and De Santis's "Verità e poesia" advised that in order to avoid fatalism and defeatism, cinema had to discover the presence throughout the nation of alternatives to the fascist ordering of bodies and desires. In *Ossessione,* the urban landscapes of Ancona and Ferrara—where Gino enjoys time, respectively, with street artist Spagnolo and the ballerina Anita—function as audiovisual counterpoints to the violent existence in the rural home, providing important glimmers of the unexplored forms of embodiment available to the Italian people.

Ancona and Ferrara of *Ossessione* are spaces of redemptive encounters, replete with exuberant vitality, light and lightness; places where the poor benefit from a system of alliance and support divorced from the market of labor exchange or the exploitative tutelage of the upper class. This is a place grounded in mutual assistance—an example of that parallel welfare structure embedded in Italian non-Stalinist communism.[39] In these cities, the film suggests, people invite you into their homes and share their meager supplies with you out of love and solidarity, with no ulterior motives. The Black man pacing Ancona and the two disabled people seen in Ferrara subtly attest to how the landscapes in which Spagnolo and Anita move are spaces of difference, not the site of the white ableist body politic prized by Fascism. Neither does the rhythm to which these localities move hew to Italian nationalism. When Giovanna, in Ferrara, tries to entice Gino with the money from Bragana's life insurance and with tales of upward social mobility, he is distracted by the upbeat music playing in the background and walks away from her to join Anita, whose demeanor was modeled on Pablo Picasso's cubist portraits (while Giovanna was based on the Italian painter Amedeo Modigliani).[40] Expanding on Minghelli's insightful account of how the *Cinema* film shifts gears whenever Gino disconnects from the fantasies of domesticity, normalcy, and heterosexuality that Giovanna represents, I hold that the opposition between urban and country lifestyles in the film is more than a displacement of Visconti's homosexual desires, or a repetition of the Aryanism–Mediterraneanism feud. It is the key element for reckoning with the film's queer interweaving of politics and sexuality.[41]

After they have sex for the first time, Gino offers Giovanna a conch shell in which she can hear the echo of the ocean and seduces her with the unbound way of life that the sea—borderless, fluid, and always in motion—evokes. Giovanna seems to be convinced and agrees to desert the inn with Gino. A few meters on the road are enough to make her waver: her old life has a gravity that tugs Giovanna back. Whereas on the road Gino perceives glimmers of hope, Giovanna is paralyzed in her existence, burdened by the weight of tradition and the fear of losing social status. She sits down on a mound of gravel. Gino sits down with her, and the camera, in a high-angle shot, embeds them in the backdrop, where a group of peasants is working in a rudimentary wheat-threshing ritual (Figure 34). As De Santis recalls in an essay penned in honor of the film's fortieth anniversary, the background in this sequence was paramount to advancing the film's proposal. First, it signals how the two lovers, by aborting their escape plan,

FIGURE 34. Gino and Giovanna pause their flight, as peasants toil in the background, in *Ossessione* (Luchino Visconti, 1943).

FIGURE 35. *The Harvesters* (Pieter Bruegel the Elder, 1565).

would be confined to an archaic existence of toil and labor. Moreover, being modeled on Pieter Bruegel the Elder's 1565 *The Harvesters* (Figure 35), the backdrop was also designed to lift the representation of the national land-scape from its provincialism and insert it in wider networks of figuration.[42]

The reference to transnational cultural affiliations carries on in the reverse shot: Gino stands up and walks away, hitting the road without hes-itation or fear in a shot that formally and tonally alludes to the endings of Charlie Chaplin's *The Tramp* (1915) and *Modern Times* (1936). A femme fatale, Giovanna allegorically indicates the tragic fate the nation will endure if it does not abandon its current way of living and loving. It is then expected that as soon as Gino cuts ties with her, his horizon dramatically changes. Now, the jobless hobo has an open road and a clear sky in front of him. There is a whole world waiting to be explored. The only thing he is missing is allies. Eve Kosofsky Sedgwick defines queerness as the "open mesh of possibilities" exceeding traditional social relations and entailing an experimentation with modes of intimacy that challenge the models endorsed by dominant discourse.[43] It is such a queer openness that Gino experiences in his oblique existence away from "home," where he encoun-ters Spagnolo and Anita—an openness the film mobilizes as foils to the Italian life embodied by Bragana and Giovanna.

Spagnolo in particular is crucial for the film's political imaginary. This character was wholly invented by the *Cinema* team; he has no analogue in Cain's novel. As Alicata would later explain, Spagnolo is a proletarian living as a street artist in order to disseminate communism across Italy; he got his nickname from enlisting with the anti-Francoist International during the Spanish Civil War.[44] In the Ancona hotel room where they share their first night together, the camera follows Spagnolo's eyes caressing Gino with affection and care. In this scene, one witnesses a coding of the male body that upsets state-sponsored machismo and heterosexuality (Figure 36). The tender intimacy here contrasts with the instinctual and animalistic passions that consume Gino and Giovanna, whether in the inn's kitchen, surrounded by dirty dishes and leftovers, or—as Mira Liehm writes—"in the bedroom with the always unmade bed whose sheets seem to exhale the odor of unwashed bodies."[45] It is true, as Gilles Deleuze points out, that in *Ossessione* homosexuality arises as the chance of salvation from the weight of a stifling past. But it is not merely sex that drives Gino to Spag-nolo. It is also that with his divergent lifestyle, this character displays a form of identity that was incompatible with fascist biopolitics. In this, one could find some resonances with the positions expressed in "Friendship as a Way of Life," a short essay in which Foucault suggests that what is oppositional in same-sex practices is their potential to lead to new forms of relationality. By depicting Spagnolo as a model Italian who differs radically from that performed "offstage" by Benito Mussolini and onscreen by his less charismatic body doubles, *Ossessione* affectively mediates that a new future for Italy would remain foreclosed until the people reconsidered their limited conceptions of living and loving. Spagnolo, and in a less obvious way Anita, evokes all that the regime feared and disavowed: liminality, mobility, ephemerality, and disinterest in childbearing and reproductive futurity.

Away from closed-off and claustrophobic rural Italy, Gino experiments with a different form of existence: an existence in common where the poor look out for each other, that alternative life that Gino had dreamed about with Giovanna while listening to the sound of the ocean in a shell. In Spagnolo's company, the sea—indeed a fluid mesh of possibilities—replaces the barren Po swamplands as background; the melodramatic gives way to a lyrical representation of the lifeworld that Gino has joined. In the most

FIGURE 36. Gino and Spagnolo in bed together, in *Ossessione* (Luchino Visconti, 1943).

emblematic visualization of the message the *Cinema* cell sought to send to the nation, the camera portrays Gino and Spagnolo looking east toward the Adriatic Sea, beyond the space and time of a crumbling Italian empire, beyond the mare nostrum, silently pondering a horizon full of potentialities (Figure 37). The melody of a diegetic flute confirms a tonal shift introduced by the mise-en-scène, and the low-angle shot rockets Gino and Spagnolo toward the sky. They are propelled toward an open future, turning their back on the authority of tradition, figured here by the San Ciriaco Cathedral, and on the precariousness of labor, materialized in the background via the construction workers renovating the church's cupola. A dog, a Blackshirt, two navy sailors, a young man napping on a bench, a man reading a book, a couple kissing: no one is doing anything even remotely productive in the square where Gino and Spagnolo are exploring their prospects. It is an open space filled only with light, the opposite of Bragana's dark, cluttered inn.

Free from work and any social obligations, disconnected from the disciplined temporality of state racism, people are enjoying their time. In this

FIGURE 37. Looking beyond the mare nostrum, in *Ossessione* (Luchino Visconti, 1943).

landscape of potentialities and possibilities, Gino begins to smile—a smile that feels very different from the outbursts of laughter in Visconti's other melodramas. Düttmann insists that in Visconti's films the move beyond the present is effected by an intensification of longing and desire, which materializes in moments of uncontrollable jouissance. In *Ossessione,* on the contrary, the future is accessed through the deactivation of the overblown system of affectivity typical of the melodramatic mode: Gino smiles, for he is free from any form of operatic attachment or investment.

Deleuze's discussion of the formal innovations introduced by Visconti's film becomes relevant at this point.[46] In *Cinema 2: The Time-Image,* Deleuze claims that *Ossessione* subtly but radically transformed filmic realism. In the old realism, characters reacted almost automatically to the situations they face and to the passions they experience. With *Ossessione,* we encounter a new realism where characters do not act immediately on reality but rather take their time to consider the environs they encounter in their meandering. The "voyage-form," Deleuze suggests, turns characters into *voyants,* into seers or clairvoyants, idle visionary beings who gaze upon reality in order to strategize possible new courses of action and systems of passion. This interruption of linear plot progression is a matter not only of film style but also of film politics. It constitutes, following David Martin-Jones, a challenge to the naturalized patterns of behavior that *genre* cinema, in its different national iterations, contributed to securing. In such a challenge one also needs to locate the disruptive charge of utopia. As José Esteban Muñoz suggests in his take on Giorgio Agamben, the *désoeuvrement* (unworking) of established ways of experiencing the world interrupts the "straight" flow of time and movement, opening up reality and the body to possible new uses.[47]

We are now in a position to appreciate the political relevance of the idleness of the lyrical interlude in Ancona. In this suspension of home life, in this shift away from the melodramatic, the still camera gives the spectator time to sense what Spagnolo is trying to make Gino see and hear. Spagnolo, a fortune teller by trade, is trying to make his travel companion realize that the future is right in front of him, in the "then and there." What Spagnolo in fact manifests is the possibility of a happy life away from authority and the police, a life at sea and on the margins; this is also a life beyond the obsession with normality, a life lived on the basis of a different moral and sexual compass. It is a life beyond the affects of melodrama and the promises of Fascism; beyond the symbolic horizon of Italy's racialized aspiration for a home, a family-owned business, a spouse, some children; beyond the relational system that undergirded twenty years of dictatorship. But, as Kadji Amin's *Disturbing Attachments* reminds us, queer futurity—a life away from reassuring social forms—can also feel difficult and demanding.[48] And Gino is not committed enough to want the future. When he accidentally runs into Bragana and Giovanna in Ancona, Gino gets pulled back to the inn and kills Bragana in a staged car crash. In the end, he will have Giovanna all for himself.

Bragana is the character most fond of melodrama in the film: he constantly sings opera and even wins, in a triumph of Italian flags, a talent competition with his performance of Verdi—a composer whose arias about lost homelands were paramount for the development of Italian nationalism. After Bragana's death, Gino and Giovanna start living the existence he sang about, a life where radical change is constantly deferred in the illusory belief that one will eventually find reasons to smile. The longed-for home turns out to be a ghostly space, haunted by the crime committed and by the weight of domesticity. Gino and Giovanna do not have it particularly bad: unlike in De Sica's postwar films such as *Sciuscià* (*Shoeshine,* 1946), *Ladri di biciclette* (*Bicycle Thieves,* 1948), *Miracolo a Milano* (*Miracle in Milan,* 1951), or *Umberto D.* (1952), they have a vehicle, a job, a steady income, and even a nice roof over their heads. Their problem is that by choosing a normal life, they have committed to a routine where one does nothing but work, eat, sleep, and wither away. In a revelatory sequence, the high-angle camera portrays Gino and Giovanna cleaning up after a hard day's work. They appear nailed to the soil they tread on, barely able to lift their feet from the ground. Giovanna eats supper alone in a gloomy and untidy kitchen. The deep staging inventories the clutter surrounding her, conveying an airless atmosphere. Giovanna does realize that the fruit of her mind-numbing labor is not a good life but only more junk, more waste, more fatigue, and more exhaustion. But she has convinced herself, and Gino, that they need to endure the pain and stay at the inn, and keep working for a better future. And as Gino accepts his duty "guarding the house of a departed," as he puts it, the grim reaper appears in the background in the guise of a peasant woman, foreshadowing that there will be no silver lining in the clichéd family melodrama that the couple has settled for. Present on the scene is also the child laborer whom Giovanna has taken in as housemaid. While in postwar neorealism children function as markers of hope—the precise trope that Lee Edelman protests—here the unnamed child who betrays her masters by setting the police on Gino and Giovanna's trails figures the endless cycle of exploitation and revenge that the cult of the "home" conjures.[49]

With the police closing in on them, and the new knowledge that Giovanna is pregnant, the murderous couple finally decides to abandon the inn for good. This move away from their home is radically different from the flight toward utopia that Gino had earlier proposed to Giovanna and experienced with Spagnolo and Anita. The life that Giovanna and Gino are now seeking is not new but merely another iteration of the life they already have. The repetitive landscape Gino and Giovanna drive through and the slow-moving truck blocking their route signal that they are not going anywhere. It is too late for them. As Gino confessed to Spagnolo, he is tired of traveling, of exploring; he just wants a place to start a family and call home. And tragedy strikes precisely as the fantasy of a traditional nuclear family seduces Gino and Giovanna, when they get lost in what Lauren Berlant describes as a relation of "cruel optimism"—the blindly optimistic attachment to a way of living that has already proven itself unsustainable and destructive.[50] As Gino reassures Giovanna, destiny is on their side; it cannot turn its back on soon-to-be parents. But Giovanna gets scared when the truck in front of them makes a sudden maneuver, and she grabs the steering wheel from Gino. Their car skids into the Po River, and Giovanna is killed in the crash. The police arrive on the scene. *Ossessione* comes to a close with a frontal medium shot of the man, in tears, as he is taken away by the police (Figure 38). This is the new Italian man Fascism made. The film began with a quote from Blasetti, and it ends with an allusion to the last frame of Rossellini's *Un pilota ritorna* (*A Pilot Returns*, 1942) (Figure 38), which confirms the effort of *Ossessione* to occupy and hijack the gaze of fascist realism.

William Van Watson has focused precisely on the system of looks that *Ossessione* sets up, analyzing how the camera—from the film's beginning to its conclusion—establishes Gino as the object of everyone's gaze. Bragana, Giovanna, Spagnolo, Anita: they all long for Gino's body. Drawing upon the framework articulated by Laura Mulvey in "Visual Pleasure and Narrative Cinema," Van Watson interprets Gino's status as a body to be looked at as a manifestation of Visconti's homosexuality.[51] While the camera's attraction to Gino is undeniable, it may be limiting to attribute the investment in his body to a displacement of the author's sexual preference. An approach that reduces *Ossessione* to a voyeuristic homosexual spectacle

FIGURE 38. The maimed men Fascism made: Massimo Girotti at the end of Rossellini's *Un pilota ritorna* (1942) and Visconti's *Ossessione* (1943).

and Gino to an objectified fetish risks overlooking the collaborative dimension of the film as well as the insurrectional moment to which it belonged.
Alicata and one of the screenwriters, Gianni Puccini, were in jail when *Ossessione* was released; Visconti would be arrested shortly afterward, during
the Nazi occupation of Rome, and only narrowly avoided execution. By
then, De Santis had gone underground, abandoning his position as Rossellini's assistant director on the later aborted *Scalo merci* (*Freight Yard*) to join
the partisan uprising. In *Ossessione*, Gino is indeed a vexed figure caught
between different gazes, horizons of desire, and systems of intimacy. But
considering the film in the context of the looming antifascist uprising allows
us to appreciate how the visual attachment to the tramp's wavering body
attests less to Visconti's homosexual desires than to the *Cinema* cell's anti-
Fascism, its commitment to assembling a different form of body politic.
In this regard, the gaze that the group chose to celebrate the regime's collapse is significant.

After his father's fall, Vittorio Mussolini was ousted from the editorial
office of *Cinema* by the *Ossessione* team. At that point, the fringe group could
come out of the closet, so to speak, and make explicit the coded nature of its
early interventions: in a collective editorial note, they explain that "cautious
and underground tactics" had guided their work in *Cinema* and national
film, but now the time for secrets and conspiracies was over.[52] In the celebratory issue following the September 8 armistice, when Italy surrendered
unconditionally to the Allies, the group continued its coming out by featuring Spagnolo on the journal's cover (Figure 39).

Spagnolo looks to an off-frame Gino for one last time, his eyes pleading
with him to take charge of his own existence instead of remaining mired
in destructive patterns of behavior. Spagnolo is about to leave for Naples
and Genoa, two crucial hubs of the partisan insurrection against Nazi Fascism, and then for Sicily—the Sicily of the *Cinema* cell interventions on
realism, which in September 1943 had already been liberated by the Allies.
"I came by thinking that maybe you would join. I wanted to go to Sicily.
Sicily is a beautiful *paese*, you know?" Spagnolo tries to entice Gino. But
Gino does not have the courage to explore this emerging and oppositional
paesaggio italiano, to echo the title of De Santis's 1941 manifesto. From the
Cinema cover, then, Spagnolo hails other comrades who might join him in
his journey. His gaze directly addresses the public, which is put into Gino's
position and made to identify with him. Understanding this gaze purely as
sublimated homosexual desire minimizes its force as a call to action and as

FIGURE 39. Spagnolo's eyes call to new comrades, on the celebratory post-armistice and post-Mussolini *Cinema* cover (September–October 1943).

a placeholder for a type of embodiment that exceeds the hegemonic social milieu. In fact, Gino's diegetic failure puts spectators in the spotlight, awakening them to their extradiegetic responsibilities and turning them into historical actors at a moment when the old country has crumbled and a new one is being invented.[53] Hijacking the cinematographic apparatus to denounce the toxicity of present Italian reality, the *Cinema* group urged a people caught between a stifling past and an unwritten future to make a decision: either kill the father and take his place at the head of the home, or understand that the only chance of moving past the evil of fascist normality was to respond to Spagnolo's soft eyes and build a new Italian life together, a lyrical existence unburdened by the chronotopes of melodrama.

The problem is that Spagnolo's address was never given the chance to reach the public. Substantially banned after its May 1943 premiere in Rome, *Ossessione* never enjoyed a proper theatrical release. Its impact on Italian popular culture cannot compare to that of the postwar neorealist films by De Sica or Rossellini. Catherine O'Rawe holds that the film's marginalization in the country's film canon is connected to its formal hybridity. *Ossessione,* she claims, could hardly fit in a mediascape hegemonized by neorealism's pseudodocumentary style. The postwar reception of the film somehow echoed the reactions it had sparked under Fascism: Visconti's debut was too French, too American, too melodramatic, not realistic or Italian enough. The treatment of *Ossessione* as stylistically foreign can also be considered in relation to the geopolitical context in which post-Mussolini Italy found itself—and hence approached as a disavowal of the *Cinema* cell's representation of national life. With its pointed indictment of Fascism as a typically Italian phenomenon, how could *Ossessione* be taken seriously in a nation being urged to forget the past and promptly return to normal life? Given the "Latin repressive phallocracy" of both the Communist and Christian Democratic Parties, to echo Lino Miccichè, how could anyone take the film's queer worldview seriously and follow its lead on the practices that authentic anti-Fascism entails? In this regard, it is important to recall, as Mira Liehm does, that no Italian scholar mentioned Spagnolo's homosexuality until the cultural revolution of the 1960s.[54]

On the basis of Karl Schoonover's reassessment of neorealism's moral conservatism, as well as Giacomo Lichtner's insights on the convenient amnesias that postwar national cinema enables, one could speculate that the failure of *Ossessione* and the success of, for example, Rossellini's films were somehow overdetermined by the political juncture Italy faced in the aftermath of World War II: the ideological vectors of a film like *Roma città aperta* (*Rome Open City*, 1945) resonated better in a country pressured both domestically and internationally to archive Fascism as a momentary parenthesis in the country's history, a temporary blunder rather than a phenomenon with profound roots in the body politic.[55] If the mythos of "good people" that neorealism streamlined was to pass as the truth about the Italian people, *Ossessione* could not be accepted as an authoritative exposé of national life.

In 1945, Elio Marcuzzo, the actor who played Spagnolo, was buried alive by a group of partisan fighters, due to either a tragic mix-up or a personal vendetta. By then, Benito Mussolini had been hanged in Piazza Loreto, Italy had been liberated, and top-ranking members of the dissolved Fascist Party were being reinstated into key social roles. The utopia of the partisan uprising had already faded away. The insurrection against the regime did not bring about radical democracy, and the resistance did not culminate in a social revolution. The subaltern, revolutionary, transnational queer new realism found in *Ossessione* was to give way to "neorealism proper" and to a proper postfascist nation. *Ossessione* was not Italy, Vittorio Mussolini had apocryphally claimed. Nor was it going to be. Returning to the film and to the context from which it emerged, returning one more time to Gino's contested body, thus remain important ways to bring to light the existence, in the archive of film history, of an unrealized future for both Italy and its cinema.

On Neorealism

The Ends of the Resistance and
the Birth of an Area

> Le cinéma américain se fait aujourd'hui en Italie, mais jamais
> le cinéma de la péninsule n'a été plus typiquement italien.
>
> —André Bazin, *Le réalisme cinématographique et*
> *l'école italienne de la liberation*

Through case studies from Italian film under Fascism, in this book I have
shown that cinema is a crucial tool in the production of a docile body politic
as well as a hijackable apparatus for fostering resistance against destructive forms of living and state control. By untangling the complex representations of race, labor, sexuality, and technology in the works examined,
I have argued that devices of mass mediation cannot neatly be identified
as the "strongest weapon" of state biopower. In the formal and affective
disruptions from Vittorio De Sica's genre comedies and Luchino Visconti's
Ossessione (*Obsession,* 1943), I located wayward configurations of desire, subjectivity, and belonging—modes of embodiment that escaped the boundaries of Fascism's racialized identity politics and that deserve attention
especially in a context of media-driven resurgence of ethno-nationalisms.

In what follows, I turn to the aftermath of Mussolini's fall, pausing on
how the established hagiographic memory of postwar Italian realist cinema,
that is, of "neorealism," contributed and still contributes to avert more transformative engagements with the realities of what Fascism was, why it took
root in the country, and how it ended. As Catherine O'Rawe points out, the
centrality of neorealism in imagining Italy, thanks largely to its consolidation in France first by André Bazin and later by Gilles Deleuze, "has remained
relatively unchallenged."[1] Here, I connect neorealism's persistent hegemony

in discussions of modern Italy with the specious accounts of national identity and history that such a category enables. First, I highlight a shared
component in Bazin's and Deleuze's foundational treatments of the cinemas of Rossellini and De Sica: their emphasis on liberated Italy's film as
a revolutionary, antinarrative, speculative register that breaks away from
the deceitful and inauthentic film forms of the past. Then, taking my cue
from Mario Mattòli's *La vita ricomincia* (*Life Begins Anew*, 1945), I suggest
that Bazin's and Deleuze's analyses have remained relatively unchallenged
because they sustain the very system of knowledge upon which contemporary Italy as a geopolitical area under the United States' "remote control" was constituted.[2] In fact, hailing respectively from the inception and
the end of the Cold War, of the sociopolitical reality that ensued from the
Allies' liberation of Europe from Nazi Fascism, Bazin and Deleuze both
sustain the feeling of a redeemed postwar Italy, of a brutalized, subaltern,
childlike population finally set free from the fascist madness and ready to
return—with the appropriate international support—to being its real self,
to go back to being a good people. An unsuccessful framework for discussing film, the trope of neorealism is successful in brushing off the aborted
"de-fascistizzazione" of post-fascist Italy and consequently also the continuity between the totalitarian world and the new world order. Although, as
Bazin conceded, neorealism as such does not exist, it does exist as a mechanism of avoidance.[3]

BAZIN'S FABLES, DELEUZE'S SAMPLES

Neither Bazin nor Deleuze considered neorealism to be a monolithic
phenomenon. Yet in writing about, respectively, the Italian school of the
liberation and the cinema of liberated senses, Bazin and Deleuze alike contributed to cementing neorealism as the crucial turning point in the history
of world cinemas—the moment where the medium's specificity finally manifests itself at the movies.[4] The subsequent global appreciation of postwar
Italian auteurs, in turn, has made it basically impossible to engage with Italian cinema without taking *Roma città aperta* (*Rome Open City*, 1945) or *Ladri
di biciclette* (*Bicycle Thieves*, 1948) as obligatory points of reference. The problem is that when neorealism rises to the status of "*via maestra* of Italian
film," as happens in the book by Millicent Marcus that coalesced Italian
film studies into an academic area in the United States in the 1980s, one
cannot but articulate normative accounts of the country's cinema, accounts

that reduce everything to anticipations, returns, or betrayals of Rossellini's or De Sica's aesthetics.[5]

In order to overcome the situation caused by viewing Italian film history in the light of neorealism, Alan O'Leary and Catherine O'Rawe proposed shunning neorealism and auteur cinema, so to redirect critical attention to the much-overlooked and often-vilified national commercial production.[6] However, while a reassessment of the politics and history of Italian genre fiction is indeed crucial, by simply ignoring neorealism one eschews the opportunity to upset the categories grounding other areas of inquiry, like the geopolitical area "Italy," or the disciplinary area "Italian film studies," or even, more fundamentally, the area of cinema studies itself, given the role that neorealism has played in defining what cinema is.

To effect a more radical reassessment of what Italy and cinema are, rather than forgetting neorealism, it might be therefore useful to *deconstruct* it—to simultaneously put pressure on this category and account for its success. Accordingly, I want to try to understand what, if anything, is this "neorealism" that Deleuze and Bazin so enthusiastically reviewed, before speculating on why we keep falling for engagements with national film that are as imprecise as they are influential. In fact, notwithstanding the radically different philosophical traditions they belong to—put simply, Christian humanism versus Nietzschean post-structuralism—Bazin and Deleuze approach their archives in a quite similar manner: it is by purging all traditional aspects from the corpus of postwar Italian cinema and telling tales about actual Italian films that they can turn Rossellini and De Sica into the heralds of a post-totalitarian redemption of cinema. As far as Bazin is concerned, the mythical foundations of his whole film theory become evident when one ponders the organic link that his 1948 essay "An Aesthetic of Reality" draws between the new Italian cinematic realism and the old realist films made under the regime.

To refute the impression that De Sica's and Rossellini's masterpieces miraculously emerged from the rotten corpse of Fascism, Bazin argues that the Italian school of the liberation was anticipated by preliberation realist films by Alessandro Blasetti, Rossellini, De Robertis, and Mario Camerini. Bazin assures his readers that Italian cinema in the 1930s had moved beyond the silent monumentality of *Quo Vadis?* (Enrico Guazzoni, 1913) and *Cabiria* (Giovanni Pastrone, 1914), films whose complicity with nationalist and imperialist agendas was apparent. He also affirms that Blasetti's fantasy film *La corona di ferro* (*The Iron Crown,* 1941), with its affected rhetoric, tasteless decor, reliance on celebrities, conventional scenario, and disregard for naturalistic acting, did not represent the true "characteristics of films made beyond the Alps."[7] To find authentic Italian cinema, a cinema that stayed true to Italy's core character, one has to move away from studios and sets.

In Cinecittà, escapism and propaganda ruled. Outside the fascist-founded studios, however, in Bazin's account, directors were shooting without following strict scripts and thus capturing life as it unfolded in front of the camera and not through the mediation of political preconceptions or an a priori thesis. It is on the basis of these imprecise insights that Bazin praises Camerini, De Robertis, and Blasetti's films I have discussed in this book. Since (again according to Bazin) they were to a large extent improvised and shot on location—in the streets and on the sea—for Bazin these films freed themselves from the fascist gaze, starting to move closer to reality and truth. This characteristically Italian interest in reality that already manifested with Blasetti, Rossellini, and Camerini under Mussolini sprouted after the regime's demise. As a matter of fact, in "An Aesthetic of Reality," neorealism stands out as the blooming of cinematic practices already present at the margins of the fascist film industry. Until Italy's entry into World War II, realist films were "modest violets flowering at the feet of the grand sequoias" of the cultural industry.[8] Then, as the resistance to Nazi Fascism grew and the regime's forest of lies burned down, accurate chronicles of national life started blossoming across Italy. The liberation further nourished this Italian aesthetic of reality, and finally allowed the cinematographic apparatus to fully develop its potential and specificity as a medium. At that point, De Sica's and Rossellini's liberated cinema flowered, changing film forever.

Bazin's history of Italian film might appear straightforward, but with its flurry of naturalistic metaphors it conceals important theoretical moves. Not only does Bazin craft a normative outlook on Italian film by claiming that realism is its defining trait. He also imbues what he considers proper Italian cinema with a necessary progressive dimension. In fact, Bazin insists that the choice to privilege improvisation, location shooting, nonprofessional actors, and long takes allows the camera to rid itself of the studio system's ideological scripts and, as a result, attain a higher degree of authenticity and proximity to the real. He then posits that the realist impulse informing such a typically Italian zero-degree style is incompatible with capitalist or political idiocies (*bêtises*), sanctioning it as a refuge of culture and intelligence that stands strong against the compromised vision dominating commercial cinema. Such an enticing proposal regarding the revolutionary ethics of new and old Italian realisms and the essence of national cinema hinges on a very dubious claim: that when it comes to Italy, the move away from studios and toward reality, to use Bazin's terminology, has historically favored modes of behavior and forms of identification that are incompatible with capitalist violence and political oppression. This conclusion is untenable. "An Aesthetic of Reality"—which is possibly the most consequential intervention in the history of neorealism specifically and film criticism more broadly—misses completely how Blasetti's and Camerini's social realism, or De Robertis's and Rossellini's racial melodramas, were unquestionably complicit with the regime's biopolitical efforts and perfectly in sync with Mussolini's projects of internal colonization and external colonialism.

Bazin's misreading of Italian film history is so egregious that it appears more than a mere blunder. It is instead a constitutive blindness that is paramount for the system of insight Bazin sets up. It is as if Bazin cannot even contemplate the existence of a fascist realist cinema because its very existence would challenge the terms of his whole ontology of cinema. Both Bazin's Manichean dismissal of genre fiction and his insistence on realism as an antitotalitarian cinematic mode become untenable once one acknowledges that the audiovisual forms and narrative strategies characteristic of liberated Italy had earlier contributed to the making of the Blackshirt race.[9]

However, it is not quite simply a matter of reckoning—speculatively and historically—with the role of old Italian realism in Mussolini's racialized identity politics, of reconsidering the politics of genre fiction, and of correcting Bazin accordingly. As soon as elements of continuity between neorealist aesthetic and fascist cinema become apparent, additional cracks appear in Bazin's framework. In this regard, Christopher Wagstaff and Karl Schoonover further challenge Bazin's mythicization of neorealism by signaling that the new Italian realism itself is less progressive (Schoonover) and unscripted (Wagstaff) than Bazin posited. Although they engage with Bazin from very different angles and with very different methodologies, Schoonover and Wagstaff reach a similar conclusion: Bazin can transform postwar Italian film into a revolution of cinema; he can invent what Wagstaff dubs the "institution of neorealism" only through a very partial account of the works he analyzes.[10] There is a strategic forgetting of the realities of Italian cinema at play in the foundational "An Aesthetic of Reality," and a similar form of selective memory in Deleuze's authoritative treatment of neorealism.

For Cesare Casarino, Deleuze convincingly identified neorealism as a cinema of absence and potentiality:

> whereas the primary political import of pre-war cinema consisted in the presence of the people . . . the political import of post-war cinema lies precisely in drawing attention to the conspicuous absence of the people, in knowing how to show that the people are what is missing.[11]

Yet, as Jacques Rancière and Alessia Ricciardi emphasize, the films associated with neorealism carried out a more complex operation.[12] Cinema, once again, highlighted the absence of a united Italian people; it insisted on differences, fractures, and friction in the nation's body. At the same time, it also tried to affectively gather the population together by providing a lost country with a new sense of belonging and identity, of position in history and the world after the end of Nazi Fascism. Do *Roma città aperta* and *Ladri di biciclette* exhibit a historical incapacity to act, or are they instead slow explorations of how Italians should dwell in the new historical reality that the Allies were busy assembling? Do these films witness the liberation of sense organs from sensory–motor reflex arcs or do they engender appropriate ways of reacting to the new world order: the world order of American hegemony, opposing blocs, post-racial racism, neocolonialism and neocapitalism, geopolitical areas and area studies?

Rancière and Ricciardi do not contest the presence of idleness ("time-images," in Deleuze's terms) in *Roma città aperta* or in other postwar Italian films. They do insist, however, that Deleuze neglects the interplay of these speculative moments with bursts of action, resoluteness, decisiveness, and motion. On the one hand, Deleuze brilliantly illuminates certain specific sequences that, with their "hieratic slowness" and uneventful episodic meandering, prompt the pensive spectator to linger on the very act of seeing.[13] On the other hand, the sequences that Deleuze discusses do not exist in isolation. One can fully appreciate what these moments accomplish, how they affect bodies and brains, only by treating them as components of the larger textual machines of which they are a part. Instead, Deleuze samples a few scenes from each film and then reedits them into his own director's cut of world cinema history. In a sense, Deleuze's *Cinema* volumes are extraordinary works of montage, where a continuous metonymic displacement presents particular *objets petit a* as representative of the whole.

This very technique of sampling is what allows Deleuze to limn a neo-realist canon identified by five distinctive features (dispersive situation, weak narrative links, voyage form, consciousness of clichés, and condemnation of a plot).[14] The very use of isolated images and moments as emblematic metonymies is also what causes Deleuze to lose sight of the films he discusses. A woman's hand on her pregnant belly stands for De Sica's *Umberto D.* (1952). A carnival party stands for Federico Fellini's *I vitelloni* (*The Bullocks*, 1953). The arrival of Rocco's family in Milan stands for Visconti's *Rocco e i suoi Fratelli* (*Rocco and His Brothers*, 1960). Only through a generalized forgetting of the bigger picture, so to speak, can Deleuze conclude that neorealism's innovation consists in the transformation of film characters into wanderers and seers who are more committed to studying the world than acting in it. After all, postwar Italian films' *balades* (strolls) do lead somewhere. No matter how slowly they unfold, how dispersive the reality they mirror, how trivial their scripts, or how reflexive they are, the films that Deleuze samples do not merely register unprecedented audiovisual situations. They also model specific forms of living and particular patterns of behavior within the context of a history that is still the history of racial capitalism. In the final instance, then, by rewriting Italian films, Deleuze also rewrites the basic social function of the cinematographic apparatus in the wake of World War II, remediating it from a weapon of social reproduction and geopolitical governmentality into the first new technology of a liberated form of human life.

To tell the fable of cinema's evolution from realist aspiration to revolutionary humanism, Bazin represses the generic aspects of Rossellini's and De Sica's works. In order to stage neorealism as the event ripening cinema's speculative potential, Deleuze occludes the force with which Pina (Anna Magnani) from *Roma città aperta* and other famous characters from post-Mussolini Italian cinema respond and react to the realities they confront. Bazin feared that traditional narrative techniques would prevent cinema from achieving the phenomenological dream of a pure rendering of all of reality's ambiguities. To preserve the very myth of a total cinema he elsewhere mocked, he erased from the filmic corpus of De Sica and Rossellini every stain of conventionality and directorial manipulation.[15] Deleuze displayed a similar mistrust of classic narrative economy—which he considered inducing naturalized behaviors—and forced Italian auteurs to stand for the possibility of a modernist cinema that evaded truisms about the world and scrutinized all commonplaces about it. There is a common anxiety about cinematographic writing, about storytelling, at the center of Bazin's and Deleuze's understanding of post-fascist Italian films. Surprisingly enough, Cesare Zavattini, the author of so many neorealist scenarios, expressed a similar suspicion of plot.

By 1952, critics were claiming that neorealism had exhausted its energies. When interviewed on the matter, though, Zavattini provided a different account of its life cycle: neorealism was not dead; it had never been born. Even the presumed strongholds of neorealism were in fact insufficiently neorealist because these films still relied on plots to communicate the large or small facts of everyday life.[16] Neorealist directors knew all too well that life could not be captured through artifice and that cinema's business was not to tell stories, to peddle fictions. Accordingly, they had explored strategies to allow life to expose itself, unmediated, to the camera. Alas, for Zavattini, no one had yet succeeded in such an enterprise. Rossellini, De Sica, and Visconti had started the battle to capture reality, and now there was an army of directors behind them ready to go on the attack and win the neorealist war. The victory, however, would not bring about a liberation *of* cinema but rather a liberation *from* cinema. For Zavattini, the birth of neorealism proper would imply the elimination of film as we know it: directors, producers, screenwriters, actors—all these roles had to be renounced. Thus, to achieve neorealism, to translate neorealism from manifestos to reels, one would have to reject the cinematic apparatus altogether.

Even Bazin was aware that the birth of neorealism would entail the death of film. Believing he had found neorealism in *Ladri di biciclette,* he commented: "No more actors, no more story, no more sets, which is to say that in the perfect aesthetic illusion of reality there is no more cinema."[17] But in later writing, he retraced his steps and admitted to making "some rather naïve statements in the past."[18] Bazin, in the end, cannot but concede that even in De Sica one can only find glimpses of what neorealism might be—two or three sequences that in *Umberto D.* bear witness to a cinema that has renounced fiction.[19] Neorealism begins when plot ends: Bazin, Zavattini, and Deleuze would agree on this. Only beyond the threshold of subjective mediation do authentic cinema and realism become possible. Such a crossing—unrealistic as it is—remains a categorical imperative, the urgency that forces theories of neorealism to speak in the future tense.

In Bazin, such a futurity takes the geometrical shape of an asymptote, the curve that approaches another line without ever connecting with it. To achieve realism, Bazin writes in 1952, one must strive to make cinema the asymptote of reality, "in order that life might in this perfect mirror be visible poetry."[20] By acknowledging that cinema can only approach reality, without ever being able to touch it, Bazin also admits that realism is only an aspiration, cinema's persistent dream. But if integral realism is always "to come," then it becomes difficult to pin down precise criteria through which one could discriminate between faithful and unfaithful captures of reality onscreen, objective and partisan takes on the world, works moved by a humanist impulse, and films informed by political motivations—neorealist and non-neorealist movies.[21]

But "An Aesthetic of Reality" already showed signs of Bazin's own hesitations in regard to the actual import and existence of a neorealist ethico-aesthetic revolution. Consider the fraught reading that Bazin's 1948 essay offers of *Paisà* (*Paisan*, 1946). In the body of the text, Bazin treats Rossellini's film as the gold standard of neorealist cinema, excavating its secrets and mining from it the norms of authentic Italian national film. At the same time, in a note, Bazin acknowledges that there are *demi-mensonges* (half lies) in Rossellini and that *Paisà* is not an unadulterated account of social reality. It would not be silly (*dupe*), Bazin suggests, to detect in the film a pro-American stance and an a priori take on the real.[22] Yet, after this concession, after admitting there are fictions and politics in *Paisà,* after admitting the film is not an objective chronicle but an ideological script, Bazin somehow goes on to argue that *Paisà* is still more "sociological" than "political," that is, an objective work rather than a partisan intervention, insofar as Rossellini's film is more concerned with capturing reality as is than with imposing a particular meaning on it.

Notwithstanding this convoluted attempt to save his own take on *Paisà* and consequently his whole film theory, Bazin cannot hide that—as in Pirandello's *Quaderni di Serafino Gubbio operatore*—as long as human hands control the movie camera, film will be a human, and thus imperfect, partial, political, interested, "fictional" representation of reality.[23] Only a redeemed humanity that has rejected all prejudices, biases, divisions, stereotypes, and subject positions will be able to invent a cinema that is true to its originating dream and finally mirrors life as it is, without telling stories about it. Yet even Bazin knows that such a liberation of the human race will not be possible while human beings remain under the yoke of capitalist political economy. So long as we are capitalist subjects, that is, bodies subjected to racialized biopolitics and racial imaginaries, neorealism as such cannot exist; it can only remain a fiction.

In Deleuze, there are no traces of the Christian overtones informing Bazin's longing for a pure humanity and pure images. Nevertheless, in his treatment of neorealism one can still hear the ring of futurity. It is true that Deleuze presents his take on postwar Italian cinema as a radical displacement of "An Aesthetic of Reality" four decades after its publication. Yet it is also true that Deleuze radicalizes Bazin's film fables, emphasizing the lack of preexisting schemas through which neorealism approaches reality and evoking the specific cinematic intelligence of the people behind this new stage in the history of human imagination. As a matter of fact, Deleuze's *Cinema* volumes offer not only a taxonomy of different species of images; they also propose an axiology of life marked by a specific evolutionary progression, an asynchronous and yet progressive history in which neorealism attests to the human brain's unbound potential for speculation.

We have seen that for Deleuze certain images are closer to speculation than other film forms; they are more just, more thought-provoking, more philosophical, and have more intellectual value. Instead of making spectators jump to conclusions and leap into action, some images lead people to pause and reflect. Since these smarter images are, for Deleuze, organically connected to the geohistorical milieux from which they originate, their differential complexity and reflectivity also manifest something about the community that generated them. The modes of the imaginary, in other words, can be brought back to the plane of effective history and used to profile its protagonists. It is the thoughtfulness of different historical forms of life that Deleuze's volumes thus end up classifying, using film forms as the markers to assess each of them.[24] But if this is true, what are the features of the people responsible for neorealism's speculative images?

Deleuze posits that the time-image emanates from bodies that ponder the world rather than automatically reacting to it on the basis of hegemonic clichés or established habits. Hence, a purely speculative film could be realized only by a life absolutely idle and autonomous, by an existence freed from the ideologies and behavioral patterns imposed by the needs of economic production and social reproduction. It is for this precise reason that Deleuze cannot help but connect neorealism with a science-fiction imaginary that takes us beyond the horizon of labor and the universe of racial capitalism. Deleuze's discussion of the time-image begins with a pregnant

Italian maid working in a Rome apartment and ends with a white American interplanetary traveler whose only occupation is watching himself eating, dying, and being reborn as a star child. This child is naked; it could not have been otherwise, since this new white life has been liberated from any habitus whatsoever. In order for neorealism to be a cinema of time-images, the white people who were responsible for it ought to be as bare and idle as the absolute life born at the end of *2001: A Space Odyssey* (1968). In the last scene of Stanley Kubrick's film on the origins and ends of white humanity (notably, there are no Black characters in this journey), "the sphere of the fetus and the sphere of the earth have the chance of entering into a new, incommensurable, unknown relation, which would convert death into a new life."[25] Somehow, it seems to me, Deleuze leans on neorealism to suggest that the futuristic evolution of white lives that *2001* features in the midst of the 1960s is not mere science fiction but a concrete historical possibility that first manifested itself in Italy's past: from Blackshirt death to time-images, and beyond.

Bazin held that the Italian school of the liberation was the cinema of a redeemed people. For Deleuze, it appears to be the film form appropriate for new species of living beings. In both cases, the evolution of cinema that neorealism would manifest can only occur after a radical reclamation of Italian life from its racial configuration under Fascism. Deleuze's emphasis on neorealism as a cinema that starts from zero unmistakably resonates with Bazin's insistence on neorealism as the cinema of a recently reborn country, of a nation that is only a few years old. Liberated Italy stands out, in Bazin and Deleuze, as a sort of miraculous void in which the essence of humanity, or the potential of a superhuman life, is set free. Their neorealism is made to attest to an epochal moment in the history of Western humanity: a metamorphosis, an evolution that is a revolution, a blank slate untouched by the evil of either capitalistic savagery or naturalized habit. It only takes a closer look at their frameworks to register that Bazin and Deleuze are writing about a zero cinema, a zero nation, and a zero people that in fact did not exist—but that we keep falling for.

FEELING FOR ITALY

Neorealism stands strong. Despite the many voices that have problematized this category, discussions of Italy and Italian film can hardly avoid the reference to this elusive, and yet fundamental, redemption of cinema. Why is this the case? Why is it almost impossible to experience the geopolitical

area known as Italy away from neorealism's blinding light, even if it is unclear what neorealism actually is and which films, if any, comprise its
canon? The attachment to a term that is manifestly fraught and aporetic
goes beyond being an ingrained habit in film discourse that could simply
be corrected. Hence, it seems important to complement treatments of
what Charles Leavitt calls the "repeated occlusions implicit in neorealism's
accepted definitions" with an explanation of why an institution with such
unsound foundations nevertheless stands so strong.[26]

Might it be that the weaknesses in neorealism as a concept, its historical
imprecisions and theoretical indecisions, are precisely what have made it
successful? In this regard, the most crucial insight into neorealism's critical hegemony belongs to Peter Bondanella, who insisted that the intertwined misrepresentation of fascist cinema and emphasis on Rossellini's
and De Sica's aesthetico-politico newness should be connected with the
need to isolate the regime from national history and establish a clear break
between totalitarianism and democracy.[27] In Bazin's "An Aesthetic of Reality," we read that the war in Italy was the end of an era, the conclusion of
an epoch. The centrality of neorealism in discussions of anything Italian
would derive, then, from its power to hide continuities between the fascist
and post-fascist nation—between the race that Italians were under Mussolini and the people they became after his fall; between the racial imaginaries and racist structures that characterize totalitarian biopolitics and
those ruling over a neoliberal society. Christina Sharpe emphasizes the need
to read the history of Western modernity in the wake of racism and colonization, that is, to read Western history in its structural complicity with
racial capitalism.[28] The category of neorealism, with its "year zero" mythologies, forecloses precisely the possibility of such a *wake work*—amplifying
the convenient fantasy that the Allies' liberation of Europe from Nazi Fascism constituted a turning point for the West and thus the start of something new and beautiful for the whole human race. But how could things
radically change, how could discriminations and hierarchies among human
beings be redressed if the capitalist-colonial order and white supremacy
with it remained unfazed?

I am not arguing that Bazin and Deleuze consciously suppressed Fascism's deep roots in Italian *and* Western history. Instead, I suggest that
Bazin and Deleuze were somehow duped—to use a term dear to Bazin—by
Italian cinema and ended up enabling specious tropes about Italy and Italians that are fundamental to a very specific postwar geopolitical ordering.

Bazin's and Deleuze's explicit confrontations with Italian film are also making implicit claims on the essence of the Italian people and their standing in the world.

In the note from "An Aesthetic of Reality" discussing *Paisà*, Bazin remarks on the relation between the film forms characteristic of proper Italian national cinema and Italy's national character. He claims that neorealism avoids artificiality, politics, and division in part because of Italians' "ethnic temperament." In a later passage from the original version of "An Aesthetic of Reality" that does not appear in the canonical English translation of the essay, Bazin reiterates that neorealism's liberation from classic cinematographic writing is somehow connected with the "génie ethnique"—the ethnic genius, spirit—that is proper to Italy.[29] So while Bazin writes about neorealism as a cinema of humanity liberated from divisions, he cannot avoid the specter of ethnic racism as he reintroduces naturalized specificities and differences between peoples and communities. In fact, Bazin's essay obliquely implies that Italians have the natural disposition to dwell closer to reality, and that this proximity to the real entails a familiarity with each other and with the world that allows them to renounce artificial divisions and focus on what is naturally common to the whole human race. It would be this very Italian simplicity that—once past the fascist blunder— pushed national cinema to embrace a raw, universalistic aesthetics.

Bazin's outlook on Italians' ethnic character, with its obvious resonances with the "Italian good people" discourse, might appear flattering at first sight. Yet one should be wary of Bazin's association of Italians with nature as well as his emphasis on their spontaneous simplicity and natural community bonds. These discourses rehash stereotypes about southern people's "rawness" and "unscriptedness" that, Gayatri Chakravorty Spivak elucidates, give rise to precise hierarchies between world locations and cultures.[30] Italian neorealism, for Bazin, is only a starting point, the beginning of a new life for cinema that other peoples and other national cinemas must sustain: given that Italian neorealism remained only an aspiration—often giving in to the temptations of genre fiction, melodrama, and sentimentalism—more sophisticated ethnicities, peoples with a more refined ethnic temperament, that is, the Americans and French, are by "An Aesthetic of Reality" implicitly assigned the task of bringing to maturity the immediate, unmediated cinematic intuitions that emerged naturally and organically, almost out of a biological or geological necessity, in Italy. The essay's effort to position Italy in a geopolitical area under U.S. sway becomes apparent in its conclusion, another section that is trimmed in the English translation by Hugh Gray for the University of California Press. Here, Bazin argues that what a film like *Paisà* showcases is the symbiotic relation between American and Italian civilizations: the cinema made in Italy in the postwar period, he writes, is simultaneously the most typically Italian filmic expression *and* American cinema.[31] So, in a certain sense, being an ethnically authentic Italian means, for Bazin, becoming Americanized.

In Deleuze, one can find similar regressive tropes about Italian identity and character as well as a similar need to embed Italy in the Western spiritual community. Ricciardi writes:

> Under Deleuze's gaze, the entire tradition of European modern cinema comes to seem a coherent and, to an extent, even a progressively evolved whole. The French philosopher attributes to the Italian neorealist directors an intuitive grasp of the new time-image that eventually advances to a reflective, intellectual awareness in the work of the *auteurs* of the French *Nouvelle Vague* at the end of the 1950s.[32]

Ricciardi righteously criticizes the indisputable biases that Bazin's and Deleuze's tales of world cinema manifest. Yet by arguing that the French critics were duped by Italian cinema, I want to suggest that their infantilizing gaze on Italy is itself, at least in part, the result of the Orientalizing tales about the Italian liberation and liberated Italians that national cinema itself circulated. As Schoonover holds, the films that we traditionally associate with the neorealist revolution precisely essentialized Italy as a childlike country that was not autonomous but in need of external support to mature and realize its full potential. Paradoxically, Italians emerged better from the war than how they had entered it, Noa Steimatsky comments— they were not thugs anymore but a people to be pitied.[33] Thanks largely to Italian film, Italians were remediated as a poor, simple, good-hearted, "worthy" ethnicity who temporarily fell for mad leaders and a monstrous ideology but then endured terrible sacrifices to make amends.

Steimatsky has noted how harsh neorealist films used the ruined landscape left behind by Fascism's downfall to project a brutal but redeeming experience of Italian history and identity.[34] What went unnoticed until Schoonover's *Brutal Vision* is that this way of feeling for Italy contributed to Italy's postwar normalization and provided a visual authorization of the Marshall plan and of U.S. meddling in national affairs, playing a crucial role in the consolidation of a North Atlantic political space in the aftermath of World War II.

The dead bodies of Benito Mussolini, Claretta Petacci, Nicola Bombacci, Achille Starace, and Alessandro Pavolini were hung upside-down and exhibited in Piazzale Loreto in Milan on July 29, 1945. On that same day, the German occupation forces and the Salò puppet state surrendered unconditionally to the Allies in Caserta. The war and the occupation were finally over. But summer 1945 also ended the resistance, and with it the fight for a radically new Italian futurity. As Francesco Filippi explains, given the country's position as a border zone between East and West, Global North and Global South, but also the presence on national soil of the strongest Communist Party in Western Europe, the forces in charge of the pacification of the country deemed it essential for both the new world order and the reproduction of capitalist supremacy—that is, of white supremacy—to avoid probing too deeply into twenty years of Blackshirt command.[35] After the Allies took control of Italy, the pressure to return to normal life mounted; it was no longer time for the revolutionary passions that had animated the years of the resistance and the civil war. It was time to go back to normalcy, to go back to being hard workers and one big happy family. It was time to go back to the status quo.

Released a few months after Mussolini's execution, less subtle and accomplished than other interventions dealing with the transition from totalitarianism to democracy, Mattòli's *La vita ricomincia* is a more transparent manifestation of the ways "neorealism" enables a strategic forgetting of history that streamlines the image of a benevolent United States and leads Italians straight back to work, straight back to heteronormativity. Written by Aldo De Benedetti, *La vita ricomincia* insists on the dialectical relation between truth and justice, articulating in the most explicit way the advantages of extracting from a devastated history a story of ruins that would allow the nation to move on and rebuild, under the watchful and benevolent eyes of the United States.

Mattòli's film takes place in postwar Rome and features two of the Ventennio's most celebrated film stars: Fosco Giachetti and Alida Valli. Paolo Martini (Giachetti) makes it back home after six years spent in a British detention camp in India, witnessing in his homecoming the devastation the regime had left behind (Figure 40). Fortunately, under the control of the U.S. military police, normality seems to have been restored. Yet the specters of the past come back to haunt the present. The police arrest

Paolo's wife, Patrizia (Valli), on a charge of murder. While her husband was
away, a wicked noblewoman of German descent convinced Patrizia to turn
to sex work to earn the money she lacked to buy medicine for her son, who
was suffering from a strange and incomprehensible illness. However, one of
Patrizia's clients wanted to keep seeing her even after the return of her husband. During a heated exchange, Patrizia confronts the man and kills him.

Patrizia is eventually found innocent, the trial by jury establishing that
she acted in self-defense. And after some thinking, Paolo forgives Patrizia
insofar as whatever she did was in a state of emergency. As their Neapolitan philosophy professor friend (Eduardo De Filippo) explains, the past is
the past, and it is now time to focus on rebuilding a normal future out of
a devastated present. This absolution does not apply only to Patrizia. It is
Italy's entire population that *La vita ricomincia* prompts the public (national
and global) to understand, forgive, and forget at the behest of a philosopher from Naples. In the film, De Filippo plays the part of a Benedetto Croce
in disguise, and Mattòli popularizes the liberal philosopher's views on Fascism as a passing phenomenon in Italian history, contributing to a process
of social normalization and geopolitical realignment based on a colossal
denial of what Fascism actually was.

In the fall 1943 *New York Times* think piece I mentioned at the beginning
of this book, Croce admitted that the vast majority of the Italian people

FIGURE 40. Ruined Italy in *La vita ricomincia* (Mario Mattòli, 1945).

had collaborated with Fascism. Such an admission of the nation's involvement with Mussolini was far from an assumption of responsibility. Croce in fact specified that Fascism was a foreign virus that had taken over a people, implying that they could not be held responsible for what they had done while sick. Foucault also resorted to a medical imaginary to define Fascism's relation with democracy. But while Foucault presents Fascism as a "disease of power," something connected with how political economy works—that is, with the racism structurally embedded in Western biopolitical modernity—for Croce it is a fluke that occasionally happens to liberal democracies and does not require any radical questioning of the people and communities falling for it. What Fascism requires is, for Croce, actually an uncompromising anticommunism because the fascist sickness can catch on only when consciousness has already been compromised by the germs of Karl Marx's materialism. In a 1944 follow-up intervention, Croce explicated the consequences of this transformation of Fascism from counterrevolution seeking to secure the capitalist order into a sort of seasonal illness taking root where Marxism has weakened the liberal ethos.[36] Since Fascism comes from the outside and does not normally belong in the Italian body politic, since appropriate remedies have been put in place to eradicate this malaise but also communism, there is no point is setting up tribunals to try fascists or Fascism.

La vita ricomincia repeats the structure of admission of guilt followed by denial of responsibility that informs Croce's interventions. Patrizia acted under German influence and out of necessity: she was misguided by the foreign noblewoman, but at the same time she could not allow her son to die, nor could she agree to sell her body again after the emergency had been resolved. Nor could Paolo be held responsible for what happened to his family and to his country: he had been detained in a British camp since 1939, the very year the Pact of Steel was signed. Because he was captured before Italy's entry in World War II, he presumably has no blood on his hands (but here the fundamental avoidance is, again, that of colonialism). Lastly and most importantly, the absolution affects all Italians. Whatever they did, the philosopher lectures, they did it to survive. In *La vita ricomincia*—which placed second at the box office in 1945–46, after *Roma città aperta*—spectatorial pleasure comes through a pseudo-confession that leads to acquittal.

The idea that Italians were not responsible for the ruination brought upon them is obviously a self-exonerating account of the nation's history, a historical fiction that is common in the neorealist canon.[37] Yet, while *Roma città aperta* and *Paisà* cloak their ideological maneuvering to the point that their absolutions of Italians dupe even Bazin and Deleuze, *La vita ricomincia* does nothing to hide its address to the nation. Through De Filippo, Mattòli's film literally tells Italians what they should be doing: letting bygones be bygones. There is no hesitation or qualm or doubt or remorse here; the only valid feeling is the desire to return to normal life, to the productive existences we had and the reproductive families we were before all this. "Chi ha avuto ha avuto ha avuto, chi ha dato ha dato ha dato, scordiamoci il passato, siamo di Napoli paisà" (Who has had has had has had, who has given has given has given, let's forget about the past—we are from Naples paisan), states a famous Neapolitan song from 1944—lyrics that the Neapolitan philosophy professor in Mattòli's film repeats almost verbatim. We should keep in mind that this film was written by De Benedetti, a Jewish man who faced discrimination under the regime, and thus in this call to forget and return to a prelapsarian "before," we could also pick up on the traumatized experience of someone for whom the times before Fascism were indeed safer. However, in forgetting and moving on, one is also leaving the regime unaddressed, and thus allowing the entanglement between fascist racism and larger, ongoing dynamics of Western history to remain unnoticed.

Yet it is not merely sociopolitical history that *La vita ricomincia* encourages its viewers to forgive and forget. The memory of past Italian cinema undergoes a similar suppression: Valli and Giachetti—among the most popular stars of fascist cinema—were hailed as stars of the new democratic Italy. "Nothing, it's life that starts again as before. Nothing happened, nothing took place," suggests the philosophy professor at the end of the film. The past has indeed disappeared into irrelevance, and the political responsibility of the Italian cinematographic apparatus in this past has likewise been eluded rather than confronted.

Notwithstanding the initial call for change, the film industry was left unbothered by the processes of "de-fascistizzazione," and the purge commission chaired by Umberto Barbaro, Mario Chiari, Mario Camerini, Mario Soldati, and Luchino Visconti granted substantial amnesties. Although Pavolini, the fascist Minister of Popular Culture, had been hanged at Piazzale Loreto, directors who had made films to suit the exigencies of the regime were steadily reintegrated into the nation's cultural industry. Simultaneously, the most radical voices of anti-Fascism at the movies, those authors

and intellectuals who denounced the persistence of more subtle and dis-
creet forms of social control and violence within the country, were being
isolated and marginalized. In 1947, Ruth Ben-Ghiat reconstructs, a young
and eager Giulio Andreotti launched a mini-purge of communist intellectuals within the film industry. For the postwar governance of Italians, the
perspectives of people like Barbaro, Visconti, or De Santis were deemed
more troubling than the presence of high-ranking fascist officials in key
positions within the film establishment—or the Italian state, for that matter.
Normal life had indeed begun again. The process of normalization was fast.
While no one spoke openly in favor of conservation and restoration, while
culture and the arts—Leavitt shows—sustained illusions of radical renewal,
a radicalization of Italian life and Italian cinema was actively prevented from
taking place.[38]

But if liberated Italian film favored a conservative agenda and foreclosed
the horizon of radical hope and radical change that the resistance conjured,
how does one explain the fact that the Communist Party was the greatest
proponent of the neorealist myth? The answer to this question was provided by Mario Cannella in the early 1970s, in an important essay where he
investigates the fetishistic attachment to neorealism displayed by communist critics in democratic Italy. According to Cannella, the identification of
"a series of organic links" between neorealism and the antifascist resistance
allowed the Communist Party to claim a moral authority over national life
after the Christian Democratic Party had achieved political hegemony in
the country.[39] By indulging in the ideological fantasy of neorealism as a
cultural revolution, leftist criticism found a way to repress the role that
culture and intellectuals (many of whom were now enlisted in the Communist Party) played during the fascist regime. Here we come to the heart
of the matter, says Cannella: the myth that throughout the fascist era, Italian
culture had remained neutral and that it rose up again thanks to the communist resistance.

Within the context of this bipartisan agreement to avoid the nation's
recent past, neorealism was, and still is, authorized as representative of a
new Italy that had finally broken with the papier-mâché regime of misrepresentation perpetuated by fascist cinema. In the final instance, Italy cannot
but be associated with neorealism because neorealism is used as a token
of the people's redemption, a redemption upon which Italy's geopolitical
realignment and its repositioning under U.S. tutelage was predicated. The
legend of neorealism as zero-degree cinema legitimizes the idea of 1945

as Italy's year zero, and vice versa. These two "zero" mythologies are grounded in a similar twofold avoidance: the relegation of Fascism and its film culture to the realm of inauthenticity (authoritarianism, falsehood, superficial consensus); and the pretense that the sociopolitical dynamics and racialized structures of feeling that brought Fascism to power had vanished with Mussolini's execution. But if they didn't, how different could the color of liberated Italy be from the Blackshirt whiteness of the ethnonation that waged war against Ethiopia and then the world?

Given the reticence in interrogating the relation between Italy's racist past and present, it is not surprising that less apologetic takes on the "good people" into which the Blackshirt racial assemblage suddenly metamorphosed—like the compilation documentaries *Giorni di gloria* (*Days of Glory,* Mario Serandrei, 1945) and *All'armi siam fascisti* (*To Arms, We're Fascists!,* Lino Del Fra, Cecilia Mangini, and Lino Miccichè, 1962)—are still virtually invisible and consistently excluded from the canon of Italian cinema.

While these projects manifest Fascism's connection to the capitalist–colonial order, the commemorative reference to neorealism is a way to whitewash Italian history in order to turn it into an edifying tale, a sort of coming-of-age story for a whole nation but also the entirety of white humanity. We keep hearing that neorealism is an antinarrative cinema, a cinema of seers rather than actors, a cinema that confronts the facts of reality without any a priori preconceptions. It may be that we should pay more attention to Zavattini confessing the imbrication of neorealist films with fictionality and focus on the fictions that neorealism enables. In this way, by switching off the blinding light of neorealism, we might catch some glimpse of what Fascism was, who we were, who we became after Mussolini's fall, but also what anti-Fascism—and "we"—could be.

Notes

PREFACE AND ACKNOWLEDGMENTS

  1. Benedetto Croce, "The Fascist Germ Still Lives," *New York Times*, November 28, 1943; Benedetto Croce, "Chi è fascista?," *Il Giornale di Napoli*, October 24, 1944; Benedetto Croce, "La libertà italiana nella libertà del mondo: Discorso al primo Congresso dei partiti uniti nei Comitati di liberazione," in *Scritti e discorsi politici*, vol. 1, ed. Angela Carella (Naples: Bibliopolis, 1993), 54–62.

  2. Claudio Fogu, "*Italiani brava gente*: The Legacy of Fascist Historical Culture on Italian Politics of Memory," in *The Politics of Memory in Postwar Europe*, ed. Richard Ned Lebow, Wulf Kansteiner, and Claudio Fogu (Durham, N.C.: Duke University Press, 2006), 147–76.

  3. See Giacomo Lichtner, *Fascism in Italian Cinema since 1945: The Politics and Aesthetics of Memory* (London: Palgrave Macmillan, 2013), especially 3–41 and 129–53; and Kriss Ravetto, *The Unmaking of Fascist Aesthetics* (Minneapolis: University of Minnesota Press, 2001), 1–20.

INTRODUCTION

  1. See Elaine Mancini, *Struggles of the Italian Film Industry during Fascism, 1930–1935* (Ann Arbor: UMI Research Press, 1985).

  2. David Forgacs, ed., *Rethinking Italian Fascism: Capitalism, Populism and Culture* (London: Lawrence & Wishart, 1986); Ruth Ben-Ghiat, *Fascist Modernities: Italy, 1922–1945* (Berkeley: University of California Press, 2001).

  3. Jacqueline Reich and Piero Garofalo, "Preface," in *Re-viewing Fascism: Italian Cinema, 1922–1943*, ed. Jacqueline Reich and Piero Garofalo (Bloomington: Indiana University Press, 2002), vii–xiv; Jacqueline Reich, "Mussolini at the Movies," in Reich and Garofalo, *Re-viewing Fascism*, 3–29.

  4. Louis Althusser, "Ideology and Ideological State Apparatuses (Notes towards an Investigation)," in *Lenin and Philosophy and Other Essays*, trans. Ben Brewster (London: New Left Books, 1971), 127–86.

5. Antonio Gramsci, "The Concept of Passive Revolution," "Elements of Politics," and "Sociology and Political Science," in *Selection from the Prison Notebooks*, ed. Quintin Hoare and Geoffrey Nowell Smith (London: Lawrence & Wishart, 1971), 106–14, 144–47, and 244.

6. Jean-Louis Baudry, "Ideological Effects of the Basic Cinematographic Apparatus," trans. Alan Williams, *Film Quarterly* 28, no. 2 (Winter 1974/75): 39–47, https://doi.org/10.2307/1211632.

7. Victoria de Grazia, *The Culture of Consent: Mass Organisation of Leisure in Fascist Italy* (Cambridge: Cambridge University Press, 1981), especially 225–45; Karen Pinkus, *Bodily Regimes: Italian Advertising under Fascism* (Minneapolis: University of Minnesota Press, 1995); Barbara Spackman, *Fascist Virilities: Rhetoric, Ideology, and Social Fantasy in Italy* (Minneapolis: University of Minnesota Press, 1996), especially 114–19; Marcia Landy, *The Folklore of Consensus: Theatricality in the Italian Cinema, 1930–1943* (Albany: State University of New York Press, 1998); Simonetta Falasca-Zamponi, *Fascist Spectacle: The Aesthetics of Power in Mussolini's Italy* (Berkeley: University of California Press, 2000).

8. Tom Gunning, "The Cinema of Attractions: Early Film, Its Spectator and the Avant-Garde," *Wide Angle* 8, nos. 3–4 (1986): 63–70, https://doi.org/10.5040/97818387 10170.0008; Miriam Hansen, "The Mass Production of the Senses: Classical Cinema as Vernacular Modernism," *Modernism/modernity* 6, no. 2 (1999): 59–77, https://doi.org/10.1353/mod.1999.0018; Giuliana Bruno, *Atlas of Emotions: Journeys in Art, Architecture, and Film* (New York: Verso Books, 2002); Jonathan Crary, *Techniques of the Observer: On Vision and Modernity in the Nineteenth Century* (Cambridge, Mass.: MIT Press, 1992).

9. Alexander G. Weheliye, *Habeas Viscus: Racializing Assemblages, Biopolitics, and Black Feminist Theories of the Human* (Durham, N.C.: Duke University Press, 2014), 33–74; Jonathan Xavier Inda, "Performativity, Materiality, and the Racial Body," *Latino Studies Journal* 11, no. 3 (2000): 74–99.

10. See, for instance, bell hooks, *Writing beyond Race: Living Theory and Practice* (New York: Routledge, 2013), 4–5.

11. Rhiannon Welch, *Vital Subjects: Race and Biopolitics in Italy* (Liverpool: Liverpool University Press, 2016), 1–33.

12. Jane Schneider, "The Dynamics of Neo-Orientalism in Italy," in *Italy's "Southern Question": Orientalism in One Country*, ed. Jane Schneider (Oxford: Berg, 1998), 1–26; Nelson Moe, *The View from the Vesuvius: Italian Culture and the Southern Question* (Berkeley: University of California Press, 2006); Pasquale Verdicchio, "The Preclusion of Postcolonial Discourse in Southern Italy," in *Revisioning Italy: National Identity and Global Culture*, ed. Beverly Allen and Mary Russo (Minneapolis: University of Minnesota Press, 1997), 191–212; Pasquale Verdicchio, "Introduction," in *The Southern Question*, by Antonio Gramsci, ed. and trans. Pasquale Verdicchio (Toronto: Guernica Editions, 2006); Miguel Mellino, "Deprovincializing Italy: Notes on Race, Racialization, and Italy's Coloniality," in *Postcolonial Italy: Challenging National Homogeneity*, ed. Cristina Lombardi-Diop and Caterina Romeo (New York: Palgrave Macmillan, 2012), 83–102.

13. Cesare Lombroso, *The Criminal Man*, ed. and trans. Mary Gibson and Nicole Hahn Rafter (Durham, N.C.: Duke University Press, 2006), originally published as

L'uomo delinquente: Studiato in rapporto alla antropologia, alla medicina legale ed alle discipline carcerarie; con incisioni (Milan: Hoepli, 1876). See also Mary Gibson, "Biology or Environment? Race and Southern 'Deviancy' in the Writings of Italian Criminologists, 1880–1920," in Schneider, *Italy's "Southern Question,"* 99–116; and Silvana Patriarca, "How Many Italies? Representing the South in Official Statistics," in Schneider, *Italy's "Southern Question,"* 99–117.

14. David Theo Goldberg, *The Racial State* (Oxford: Blackwell, 2002), 98–132; Walter Mignolo, "Introduction: Coloniality of Power and De-colonial Thinking," *Cultural Studies* 21, nos. 2–3 (2007): 155–67, https://doi.org/10.1080/09502380601162498.

15. See de Grazia, *The Culture of Consent*, 1–3.

16. Suzanne Stewart-Steinberg, *The Pinocchio Effect: On Making Italians, 1860–1920* (Chicago: University of Chicago Press, 2008), 1–20.

17. Gaia Giuliani, *Race, Nation and Gender in Modern Italy: Intersectional Representations in Visual Culture* (New York: Palgrave Macmillan, 2019), 65–108. On Fascism's racial imaginary, see also Aaron Gillette, *Racial Theories in Fascist Italy* (New York: Palgrave Macmillan, 2002), 35–153; and Mauro Raspanti, "I razzismi del fascismo," in *La menzogna della razza: Documenti e immagini del razzismo e dell'antisemitismo fascista,* ed. Centro Furio Jesi (Bologna: Grafis, 1994), 73–89.

18. Emil Ludwig, *Talks with Mussolini,* trans. Eden Paul and Cedar Paul (Boston: Little, Brown, 1933), 69–70, quoted in Gillette, *Racial Theories in Fascist Italy,* 44. On the role of sentiments for biopolitical projects of nation building in the romantic tradition, see Alistair Hunt and Matthias Rudolf, eds., "Romanticism and Biopolitics," special issue of *A Romantic Circles Praxis* (December 2012).

19. I derive the "fare razza" from Welch, *Vital Subjects,* 70. In her formidable book, an invaluable resource for my own thinking about Italian history and culture, Welch traces how this expression—originally used in regard to animal breeding—came to encapsulate the racializing and reproductive imperatives of the Italian colonial-capitalist order.

20. See Eden K. McLean, *Mussolini's Children: Race and Elementary Education in Fascist Italy* (Lincoln: University of Nebraska Press, 2018); James Hay, "Revisiting the Grand Hotel (and Its Place in the Cultural Economy of Fascist Italy)," in *Moving Images / Stopping Places,* ed. David B. Clarke, Valerie Crawford Pfannhauser, and Marcus A. Doel (Lanham, Md.: Rowman & Littlefield, 2009), 13–47.

21. André Bazin, "An Aesthetic of Reality: Neorealism," in *What Is Cinema?*, vol. 2, trans. Hugh Gray (Berkeley: University of California Press, 1971), 16–40; Millicent Marcus, *Italian Film in the Light of Neorealism* (Princeton, N.J.: Princeton University Press, 1986); Gilles Deleuze, *Cinema 2: The Time-Image,* trans. Hugh Tomlinson and Robert Galeta (Minneapolis: University of Minnesota Press, 1989).

22. David Forgacs, "Sex in the Cinema: Regulation and Transgression in Italian Films, 1930–1943," in Reich and Garofalo, *Re-viewing Fascism,* 143.

23. Ben-Ghiat, *Fascist Modernities*; Ruth Ben-Ghiat, *Italian Fascism's Empire Cinema* (Bloomington: Indiana University Press, 2015).

24. Catherine O'Rawe, *Stars and Masculinities in Contemporary Italian Cinema* (New York: Palgrave Macmillan, 2014), 70–72; Linda Williams, "Melodrama Revised," in

Refiguring American Film Genres: History and Theory, ed. Nick Browne (Berkeley: University of California Press, 1998), 42–88.

25. Shelleen Greene, *Equivocal Subjects: Between Italy and Africa—Constructions of Racial and National Identity in the Italian Cinema* (London: Continuum, 2012); Edward W. Said, *Orientalism* (New York: Pantheon Books, 1978).

26. Richard Dyer, *White,* 20th Anniversary Edition (New York: Routledge, 2017), 13.

27. Marla Stone, *The Patron State: Culture and Politics in Fascist Italy* (Princeton, N.J.: Princeton University Press, 1998), 65–70.

28. Lauren Berlant, *Cruel Optimism* (Durham, N.C.: Duke University Press, 2011), 1–46.

29. Antonio Gramsci, *Prison Notebooks,* vol. 3, trans. Joseph A. Buttigieg (New York: Columbia University Press, 2010), 168. On the effectiveness of entryism as a political tactic, see de Grazia, *The Culture of Consent,* 225–45.

30. Silvia Federici, *Caliban and the Witch: Women, The Body, and Primitive Accumulation* (New York: Autonomedia, 2004); Sara Ahmed, *The Cultural Politics of Emotion* (New York: Routledge, 2014).

31. Brady Thomas Heiner, "Foucault and the Black Panthers," *City* 11, no. 3 (2007): 313–56, https://doi.org/10.1080/13604810701668969.

32. Michel Foucault, *Discipline and Punish: The Birth of the Prison,* trans. Alan Sheridan (New York: Vintage Books, 1995). On the relation between Foucault and Althusser, see Warren Montag, "'The Soul Is the Prison of the Body': Althusser and Foucault, 1970–1975," *Yale French Studies,* no. 88 (1995): 53–77, https://doi.org/10.2307/2930102.

33. Michel Foucault, "Film, History, and Popular Memory," in *Foucault at the Movies,* ed. and trans. Clare O'Farrell (New York: Columbia University Press, 2018), 103–23. On the relation between Foucault and *Cahiers du Cinéma,* see Emilie Bickerton, *A Short History of Cahiers du Cinéma* (New York: Verso Books, 2009), 90–100.

34. Alessandro Fontana and Mauro Bertani, "Situating the Lectures," in *"Society Must Be Defended,"* by Michel Foucault, ed. Mauro Bertani and Alessandro Fontana, trans. David Macey (New York: Picador, 2003), 273–79.

35. Foucault, *"Society Must Be Defended,"* 25.

36. Antonio Gramsci, "Some Considerations on the Southern Question," in *The Southern Question,* 24.

37. Foucault, *"Society Must Be Defended,"* 56–57.

38. Foucault, 57.

39. See, for instance, Weheliye, *Habeas Viscus,* 1–33.

40. Ann Laura Stoler, *Race and the Education of Desire: Foucault's History of Sexuality and the Colonial Order of Things* (Durham, N.C.: Duke University Press, 1995), 55–73; Timothy Campbell, *Improper Life: Technology and Biopolitics from Heidegger to Agamben* (Minneapolis: University of Minnesota Press, 2011).

41. Foucault, *"Society Must Be Defended,"* 43–63.

42. Lee Grieveson, "On Governmentality and Screens," *Screen* 50, no. 1 (Spring 2009): 180–87, https://doi.org/10.1093/screen/hjn079; Mark B. N. Hansen, "Foucault

and Media: A Missed Encounter?," *South Atlantic Quarterly* 111, no. 3 (June 20, 2012): 497–528, https://doi.org/10.1215/00382876-1596254; Gilles Deleuze, "Postscript on the Societies of Control," *October* 59 (1992): 3–7, https://www.jstor.org/stable/7788 28.

43. Hansen, "Foucault and Media," 498.

44. Hunter Hargraves, "The Urgency and Affects of Media Studies," *Cinema Journal* 57, no. 2 (2018): 137–42, https://doi.org/10.1353/cj.2018.0010; Paola Bonifazio, *Schooling in Modernity: The Politics of Sponsored Films in Postwar Italy* (Toronto: Toronto University Press, 2014), 3–24.

45. Eugenie Brinkema, *The Forms of the Affects* (Durham, N.C.: Duke University Press, 2014), 26–46.

46. Foucault, *"Society Must Be Defended,"* 10.

47. Michel Foucault, "Preface to the English Edition," in *Anti-Oedipus: Capitalism and Schizophrenia,* by Gilles Deleuze and Félix Guattari, trans. Robert Hurley, Mark Seem, and Helen R. Lane (New York: Penguin, 2009), xi–xiv.

1. THE GOVERNMENT OF THE UNGOVERNABLE

1. Max Horkheimer and Theodor W. Adorno, *Dialectic of Enlightenment*, trans. Edmund Jephcott (Stanford: Stanford University Press, 2002), 119.

2. Stephanie Malia Hom, "On the Origins of Making Italy: Massimo D'Azeglio and 'Fatta l'Italia, bisogna fare gli Italiani,'" *Italian Culture* 31, no. 1 (2013): 1–16, https://doi.org/10.1179/0161462212Z.00000000012; see also Rhiannon Welch, *Vital Subjects: Race and Biopolitics in Italy* (Liverpool: Liverpool University Press, 2016), 75–178.

3. Suzanne Stewart-Steinberg, *The Pinocchio Effect: On Making Italians, 1860–1920* (Chicago: University of Chicago Press, 2008), 21–63.

4. Gualtiero Fabbri, *Al Cinematografo,* ed. Sergio Raffaelli (1907; repr., Rome: Associazione italiana per le ricerche di storia del cinema, 1993); Luigi Pirandello, *Shoot! The Notebooks of Serafino Gubbio, Cinematograph Operator,* trans. C. K. Scott Moncrieff (1925; repr., Chicago: University of Chicago Press, 2005), first published in serial format in the journal *La nuova antologia* in 1915 with the title "Si gira" (Shoot), published as a book in 1916, and rereleased with slight revisions and a new title, *Quaderni di Serafino Gubbio operatore* (Milan: Mondadori, 1925). Translations from Fabbri, *Al Cinematografo,* are mine.

5. Aaron Gillette, *Racial Theories in Fascist Italy* (New York: Palgrave McMillan, 2002), 1–19; Shelleen Greene, *Equivocal Subjects* (London: Continuum, 2012), 1–20.

6. See Luca Giuliani, "From Wonder to Propaganda: The Technological Context of Italian Silent Cinema," in *Italian Silent Cinema: A Reader,* ed. Giorgio Bertellini (Bloomington: Indiana University Press, 2013), 135–42.

7. John P. Welle, "Film on Paper: Early Italian Cinema Literature, 1907–1920," *Film History* 12, no. 3 (January 2000): 288–99, https://www.jstor.org/stable/3815358; Gavriel Moses, *The Nickel Was for the Movies: Film in the Novel from Pirandello to Puig* (Berkeley: University of California Press, 1995), 99. See also Davide Turconi, "Prefazione," in *Cinema scritto: Il catalogo delle riviste italiane di cinema, 1907–1944,* ed. Riccardo Redi (Rome: Associazione italiana per le ricerche di storia del cinema, 1992), vii–ix.

8. Pietro Tonini, "L'Editore: Presentazione," in Fabbri, *Al Cinematografo*, 9.

9. Jay Leyda, *Kino: A History of the Russian and Soviet Film* (Princeton, N.J.: Princeton University Press, 1983), 41.

10. See Sergio Raffaelli, "Un pioniere," in Fabbri, *Al Cinematografo*, 81–102.

11. John David Rhodes, "'Our Beautiful and Glorious Art Lives': The Rhetoric of Nationalism in Early Italian Film Periodicals," *Film History* 12, no. 3 (2000): 308–21, www.jstor.org/stable/3815360; Francesco Casetti, *Eye of the Century: Film, Experience, Modernity* (New York: Columbia University Press, 2008), 7–26.

12. Jay David Bolter and Richard Grusin, *Remediation: Understanding New Media* (Cambridge, Mass.: MIT Press, 2000), 2–19.

13. Fabbri, *Al Cinematografo*, 22. Subsequent citations are given parenthetically in text.

14. On the spread of movie halls in Italy, see Elena Mosconi, "Uno spazio composito: Il politeama," in *Spettatori italiani: Riti e ambienti del consumo cinematografico (1900–1950)*, ed. Francesco Casetti and Elena Mosconi (Rome: Carocci, 2006), 17–29.

15. Guido Cincotti, "Il risorgimento nel cinema," in *Il Risorgimento italiano nel teatro e nel cinema*, ed. Giovanni Calendoli (Rome: Editalia, 1962), 129–71.

16. Welch, *Vital Subjects*, 191.

17. Welch, 26.

18. Alfredo Niceforo and Scipio Sighele, *La mala vita a Roma* (Turin: Frassati, 1898), 185.

19. Miguel Mellino, "Deprovincializing Italy: Notes on Race, Racialization, and Italy's Coloniality," in *Postcolonial Italy: Challenging National Homogeneity*, ed. Cristina Lombardi-Diop and Caterina Romeo (New York: Palgrave Macmillan, 2012), 83–102.

20. Ann Laura Stoler, *Race and the Education of Desire: Foucault's History of Sexuality and the Colonial Order of Things* (Durham, N.C.: Duke University Press, 1995), 95–137.

21. Antonio Gramsci, "Some Considerations on the Southern Question," in *The Southern Question*, ed. and trans. Pasquale Verdicchio (Toronto: Guernica Editions, 2006).

22. Philip V. Cannistraro, *La fabbrica del consenso: Fascismo e mass media* (Rome: Laterza, 1975).

23. Pirandello, *Shoot!*, 93. Subsequent citations are given parenthetically in text.

24. Gaetano Salvemini, *Il ministro della mala vita* (Rome: La voce, 1919). On the relationship between the crisis of Giolitti's liberal governance and the rise of the fascist state, see Emilio Gentile, *Il mito dello Stato nuovo dall'antigiolittismo al fascismo* (Rome: Laterza, 1982).

25. Fabrizio De Donno, "La Razza Ario-Mediterranea: Ideas of Race and Citizenship in Colonial and Fascist Italy, 1885–1941," *Interventions: International Journal of Postcolonial Studies*, 8, no. 3 (2006): 394–412, https://doi.org/10.1080/13698010600955958.

26. Giuseppe Sergi, *The Mediterranean Race: A Study of the Origin of European Peoples* (London: Walter Scott, 1909); Giuseppe Sergi, *Arii e Italici: Attorno all'Italia preistorica* (Turin: Fratelli Bocca, 1898): in these works, Sergi uses "stirpe" and "razza" interchangeably. On Sergi's broad influence and impact, see Fedra Pizzato, "Per una storia antropologica della nazione: Mito mediterraneao e construzione nazionale in

Giuseppe Sergi (1880–1919)," *Storia del pensiero politico,* no. 1 (June–April 2015): 25–52, http://www.rivisteweb.it/doi/10.4479/79421.

27. See Gavriel Moses, "'Gubbio in Gabbia': Pirandello's Cameraman and the Entrapments of Film Vision," *MLN* 94, no. 1 (January 1979): 36–60, https://doi.org/10.2307/2906329; Gavriel Moses, "Film Theory as Literary Genre in Pirandello and the Film-Novel," *Annali d'Italianistica,* no. 6 (1988): 38–68, https://www.jstor.org/stable/24004190; Alessandro Vettori, "Serafino Gubbio's Candid Camera," *MLN* 113, no. 1 (January 1998): 79–107, https://doi.org/10.1353/mln.1998.0017; Francesco Casetti, "Italian Early Film 'Theories': Borders and Crossings," in Bertellini, *Italian Silent Cinema,* 275–84; Michael Subialka, "The Meaning of Acting in the Age of Cinema: Benjamin, Pirandello, and the Italian Diva," *Comparative Literature* 68, no. 3 (September 2016): 312–31, https://doi.org/10.1215/00104124-3631587; and Tom Gunning, "Introduction: The Diva, the Tiger, and the Three-Legged Spider," in Pirandello, *Shoot!,* vii–xiv.

28. Fiora Bassanese, *Understanding Luigi Pirandello* (Columbia: University of South Carolina Press, 1997), 70–74.

29. Sianne Ngai, *Our Aesthetic Categories: Zany, Cute, Interesting* (Cambridge, Mass.: Harvard University Press, 2015), 7–10.

30. Sianne Ngai, *Theory of the Gimmick: Aesthetic Judgment and Capitalist Form* (Cambridge, Mass.: Belknap Press of Harvard University Press, 2020), especially 53–82.

31. Walter Benjamin, "The Work of Art in the Age of Its Technological Reproducibility: Second Version," in *The Work of Art in the Age of Its Technological Reproducibility, and Other Writings on Media,* ed. Michael W. Jennings, Brigid Doherty, and Thomas Y. Levin, trans. Edmund Jephcott and Harry Zohn (Cambridge, Mass.: Harvard University Press, 2008), 31–32; Robert S. Dombroski, *La totalità dell'artificio: Ideologia e forma nel romanzo di Pirandello* (Padua: Liviana, 1978).

32. See Thomas Harrison, *Essayism: Conrad, Musil, and Pirandello* (Baltimore: Johns Hopkins University Press, 1991), 197.

33. Bernard Stiegler, "Derrida and Technology: Fidelity at the Limits of Deconstruction and the Prosthesis of Faith," in *Jacques Derrida and the Humanities: A Critical Reader,* ed. Tom Cohen (Cambridge: Cambridge University Press, 2001), 238–70.

34. Michael Syrimis, *The Great Black Spider on Its Knock-Kneed Tripod: Reflections of Cinema in Early Twentieth-Century Italy* (Toronto: University of Toronto Press, 2012), 199–240.

35. Alberto Asor Rosa, *La cultura,* book 2 of *Storia d'Italia,* ed. Ruggiero Romano and Corrado Vivanti, vol. 4, *Dall'Unità ad oggi* (Turin: Einaudi, 1975); Giuseppe Panella, "Pirandello fascista ovvero Del demiurgo indispensabile," in *La scrittura memorabile: Leonardo Sciascia e la letteratura come forma di vita* (Avellino: Delta 3 Edizioni, 2012), 97–122.

36. See Gian Venè, *Pirandello fascista: La coscienza borghese tra ribellione e rivoluzione* (Venice: Marsilio, 1981). The first scholar to make the connection between Pirandello's art and his politics was Adriano Tilgher in 1923—the year before Fascism's inception—who drew Pirandello's Fascism out of his opposition between life and form. Scholars have usually discarded Tilgher's interpretation, but—as Luca Barattoni has recently

argued—this has more to do with the attempt to save Pirandello than to understand his work. See Adriano Tilgher, *Studi sul teatro contemporaneo, preceduti da un saggio su l'arte come originalità e i problemi dell'arte* (Rome: Libreria di scienze e lettere, 1928); and Luca Barattoni, "Ritornare a Tilgher: Bergsonian Themes and the Human Condition in the *Notebooks of Serafino Gubbio, Cinematograph Operator*," *Forum Italicum: A Journal of Italian Studies* 45, no. 1 (March 2011): 80–99, https://doi.org/10.1177/001458 581104500104.

37. Luigi Pirandello, "La vita creata," in *Saggi e interventi,* ed. Ferdinando Taviani (Milan: Mondadori, 2006), 1249; Siegfried Kracauer, *From Caligari to Hitler: A Psychological History of the German Film* (Princeton, N.J.: Princeton University Press, 2004), 184–87.

38. Étienne Balibar, "Is There a Neo-Racism" and "Racism and Nationalism," in *Race, Nation, Class: Ambiguous Identities,* by Étienne Balibar and Immanuel Wallerstein, trans. Chris Turner (New York: Verso, 1991), 17–28 and 37–68.

2. WORKERS ENTERING THE MILITARY-INDUSTRIAL COMPLEX

1. Harun Farocki, "Workers Leaving the Factory," *Senses of Cinema,* no. 21 (July 2002), http://sensesofcinema.com. On Farocki's piece, see also Karen Pinkus, *Clocking Out: The Machinery of Life in 1960s Italian Cinema* (Minneapolis: University of Minnesota Press, 2020), 45–46.

2. Luigi Pirandello, "La vita creata," in *Saggi e interventi,* ed. Ferdinando Taviani (Milan: Mondadori, 2006), 1249.

3. Franco Bonelli, *Lo sviluppo di una grande impresa in Italia: La Terni dal 1884 al 1962* (Turin: Einaudi, 1975), 233–44. On Terni, see also Alessandro Portelli's oral histories, *Biografia di una città* (Turin: Einaudi, 1985) and *La città dell'acciaio: Due secoli di storia operaia* (Rome: Donzelli, 2017).

4. For a more detailed description of the genealogy of *Acciaio,* see Elaine Mancini, *Struggles of the Italian Film Industry during Fascism, 1930–1935* (Ann Arbor, Mich.: UMI Research Press, 1985), 70–85; and Claudio Camerini, ed., *Acciaio: Un film degli anni trenta: Pagine inedite di una storia italiana* (Rome: Centro Sperimentale di Cinematografia, 1990).

5. Jean A. Gili, *Stato fascista e cinematografia: Repressione e promozione* (Rome: Bulzoni, 1981), 100–130.

6. See Marla Stone, *The Patron State: Culture and Politics in Fascist Italy* (Princeton, N.J.: Princeton University Press, 1998); and Emilio Gentile, *La via italiana al totalitarismo: Il partito e lo Stato nel regime fascista* (Rome: Nuova Italia Scientifica, 1995).

7. Vincenzo Buccheri, *Stile Cines: Studi sul cinema italiano 1930–1934* (Milan: Vita e Pensiero, 2004), 21–26; Gian Piero Brunetta, "Les ferments realistes dans le cinéma italien de l'epoque fasciste," in *Le cinéma italien,* ed. Aldo Bernardini and Jean A. Gili (Paris: Centre Pompidou, 1986). On cinema as a vernacular producing specific experiences of the real, see Miriam Hansen, "The Mass Production of the Senses: Classical Cinema as Vernacular Modernism," *Modernism/modernity* 6, no. 2 (1999): 59–77, https://doi.org/10.1353/mod.1999.0018.

8. Luigi Pirandello, *Quaderni di Serafino Gubbio operatore* (Milan: Mondadori, 1925).

9. Luigi Pirandello, *Gioca, Pietro!*, booklet distributed with *Scenario* 2, no. 1 (January 1933).

10. Piero Garofalo, "Seeing Red: The Soviet Influence on Italian Cinema in the Thirties," in *Re-viewing Fascism*, ed. Jacqueline Reich and Piero Garofalo (Bloomington: Indiana University Press, 2002), 223–49.

11. See Michael Cowan, *Walter Ruttmann and the Cinema of Multiplicity: Avant-Garde Film—Advertising—Modernity* (Amsterdam: Amsterdam University Press, 2014), 55–130.

12. Bucchieri, *Stile Cines*, 69–70.

13. Luigi Pirandello, "Se il film parlante abolirà il teatro?," *Corriere della Sera*, June 19, 1929.

14. Siegfried Kracauer, *From Caligari to Hitler: A Psychological History of the German Film* (Princeton, N.J.: Princeton University Press, 2004), 184–87; Siegfried Kracauer, "Film of 1928," in *The Mass Ornament: Weimar Essays*, trans. Thomas Levin (Cambridge, Mass.: Harvard University Press, 2005), 318.

15. Cowan, *Walter Ruttmann and the Cinema of Multiplicity*, 139.

16. Rossano Vittori, "Una trama di Pirandello tradita dalla sceneggiatura," *Cinema Nuovo*, no. 295 (June 1985): 32–38. For accounts of the artistic divergences between Pirandello on one side, and Ruttmann, Cecchi, and Soldati on the other, see Giorgio Bertellini, "Dubbing *L'Arte Muta*: Poetic Layerings around Italian Cinema's Transition to Sound," in Reich and Garofalo, *Re-viewing Fascism*, 49–56.

17. Garofalo, "Seeing Red," 243.

18. Garofalo, 241.

19. Siegfried Kracauer, "The Mass Ornament," in *The Mass Ornament*, 78.

20. See Cowan, *Walter Ruttmann and the Cinema of Multiplicity*, 138–72.

21. Alberto Spaini, "A Pure but Intelligible Art," *International Review of Educational Cinematography* 5, no. 6 (June 1933): 409–10.

22. Susan Sontag, "Fascinating Fascism," in *Under the Sign of Saturn* (New York: Picador, 1980), 73–105.

23. James Hay, *Popular Film Culture in Fascist Italy: The Passing of the Rex* (Bloomington: Indiana University Press, 1987), 102.

24. Furio Jesi, *Germania segreta* (Milan: Silva, 1967); Furio Jesi, *Cultura di destra: Con tre inediti e un'intervista* (Rome: Nottetempo, 2011).

25. Philippe Lacoue-Labarthe and Jean-Luc Nancy, "The Nazi Myth," trans. Brian Holmes, *Critical Inquiry* 16, no. 2 (Winter 1990): 291–312, https://doi.org/10.1086/448535.

26. Jesi, *Germania segreta*, 106.

27. Bruno Vespa, *Perché l'Italia amò Mussolini* (Rome: Mondadori, 2020).

3. WHITE, RED, BLACKSHIRT

1. Benito Mussolini, "Il discorso alla 'Sciesa' di Milano," in *Opera omnia di Benito Mussolini*, vol. 18, *Dalla conferenza di Cannes alla Marcia su Roma*, ed. Edoardo Susmel

and Dulio Susmel (Florence: La Fenice, 1956), 433–40. For an exemplary foreclosure of Fascism's racism, see Renzo De Felice, *Storia degli ebrei italiani sotto il fascismo* (Turin: Einaudi, 1961).

2. Alexander G. Weheliye, *Habeas Viscus: Racializing Assemblages, Biopolitics, and Black Feminist Theories of the Human* (Durham, N.C.: Duke University Press, 2014), 60.

3. Ruth Wilson Gilmore, *Golden Gulag: Prisons, Surplus, Crisis and Opposition in Globalizing California* (Berkeley: University of California Press, 2007); Rhiannon Welch, *Vital Subjects: Race and Biopolitics in Italy* (Liverpool: Liverpool University Press, 2016), 22; Michel Foucault, *"Society Must Be Defended,"* ed. Mauro Bertani and Alessandro Fontana, trans. David Macey (New York: Picador, 2003), 273–79; Weheliye, *Habeas Viscus*, 55–56.

4. See Carlo Celli, "Alessandro Blasetti and Representations of Fascism in the 1930's," *Italian Culture* 16, no. 2 (1998): 99–109, https://doi.org/10.1179/itc.1998.16.2.99.

5. Stephen Gundle and Michela Zegna, "Art, Entertainment and Politics: Alessandro Blasetti and the Rise of the Italian Film Industry, 1929–1959," *Historical Journal of Film, Radio and Television* 40, no. 1 (2020): 6–28, https://doi.org/10.1080/01439685.2020.1715592.

6. Alessandro Blasetti, "Lettera aperta ai banchieri italiani," *Lo schermo,* August 1926, cited in Riccardo Redi, *"Sole* film della rinascita," in *Sole: Soggetto, sceneggiatura, note per la realizzazione,* ed. Adriano Aprà and Riccardo Redi (Rome: Di Giacomo Editore, 1985), 16.

7. Fredric Jameson, "The Existence of Italy," in *Signatures of the Visible* (New York: Routledge, 2007), 213–314.

8. Alfredo Niceforo and Scipio Sighele, *La mala vita a Roma* (Turin: Frassati, 1898); Luigi Pirandello, *Quaderni di Serafino Gubbio operatore* (Milan: Mondadori, 1925).

9. LUCE president Giacomo Paulucci de' Calboli discusses the connection between the "Great Rome" zoning plan and the decision to build Cinecittà in the city's southern outskirts in "La città del cinema," *Cinema,* no. 1 (July 10, 1936): 12–14.

10. Steen Bo Frandsen, "'The War That We Prefer': The Reclamation of the Pontine Marshes and Fascist Expansion," *Totalitarian Movements and Political Religions* 2, no. 3 (2001): 69–82, https://doi.org/10.1080/714005458.

11. Suzanne Stewart-Steinberg, "Grounds for Reclamation: Fascism and Postfascism in the Pontine Marshes," *differences* 27, no. 1 (2016): 94, https://doi.org/10.1215/10407391-3522769.

12. Stewart-Steinberg, 108.

13. Federico Caprotti, *Mussolini's Cities: Internal Colonialism in Italy, 1930–1939* (Youngstown, N.Y.: Cambria Press, 2007); Mia Fuller, "Wherever You Go, There You Are: Fascist Plans for the Colonial City of Addis Ababa and the Colonizing Suburb of EUR '42," *Journal of Contemporary History* 31, no. 2 (1996): 397–418, http://www.jstor.org/stable/261172.

14. Ruth Ben-Ghiat, *Italian Fascism's Empire Cinema* (Bloomington: Indiana University Press, 2015).

15. See Gianfranco Graziani, ed., *Pratiche basse e telefoni bianchi: Cinema italiano 1923–1943* (Pescara: Traccie, 1986), 60. Admitting the influence of Ferri, Blasetti

mischaracterizes this racial scientist as a "liberal" and *Sole!* as a liberal film. In fact, Ferri was initially a socialist, as were most Italian racial scientists, and then embraced Fascism after World War II.

16. On mechanical reproduction as a means of surveillance and identification, see John Tagg, "Power and Photography: A Means of Surveillance," in *Culture, Ideology and Social Process: A Reader,* ed. Tony Bennett, Graham Martin, Colin Mercer, and Janet Woollacott (London: Open University, 1981), 285–308.

17. Aldo Vergano, "La sceneggiatura," in Aprà and Redi, *Sole,* 61–112.

18. Graziani, *Pratiche basse e telefoni bianchi,* 60.

19. Lara Pucci, "Remapping the Rural: The Ideological Geographies of *Strapaese*," in *Film, Art, New Media: Museum without Walls?,* ed. Andrea Dalle Vacche (New York: Palgrave Macmillan, 2012), 184.

20. Natasha Chang, *The Crisis Woman: Body Politics and the Modern Woman in Fascist Italy* (Toronto: University of Toronto Press, 2015), 3.

21. Pirandello, *Quaderni di Serafino Gubbio operatore*; Ada Negri, "Cinematografo," *Corriere della Sera,* November 27, 1928.

22. Gaia Giuliani, "L'Italiano Negro: The Politics of Colour in Early Twentieth-Century Italy," *Interventions* 16, no. 4 (2014): 577, https://doi.org/10.1080/1369801X.2013.851828.

23. James Hay, "Revisiting the Grand Hotel (and Its Place in the Cultural Economy of Fascist Italy)," in *Moving Images / Stopping Places,* ed. David B. Clarke, Valerie Crawford Pfannhauser, and Marcus A. Doel (Lanham, Md.: Rowman & Littlefield, 2009), 13–47.

24. Richard Dyer, *White,* 20th Anniversary Edition (New York: Routledge, 2017), 207–23.

25. Jameson, "The Existence of Italy."

4. THE SHAME OF ESCAPISM

1. Riccardo Redi, *"Sole* film della rinascita," in *Sole: Soggetto, sceneggiatura, note per la realizzazione,* ed. Adriano Aprà and Riccardo Redi (Rome: Di Giacomo Editore, 1985), 15–19.

2. Marcia Landy, *The Folklore of Consensus: Theatricality in the Italian Cinema, 1930–1943* (Albany: State University of New York Press, 1998), 2–4; Lara Pucci, "Remapping the Rural: The Ideological Geographies of *Strapaese*," in *Film, Art, New Media: Museum without Walls?,* ed. Andrea Dalle Vacche (New York: Palgrave Macmillan, 2012), 178–95.

3. Mark Antliff, *Avant-Garde Fascism: The Mobilization of Myth, Art, and Culture in France, 1909–1939* (Durham, N.C.: Duke University Press, 2007), 60. On "polyvalent mobility" as a tool of racial government, see Ann Laura Stoler, *Race and the Education of Desire: Foucault's History of Sexuality and the Colonial Order of Things* (Durham, N.C.: Duke University Press, 1995), 89.

4. Emanuel Levinas, *On Escape: De l'évasion,* trans. Bettina Bergo (Stanford: Stanford University Press, 2003); Eve Kosofsky Sedgwick, *Touching Feeling: Affect, Pedagogy,*

Performativity (Durham, N.C.: Duke University Press, 2003), 37; Jean-Paul Sartre, *Being and Nothingness,* trans. Hazel E. Barnes (New York: Philosophical Library, 1956), 221.

5. Lisa Guenther, "Shame and the Temporality of Social Life," *Continental Philosophy Review,* no. 44 (2011): 23–29, https://doi.org/10.1007/s11007-011-9164-y; Frantz Fanon, *Black Skin, White Masks,* trans. Charles Lam Markmann (London: Pluto, 1986), 109.

6. Fanon, *Black Skin, White Masks,* 112.

7. Alberto Farassino, "Camerini, au-delà du cinéma italien," in *Mario Camerini,* ed. Alberto Farassino (Locarno: Editions du Festival international du film de Locarno, 1992), 17, translation mine. For the biographical information regarding Camerini, I rely on Stephen Gundle, *Mussolini's Dream Factory* (New York: Berghahn Books, 2013), 145–50.

8. Ruth Ben-Ghiat, *Italian Fascism's Empire Cinema* (Bloomington: Indiana University Press, 2015), 35.

9. The connection between regimes of premature death and racializing practices is explored by Ruth Wilson Gilmore, "Race and Globalization," in *Geographies of Global Change: Remapping the World,* ed. Ronald John Johnston, Peter James Taylor, and Michael Watts (Malden, Mass.: Wiley-Blackwell, 2002), 261–74.

10. The expression "logic of coloniality" is derived from Walter Mignolo, "Delinking: The Rhetoric of Modernity, the Logic of Coloniality and the Grammar of De-coloniality," *Cultural Studies* 21, nos. 2–3 (March–May 2007): 449–514, https://doi.org/10.1080/09502380601162647. Mignolo uses this expression to point out racial modernity's impulse to control and colonize (literally and figuratively) all aspects of human living.

11. Judith Butler, *Gender Trouble: Feminism and the Subversion of Identity* (New York: Routledge, 1990).

12. Gian Piero Brunetta, *Il cinema italiano di regime: Da "La canzone dell'amore" a "Ossessione,"* digital edition (Rome: Laterza, 2015), location 5779.

13. Giorgio Agamben, *The Open: Man and Animal,* trans. Kevin Attell (Stanford: Stanford University Press, 2003), 31–38; Sylvia Wynter, "Beyond the Word of Man: Glissant and the New Discourse of the Antilles," *World Literature Today* 63, no. 4 (Autumn 1989): 637–48, especially 640–42, https://doi.org/10.2307/40145557.

14. Silvan Tomkins, "Shame-Humiliation and Contempt-Disgust," in *Shame and Its Sisters: A Silvan Tomkins Reader,* ed. Eve Kosofsky Sedgwick and Adam Frank (Durham, N.C.: Duke University Press, 1995), 135.

15. For more on *dopo-lavoro* as a realm of control and discipline, see Victoria de Grazia, *The Culture of Consent: Mass Organisation of Leisure in Fascist Italy* (Cambridge: Cambridge University Press, 1981), 24–60.

16. Farassino, "Camerini, au-delà du cinéma italien," 18.

17. Piero Garofalo, "Seeing Red: The Soviet Influence on Italian Cinema in the Thirties," in *Re-viewing Fascism: Italian Cinema, 1922–1943,* ed. Jacqueline Reich and Piero Garofalo (Bloomington: Indiana University Press, 2002), 239.

18. After *Kif Tebbi,* Camerini worked abroad for a while (Germany, France, and the United States), and thus *Rotaie* can be thought of as an anthology attesting to the

director's proficiency in different cinematic idioms and jargons. See Mira Liehm, *Passion and Defiance: Film in Italy from 1942 to the Present* (Berkeley: University of California Press, 1984), 30.

19. On the critical reception of *Gli uomini che mascalzoni* . . . , see Francesco Savio, *Ma l'amore no: Realismo, formalismo, propaganda e telefoni bianchi nel cinema italiano di regime, 1930–1943* (Venice: Sonzogno, 1975), xiv.

20. I talk more about De Benedetti in chapter 6, when discussing his contributions to the first films directed by De Sica.

21. Filippo Sacchi, "Rassegna cinematografica," *Corriere della Sera*, October 7, 1932, translation mine.

22. Francesco Savio, *Cinecittà anni trenta* (Rome: Bulzoni, 1979), 208.

23. James Hay, *Popular Film Culture in Fascist Italy: The Passing of the Rex* (Bloomington: Indiana University Press, 1987); James Hay, "Revisiting the Grand Hotel (and Its Place in the Cultural Economy of Fascist Italy)," in *Moving Images / Stopping Places*, ed. David B. Clarke, Valerie Crawford Pfannhauser, and Marcus A. Doel (Lanham, Md.: Rowman & Littlefield, 2009), 13–47.

24. Ben-Ghiat, *Italian Fascism's Empire Cinema*, 21–43.

25. Stuart Hall, Chas Critcher, Tony Jefferson, John Clarke, and Brian Roberts, *Policing the Crisis: Mugging, the State, and Law and Order* (London: Macmillan, 1978), 394.

26. Gayle Rubin, "The Traffic in Women: Notes on the 'Political Economy' of Sex," in *Toward an Anthropology of Women*, ed. Rayna R. Reiter (New York: Monthly Review Press, 1975), 157–210.

27. Ruth Ben-Ghiat, *Fascist Modernities: Italy, 1922–1945* (Berkeley: University of California Press, 2001), 80–88. See also Jacqueline Reich, "Consuming Ideologies: Fascism, Commodification, and Female Subjectivity in Mario Camerini's *Grandi magazzini*," *Annali d'Italianistica* 16 (1998): 195–212, https://www.jstor.org/stable/24007515.

28. Barbara Spackman, "Shopping for Autarchy: Fascism and Reproductive Fantasy in Mario Camerini's *Grandi Magazzini*," in Reich and Garofalo, *Re-viewing Fascism*, 276–92.

29. See Karen Pinkus, *Bodily Regimes: Italian Advertising under Fascism* (Minneapolis: University of Minnesota Press, 1995), 161.

5. THE WHITE ITALIAN MEDITERRANEAN

1. See Olga Khazan, "How White Supremacists Use Victimhood to Recruit," *The Atlantic*, August 15, 2017; and Jacques Derrida, *Rogues: Two Essays on Reason*, trans. Pascale-Anne Brault and Michael Naas (Stanford: Stanford University Press, 2005).

2. Quoted in Khazan, "How White Supremacists Use Victimhood to Recruit."

3. Fredric Jameson, "Cognitive Mapping," in *Marxism and the Interpretation of Culture*, ed. Cary Nelson and Lawrence Grossberg (Urbana: University of Illinois Press, 1988), 347–60.

4. Elisabeth Anker, *Orgies of Feeling: Melodrama and the Politics of Freedom* (Durham, N.C.: Duke University Press, 2014).

5. Sianne Ngai, *Ugly Feelings* (Cambridge, Mass: Harvard University Press, 2007).

6. Angelica Pesarini, "When the Mediterranean 'Became' Black: Diasporic Hopes and (Post)Colonial Traumas," in *The Black Mediterranean: Bodies, Borders and Citizenship*, ed. Gabriele Proglio, Camilla Hawthorne, Ida Danewid, P. Khalil Saucier, Giuseppe Grimaldi, Angelica Pesarini, Timothy Raeymaekers, Giulia Grechi, and Vivian Gerrand (New York: Palgrave Macmillan, 2021), 23.

7. Karl Schoonover, *Brutal Vision: The Neorealist Body in Postwar Italian Cinema* (Minneapolis: University of Minnesota Press, 2012); Claudio Fogu, *The Fishing Net and the Spider Web: Mediterranean Imaginaries and the Making of Italians* (New York: Palgrave Macmillan, 2020); Valerie McGuire, *Italy's Sea: Empire and Nation in the Mediterranean, 1895–1945* (Liverpool: Liverpool University Press, 2020).

8. Linda Williams, "Film Bodies: Gender, Genre, and Excess," *Film Quarterly* 44, no. 4 (Summer 1991): 4, https://doi.org/10.2307/1212758.

9. Ida Danewid, "White Innocence in the Black Mediterranean: Hospitality and the Erasure of History," *Third World Quarterly* 38, no. 7 (2017): 1674–89, https://doi.org/10.1080/01436597.2017.1331123.

10. Nicola Labanca, "Exceptional Italy? The Many Ends of the Italian Colonial Empire," in *The Oxford Handbook of the Ends of Empire*, ed. Martin Thomas and Andrew S. Thompson (Oxford: Oxford University Press, 2018), 123–43.

11. Carl Schmitt, *Land and Sea: A World-Historical Meditation*, trans. Samuel Garrett Zeitlin (Candor, N.Y.: Telos Press, 2015).

12. Michel Foucault, *The History of Sexuality: Introduction*, trans. Robert Hurley (New York: Vintage, 1990), 137.

13. David Rodogno, "Le nouvel ordre fasciste en Méditerranée, 1940–1943: Présupposés idéologiques, visions et velléités," *Revue d'histoire moderne & contemporaine* 55, no. 3 (2008): 138–56, https://doi.org/10.3917/rhmc.553.0138.

14. See Giuseppe Bottai, *Diario, 1935–1944* (Milan: Rizzoli, 1989), 141.

15. Giuliana Minghelli, *Landscape and Memory in Post-Fascist Italian Film: Cinema Year Zero* (New York: Routledge, 2013), 52–53.

16. This is true not only for *Fantasia sottomarina* but also for the other three shorts taking place in the animal world that Rossellini realized under Fascism: *La vispa Teresa* (*Lively Teresa*, 1939), *Il tacchino prepotente* (*The Prepotent Turkey*, 1939) and *Il ruscello di Ripasottile* (*Ripasottile's Creek*, 1941). See Luca Caminati, *Roberto Rossellini documentarista: Una cultura della realtà* (Rome: Carocci, 2012), 34–37.

17. Enrique Seknadje-Askénazi, *Roberto Rossellini et la seconde guerre mondiale: Un cinéaste entre propagande et réalisme* (Paris: L'Harmattan, 2000); Fredric Jameson, *The Political Unconscious: Narrative as a Socially Symbolic Act* (Ithaca, N.Y.: Cornell University Press, 1981), 1.

18. Guido Aristarco, "Film di questi giorni," *Cinema*, n.s., no. 5 (December 30, 1948): 156–57; Francesco De Robertis, "Libertas, Unitas, Caritas," *Cinema*, n.s., no. 7 (January 30, 1949): 212.

19. Peter Sloterdijk, *Terror from the Air*, trans. Amy Patton and Steve Corcoran (Los Angeles: Semiotext(e), 2009).

20. On atmospheric film, see Ruth Ben-Ghiat, *Italian Fascism's Empire Cinema* (Bloomington: Indiana University Press, 2015), 233.

21. See Francesco Zucconi, "La forma del mare: Il cinema di Francesco De Robertis e la crisi del Mediterraneo," *Fata Morgana Web,* March 4, 2019, https://www.fatamor ganaweb.it.

22. Alexander G. Weheliye, *Habeas Viscus: Racializing Assemblages, Biopolitics, and Black Feminist Theories of the Human* (Durham, N.C.: Duke University Press, 2014), 1–16, 33–45.

23. D'Annunzio's play was turned into a film by his son Gabriellino in 1921.

24. "Manifesto della razza," in *Scienza italiana e razzismo fascista,* by Roberto Maiocchi (Florence: La Nuova Italia, 1999).

25. Fogu, *The Fishing Net and the Spider Web,* 233–35.

26. Gian Piero Brunetta, *Il cinema italiano di regime: Da "La canzone dell'amore" a "Ossessione,"* digital edition (Rome: Laterza, 2015), location 3374; André Bazin, "An Aesthetic of Reality: Neorealism," in *What Is Cinema?,* vol. 2, trans. Hugh Gray (Berkeley: University of California Press, 1971), 17. Bazin mentions *Uomini sul fondo* with its French title (*SOS 13*) and describes it as a film that, as with *La nave bianca,* makes no concessions to the regime.

27. Samuel Agbamu, "Mare Nostrum: Italy and the Mediterranean of Ancient Rome in the Twentieth and Twenty-First Centuries," *Fascism* 8, no. 2 (2019): 250–74, https://doi.org/10.1163/22116257-00802001.

28. Maria Antonietta Macciocchi, *La donna nera: "Consenso" femminile e fascismo* (Milan: Feltrinelli, 1976), 156.

29. Ruth Ben-Ghiat, "The Fascist War Trilogy," in *Roberto Rossellini: Magician of the Real,* ed. David Forgacs, Sarah Lutton, and Geoffrey Nowell-Smith (London: British Film Institute, 2000), 24.

30. David Forgacs, *Rome Open City* (London: British Film Institute, 2000), 62–63.

31. Ben-Ghiat, "The Fascist War Trilogy," 24.

32. Naoki Sakai, "The West—A Dialogic Prescription or Proscription?," *Social Identities* 11, no. 3 (May 2005): 177–95, https://doi.org/10.1080/13504630500256910.

33. Aimé Césaire, *Discourse on Colonialism,* trans. Joan Pinkham (New York: Monthly Review Press, 2000), 73, quoted in Weheliye, *Habeas Viscus,* 7.

34. Gabriele Proglio, Camilla Hawthorne, Ida Danewid, P. Khalil Saucier, Giuseppe Grimaldi, Angelica Pesarini, Timothy Raeymaekers, Giulia Grechi, and Vivian Gerrand, "Introduction," in Proglio et al., *The Black Mediterranean,* 23. On the Black Mediterranean, see Alessandra Di Maio, "The Mediterranean; or, Where Africa Does (Not) Meet Italy: Andrea Segre's *A Sud di Lampedusa* (2006)," in *The Cinemas of Italian Migration: European and Transatlantic Narratives,* ed. Sabine Schrader and Daniel Winkler (Cambridge: Cambridge Scholars Publishing, 2013), 41–52; SA Smythe, "Black Italianità: Citizenship and Belonging in the Black Mediterranean," *California Italian Studies* 9, no. 1 (2019), https://doi.org/10.5070/C391042328; Pesarini, "When the Mediterranean 'Became' Black"; and Camilla Hawthorne, *Contesting Race and Citizenship: Youth Politics in the Black Mediterranean* (Ithaca, N.Y.: Cornell University Press, 2022).

35. Pesarini, "When the Mediterranean 'Became' Black." On the colors of the Mediterranean, see also Danewid, "White Innocence in the Black Mediterranean";

and Gabriele Proglio, "Is the Mediterranean a White Italian-European Sea? The Multiplication of Borders in the Production of Historical Subjectivity," *Interventions* 20, no. 3 (2018): 406–27, https://doi.org/10.1080/1369801X.2017.1421025.

36. Shelleen Greene, *Equivocal Subjects* (London: Continuum, 2012), 116–84.

37. Catherine O'Rawe, *Stars and Masculinities in Contemporary Italian Cinema* (New York: Palgrave Macmillan, 2014), 70–72; Catherine O'Rawe, "Back for Good: Melodrama and the Returning Soldier in Post-war Italian Cinema," *Modern Italy* 22, no. 2 (2017): 123–42, https://doi.org/10.1017/mit.2017.18; Dana Renga, *Watching Sympathetic Perpetrators on Italian Television: Gomorrah and Beyond* (New York: Palgrave Macmillan, 2019), 1–38; Williams, "Film Bodies."

38. Peter Brunette, *Roberto Rossellini* (Berkeley: University of California Press, 1996), 21.

39. Noa Steimatsky, *Italian Locations: Reinhabiting the Past in Postwar Cinema* (Minneapolis: University of Minnesota Press, 2008), 17.

40. Renzo Rossellini, "Al fratello," *Cinema,* no. 158 (January 25, 1943): 62; Mino Argentieri, *Il cinema in guerra: Arte, comunicazione e propaganda in Italia, 1940–1944* (Rome: Editori riuniti, 1998), 274.

41. In a 1953 note published in *Cinema Nuovo,* Renzo Renzi proposed to explore these themes in a film. The idea warranted Renzi and Guido Aristarco, *Cinema Nuovo's* editor in chief, a seven-month sentence in military prison. Renzo Renzi, "L'armata s'agapò," *Cinema Nuovo* 2, no. 4 (February 1, 1953): 73–75, republished in Piero Calamandrei, Renzo Renzi, and Guido Aristarco, eds., *Dall'Arcadia a Peschiera: Ol processo s'agapò* (Rome: Laterza, 1954).

42. Ben-Ghiat, "The Fascist War Trilogy," 32.

43. See Peter Bondanella, *The Films of Roberto Rossellini* (Cambridge: Cambridge University Press, 1993), 32–41.

44. See, for instance, Asvero Gravelli, *Razza in Agonia* (Rome: Nuova Europa, 1939).

45. Brunette, *Roberto Rossellini*, 32.

46. Argentieri, *Il cinema in guerra*, 120–30.

47. Marla Stone, "Italian Fascism's Soviet Enemy and the Propaganda of Hate, 1941–1943," *Journal of Hate Studies* 10, no. 1 (2012): 73–97, http://doi.org/10.33972/jhs.114.

6. DE SICA'S GENRE TROUBLE

1. Giorgio Agamben, *Stasis: Civil War as a Political Paradigm,* trans. Nicholas Heron (Stanford: Stanford University Press, 2015), 25–35.

2. Agamben, 44.

3. Giorgio Agamben, *Pulcinella: Or Entertainment for Children,* trans. Kevin Attell (Chicago: University of Chicago Press, 2018), 41–43.

4. André Bazin, "De Sica: Metteur en Scène," in *What Is Cinema?,* vol. 2, trans. Hugh Gray (Berkeley: University of California Press, 1971), 61–78.

5. David Bruni, *Dalla parte del publico: Aldo De Benedetti sceneggiatore* (Rome: Bulzoni, 2011), 134–39.

6. Michele Sarfatti, *The Jews in Mussolini's Italy: From Equality to Persecution*, trans. John and Anne C. Tedeschi (Madison: University of Wisconsin Press, 2006), 122–210.

7. Giorgio Almirante, "Fotogrammi: Discussioni sul cinema italiano," *Il Tevere*, March 9–10, 1943, 3.

8. Enzo Maurri, *Rose scarlatte e telefoni bianchi* (Rome: Abete, 1981), 27–32.

9. David Forgacs, "Sex in the Cinema: Regulation and Transgression in Italian Films, 1930–1943," in *Re-viewing Fascism: Italian Cinema, 1922–1943*, ed. Jacqueline Reich and Piero Garofalo (Bloomington: Indiana University Press, 2002), 141–71.

10. Giuseppe De Santis, "Film di questi giorni," *Cinema*, no. 20 (April 4, 1942): 198–99; Giuseppe De Santis, "Film di questi giorni," *Cinema*, no. 168 (June 25, 1943): 374–75.

11. Alan O'Leary, "The Phenomenology of the *Cinepanettone*," *Italian Studies* 66, no. 3 (2011): 431–43, https://doi.org/10.1179/0075163113134938380526; Lauren Berlant and Sianne Ngai, "Comedy Has Issues," *Critical Inquiry* 43, no. 2 (Winter 2017): 233–49, https://doi.org/10.1086/689666.

12. Arpad Szakolczai, *Comedy and the Public Sphere: The Rebirth of Theatre as Comedy and the Genealogy of the Modern Public Arena* (New York: Routledge, 2013), 4. The concept of a global reactionary cycle is derived from Alberto Di Nicola, "L'Italia nel ciclo politico reazionario," *Dinamo Press*, February 14, 2018, https://www.dinamopress.it.

13. See Emma Bond, "Discourses of Italian Colonialism on the Global Stage: The Collections of the Wolfsonian-FIU" (presentation, American Association for Italian Studies, Sorrento, Italy, June 14–17, 2018).

14. See Elaine Mancini, *Struggles of the Italian Film Industry during Fascism, 1930–1935* (Ann Arbor: University of Michigan Press, 1985), 92–93.

15. Carlo Celli, "The Legacy of Mario Camerini in Vittorio De Sica's *The Bicycle Thief* (1948)," *Cinema Journal* 40, no. 4 (Summer 2001): 3–17, http://www.jstor.org/stable/1225867.

16. Mino Argentieri, *Risate di regime* (Venice: Marsilio, 1991).

17. Henri Bergson, *Laughter: An Essay on the Meaning of the Comic*, trans. Cloudesley Brereton and Fred Rothwell (Mansfield Centre, Conn.: Martino Publishing, 2014).

18. Emily Herring, "Laughter Is Vital," *aeon*, July 7, 2020, https://aeon.co.

19. See John Morreal, "Philosophy of Humor," *The Stanford Encyclopedia of Philosophy* (Fall 2020 edition), ed. Edward N. Zalta, https://plato.stanford.edu.

20. On Montessori, see Suzanne Stewart-Steinberg, *The Pinocchio Effect: On Making Italians, 1860–1920* (Chicago: University of Chicago Press, 2008), 326–64; and Erica Moretti, *The Best Weapon for Peace: Maria Montessori, Education, and Children's Rights* (Madison: University of Wisconsin Press, 2021), 18–69. On French feminism, see Ann Rosalind Jones, "Writing the Body: Toward an Understanding of 'L'Ecriture Feminine,'" *Feminist Studies* 7, no. 2 (Summer 1981): 247–63, https://doi.org/10.2307/3177523.

21. Ramsey McGlazer, "Learning by Hart: Gender, Image, and Ideology in Vittorio De Sica's *Maddalena zero in condotta*," *The Italianist* 36, no. 2 (2016): 187–213, https://doi.org/10.1080/02614340.2016.1176703.

22. McGlazer, 195.

23. Celli, "The Legacy of Mario Camerini," 13.

24. Marcia Landy, *Fascism in Film: The Italian Commercial Cinema, 1931–1943* (Princeton, N.J.: Princeton University Press, 1986), 46–49.

25. McGlazer arrives at the opposite conclusion in his reading of these moments from *Maddalena*, arguing that the teacher's "soaring rhetoric and passionate cadences colour, even while they contrast with, the faces and bodies [of Harman and his cousin] we behold again." See McGlazer, "Learning by Hart," 190.

26. I discuss *Un garibaldino al convento* at length in Lorenzo Fabbri, "'Non è ancora venuto il momento di cantare': *Un garibaldino al convento* tra revisionismo storico e impegno antifascista," in *Cinema e Risorgimento: Visioni e re-visioni,* ed. Fulvio Orsitto (Rome: Vecchiarelli, 2012), 69–81.

27. Walter Benjamin, "The Work of Art in the Age of Its Technological Reproducibility (First Version)," trans. Michael W. Jennings, *Grey Room,* no. 39 (Spring 2010): 11–38.

28. See Miriam Bratu Hansen, "Room-for-Play: Benjamin's Gamble with Cinema," *October,* no. 109 (Summer 2004): 3–45, https://doi.org/10.1162/0162287041886511.

29. On reenchantment as a political strategy, see Silvia Federici, *Re-enchanting the World: Feminism and the Politics of the Commons* (Oakland, Calif.: PM Press, 2018); for a critique of it, see Jason Crawford, "The Trouble with Re-enchantment," *Los Angeles Review of Books,* September 7, 2020, https://www.lareviewofbooks.org.

30. Sara Ahmed, "Feminist Killjoys (and Other Willful Subjects)," *Cahiers du Genre* 53, no. 2 (2012): 77–98, https://doi.org/10.3917/cdge.053.0077.

31. Landy, *Fascism in Film,* 53–55; Jacqueline Reich, "Reading, Writing, and Rebellion: Collectivity, Specularity, and Sexuality in the Italian Schoolgirl Comedy, 1934–1943," in *Mothers of Invention: Women, Italian Fascism, and Culture,* ed. Robin Pickering-Iazzi (Minneapolis: University of Minnesota Press, 1995), 238.

32. McGlazer, "Learning by Hart," 209–10.

33. Castor oil is a very powerful laxative, and political opponents would be obliged to drink a whole bottle without being allowed to use the restroom. After they inevitably shit their pants, they would be paraded through the streets and exposed to public mockery—another example of how laughter can be weaponized for the worst.

34. Reich, "Reading, Writing, and Rebellion," 245.

35. On parrhesia, see Michel Foucault, *The Courage of Truth: The Government of Self and Others II; Lectures at the Collège de France, 1983–1984,* ed. Arnold Davidson, trans. Graham Burchell (New York: Picador, 2012), 1–22.

36. Aldo De Benedetti, "Scusatemi ma le commedie so scriverle soltanto così . . ." [Apologies but I only know how to write comedies like this], *Il dramma* 12, no. 247 (December 1936): 23–24.

7. QUEER ANTIFASCISM

1. Karl Schoonover and Rosalind Galt, *Queer Cinema in the World* (Durham, N.C.: Duke University Press, 2016), 1–34.

2. David Forgacs, "Sex in the Cinema: Regulation and Transgression in Italian Films, 1930–1943," in *Re-viewing Fascism: Italian Cinema, 1922–1943,* ed. Jacqueline Reich and Piero Garofalo (Bloomington: Indiana University Press, 2002), 141–71.

3. André Bazin, "An Aesthetic of Reality: Neorealism," in *What Is Cinema?*, vol. 2, trans. Hugh Gray (Berkeley: University of California Press, 1971), 16–40.

4. Ennio Di Nolfo, "Intimations of Neorealism in the Fascist Ventennio," in Reich and Garofalo, *Re-viewing Fascism*, 93.

5. Millicent Marcus, *Italian Film in the Light of Neorealism* (Princeton, N.J.: Princeton University Press, 1986), 31–31–117; Tom Gunning, "'Now You See It, Now You Don't': The Temporality of the Cinema of Attractions," *The Velvet Light Trap*, no. 32 (Fall 1993): 3–12; William Van Watson, "Luchino Visconti's (Homosexual) *Ossessione*," in Reich and Garofalo, *Re-viewing Fascism*, 172–93; Giuliana Minghelli, "Haunted Frames: History and Landscape in Luchino Visconti's *Ossessione*," *Italica* 85, nos. 2–3 (2008): 173–96, https://www.jstor.org/stable/40505801. On the *Cinema* cell realism, see Orio Caldiron, ed., *Il lungo viaggio del cinema italiano: Antologia di "Cinema" 1936–1943* (Venice: Marsilio, 1965); Peter Bondanella, *A History of Italian Cinema* (London: Continuum, 2009), 55–60; Di Nolfo, "Intimations of Neorealism in the Fascist Ventennio"; and David Overbey, introduction to *Springtime in Italy: A Reader on Neorealism*, ed. David Overbey (London: Talisman Books, 1978), 10–16. Key sources for understanding Bazin's and Baudry's opposite takes on the ontology and politics of realism in cinema are Bazin, "An Aesthetic of Reality"; Bazin, "The Ontology of the Photographic Image," in *What Is Cinema?*, vol. 1, trans. Hugh Gray (Berkeley: University of California Press, 1967), 9–16; and Jean-Louis Baudry, "Ideological Effects of the Basic Cinematographic Apparatus," trans. Alan Williams, *Film Quarterly* 28, no. 2 (1974/75): 39–47, https://doi.org/10.2307/1211632.

6. Jonathan Mullins, "Desiring Desire in Visconti's *Ossessione*," *Journal of Romance Studies* 12, no. 2 (2012): 33–58, https://doi.org/10.3828/jrs.12.2.33.

7. Sergio J. Pacifici, "Notes toward a Definition of Neorealism," *Yale French Studies*, no. 17 (1956): 44–53, https://doi.org/10.2307/2929117; Duncan Petrie, "A New Art for a New Society? The Emergence and Development of Film Schools in Europe," in *The Emergence of Film Culture: Knowledge Production, Institution Building, and the Fate of the Avant-Garde in Europe, 1919–1945*, ed. Malte Hagener (New York: Berghahn Books, 2014), 268–82.

8. Maurizio Rava, "I popoli africani dinanzi allo schermo," *Cinema*, no. 1 (July 10, 1936): 9–11. For a broader discussion of Fascism's politics of natality and the role that cinema played in its enforcement, see Shelleen Greene, *Equivocal Subjects: Between Italy and Africa—Constructions of Racial and National Identity in the Italian Cinema* (London: Continuum, 2012), 50–117.

9. Rava, "I popoli africani dinanzi allo schermo."

10. See Ann Laura Stoler, *Race and the Education of Desire: Foucault's History of Sexuality and the Colonial Order of Things* (Durham, N.C.: Duke University Press, 1995), 95–137.

11. Vittorio Mussolini, "Ordine e disciplina," *Cinema*, no. 71 (June 10, 1939): 355; Vittorio Mussolini, "Razza italiana e cinema italiano," *Cinema*, no. 53 (September 10, 1938): 143. See also the following works by Vittorio Mussolini: "Emancipazione del cinema italiano," *Cinema*, no. 6 (September 25, 1936): 213–14; "Cinema per gli indigeni," *Cinema*, no. 64 (February 25, 1939): 109; "Cinema di guerra," *Cinema*, no. 96 (June 25,

1940): 423; and "Constatazioni," *Cinema*, no. 117 (May 10, 1941): 297. For a longer engagement with Mussolini as a film theorist and scenario writer, see Giovanni Sedita, "Vittorio Mussolini, Hollywood and Neorealism," *Journal of Modern Italian Studies* 15, no. 3 (2010): 431–57, https://doi.org/10.1080/13545711003768618.

12. Vittorio Mussolini, "In cerca della formula italiana al cinema," *Cinema*, no. 15 (February 10, 1937): 88–89.

13. Ernesto Laclau, *Politics and Ideology in Marxist Theory: Capitalism, Fascism, Populism* (London: Verso, 1979), 120.

14. Gian Piero Brunetta, *Cinema italiano tra le due guerre: Fascismo e politica cinematografica* (Palermo: Mursia, 1975), 44, translation mine. For the history of the *Cinema* cell, I rely on Gianni Puccini, "Storia di *Cinema*," in Caldiron, *Il lungo viaggio del cinema italiano*, lxxxiii.

15. The political registry of antifascist activities is available online at http://dati.acs.beniculturali.it/CPC/.

16. Antonio Gramsci, *Prison Notebooks*, vol. 3, trans. Joseph A. Buttigieg (New York: Columbia University Press, 2010), 168. On the effectiveness of entryism as a political tactic, see Victoria de Grazia, *The Culture of Consent: Mass Organisation of Leisure in Fascist Italy* (Cambridge: Cambridge University Press, 1981), 225–45; on Fascism's strategic "aesthetic pluralism," see Marla Susan Stone, *The Patron State: Culture and Politics in Fascist Italy* (Princeton, N.J.: Princeton University Press, 1998), 65–70.

17. See Ruth Ben-Ghiat, *Fascist Modernities: Italy, 1922–1945* (Berkeley: University of California Press, 2001), 32–33.

18. Giuseppe De Santis, "Per un paesaggio italiano," *Cinema*, no. 116 (April 25, 1941): 262–63. English translations for De Santis's "Per un paesaggio italiano" and for two other essays I discuss in this chapter (Alicata and De Santis's "Verità e poesia: Verga e il cinema italiano" and Visconti's "Cinema antropomorfico") can be found in Overbey, *Springtime in Italy*, 83–86, 125–30, and 131–38.

19. Mussolini, "Razza italiana e cinema italiano," 9. The illustrious scientists evoked by Mussolini are in all probability the ones who penned and signed the "Manifesto della razza," which had been published two short months earlier.

20. De Santis, "Per un paesaggio italiano," 262.

21. De Santis, "Il linguaggio dei rapporti," *Cinema*, no. 132 (December 25, 1941): 388, translation mine.

22. Noa Steimatsky, *Italian Locations: Reinhabiting the Past in Postwar Cinema* (Minneapolis: University of Minnesota Press, 2008), 79–85.

23. See Derek Duncan, *"Ossessione,"* in *European Cinema: An Introduction,* ed. Jill Forbes and Sarah Street (New York: Palgrave, 2000), 95–108.

24. Roman Jakobson, "On Realism in Art," in *Language in Literature*, ed. Krystyna Pomorska and Stephen Rudy (Cambridge, Mass.: Belknap Press of Harvard University Press, 1987), 19–27.

25. Mario Alicata and Giuseppe De Santis, "Verità e poesia: Verga e il cinema italiano," *Cinema*, no. 127 (October 10, 1941): 216–17.

26. Umberto Barbaro, "Documento e didattico (1939)," in *Neorealismo e realismo*, vol. 2 (Rome: Editori riuniti, 1976), 495–99; Mario Alicata and Giuseppe De Santis, "Ancora su Verga e il cinema italiano," *Cinema*, no. 130 (November 25, 1941): 314.

27. Noa Steimatsky, "Photographic *Verismo,* Cinematic Adaptation, and the Staging of Neorealistic Landscape," in *A Companion to Literature and Film,* ed. Robert Stam and Alessandra Raengo (Malden, Mass.: Blackwell, 2004), 207.

28. See Pietro Ingrao, "Luchino Visconti: L'antifascismo e il cinema," *Rinascita,* no. 13 (March 26, 1976): 33–34; and Mario Alicata, "Lingua e popolo," in *Intellettuali e vita politica* (Rome: Editori riuniti, 1975), 60–61.

29. On the importance of new national heroes for progressive movements, see Mario Alicata, "Ambiente e società nel racconto cinematografico," *Cinema,* no. 135 (February 10, 1942): 74–75.

30. Alicata and De Santis, "Verità e poesia," 217, translation mine.

31. Fausto Montesanti, "Della ispirazione cinematografica," *Cinema,* no. 129 (November 10, 1941): 280–81.

32. Luchino Visconti, "Cadaveri," *Cinema,* no. 119 (June 10, 1941): 445.

33. Luchino Visconti, "Tradizione e invenzione" (1941), in *Luchino Visconti: Un profilo critico,* ed. Lino Miccichè (Venice: Marsilio, 1996), 78–79, translation mine.

34. Mario Alicata, *Lettere e taccuini di Regina Coeli,* ed. Giorgio Amendola (Turin: Einaudi, 1977), 42; Luchino Visconti, "Cinema antropomorfico," *Cinema,* nos. 173–74 (September 25, 1943): 108–9. For a more detailed discussion of Visconti's primitivistic fascination with Verga and Sicily, see Lorenzo Fabbri, "Chrono-Maps: The Time of the South in Antonio Gramsci, Luchino Visconti, and Emanuele Crialese," *Senses of Cinema,* no. 81 (2016), https://www.sensesofcinema.com.

35. Umberto Barbaro, "'Neo-realismo' (1943) and 'Realismo e moralità' (1943)," in *Neorealismo e realismo,* vol. 2 (Rome: Editori riuniti, 1976), 500–509. For a contemporary account of the reactions to *Ossessione,* see Massimo Mida, "A proposito di Ossessione," *Cinema,* no. 169 (July 10, 1943): 19–20; for a more recent one, see Henry Bacon, *Visconti: Explorations of Beauty and Decay* (Cambridge: Cambridge University Press, 1998), 14–16.

36. Peter Brooks, *Realist Vision* (New Haven, Conn.: Yale University Press, 2008), 3.

37. Alexander García Düttmann, *Visconti: Insights into Flesh and Blood,* trans. Robert Savage (Stanford: Stanford University Press, 2009), 85–132; Jonathan Goldberg, *Melodrama: An Aesthetics of Impossibility* (Durham, N.C.: Duke University Press, 2016), 160; Alexander García Düttmann, "Melodrama and Laughter: On Visconti" (conference presentation, The Positive Negative—Cinema and Comedy, Berlin, May 5–6, 2017).

38. Bacon, *Visconti,* 16–25.

39. Carlo Vercellone, "The Anomaly and Exemplariness of the Italian Welfare State," in *Radical Thought in Italy: A Potential Politics,* ed. Paolo Virno and Michael Hardt (Minneapolis: University of Minnesota Press, 2006), 81–98.

40. De Santis, "Quando Visconti girava *Ossessione* tra Ferrara e Pontelagoscuro e io . . . ," *Bologna incontri: Mensile dell'Ente Provinciale per il Turismo di Bologna,* April 1983, 39–42. Parts of this essay appeared in English: see Giuseppe De Santis, "Visconti's Interpretation of Cain's Setting in *Ossessione,*" trans. Luciana Bohne, *Film Criticism* 9, no. 3 (1985): 23–32, http://www.jstor.org/stable/44019015.

41. Minghelli, "Haunted Frames."

42. De Santis, "Visconti's Interpretation of Cain's Setting in *Ossessione,*" 31.

43. Eve Kosofsky Sedgwick, *Tendencies* (Durham, N.C.: Duke University Press, 1993), 8.

44. See Mario Alicata, "Ricordi," in *Il cinema italiano dal fascismo all'antifascismo,* ed. Giorgio Tinazzi (Venice: Marsilio, 1966). Alicata blamed Visconti for Spagnolo's "moral ambiguity," possibly alluding to the character's implicit homosexuality.

45. Mira Liehm, *Passion and Defiance: Film in Italy from 1942 to the Present* (Berkeley: University of California Press, 1984), 54.

46. Gilles Deleuze, *Cinema 2: The Time-Image,* trans. Hugh Tomlinson and Robert Galeta (Minneapolis: University of Minnesota Press, 1989), 3–5.

47. David Martin-Jones, *Deleuze and World Cinemas* (New York: Continuum, 2011), 69–71; José Esteban Muñoz, *Cruising Utopia: The Then and There of Queer Futurity* (New York: New York University Press, 2009), 90–96.

48. Kadji Amin, *Disturbing Attachments: Genet, Modern Pederasty, and Queer History* (Durham, N.C.: Duke University Press, 2017).

49. Lee Edelman, *No Future: Queer Theory and the Death Drive* (Durham, N.C.: Duke University Press, 2004), 29.

50. Lauren Berlant, *Cruel Optimism* (Durham, N.C.: Duke University Press, 2011), 1–49.

51. Van Watson, "Luchino Visconti's (Homosexual) *Ossessione,*" 178–80; Laura Mulvey, "Visual Pleasure and Narrative Cinema," *Screen* 16, no. 3 (1975): 6–18, https://doi.org/10.1093/screen/16.3.6.

52. Editorial Office, "Note," *Cinema,* no. 170 (July 25, 1943): 33.

53. For onscreen parapraxis as a way to ignite agency in the spectatorship, see Thomas Elsaesser, *German Cinema—Terror and Trauma: Cultural Memory since 1945* (New York: Routledge, 2013), 1–31.

54. See Catherine O'Rawe, "Gender, Genre, and Stardom: Fatality in Neorealist Cinema," in *The Femme Fatale: Images, Histories, Contexts,* ed. Helen Hanson and Catherine O'Rawe (New York: Palgrave Macmillan, 2010), 127–42; Lino Miccichè, *Visconti e il neorealismo* (Venice: Marsilio, 1990), 58–59n63. See also Liehm, *Passion and Defiance,* 328; and, for the troubled exhibition history of *Ossessione,* Gianni Rondolino, *Luchino Visconti* (Turin: Unione Tipografico-Editrice Torinese, 1981), 114–24.

55. See Giacomo Lichtner, *Fascism in Italian Cinema since 1945: The Politics and Aesthetics of Memory* (London: Palgrave Macmillan, 2013), 171–214; and Karl Schoonover, *Brutal Vision: The Neorealist Body in Postwar Italian Cinema* (Minneapolis: University of Minnesota Press, 2012), 69–108.

CONCLUSION

1. Catherine O'Rawe, "'I padri e i maestri': Genre, Auteurs, and Absences in Italian Film Studies," *Italian Studies* 63, no. 2 (2008): 178, https://doi.org/10.1179/007516308X344342. For a precise review of the status of Italian film studies confirming neorealism's persisting centrality in the field, see Dana Renga, "Italian Screen Studies in the Anglophone Context: 2008–2013," *The Italianist* 34, no. 2 (2014): 242–49, https://doi.org/10.1179/0261434014Z.00000000077.

2. The discussion of U.S. postwar hegemony, geopolitical areas, and area studies I develop in this chapter is deeply indebted to Gavin Walker and Naoki Sakai,

"The End of Area," *Positions: Asia Critique* 27, no. 1 (2019): 1–31, https://doi.org/10.1215/10679847-7251793.

3. André Bazin, "In Defense of Rossellini," in *What Is Cinema?*, vol. 2, trans. Hugh Gray (Berkeley: University of California Press, 1971), 99.

4. André Bazin, "An Aesthetic of Reality: Neorealism," in *What Is Cinema?*, 2:16–40; Gilles Deleuze, *Cinema 1: The Movement-Image,* trans. Hugh Tomlinson and Barbara Habberjam (Minneapolis: University of Minnesota Press, 1986), 205–16; Gilles Deleuze, *Cinema 2: The Time-Image,* trans. Hugh Tomlinson and Robert Galeta (Minneapolis: University of Minnesota Press, 1989), 1–13.

5. Millicent Marcus, *Italian Film in the Light of Neorealism* (Princeton, N.J.: Princeton University Press, 1986), xvii.

6. Alan O'Leary and Catherine O'Rawe, "Against Realism: On a 'Certain Tendency' in Italian Film Criticism," *Journal of Modern Italian Studies* 16, no. 1 (2011): 107–28, https://doi.org/10.1080/1354571X.2011.530767. For reactions to this intervention, see Millicent Marcus, "Responses: Against Realism," *Journal of Modern Italian Studies* 16, no. 1 (2011): 121–23, https://doi.org/10.1080/1354571X.2011.530767; and Charles L. Leavitt IV, "*Cronaca, Narrativa,* and the Unstable Foundations of the Institution of Neorealism," *Italian Culture* 31, no. 1 (2013): 28–46, https://doi.org/10.1179/01614622 12Z.00000000014.

7. Bazin, "An Aesthetic of Reality," 18.

8. Bazin, 19.

9. See Shelleen Greene, *Equivocal Subjects: Between Italy and Africa—Constructions of Racial and National Identity in the Italian Cinema* (London: Continuum, 2012), 129–40.

10. Christopher Wagstaff, *Italian Neorealist Cinema: An Aesthetic Approach* (Toronto: University of Toronto Press, 2007), 184; Karl Schoonover, *Brutal Vision: The Neorealist Body in Postwar Italian Cinema* (Minneapolis: University of Minnesota Press, 2012).

11. Cesare Casarino, "Three Theses on the Life-Image (Deleuze, Cinema, Biopolitics)," in *Releasing the Image: From Literature to New Media,* ed. Jacques Khalip and Robert Mitchell (Stanford: Stanford University Press, 2011), 166.

12. See Jacques Rancière, "Falling Bodies: Rossellini's Physics," in *Film Fables,* trans. Emiliano Battista (New York: Berg, 2006), 125–42; and Alessia Ricciardi, "The Italian Redemption of Cinema: Neorealism from Bazin to Godard," *Romanic Review* 97, nos. 3–4 (May 2006): 483–500, https://doi.org/10.1215/26885220-97.3-4.483.

13. Deleuze, *Cinema 2*, 97.

14. Deleuze, *Cinema 1*, 210.

15. André Bazin, "The Myth of Total Cinema," in *What Is Cinema?*, vol. 1, trans. Hugh Gray (Berkeley: University of California Press, 1967) 17–22.

16. Cesare Zavattini, "Alcune idee sul cinema," in *Neorealismo Ecc.,* ed. Mino Argentieri (Milan: Bompiani, 1979), 99. For an English translation, see Zavattini, "Some Ideas on the Cinema," trans. Pier Luigi Lanza, *Sight & Sound* 23, no. 2 (1953): 66, https://doi.org/10.1525/9780520957411-042.

17. André Bazin, "Bicycle Thief," in *What Is Cinema?*, 2:60.

18. "I myself have made some rather naïve statements in the past about De Sica's sentimentality": André Bazin, "Cruel Naples," in *André Bazin and Italian Neorealism,*

ed. Bert Cardullo (New York: Continuum, 2011), 162. In *André Bazin and Italian Neo-realism,* see also Bazin's reviews, specifically "A Saint Becomes a Saint Only after the Fact: *Heaven over the Marshes,*" 89–93; and "Neorealism, Opera, and Propaganda," 94–102.

19. André Bazin, "*Umberto D*: A Great Work," in *What Is Cinema?,* 2:82.

20. Bazin, 82.

21. Bazin, "The Myth of Total Cinema," 21.

22. Bazin, "An Aesthetic of Reality," 21–22.

23. Luigi Pirandello, *Quaderni di Serafino Gubbio operatore* (Milan: Mondadori, 1925).

24. Jacques Rancière, "From One Image to Another? Deleuze and the Ages of Cinema," in *Film Fables,* 107–24.

25. Deleuze, *Cinema 2,* 205–6.

26. Leavitt, "*Cronaca, Narrativa,* and the Unstable Foundations of the Institution of Neorealism," 41.

27. Peter Bondanella, *The Films of Roberto Rossellini* (Cambridge: Cambridge University Press, 1993), 5.

28. Christina Sharpe, *In the Wake: On Blackness and Being* (Durham, N.C.: Duke University Press, 2016), 1–24.

29. André Bazin, "Le réalisme cinématographique et l'école italienne de la libera-tion," *Esprit* 1, no. 141 (January 1948): 73, http://www.jstor.org/stable/24250145.

30. Gayatri Chakravorty Spivak, *A Critique of Postcolonial Reason: Toward a History of the Vanishing Present* (Cambridge, Mass.: Harvard University Press, 1999), especially 1–37.

31. Bazin, "Le réalisme cinématographique et l'école italienne de la liberation," 83. For an unabridged and unauthorized translation of Bazin's essay on neorealism, see André Bazin, "Cinematic Realism and the Italian School of Liberation," in *What Is Cinema?,* trans. Timothy Barnard (Montreal: caboose, 2009), 215–49.

32. Ricciardi, "The Italian Redemption of Cinema," 495.

33. Noa Steimatsky, *Italian Locations: Reinhabiting the Past in Postwar Cinema* (Minneapolis: University of Minnesota Press, 2008), 47.

34. Noa Steimatsky, "The Cinecittà Refugee Camp (1944–1950)," *October,* no. 128 (Spring 2009): 27, https://doi.org/10.1162/octo.2009.128.1.22.

35. Francesco Filippi, *Ma perché siamo ancora fascisti?* (Turin: Bollati Boringhieri, 2020), 17–149.

36. Benedetto Croce, "The Fascist Germ Still Lives," *New York Times,* November 28, 1943; Benedetto Croce, "Intorno ai criteri dell'"epurazione,'" in *Scritti e discorsi politici,* vol. 1, ed. Angela Carella (Naples: Bibliopolis, 1993), 50–53; Michel Foucault, "The Subject and Power," *Critical Inquiry* 8, no. 4 (Summer 1982): 780, https://doi.org/10.1086/448181.

37. See David Forgacs, *Rome Open City* (London: British Film Institute, 2000); and Ruth Ben-Ghiat, "Liberation: Italian Cinema and the Fascist Past, 1945–50," in *Italian Fascism: History, Memory and Representation,* ed. R. J. B. Bosworth and Patrizia Dogli-ani (New York: Palgrave Macmillan, 1999), 83–101. For a comparison of the represen-tation of sex work in Rossellini's and Mattòli's films, see Danielle Hipkins, "Were

Sisters Doing It for Themselves? Prostitutes, Brothels and Discredited Masculinity in Postwar Italian Cinema," in *War-Torn Tales: Literature, Film and Gender in the Aftermath of World War II*, ed. Danielle Hipkins and Gill Plain (Oxford: Peter Lang, 2007), 80–103.

38. Ruth Ben-Ghiat, *Fascist Modernities: Italy, 1922–1945* (Berkeley: University of California Press, 2001), 207; Charles L. Leavitt IV, *Italian Neorealism: A Cultural History* (Toronto: University of Toronto Press, 2020). See also Salvatore Ambrosino, "Il cinema ricominica: Attori e registi fra 'continuita' e 'frattura,'" in *Neorealismo: Cinema italiano, 1945–1949*, ed. Alberto Farassino (Turin: EDT, 1989), 60–77.

39. Mario Cannella, "Ideology and Aesthetic Hypotheses in the Criticism of Neo-Realism," *Screen* 14, no. 4 (1973): 9, https://doi.org/10.1093/screen/14.4.5. For a discussion of Cannella's position in relation to the emergence of the New Left and the critique of late 1960s "compromesso storico," see Angela Dalle Vacche, *The Body in the Mirror: Shapes of History in Italian Cinema* (Princeton, N.J.: Princeton University Press, 1992), 196–97.

Index

Page references in italics refer to figures.

Abject, as dysgenic Other, 116
abjection: of northern European
whiteness, 162; performance of, 177;
of wartime assignments, 197; in
Western modernity, 116; of white
elites, 116, 119–20, *120*
Acciaio (Ruttmann), 17, 29, 66–78, 121;
audience of, 67; cult of machine in, 76;
dangers of work in, 69, 71; dehuman-
ization in, 77; diegetic universe of, 74;
factory symphony sequence, 69; factory visitors in, 67, 68; failure of, 77–78;
formalism of, 67; genealogy of, 256n4;
German appreciation of, 77; German
cultural tropes of, 78; German title
of, 74; human-machine assemblage
in, 72; individuals in, 68–69, 71, 76–77;
individual/state conflict in, 80; innocence of the state in, 69; isolation in,
74; Italian workforce of, 60, 64, *70, 74,
76,* 76–77; lightscape of, 69; military-
industrial complex in, 73; mythologi-
zation of Fascism, 76; national bodies
in, 73; noncompliance in, 77; Pirandello's treatment and, 72–73, 257n16;
plot of, 67–68; private/nationalized
sphere in, 75; reality of, 73–74, 75, 78;

reunited community of, 71; ritual cave
of, 78, *79*; score of, 73; shot-reverse-
shots of, 69; sociopolitical docility
in, 72; Soldati's role in, 66–67; sonic-
photo montage of, 75; spectatorial
pleasure at, 77; state authority in, 69,
71, 75–76; steelworks floor in, 75; symbolism of, 78; Terni in, 67–69; tone
of, 67–68; water in, 75; worker discipline in, 71. *See also Gioca, Pietro!*
Adorno, Theodor W.: *Dialectic of
Enlightenment,* 33
aesthetics: politics and, 27; of security
cameras, 195
affectivity: of Italian Fascism, xi; knowl-
edge-power networks of, 15, 21–22; in
media scholarship, 26–27; racism in,
31; state use of, 20
affectivity, cinematic, 27, 28; power of,
39, 60; of De Sica's landscapes, 184;
realism in, 15
Africa, Italian: depictions of whiteness
in, 202
Agamben, Giorgio, 8, 146, 220; on
anthropological machines, 115; on
comedy, 170; on *Leviathan,* 179;
on sovereignty, 170

Agbamu, Samuel, 150
Ahmed, Sara, 18
Akbaba (Turkish magazine), critique of Mussolini, 177
Alberini, Filoteo: *La presa di Roma,* 40
Alessandrini, Goffredo, 86; *Luciano Serra, pilota,* 97, 150; *Seconda B,* 188; *La segretaria privata,* 126
Alicata, Mario, 201, 217; at *Cinema,* 205; imprisonment of, 211; on realism, 206; "Verità e poesia: Verga e il cinema italiano," 209, 210, 214
All'armi siam fascisti (Del Fra, Mangini, Miccichè), 248
Almirante, Giorgio, 173
Althusser, Louis: on consent to capitalism, 19; "Ideology and Ideological State Apparatuses," 4, 5
Amato, Giuseppe, 173
Americans, white: assumptions of superiority, 136
Amin, Kadji: *Disturbing Attachments,* 221
Andreotti, Giulio, 247
Anker, Elisabeth, 136
antifascism, 83; as degenerate, 90; Italian repression of, 140; political registry of, 268n15
Antliff, Mark, 110
antisemitism, Italian, 172–73; in fascist cinema, 172
apparatus theory, 4, 7, 27; bodily sensations in, 26
Arbeit macht frei (slogan), 74
Argentieri, Mino, 161; on laughter, 180
Aristarco, Guido, 144; imprisonment of, 264n41
Aryanism: disposition to order, 46; Italian, 149; Nordic, 42
askari (soldier), at LUCE groundbreaking, 2, 6, 7
Attori e Direttori Italiani Associati (ADIA) consortium, 112
audiences: racialized sense of self, 16; self-misrecognition of, 4

Augustus (film company), 86, 92, 121
authority, state: embodiment of, 19; virtuous disregard for, 171
autonomy: biopolitical anxiety over, 58; of submarines, 270n1

Bacon, Henry, 214
Baldwin, James: *The Fire Next Time,* 139
Balibar, Étienne, 58
Barbaro, Umberto, 204, 209, 246; on neorealism, 212
Barratoni, Luca, 255n36
Barthes, Roland, 144
Baudelaire, Charles, 37
Baudry, Jean-Louis, 27; on movie theaters, 4
Bazin, André, 14, 56; "An Aesthetic of Reality," 231–34, 237–38, 241; on *La corona di ferro,* 231; on De Sica, 171–72, 271n16; on fascist cinema, 138, 232; on genre fiction, 233; on imperfect humanity, 237–38; infantilizing of Italy, 242; on Italian ethnic character, 241; on narrative, 235; on neorealism, 30, 200, 229–40; on *Paisà,* 241; pro-realism of, 30; on realism, 144, 233; on *Uomini sul fondo,* 150; on *L'uomo dalla croce,* 263n26
Benelli, Sam: *La cena delle beffe,* 204
Ben-Ghiat, Ruth: on communist purge, 247; *Fascist Modernities,* 2, 15; on Italian colonialism, 89, 125; *Italian Fascism's Empire Cinema,* 15; on *La nave bianca,* 155
Benjamin, Walter, 30; on cinema, 192; on comedy, 171; on *Quaderni di Serafino Gubbio operatore,* 52; "The Work of Art in the Age of Its Technological Reproducibility," 191
Berbrier, Mitch, 135
Bergman, Vera, 174
Bergson, Henri, 30; on comedy, 171, 180–81, 192; *Creative Evolution,* 180–81; *Laughter,* 180–81, 183

Berlant, Lauren, 17; on comedy, 176–77; on cruel optimism, 222
Bertani, Mauro, 21
Bertolucci, Bernardo, x
biopolitics: apparatuses of, 8; comedy's opposition to, 170; De Sica's contestation of, 180, 197; effect of laughter on, 176; embodiment of, 8, 83; feminist, 199; Foucault on, 22, 24, 31; intervention in liberal state, 11; of Italian cinema, 8, 62; mediation practices, 28; perception of rulers in, 100; racial dimension of, 8, 83, 111, 238, 240; remaking of collective living, 58; reproduction of patriarchy, 8; technologies of governance, 17; truth-weapons of, 26. *See also* warfare, biopolitical
biopower, Foucault on, 18
biopower, state: historical formation of, 27; mass mediation devices, 229
Birth of Jesus (film, 1906), 41
Black men, racist imaginaries of, 127, 129
Blackness: in Italian labor spaces, 117; of Mediterranean Sea, 158; in *Sole!*, 29; in *Vecchia guardia*, 29; white existence and, 16
Black Panther Party (BPP), 19
Black people, colonized, 125, 149
Blackshirts: in fascist cinema, 202; genealogy of, 10–11; industriousness of, 110, 124; internal enemies of, 29; jazz orchestras, 117, 118; model of humanity, 116; narratives contributing to, 233; political strategies of, 13–14; in Rossellini's oeuvre, 160; supremacy in national life, 126; survival of, 204; in *Vecchia guardia*, 105; whiteness of, 29, 88, 92, 158, 248; white supremacy of, 83–84, 88, 92
Blasetti, Alessandro, 15, 28, 222; anticipation of liberation, 231; cinematic language of, 80; depiction of Blackshirts,

110; ecofascist realism of, 90, 97; on Ferri, 258n15; film criticism of, 84–85; film language of, 105; fundraising by, 86, 109; on race, 81–82
Blasetti, Alessandro, works: *Aldebaran*, 97, 151; *La corona di ferro*, 231; *La crociata degli innocenti*, 84; *1860*, 107; *Ettore Fieramosca*, 107; *Quattro passi fra le nuvole*, 199. See also *Sole!*; *Terra madre*; *Vecchia guardia*
body: in apparatus theory, 26; as capitalist subject, 238; in film theory, 18; incorporation into state, 169; shaming of, 110, 111–12; truth in, 25–26; without identity, 26
body, Black: cinematic reclamation of, 6; disposable, 137; in fascist Italy, 88
body, Italian: arming of, 134; authentic, 114; autonomy of, 197; cinematic representation of, 202; in De Sica's comedies, 183–84; disciplining of, 34; ethno-national, 109; fascist expectation of, 73; fascist ordering of, 214; fictions restraining, 58; gendered, 192; nonconforming, 139; reclamation of control over, 197; ways of being, 182; White-Dark division, 10, 42, 47, 52, 73, 81; woundedness of, 154
body, racialized, 192; cinema in governance of, 30
Bolter, Jay David: on remediation, 36–37
Bombacci, Nicola, 243
Bondanella, Peter, 240
Bonifazio, Paola: *Schooling in Modernity*, 27
Bonitzer, Pascal, 20
Boulainvilliers, Henri de, 23
Bragaglia, Carlo Ludovico, 173
Brambilla, Franco, 103, 108
brava gente, Italian, x, xi
Brinkema, Eugenie: *The Forms of the Affects*, 27
Brooks, Peter, 213
Bruegel, Pieter: *The Harvesters*, 216, 217

Brunetta, Gian Piero, 63, 115; on *Uomini sul fondo*, 150
Brunette, Peter, 160
Bruni, David, 172; on racial discrimination, 173
Bruno, Giuliana, 5
Buccheri, Vincenzo, 63, 66

Cahiers du Cinéma (journal), 4
Cain, James M.: *The Postman Always Rings Twice*, 199
Calamai, Clara, 213
Calboli de' Paulucci, Giacomo, 61, 258n9
camera, weaponization, 54
Camerini, Mario, 15, 28, 246; abjectification of white elites, 116; anticipation of liberation, 231; biography of, 260n7; cinematic language of, 80, 115–16; depiction of urban underclasses, 110; diegetic universe of, 114; escapism of, 115, 195; gender compliance in, 119; race-making in, 110; racial subjugation in works of, 112; relatable characters of, 115; shame in works of, 110, 112, 115, 131; social position in, 117; urban films of, 109; weaponization of irony, 180; work abroad, 260n18; World War I service, 178
Camerini, Mario, works: *Come le foglie*, 114; *Darò un milione*, 114; *Maciste contro lo sceicco*, 112; *Ma non è una cosa seria*, 114; *I promessi sposi*, 204. See also *cappello a tre punte, Il*; *grande appello, Il*; *grandi magazzini, I*; *Kif Tebbi*; *Rotaie*; *signor Max, Il*; *uomini che mascalzoni . . . , Gli*
Caminati, Luca, 143
Campbell, Timothy, 24
Canal grande (film), 41
Cannella, Mario, 247
Cannistraro, Philip V., 45
capitalism: alienation in, 52; biopolitical warfare of, 7–8; consent to, 5, 19; division of labor, 59; modes of production, 59, 125–26; state power and, 20; technologies of, 191
capitalism, fascist, 5, 19, 60; expendability of life under, 132
capitalism, Italian, 251n19; conflict with labor, 45–46, 81; Italian people under, 49; liberal, 11, 49, 83; in modern nation-state, 9; rural/urban unity against, 110; in traditional life, 67
capitalism, racial, 24; transnational, 18; Western history of, x
capitalism-colonialism: biological warfare under, 7–8; fascist connection to, 248; following liberation of Europe, 240; gender under, 8; Italian, 8, 10–11, 18, 53; production/reproduction of, 137; racial, 146. *See also* colonialism, Italian
Capitol Riot, Washington, D.C., 2021, 135
cappello a tre punte, Il (Camerini), 178–80; abjectification of ruler in, 179; nationalism in, 178; reinstatement of order in, 179; satirization of Mussolini, 178–79; schadenfreude in, 179; sovereign/people reconciliation in, 179
Caprotti, Federico, 88
Carné, Marcel, 212
Casarino, Cesare, 234
Casetti, Francesco, 36
Castellani, Renato, 209
castor oil, fascist use of, 194, 266n33
catharsis, Aristotelian, 175
Catholic Church, Italian fascism and, 97–98
Cavani, Liliana, x
Cecchi, Emilio, 63, 66
Celli, Carlo, 179; on *Maddalena zero in condotta*, 187–88
Centro Cinematografico del Ministero della Marina, 143, 150, 155; De Robertis's work for, 158

Centro Sperimentale di Cinematografia: alternate film forms at, 17;
anti-fascist intelligentsia of, 204;
construction of, 1; training at,
204–5
Césaire, Aimé, 156
Chaplin, Charlie: *City Lights*, 111, 129;
Modern Times, 217; *The Tramp*, 217
Chiari, Mario, 246
children, Italian: in neorealism, 221–22
Christian Democratic Party, 247
Cincotti, Guido, 39
Cinecittà studios: Camerini's films at,
131; construction of, 87, 258n9;
escapism of, 232; Mussolini's organization of, 1–2; propaganda from,
232
Cine-GUFS (film clubs), 92
cinema: as apparatus of ideological
warfare, 4; atmospheric, 262n20;
experience of the real in, 4, 256n7;
influence on children, 202; as
language, 27; Leninist claims for,
2; liberation from, 236; power-
knowledge-affect in, 36; processes
of racialization, 30, 16, 201; role in
nation-building, 39; textuality of, 4;
whiteness in, 38, 41, 44–45, 99
Cinema (journal): media activists of, 171;
post-Mussolini cover, 224, *225*
Cinema (journal), Communist cell, 30,
219; on authenticity, 201; challenges
to Italian unity, 210; contesting of
racism, 200; on domestic life, 213;
establishment of, 205; on Fascism,
211, 213; on film style, 200; on Italian
landscape, 208; on Italian reality, 208;
on negative Italian present, 213; *Ossessione* and, 30, 213, 224; on realism, 200,
201, 204, 206; on Sicily, 224; smear
campaign against, 212; on technical
perfection, 209; underground tactics,
224; and Verga's fiction, 209–10, 224;
Vittorio Mussolini and, 201, 203,

205–6, 212, 224. *See also* Communist
Party, Italian
cinema, American: in fascist Italy, 84;
noir, 212
cinema, French: educational, 40, 41;
naturalism of, 212; New Wave, 209;
WWII resistance in, 20
cinema, Italian: authentic, 231, 237; calligraphic mode of, 208–9; collective
endeavor of, 84–85; colonized and
colonizers in, 125; in "culture war,"
109; fascist suspicion of, 204; film
clubs, 92; filmmaking courses, 86;
future of, 227; improvisation in, 232;
location in, 232; national character
of, 85; before neorealism, 171–76;
nonprofessional actors in, 232; production companies, 85; realism of, 15,
56, 232–33; as refuge of culture, 232;
representations of labor, 28–29; role
in national health, 194; "schoolgirl
films," 188, 195; Soviet influence on,
89, 260n18; state-funded, 84; *stracittà–
strapaese* rift in, 109; U.S. study of,
230–31; weaponization of, 28, 43, 55,
60, 182; whiteness in, 38, 41, 44–45,
99; zero-degree style, 232, 239, 240,
247–48
cinema, Italian early: comparison with
theater, 39; complicity with nationalism, 231; crisis of 1910s, 45; in crisis of
1920s, 109; educational, 39, 43–44; as
governmental technology, 40; healer-
artists of, 56; historical reenactments
in, 41; improving features of, 39;
invention of, 36; and Italian national
life, 47; manipulation of affect, 60;
melodrama in, 54; myth of, 56;
Orientalizing, 54; prejudices against,
35; racialized anxieties in, 34; redemptive power of, 41; as regenerative
apparatus, 40; reproduction of reality,
56; under Risorgimento, 39–50; as
security apparatus, 45; social benefits

of, 37; success of, 34–35; transition to
sound, 119; weaponization of, 55
cinema, Italian fascist: antisemitism in,
172–73; biopolitical, 8, 62, 203; British
naval power in, 140–41; brutal vision
of, 137; censorship system, 205;
contribution to political history,
143; "corpo-realism" of, 29; as denial
of reality, 14–15; as disciplinary, 14;
end of, 163; escapist, 5, 14, 115, 126, 131,
176, 195, 232; ethno-nationalism of,
85, 159; ideological scripts of, 232;
independence from patron state, 17;
labor in, 59–60; legitimization of
Fascism, 204; locations of, 16; "made
in Italy" narratives of, 14; Marxist
ideology critique of, 4; masculinity
in, 97, 190–91; media archaeology of,
5; Mussolini's investment in, 1–2;
national life in, 15–16, 170–71; national
reality in, 29, 63; order in, 210; performance of racism, 203–4; post–WWI
crisis, 1; production of docile bodes,
229; proper/improper lives in, 16;
racialized tropes of, 93, 203, 210;
racially appropriate behaviors in,
201; as racial melodramas, 138; racial
unity in, 203; realist, 29, 63, 206, 232;
resistance in, 17–18, 229; restorative
function of, 97; rule through, 6;
social normalization through, 201;
soldiers in, 138; state control of,
210–11; territorial expansion in, 201;
threat from sea in, 138; unity in, 210;
weaponization of, 2–3, 8, 204; white
supremacy in, 201; women's sacrifice
in, 138
cinema, Italian postwar, x–xi; auteur,
x, 84, 200, 230, 231, 235; conservative
agenda of, 247; eco-cinema, 92;
educational, 27; in geopolitical order,
240; hagiographic memory of, 229;
liberated senses in, 230; liberation
school of, 30, 231, 247; moral

conservatism of, 226–27; national
life in, 30–31; normalization in, ix,
230; post-totalitarian redemption of,
231; purge of communists from, 247;
as revolutionary antinarrative, 230;
Sicily in, 209–11; social function of,
235. *See also* neorealism, Italian
cinema, queer: modes of embodiment,
199; of *Ossessione*, 201, 214, 226. *See
also* queerness
cinema, Soviet: fascist admiration for,
66; influence on Blasetti, 89
Cinematografo, Al (Fabbri), 28, 34–45, 55;
artistic merits of, 36; benefits of
cinema in, 39; cinema's respectability
in, 35; educational cinema in, 43–44;
emotivity in, 40, 41; ethnicity in, 41;
on generative apparatuses, 37; *genia*
in, 41; history of cinema in, 36;
modernity in, 44; movie audiences
in, 38–39; national regeneration in,
40; national unity, 39; patriotism in,
40; redemptive cinema in, 41; redis-
covery of, 36; remediation in, 37;
technology in, 36
Cines (production company), 61–62;
nationalization of, 62; prototypical
film forms of, 63
Civil War, Spanish, 217
class, enactment through race, 127
class conflict, pathologization of, 82
classes, Italian: in Camerini's films,
116–17; racialized, 44–45, 114; separation in theaters, 38. *See also* elites;
peasants, Italian; working class,
Italian
Coke, Edward, 23
colonialism, Italian, 8, 10–11, 88,
251n19; Black subjects of, 202; in
Camerini's films, 112–14; as European phenomenon, 113; internal,
16; mare nostro in, 148; racialized
imaginaries of, 83; violence of, 89.
See also capitalism-colonialism

comedians, acquisition of power, 177
comedy: ancient Greek, 170; anti-
disciplinarian, 30; as challenge to
depotentiation, 181; in construction
of community, 170; Italian film criticism on, 176; Jewish philosophers on,
171; liberation in, 192; opposition to
biopolitics, 170; revelation of alienation, 192. *See also* laughter
Communism: as biological threat, 104;
as biospiritual illness, 163; degenerate
subjects of, 82; in *Un pilota ritorna*,
163; in *Vecchia guardia*, 104–5
Communist Party, Italian, 205, 243; as
proponent of neorealism, 247. See
also *Cinema* (journal), Communist
cell
community: comedy in construction
of, 170; ecofascist landscapes of, 28;
Romantic view of, 13; of victimhood,
136
Comolli, Jean-Louis, 20, 27
conformista, Il (1970), x
Cortese, Leonardo, 175
Cowan, Michael, 69
Crary, Jonathan, 5
creativity, human: neglect of, 180–81;
normalization and, 181
Crespi, Daniele, 119
Creti, Vasco, 90
Cristiani, Dhia, 213
critical race theory, Mediterranean in,
158
Croce, Benedetto: interpretation of
Fascism, ix–x, 244–45

D'Ancora, Maurizio, 115, 119
Daney, Serge, 20
D'Annunzio, Gabriele, 84; in Fiume
expedition, 164; *La nave*, 148, 263n23
D'Annunzio, Gabriellino, 263n23
Darwin, Charles, 116
D'Azeglio, Massimo, 33
De Amicis, Edmondo: *Cuore*, 40

De Benedetti, Aldo, 29, 261n20; collaborations with De Sica, 172, 176, 180;
Due dozzine di rose scarlatte, 173;
persecution of, 172–73, 190, 197, 246;
screenplay for *La vita ricomincia*, 243,
246; uncredited work of, 172
De Filippo, Eduardo, 178, 244, 246
De Filippo, Peppino, 178
de Grazia, Victoria: *The Culture of
Consent*, 5
de Landa, Juan, 213
de Lauretis, Teresa, 27
Deleuze, Gilles, 14, 31; on hieratic slowness, 234; infantilizing of Italy, 242; on
Italian people's essence, 241; modes
of the imaginary, 238; on narrative,
235; on naturalized behaviors, 235;
on neorealism, 30, 229–30, 234–37, 240,
242; on *Ossessione*, 217, 220; sampling
technique, 235; taxonomy of images,
238; on time-images, 238–39.
Deleuze, Gilles, works: *Cinema* volumes,
220, 234–36, 238; "Postscript on the
Societies of Control," 26
Del Fra, Lino, 248
Del Poggio, Carla, 174–75
De Robertis, Francesco, 15; anticipation
of liberation, 231; war cinema of, 144;
work for Navy Ministry Film Center,
158. See also *La nave bianca*
De Robertis, Francesco, works: *Alpha
Tau!*, 158–59; *Il mulatto*, 159; *La vita
semplice*, 159. See also *Uomini sul fondo*
Derrida, Jacques: on performance of
weakness, 135
De Santis, Giuseppe, 29, 176, 224; at
Cinema, 205; on De Sica's comedies,
180; on diversity, 206–7; eco-cinema
of, 92; Jewish collaborators of, 173;
liberated cinema of, 232; on new
national cinema, 207; on *Ossessione*,
215; peasant origins of, 208; on realism, 206; remediation in, 201; on
Verga, 209, 210. Works: "Il linguaggio

dei rapporti," 207; *Non c'è pace tra gli ulivi*, 92; "Per un paesaggio italiano," 206–8, 211; *Riso amaro*, 92; "Verità e poesia: Verga e il cinema italiano," 209, 210, 214
De Sica, Vittorio: abject female subjects of, 186; affective landscapes of, 184; antifascism of, 182, 192; anti-utopic endings, 195; in Camerini's films, 115, 126, 127, 180, 183; catharsis in, 175; collaborations with De Benedetti, 172, 176, 180; collaborations with Zavattini, 171; collaborators of, 172; comedic settings of, 182–83; commercial fictions of, 195; conception of virtue, 171; contestation of fascist biopolitics, 180, 197; disciplinary spaces in, 182; dreams in, 194, 195; early films of, 261n20; empowerment of viewers, 182; escapist films of, 176; exuberance in, 191; fantasy of freedom in, 194; futurity in, 195; in *Un garibaldino al convento*, 191; humanity in films of, 176; Italian body in, 183–84; laughter in comedies of, 181; in *Maddalena zero in condotta*, 174, 192; mocking of inefficacy, 194; modification of life ways in, 180; narrative structures of, 189, 191, 195; national reality in, 183; neorealism's possibilities in, 236; noncompliance in films of, 182; nuclear family in, 194; patterns of affect, 167; playfulness in films of, 187; postwar films, 221, 226; pre-neorealist films, 171–76; pursuit of happiness in, 193; realist films of, 171, 236; in redemption of postwar cinema, 231; reenchantment of Italy, 192; rhetorical structure of, 195; romantic comedies of, 29–30, 172–76, 180–97, 229; in *Rose scarlatte*, 173; sentimentality of, 271n18; in *Teresa Venerdì*, 174, 175; transgressive desires in, 172; utopic imaginaries of, 195;

vital optimism of, 180–97; women protagonists of, 184, 186; women's resistance in, 197; works created under fascism, 29–30
De Sica, Vittorio, works: *I bambini ci guardano*, 171; *Miracolo a Milano*, 221; *Sciuscià*, 221; *Umberto D.*, 221, 235. See also *garibaldino al convento, Un*; *Ladri di biciclette*; *Maddalena zero in condotta*; *Rose scarlatte*; *Teresa Venerdì*
desire, proper representation of, 202
Dilián, Irasema, 193
Di Maio, Alessandra, 158
Di Nicola, Alberto, 265n12
discipline: class, 112; of excesses, 55; of fascist cinema, 14; of Italian body, 34; for Italian national life, 81–82; workers', 60, 71
documentaries, cinematic, 40–41
Dombroski, Robert S., 52
domus (home and family): in Italian Fascism, 79–80, 220–21; in Italian national life, 214
dopo-lavoro (work clubs), 117, 260n15
Doro, Mino, 103
Duncan, Derek, 208
Dyer, Richard, 99

ecofascism, 84; community, 28; in *Sole!*, 90; in *Terra madre*, 97; in *Vecchia guardia*, 107
education: fascist, 187–88; in Italian early cinema, 39, 43–44; Montessori method, 183
Eisenstein, Sergei, 66
elites: abjection of, 116, 119–20, *120*; account of progress, 55; in Camerini's films, 114, 116; learning from underclass, 114; modernity of, 98; Mussolini on, 81; resentment of, 63, 93, 99; in *Il signor Max*, 117–19; spoiling of national life, 82; in *Terra madre*, 99, 101, *102*; as vampires, 99; whiteness of, 117. *See also* classes, Italian; liberalism, Italian

embodiment: biopolitical, 8, 83; discursive forms of, 40; Foucault on, 19; of Italian femininity, 98; Italian modes of, 229; of Italian people, 214; queerness modes of, 199; shame in, 110; in state authority, 19; subjection and, 13

emotion, politics of, 18, 110–11

Epstein, Jean: *Faithful Heart,* 68

escapism, cinematic, 5, 14, 232; Camerini's, 115, 126, 131, 195; De Sica's, 176

Ethiopia, Italian invasion, 6, 84, 140; gas attacks in, 144; war crimes in, 157

Europe: biospiritual warfare in, 23; ethnicities of, 22; mythological ancestries of, 23; proto-capitalism of, 23–24; racial allegiances in, 23

evil, sexualized tropes of, x

Evola, Julius, 79

excess: cultural disciplining of, 55; of Italian people, 41, 48, 51–53

Fabbri, Gualtiero: film theory of, 36; rules of screenplay, 36; weaponization of cinema, 60. See also *Cinematografo, Al*

Falasca-Zamponi, Simonetta, 5

Fanon, Frantz: *Black Skin, White Masks,* 111–12, 127

Fantasia sottomarina (Rossellini): moral of, 143; spectatorial body of, *142, 143;* warfare in, 141–43

Farassino, Alberto, 112

fare razza (making race), 14, 65, 251n19

Farocki, Harun: *Workers Leaving the Factory in Eleven Decades,* 59, 256n1

Fascism, American: Black bodies in, 137

Fascism, Italian: as abjection, x; ableism of, 215; affective mediation of, 137; after-work clubs of, 117; appeal to labor, 119; approach to governing, 110; attitude toward popular culture, 1; being-together in, 109–10; biological body of, 109; biopolitics of, 8, 17,

62, 110, 180, 197, 203; capitalist, 5, 19, 60, 132, 248; Catholic Church and, 97–98; challenge by love, 201; in cinematic realism, 15, 29, 90, 97, 171, 233; class/gender exploitation, 115; consent to, 5; "created life" of, 131; defeat of, 30, 212, 229, 243; disciplined workers of, 60; domesticity in, 79–80, 220–21; economic development models, 109; education under, 187–88; ethno-nationalism of, 11–12, 82–83, 85, 132, 139; as foreign virus, 245; forms of affect, xi; gendered racial assemblage of, 9; global affirmation of, 204; ideal cities of, 88; ideological confusion in, 3–4, 5; intellectuals during, 247; internal colonization, 16; *jus soli* (birthright citizenship) in, 159, 267n8; land reclamation projects, 84, 86, 88–89, 124; media activists in, 17; *Me ne frego* slogan, 80; naturalization into landscape, 106; versus Nazism, 3; non-state actions in, 17; parodies of, 177; as passing phenomenon, ix–xi, 11, 227, 244; politics of natality, 267n8; popular commitment to, xi–xii; popular culture of, 1, 206; postwar purge of, 246–47; postwar reinstatement of, 227; queer alternative to, 201; race-empire-nation project, 98; race-making in, 171, 202, 204; race wars of, 80, 83, 167, 212; on racial degeneration, 89–91; Racial Laws of, 43, 132, 138, 139, 153, 172; racism of, 81–84; recovery from, ix–x; resistance to, x, 17–18, 107, 197, 199, 229, 247; rule through cinema, 6; securitarian fixation of, 79; sexual behavior concerns, 202; structures of living under, 60; unifying project of, 8; victimhood in, 139, 151; as war for security, 80; in Western press, 177–78; whitening of, 157; white supremacy of, 99, 201; winning of working class,

60. *See also* cinema, Italian fascist; Italy, fascist

Fascism, Nazi, 232; aestheticization of politics, 191; importance of water for, 139

fear: affective geographies of, 16; governance by, 161–62; white, 135–36

Federici, Silvia, 18

Fellini, Federico: *I vitelloni*, 195, 235

femininity, Italian: racially appropriate, 98

feminism, Black, 8

Ferri, Enrico, 89, 258n15

Filippi, Francesco, 243

film culture, early twentieth-century: in Italian social health, 34

flâneurs, French, 37

Fogu, Claudio, x, 137; on Aryanism, 149

Fontana, Alessandro, 21

Forgacs, David: *Rethinking Italian Fascism*, 2; "Sex in the Cinema," 14–15, 175–76; on Visconti, 199

Forzano, Giovanni: *Camicia nera*, 17

Foscolo, Ugo: *Le ultime lettere di Jacopo Ortis*, 175, 181

Foucault, Michel: on Althusser, 19; analytics of power, 18–19; on biopolitical warfare, 7, 140; on biopolitics, 22, 24, 31; on biopower, 18; on consent building, 19; on Enlightenment discourse, 19–20; on Fascism, 245; on governance, 26; on Marxism, 20; on penal apparatus, 20; on resistance, 31; on state racism, 23–24; on subjugated knowledges, 21; on weaponization of truth, 1

Foucault, Michel, works: *Cahiers du Cinéma* interview, 20; *Discipline and Punish*, 19–20; "Friendship as a Way of Life," 218; *Society Must Be Defended*, 21–23, 25, 27–28

Franca, Lisa, 115, 124

France: conservative Right of, 22; Popular Front, 205; state violence in, 18

Freddi, Luigi, 85

Fréret, Nicolas, 23

Fuller, Mia, 88

Galt, Rosalind: *Queer Cinema in the World*, 199

García Düttmann, Alexander: *Visconti: Insights into Flesh and Blood*, 214

garibaldino al convento, Un (De Sica), 174–75; credits for, 172; De Benedetti's work in, 172; disciplined female body in, 184, *185*; escape from fascist biopolitics, 197; forbidden reading in, 184; masculinity in, 190–91; Risorgimento fighters in, 190–91, 197

Garofalo, Piero, 74, 89; *Re-viewing Fascism*, 3

gas di guerra sul mare, I (Navy training film), 152

gender: under capitalism-colonialism, 8; under capitalist-patriarchal-colonial order, 8; of Italian body, 192; in Italian workforce, 103, 154; racial assemblage of, 9

genia, Italian, 43; deviation from norms, 41; unevolved, 45

Genina, Augusto: *Lo squadrone bianco*, 97, 150

genre fiction, 63, 233; De Sica's, 29; paratextual outrage against, 97; politics of, 233; schoolgirl comedies and, 195

Gentile, Emilio, 62

Gentile, Giovanni, 187, 188

geopolitics, Italian: of Mediterranean Sea, 137; of postwar cinema, 240; racialized, 46–47; skeletal morphology in, 46

Germany, Nazi: surrender of, 243

Giachetti, Fosco, 243, 246

Giachetti, Gianfranco, 103

Gillette, Aaron, 34

Gioca, Pietro! (Piranello), 60, 63–66; *Acciaio* and, 72–73, 257n16; common

good in, 65; discipline in, 66; *fare razza* in, 65; good capitalism in, 73; the individual in, 72–73; Italian ingenuity in, 65; labor in, 60, 63–66; masculinity in, 65, 73; national subjects in, 73; score of, 64; spiritual/authentic liberty in, 65; steelworks in, 64, 65; synchronicity in, 64. See also *Acciaio*
Giolitti, Giovanni, 45, 63; liberal governance of, 254n24; socialist critics of, 46
Girotti, Massimo, 160, 162, 213, *223*
Giuliani, Gaia, 98
Giuliani, Luca, 34–35
Giuliani, Reginaldo, 164
Gloria, Leda, 94, 178
Goebbels, Joseph: Ruttman's work for, 77; at Venice Film Festival, 132
Goldberg, David Theo, 10
Goldberg, Jonathan, 214
Good Judge, The (film, 1906), 40
Goose That Laid the Golden Eggs, The (film, 1905), 41
Gramsci, Antonio, 4, 9, 107; on capitalist exploitation, 22; interpretation of Fascism, 22, 79; on rural-urban unity, 109–10; on war of position, 17–18, 206
grande appello, Il (Camerini), 97; biopolitics of, 114; masculinity in, 113; racial imaginary of, 113–14
grandi magazzini, I (Camerini), 29, 115; biopolitical fantasy of, 131; class difference in, 118; consumerism in, 131; heteronormal bodies of, 131; hyperstaged reality of, 131; mannequins in, 131–32, *133*; organic/inorganic bodies in, *133*; as transitional film, 132; at Venice Film Festival, 132; white space in, 125
Gravelli, Asvero: hate campaigns of, 164
Gray, Hugh, 241
Greene, Shelleen, 34; *Equivocal Subjects*, 16

Grieveson, Lee, 26
Griffith, D. W.: *Birth of a Nation,* 105
Grillo, Beppe, 180; political satire of, 177
Grusin, Richard: on remediation, 36–37
Guazzoni, Enrico: *Quo Vadis,* 62, 231
Guenther, Lisa, 111
Guerzoni, Fausto, 190
Gundle, Stephen, 85
Gunning, Tom, 5, 200

Hall, Stuart, 127
Haneke, Michael: *Hidden,* 195
Hansen, Mark, 26
Hansen, Miriam, 5, 192
Hargraves, Hunter, 26–27
Hawthorne, Camilla, 158
Hay, James, 14, 78; on whiteness, 99, 125
Heath, Stephen, 27
Heiner, Brady Thomas, 18–19
Herring, Emily, 181
heteronormativity, 131; aid to racial identity, 30
historiography, cinema: engagement with filmic texts, 27
historiography, Italian: racism in, 81
Hitler, Adolf: interest in naval power, 139; Nero Decree of, 79; rise of, 66
Hobbes, Thomas: *Leviathan* frontispiece, 169–70, 179
Hollywood, Italian audiences' love of, 66
Hom, Stephanie Malia, 33
hooks, bell, 8
Horkheimer, Max: *Dialectic of Enlightenment,* 33
humanism, Christian, 231
humanism, Western: "the Rest" in, 156
hyper-regulation, disruption by laughter, 181

identity: impact of shame on, 110; white, 135–36
identity, Italian: collective, 206; crisis in, 55; destabilization of, 183; diversity in,

206–7; in exteriority, 207, 208; hard
work in, 29; history of, 27; in liberated Italy, 30; modes of embodiment,
229; racial, 29, 34, 202; regressive
tropes of, 242; struggle for truth in,
30; "two Italies" of, 12. *See also* Italian
people; national life, Italian
ideology critique, 7; Althusser's, 4;
cognitivism of, 21; in media studies,
26; waning of, 18
imagination, historical: new forms of,
22–23
immediacy, redemptive dimension of,
54
imperialism: patriarchal, 8; "ragamuffin," 139
imperialism, fascist, 163; cinematic
performers of, 159; melodramatic,
29, 139, 149, 151, 156; victimhood and,
140
Inda, Jonathan Xavier, 8
individual, the: in *Acciaio,* 68–69, 71,
76–77; in *Gioca, Pietro!,* 72–73; in narrative cinema, 59
industrialization, 11, 38; authenticity in,
109; effect on Italian people, 47, 48;
effect on relationality, 55; Pirandello
on, 63, 64
Italian literature, postunification, 33–34
Italian people: abject wartime assignments, 197; "*alla bula,*" 41–42; antago-
nisms among, 210; association with
nature, 241; authentic, 24–25, 28, 41,
55, 104, 107, 109; as biracial, 42; *brava
gente,* x, xi; collaboration with Fascism, 15, 244–45; correct reproduction
of, 203; decline in, 46; disciplining
of, 34; diversity of, 206–7; effect of
industrialization on, 48; excessivity
of, 41, 48, 51–53, 64, 66; exuberance
of, 73; fascist reclamation of, 87–88;
genia, 41, 43, 45; *genio e sregolatezza*
of, 73; global representation of, 204;
"good people" discourse, 139, 150, 157,

227, 241, 248; historically minoritized,
149–50; *jus soli* (birthright citizenship) of, 159, 267n8; under liberal
capitalism, 49; *mala vita* of, 46, 63;
mascalzoni, 127; of Mediterranean
ethnicity, 42, 47, 52, 73; northern /
Mediterranean divide in, 10, 82, 87,
109, 113; postwar redemption of, 230,
231, 247; "poveri ma belli," 114; as
quasi-African, 9, 12, 46, 86; quasi-
feminist, 17; racial anthropology of,
10, 57, 82; racial assemblages of, 60;
racial difference in, 206, 207; racially
appropriate, 28; relationship to landscape, 207, 208; self-destructive nature
of, 55; spiritual-biological destiny of,
208; stereotypes of, 241; structures of
living for, 60; suffering of, 147–48, 155,
157, 159; survival of, 154; ungovernability of, 33; unity of, 109–10, 203,
206, 210; unsustainable hyperactivity
of, 49; as victim race, 139, 140, 150.
See also body, Italian; identity, Italian;
Jews, Italian; national life, Italian;
whiteness, Italian
Italy: colonial / capitalist, 7–8, 10–11, 18,
53; color line in, 10; contribution to
world culture, 12; danger from the
sea, 29, 137, 138, 144, 147, 151; industrial
apparatus of, 27; as modern capitalist
nation-state, 9; Other within, 98;
racial health of, 28; racial whiteness
of, 12, 15, 149, 248; reenchantment of,
192; right-wing resurgence in, x; "two
Italies" myth, 12; unification of, 11;
white supremacy and, 16. *See also*
Kingdom of Italy
Italy, fascist: Allied takeover of, ix, 230;
American cinema in, 84; assistance
to Nazi Germany, 139; Battle for
Births, 12–13; Battle for Grain, 13;
Battle for Land, 13; cinematographic
apparatus sustaining, 62; continuity
with postwar Italy, 240; creativity in,

205; dissent in, 205–6; entry into World War II, 204, 232; ethno-nation of, 12; fall of, 212, 229; free-speech zones, 205; during Great Depression, 60; logic of coloniality, 114, 260n10; management of race, 28; marine dominance plans, 139–40; melodramatic imperialism of, 29, 149, 151; postliberal state of, 11; race war in, 80, 83, 167, 212; racial exceptionalism of, 149–58; Racial Laws of, 43, 132, 138, 149, 153, 172; resistance to, x, 17–18, 107, 197, 199, 229, 247; return to normalcy, ix, 242; rural-urban unity in, 109–10; social health campaigns, 12; *Spielraum* in, 192; transnational expansion of, 204; vulnerability from sea, 137, 138; whitening of, 12; worker strikes in, 212. *See also* Kingdom of Italy; Ventennio

Italy, postwar: as border zone, 243; cinematic view of, 30; continuity with fascist Italy, 240; "de-fascistizzazione" of, 246; fascist officials in, 247; geopolitical context of, 226–27; liberated, 30, 230–32; national culture of, ix; normalization of, ix, 242; purge commission, 246; sociopolitics of, ix; under U. S. hegemony, 230, 234, 241–43, 270n2; "zero" mythologies of, 248

Jakobson, Roman, 209
Jameson, Fredric, 28; on conspiracy theories, 136; "The Existence of Italy," 85; on realism, 108
Jesi, Furio, 28, 78; on *domus*, 79; on fascist mythology, 79–80
Jewish philosophers, on comedy, 171
Jews, Italian: discrimination against, 13, 149, 157, 172; minoritization of, 184
Joon-ho, Bong: *Parasite*, 99

Kafka, Franz, 171
Khazan, Olga, 135

Kif Tebbi (Camerini), colonialism in, 112–13; femonationalism of, 113; restoration of, 112

Kingdom of Italy: authentic national life of, 41, 55; cheap attractions in, 48; depopulation of, 13; differences within, 9; economic growth in, 45; extractive capitalism of, 11; foreign life patterns in, 49–50; foundation of, 33; internal emigration in, 126; liquidity crisis, 60, 62; Nordic Aryanism in, 42; nostalgia for tradition in, 55; occupation of Somalia, 10; post-unification, 33–34, 40; post–World War I, 10; racial background of, 10; racial geopolitics, 46; racialized, 34, 36, 44–45; social health of, 34; sociopolitical volatility of, 34; structural problem of, 10; system of exploitation, 11; tempo of life in, 49–51; unifying technology of, 40; will to govern, 33. *See also* nation-state, Italian; Risorgimento

knowledge, subjugated, 21
knowledge production, state appropriation of, 31
Kracauer, Siegfried, 47, 57, 76; *From Caligari to Hitler*, 78; on Ruttmann, 67
Kubrick, Stanley: *2001: A Space Odyssey*, 239

labor, Italian: Blackness in, 117; child, 221–22; cinematic, 28–29, 59–60; conflict with capital, 45–46, 81; Fascism's appeal to, 119; gendered figurations of, 121, *122*, 154; in Italian identity, 29; romanticization of, 123; rural-urban unity in, 109–10; in *Terra madre*, 93, 99–101, 102; women's, 130. *See also* working class, Italian
Lacan, Jacques, 4
Laclau, Ernesto, 204
Lacoue-Labarthe, Philippe, 78

Ladri di biciclette (De Sica), 221, 230;
Bazin on, 236; historical reality in,
234; pessimism of, 172
landscape, Italian: in Blasetti's films, 93,
96–97, 106; Christianity in, 98; De
Sica's, 184; ecofascist, 28; Italian
people's relationship to, 207, 208;
labor in, 93; in *Ossessione*, 213, 214–15,
218, 220, 222; provincialism of, 217
Landy, Marcia, 5, 188, 194
Lateran Treaty, 97–98
laughter: challenge to heteronormativity, 30; delegitimization by, 177;
deployment against racism/sexism,
176; effect on biopolitics, 176; reaffirmation of status quo, 177; in theory
of incongruity, 181; as tool of government, 179–80; as warning affect, 181.
See also comedy
Leavitt, Charles L., IV, 240, 247
Le Bon, Gustave, 5
Lenin, Vladimir: on ragamuffin imperialism, 139
Levinas, Emmanuel, 28; *On Escape*, 110,
111, 183; on shame, 129
Leyda, Jay, 36
liberalism, Italian, 11; apparatuses of,
55; capitalist, 11, 49, 83; catastrophe
of, 80; crisis of 1910s, 45; dissolute
capitalism of, 83; exhaustion under,
49; failure to unify, 40; film forms of,
55; frustrations with, 34; internal
colonialism in, 44–45; life expectancy
under, 51; Mussolini on, 81; racial
order of, 45–46; racial science under,
42, 259n15; in *Vecchia guardia*, 104;
weaponization of film, 28. *See also*
elites
Libya, Italian colonization of, 10, 113
Lichtner, Giacomo, 226
Liehm, Mira, 217
lifeworlds, alternative, 218, 220–21
Lilburne, John, 23
Lizzani, Carlo, 205

Lombroso, Cesare, 42; *L'uomo delin-
quente*, 10
LUCE. *See* L'Unione Cinematografica
Educativa (LUCE) Institute
Lumière brothers: film of workers, 59;
tour of Italy, 34

Maddalena zero in condotta (De Sica), 171,
186–90, *189*; bodily desires in, 195;
credits for, 172; De Benedetti's work
in, 172; disciplined female bodies of,
186–87; disciplined spaces of, 182;
docile subjects in, 194; escape from
fascist biopolitics, 197; loss of dreams
in, 192–93; male gaze in, 186, *187*,
188; narrative style of, 189; power
of writing in, 181; racial science in,
188–90; release from societal impositions in, 194; sadism in, 188; transgressive appetites in, 184, *185*; truth
and fiction in, 197; white race in,
189–90
Maglione, Margherita, 172
Magnani, Anna, 193, 235
Malevich, Kazimir, 71
Malipiero, Gian Francesco, 73
Mangini, Cecilia, 191, 248
"Manifesto dalla razza" (1938), 149,
269n19
Marc' Aurelio (satiric journal), on Musso-
lini, 178
March on Rome, fascist, 13, 56
Marconi, Guglielmo, 148
Marcus, Millicent, 14, 230; on neoreal-
ism, 200
Marcuse, Herbert: Freudo-Marxism
of, x
Marcuzzo, Elio, 213
Marshall Plan, 242
Martin-Jones, David, 220
Marx, Karl: materialism of, 245; vampire
mythology of, 99
Marxism: fascist cinema and, 4; post-
Althusserian, 5

masculinity, Italian: in cinema, 97, 190–91; crisis of, 53, 54; state-sponsored, 217

Masier, Gaetano, 160

Matarazzo, Raffaello: *Treno popolare,* 78

Mattòli, Mario, 173. See also *vita ricomincia, La*

McGlazer, Ramsey, 186; on De Sica's comedies, 194

McGuire, Valerie, 137

media: racialization of, 21; relationship to politics, 20

media, fascist, xi; biopolitical command in, 30; links to government, 14; productive dimension of, 15; weaponization of, 31

media archaeology, of Italian cinema, 5

mediascape, fascist: aesthetic-political conflict in, 18

mediation, technologies of, 36

Medin, Gastone, 71, 86; collaboration with De Sica, 180; designs for Rossellini, 163; set décors of, 116, 125

Mediterranean Sea: anxiety concerning, 143; Blackness of, 158; British hegemony over, 139–40; as cradle of Western civilization, 149; in critical race theory, 158; in fascist cinema, 143–49; in fascist geopolitics, 137; in fascist imaginary, 150–51; in "Manifesto della razza," 149; as mare nostrum, 148–49, 158, *219*; reclamation of, 149, 158; romanticization of, 158; threat from, 137, 138, 144, 147, 151; whiteness of, 150, 158. See also Italian people: northern / Mediterranean divide

Mellino, Miguel, 9; on state racism, 42–43

melodrama: in American public discourse, 136–37; cinematic, 15

melodrama, fascist, 30, 226, 229; imperialistic, 29, 139, 149, 151, 156; male, 159; racial, 138

melodrama, Italian: early, 54; high-contrast lighting of, 171; Visconti's, 30, 171

Meloni, Giorgia: fascism of, 31

Melville, Herman, 184

memory, popular: reprogramming of, 20

Mercader, Maria, 175

Miccichè, Lino, 226, 248

Mignolo, Walter, 10, 260n10

Milan, vitality of, 124

Minghelli, Giuliana, 200; on *Cinema,* 215

modernity, capitalist: realism under, 85

modernity, Italian, 10–11, 29; in *Al Cinematografo,* 44; displacement in, 53; excessive nature of, 51; industrial, 55; means of reproduction, 14; mechanization of, 47; Sicilian alternative to, 211; tragic consequences of, 50–51; white, 12; workers' role in, 115

modernity, racial: water in, 170

modernity, Western: the Abject in, 116; racial antagonism in, 24; ugly feelings in, 137

Modigliani, Amedeo, 215

Moe, Nelson, 9

Montessori, Maria: theory of education, 183

Moravia, Alberto, 205

morphology, skeletal: in Italian geopolitics, 46

Moses, Gavriel, 35

movie theaters: as heterotopias, 45; as Platonic caves, 4; spread in Italy, 254n14; as transformative spaces, 39

Movimento Sociale Italiano, antisemitism of, 173

Mullins, Jonathan, 201

Mulvey, Laura, 27; "Visual Pleasure and Narrative Cinema," 222

Muñoz, José Esteban, 220

Murnau, F. W.: *Tabu,* 211

Mussolini, Benito: anti-Asian stance, 82; banality of evil under, x; biospiritual unity under, 12; capitalist-colonial order of, 18; fall of, 212, 229, 243; Grand Council of Fascism speech, 140–41, 149; "Great Rome" plan, 86–87, 258n9; interest in naval power, 139; investment in cinema, 1–2, 14; on liberal state, 81; LUCE iconography of, 100; at LUCE inauguration, 2, *3,* 6; as maker of life, 60; onscreen body doubles, 218; Pirandello on, 57, 60; race war under, 83; racial assemblages of, 13, 31, 60, 233; rise of, 1, 22; satirization of, 177–79; social eugenics efforts, 17; symbiotic relationships of, 7

Mussolini, Vittorio: admiration of Jean Renoir, 205; and Camerini, 178; and *Cinema* journal, 201, 203, 205–6, 212, 224; as film theorist, 268n11; "Ordine e disciplina," 203; on *Ossessione,* 212, 227; ousting from *Cinema,* 224; *Un pilota ritorna* scenario, 160; racial strategy of, 203; "Razza italiana e cinema italiano," 206; on weaponization of film, 203

Nancy, Jean-Luc, 78

nationalism, Italian, 9; in *Il cappello a tre punte,* 178; romantic comedies in, 184; Verdi's, 221

national life, Italian: authentic, 41, 55, 83; Blackshirt supremacy in, 126; capacity to re-form, 180; domesticity in, 214; dread in, 171; early cinema and, 47; elites' spoiling of, 82; in fascist cinema, 15–16, 170–71; fascist violence in, 11, 13, 82; group / environment interaction, 208; impact of foreign film on, 84; multiplicity of, 109; in postwar cinema, 30–31; proper / improper, 16, 44, 82, 140; racialized traditionalism in, 213; reclamation from Fascism, 239; undisciplined, 81–82. *See also* identity, Italian; Italian people

nation-building, role of cinema in, 39

nation-state, Italian: founding of, x; Italian life under, 33; medical-penal apparatus, 42; nation-building in, 40, 148. *See also* Kingdom of Italy; Risorgimento

nation-states: racialization of sensibility, 22–23; social war in, 24–25

naval power: labor and materials for, 139; in racial modernity, 170

naval power, British: Italian war against, 139–41; Mediterranean hegemony of, 139–40; in *La nave bianca,* 152, 155

nave bianca, La (Rossellini and De Robertis), 29, 150–58; British navy in, 152, 155; Christian charity in, 156; dedication of, 154; demonization of enemies, 156; ethno-survival in, 157; expansionism in, 155; fascist jouissance in, 153; funding of, 158; gendered division of labor in, 154; geopolitical *vulnus* in, 152–53; humanism of, 156; Italian suffering in, 157; justification of Fascism, 155; Nazi soldiers in, 153; patriotism in, 153, *154;* phallic arsenal in, 153; postwar scholarship on, 138; racial affects in, 138; racial geopolitical anxiety in, 155; racial laws in, 153; reenactment in, 152; representation of evil, 155; romantic subplot of, 155; Rossellini's disavowal of, 154–55; sailor-actors in, 151–52; score of, 151, 157; subliminal pleasures in, 138; use of training film, 152; vulnerable bodies in, 152, 155; whiteness in, 150, *152,* 153, *154,* 157–58, 158; women in, 151, 153–54

Nazism: versus Fascism, 3; mysticism of, 80; "secret Germany" fantasy, 78; state myth of, 78–79

neocapitalism, postwar, 234

neorealism, Italian, x, 97; as antinarrative cinema, 248; as asymptote of reality, 237; barriers to, 238; benevolent U.S. in, 243; canon of, 240;

children in, 221–22; cinema before, 171–76; in cinema history, 230–31; as cinema of absence, 234; Communist proponents of, 247; consciousness of clichés, 235; deconstruction of, 231; in definition of cinema, 231; definitions of, 240; ethico-aesthetical revolution of, 159, 237; during fascist era, 232; fascist reality and, 229; fictions enabled by, 248; forgetting of history in, 243; futurity in, 237; historical context of, 235, 238; in Italian cultural history, 30; links to resistance, 247; as mechanism of avoidance, 230; moral conservatism of, 226; mythic status of, 159; narrative in, 235; new world order in, 234; origins of, 92; *Ossessione* and, 200; pace of, 161; persistent centrality of, 270n1; plot in, 236; potential for speculation in, 238; pseudodocumentary style, 226; redemption of cinema in, 239–40; rejection of cinematic apparatus, 236; as representative of new Italy, 247; speculative images of, 238; subjective mediation of, 236; as token of redemption, 239–40, 247; voyage format, 235; weaknesses of, 240; as zero-degree cinema, 240, 247–48. *See also* cinema, Italian postwar

Neri, Donatella, 112
Ngai, Sianne, 48, 50, 137; on comedy, 177
Niceforo, Alfredo: *La mala vita a Roma*, 41–42, 46, 86
Nietzsche, Friedrich, 25
Noris, Assia, 115, 131
Nuremberg trials, ix

O'Leary, Alan, 231, 271n6; "The Phenomenology of the *Cinepanettone*," 176
Opera Nazionale Balilla (fascist youth organization), 2, 104
O'Rawe, Catherine, 15, 271n6; on melodrama, 159; on neorealism, 229, 231; on *Ossessione*, 226

Ossessione (Visconti), 212–24, *218, 223,* 226–27; aesthetic-political disruption of, 200; agency in, 211; airlessness in, 221; allegory of nation in, 217; alternative lifeworld of, 218; antifascism of, 200; as anti-Italian, 212; Blackshirts in, 213; on *Cinema* cover, 224, *225*; collaborative dimension of, 224; contested body in, 227; diegetic/ extradiegetic frame of, 226; effect on film realism, 220; family life in, 213–14, 215, 221; fascist response to, 212; film politics of, 220; futurity in, 218, 220, 226; heteronormativity in, 214; homosexuality in, 217, 222, 224; hybrid style of, 212; impact on popular culture, 226; Italian realism and, 213; landscape in, 213, 214–15, 218, 220, 222; mare nostrum in, 219, *219*; marshes in, 92; melodrama in, 30, 214, 218, 221; nonconforming body politic in, 199–200; opening sequence, 213; peasants in, 215, *216,* 217; political imaginary of, 217; proletariat in, 217; queer living in, 201, 214, 226; realism of, 30; reception of, 226–27, 269n35; redemption in, 30, 215; scholarship on, 200; social status in, 215; sociosexual imaginary of, 199; soundscape of, 214, 219; spaces of difference in, 215; spectators of, 226; system of looks in, 222, 224; transgressive figuration in, 200; transnational aesthetics of, 200; voyage-form of, 220
Other: Abject, 116; conspiracy theories concerning, 25; racialized, 16
Oxilia, Nino: *Rapsodia satanica,* 62

Pact of Steel, 245
Painlevé, Jean, 143
Paisà (Rossellini), 92; absolution of Italians in, 246; Bazin on, 241; reality in, 237

Panella, Giuseppe, 55
Paola, Dria, 90
"Parlami d'amore Mariù" (song), 126
Pasolini, Pier Paolo, x
Pasqualino Settebellezze (1975), x
Pastrone, Giovanni: *Cabiria,* 231
Pavolini, Alessandro, 246; death of, 243
peasants, Italian: in *Ossessione,* 215, *216,*
    217; racial virtue of, 98; women, *95,*
    98, 103. *See also* labor, Italian; working
    class, Italian
Peele, Jordan: *Get Out,* 99, *100*
Pesarini, Angelica, 137, 158
Petacci, Claretta: death of, 243
petty bourgeoisie, Italian: rural, 109
Picasso, Pablo, 215
Pietrangeli, Antonio, 205
pilota ritorna, Un (Rossellini), 29, 159,
    160–63; antinarrative stance of, 161;
    banality of war in, 160; colonized
    and colonizer in, 162; communism in,
    163; doubt in, 163; elliptical style of,
    160; fascist imperialism in, 163; forced
    prostitution in, 161; German bomb-
    ing in, 162; immigrants in, 161; Italian
    suffering in, 161; last frame of, 222,
    223; masculinity in, *165;* national alibis
    in, 160; naturalization of pain, 162;
    prisoners of war in, 161; realism of,
    162; refugees in, 161; repetition in,
    160; scenario for, 160; score, 161;
    shared humanity in, 163; shot-
    reverse-shot patterns, 162; wartime
    suffering in, 161–62; wounded
    bodies/landscape in, 162, 164
Pilotto, Camillo, 113
Pinkus, Karen, 5; *Bodily Regimes,* 132
Pinocchio, Italian people as, 34
Pirandello, Luigi: on *cine-melo-grafia,* 67;
    Cines and, 63; conception of life, 58;
    on created life, 131; cruel vitalism of,
    57; on industrialization, 63, 64; on
    Mussolini, 57; Nobel Prize of, 49;
    support of Fascism, 56–58, 255n36;

weaponization of cinema, 60. See
    also *Gioca, Pietro!; Quaderni di Serafino
    Gubbio operatore;* "Se il film parlante
    abolirà il teatro?"; "vita create, La"
Pirelli Tire Company (Milan), arms
    supplies from, 132, 134
Pittaluga, Stefano: Cines under, 62
Poggioli, Ferdinando Maria: *Addio,
    giovinezza!,* 199
Pola, Isa, 67, 68, 94
Pontine Marshes: reclamation of, 86,
    88–89, 124; relocation from, 87–88
Poor Mother, The (film, 1906), 40, 43
Popular Front, French, 205
Porta Pia, battle of, 40
portiere di note, Il (1974), x
post-structuralism, Nietzschean, 231
poverty, Italian: resourcefulness in, 35
power: repressive hypothesis of, 14;
    seductive, 20. *See also* state power
public sphere, "commedification" of,
    177
Puccini, Dario, 205
Puccini, Gianni, 205, 224

Quaderni di Serafino Gubbio operatore
    (Pirandello), 28, 34, 41, 45–58, 237;
    alienation in, 52; animal contentment
    in, 52; antimodernism in, 48; apoca-
    lyptic aspect of, 56; audience in, 46;
    author/protagonist separation in, 54;
    camera in, 45, 48, 54; capitalist alien-
    ation in, 53; Cines's work with, 63;
    commodity fetishism in, 53; crisis of
    liberalism in, 45; destabilization in,
    80; diegetic universe of, 54; excess in,
    51–53, 55, 64; Fascism and, 57; identity
    crisis in, 55; illusion in, 56; insatiability
    in, 52; Italian character in, 48–49; lib-
    eralism in, 45, 47; masculine crisis in,
    53, 54; mechanical reproduction in,
    46, 47, 50, 52; mechanization in, 49–50,
    53, 64; misogyny in, 51; modernism
    of, 55; production-consumption cycle

in, 49; publishing history of, 253n4; race-making in, 46; "razza di donna" in, 51; role of cinema in, 50–51; Rome in, 86; on ruling liberals, 53; scholarship on, 46; separation from nature in, 52; serial format of, 56; tempo of life in, 49–51; textual layers of, 47; violence in, 50–51, 55; xenophobia in, 51

queerness: challenge to dominant discourses, 217; futurity of, 221; modes of embodiment, 199; in *Ossessione*, 201, 214, 226. *See also* cinema, queer

race: boundaries of, 149; under capitalist-patriarchal-colonial order, 8, 11; enactment through class, 127; in Italian behavior, 34; Italian exceptionalism concerning, 149–58; Mussolini on, 13; seventeenth-century reinvention of, 23

racialization: of biopolitical warfare, 8; cinematic processes of, 16; of Italian geopolitics, 46–47; of Italian people, 9, 11–12; premature death and, 260n9; shame in, 111

Racial Laws, fascist, 43, 132, 138, 139, 153, 172

racial science, Italian, 42, 259n14

racism: affects of, 31; "antiracist," 46; biopolitical, 11, 83, 245; of Italian Fascism, 81–84; in Italian historiography, 81; persistence of, 22; weaponization of, 31

racism, state, 24–25; affective mediation of, 18; disciplined temporality of, 219; Foucault on, 23–24, 31; as means of governance, 19; perception of rulers in, 100; in postunification Italy, 42–43; of proto-capitalist Europe, 23–24

radicalism, African American, 18

Raffaelli, Sergio, 36

Rancière, Jacques, 234

Rand, Ayn: *We the Living*, 204

Rava, Maurizio: "I popoli africani dinanzi allo schermo," 201

reactionary cycles, global, 265n12

realism, cinematic, 15, 56, 232–33; achievements of, 237; affective affordances of, 15; antifascism of, 206; biopolitical register of, 121; *Cinema's*, 224; differing iterations of, 15; effect of *Ossessione* on, 220; falsification of, 15; fictional lives in, 108; film theory on, 143–44; ideological operations of, 4; political malleability of, 200; racial affects of, 15

realism, fascist: gaze in, 171, 222; in Italian cinema, 15, 29, 90, 97, 171, 233; tenets of, 207

reality: fascist denial of, 14–15; liberation aesthetic of, 232; national, 29, 63

red biennium (Italy), defeat of, 22

Red Scare, 80; Italian, 13

reenchantment: of Italy, 192; as political strategy, 266n29

Reich, Jacqueline, 17, 193; "Mussolini at the Movies," 3–4, 5; "Reading, Writing, and Rebellion," 194; *Re-viewing Fascism*, 3; on schoolgirl comedies, 195

relationality, modern forms of, 57

remediation, 36–37; in Visconti, 201

Renga, Dana, 159

Renoir, Jean, 205, 212

Renzi, Renzo: imprisonment of, 264n41

Republican Party, U.S.: on white identity, 135–36

resistance: Foucault on, 31; in Italian fascist cinema, 17–18, 229; in Italian neorealism, 247; by Italian women, 197; queer cinematic, 199

Ricciardi, Alessia, 234, 242

Riefenstahl, Leni: *The Triumph of the Will*, 77

Righelli, Gennaro: *La canzone dell'amore*, 62, 63

right, radical: resurgence of, x

Risorgimento, 12; cinema's weaponization of, 43; Italian film's birth under, 39–40; unified national space under, 9. *See also* Kingdom of Italy; nation-state, Italian

Robb, Tom, 136

Rodogno, David, 140

Roma città aperta (Rossellini), 230; absolution of Italians in, 246; ideology of, 227; reality in, 234, 235

Romanticism, view of community, 13

Rome: annexation (1870), 40; criminality tropes of, 86; EUR neighborhood, 87; Nazi occupation of, 224; underground of, 42; U.S. occupation of, 243

Romero, George: *Land of the Dead,* 99

Rosa, Alberto Asor, 55

Rose scarlatte (De Sica), 171–74, *182*; De Benedetti's work in, 172; disciplined spaces of, 182; escape from fascist biopolitics, 197; futurity in, 195; masculinity in, 190; mystery lover of, 173–74; power of writing in, 181; reenchanted Italy in, 192, *193*; the unknown in, 184

Rossellini, Renzo: score for *La nave bianca,* 151, 157

Rossellini, Roberto, 15; audiovisual strategies of, 159; "democratic" films of, 155; disavowal of *La nave bianca,* 154–55; eco-cinema of, 92; fascist corpus of, 158–60; humanism of, 155, 156; ideological script of, 237; liberated cinema of, 232; neorealism of, 159; pity for fascists in, 159–60; post-fascist cinema of, 159, 226–27; realism of, 176, 236; in redemption of postwar cinema, 231; themes of, 155. *See also La nave bianca*

Rossellini, Roberto, works: *Il ruscello di Ripasottile,* 262n16; *Scalo merci,* 224; *Stromboli,* 92; *Il tacchino prepotente,* 262n16; *La vispa Teresa,* 262n16. See

also *Fantasia sottomarina*; *Paisà*; *pilota ritorna, Un*; *Roma città aperta*; *L'uomo dalla croce*

Rotaie (Camerini), 29, 114, 119–23; acceptance of work, 121; aesthetics of, 121, 123; cityscape of, 119; class/gender compliance in, 119; elites' abjection in, 119–20, *120*; German expressionism of, 123; Italian humanity in, 120; labor in, 121, *122*; POV shots, 120–21; production/reproduction in, 120–21; realism of, 121; socioeconomic status in, 119; underclass bodies in, 120; working-class shame in, 119–20, *120*

Rubin, Gayle, 129

Ruttmann, Walter, 15, 28; *Berlin: Symphony of a Great City,* 60; formalism of, 60; German propaganda films of, 77. *See also Acciaio*

Sacchi, Filippo, 124

Said, Edward: *Orientalism,* 16

Saint-Cyr, Renée, 173

Sakai, Naoki, 156

Salò o le 120 giornate di Sodoma (1975), x

Salò puppet state, surrender of, 243

Salvini, Matteo, 177

Santa Cecilia public conservatory, filmmaking courses, 86

Sartre, Jean-Paul: *Being and Nothingness,* 111

Savio, Francesco, 124

Savoy, House of: hegemony over Italy, 9; national rebirth program, 43. *See also* Kingdom of Italy

Scaligero, Massimo, 79

schadenfreude, cinematic, 179

Schmitt, Carl: *Land and Sea,* 139

Schneider, Jane, 9

Schoonover, Karl, 137; *Brutal Vision,* 242; on Italian national character, 242; on neorealism, 226, 233; *Queer Cinema in the World,* 199

Screen (journal), 4
Sedgwick, Eve Kosofsky: on politics of
    emotion, 110–11; on queerness, 217
"Se il film parlante abolirà il teatro?"
    (Pirandello), 67
Seknadje-Askénazi, Enrique, 143
self, embodied: escape from, 111
self, oppositional processes of, 116
self-realization, racial, 53
Serandrei, Mario: *Giorni di gloria*, 248
Sergi, Giuseppe, 64, 66; influence of,
    254n26; on Mediterranean suprem-
    acy, 149; *Origine e diffusione della
    stirpe mediterranea*, 46–47, 52; racial
    anthropology of, 57, 254n26; racial-
    ized antiliberalism, 46
sex, political economy of, 129–30
sexual behavior, fascist anxiety over,
    202
shame: in Camerini's films, 110, 112, 115,
    131; in De Sica's films, 171; impact on
    identity, 110; operation of, 117; in
    racialization, 111; social dimension
    of, 111; weaponization of, 180
Sharpe, Christina, 240
Sicilians, as Italian popular heroes, 210,
    211
Sicily: as alternate reality, 211; *Cinema*
    on, 224; liberation of, 224; in postwar
    cinema, 209–11; Visconti on, 210–11,
    269n34
Sighele, Scipio: *La mala vita a Roma*,
    41–42, 46, 86
signor Max, Il (Camerini), 29, 114–19;
    Blackshirts in, 117, *118*; class in, 116–18;
    elites in, 117–19; shame in, 117; white-
    ness in, 117; white space in, 125
Silverman, Kaja, 27
Sloterdijk, Peter, 144
Smythe, SA, 158
social control: cultural imaginaries and,
    20; invasive strategies of, 18
Soldati, Mario, 66, 209, 246; *Piccolo
    mondo antico*, 74. See also *Acciaio*

Sole! (Blasetti), 86, 88–92; Communism
    in, 163; distribution of, 92; ecofascism
    in, 90; Fascism in, 89–90; gate
    imagery of, 88, 123; homesteaders in,
    90; influence of Soviet cinema, 89; as
    liberal film, 259n9; light / darkness in,
    90–91; pathological subjects of, 90–91,
    91; reception of, 92; reclamation in,
    88–89, 91–92; verticality of, 89
Somalia, Italian occupation of, 10
Sontag, Susan, 78
South, Global: minoritized peoples of,
    149
sovereignty, as optical illusion, 170
Spackman, Barbara, 5, 132
Spada, Marcello, 83; in Camerini's films,
    112, 113
spectatorship, agency in, 270n53,
    270n54
Spielraum (field of action), 191–92
Spivak, Gayatri Chakravorty, 241
squadristi cattolici (Catholic paramilitary
    squads), 164
Starace, Achille: death of, 243
state: appropriation of knowledge
    production, 31; authentic people
    of, 24–25; control of individuals, 7;
    counterdiscourses to, 21; incorpora-
    tion of body into, 169; noncompliant
    modes of being, 25; relationality
    in, 24; social acceptability codes,
    20; sociopolitical indocility in, 170;
    sociopolitical reproduction, 25; use
    of affective attachment, 20. See also
    nation-states; racism, state
state, biopolitical: intervention in liber-
    alism, 11; socio-racial profile of, 8
state power: capitalism and, 20; propa-
    gation of subjectivity, 170; securitar-
    ian logics of, 170
steelworks, Italian: nationalization of,
    60. See also *Acciaio*
Steimatsky, Noa, 208, 242
Stephan, Maria, 172

Stewart-Steinberg, Suzanne, 11, 33–34; on reclamation projects, 87–88

Stiegler, Bernard, 53

Stoler, Ann Laura, 24, 202

Stone, Marla, 17; *The Patron State*, 62

stracittà movement, urban values of, 109

strapenese movement, traditional values of, 109

Strike, The (film, 1904), 40

subject: docile, 194; pathological, 90–91, 91; regulatory representations of, 116; unproductive, 124

subjectivity: Deleuze on, 26; state power's propagation of, 170

Tavazzi, Alberto, 164

Teresa Venerdì (De Sica), 171; credits for, 172; De Benedetti's work in, 172; disciplined spaces of, 182; escape from fascist biopolitics, 197; female gaze in, 184; gaze of control in, 195–96, *196*; masculinity in, 190; performance in, 194; POV shots, 195; power of writing in, 181; redemptive flight in, 195–96; regenerative imagination in, 193

Terni (Umbria): *acciaierie* (steelworks) of, 60, 71, 74, 76; history of, 60; hydroelectric basin of, 71, *72*; Marmore Falls of, 61, 71, 74, 75

Terra madre (Blasseti), 29, 92, 93–103; Christianity in, 94; chromatic strategy of, 99; city dwellers in, 94, 97; cowherds, 100–101; diegetic sound of, 93; *donna-crisi* figure, 94, *95*, 99; elites in, 99, 101, *102*; gendered workforce of, 103; heteronormativity of, 103; Italian landscape in, 93, 96–97; *padrone* in, 93–94, 96–101, 103; peasantry, 98–99, *102*; peasant woman of, *95*, 98, 103; *razza* in, 96, 99; rural labor in, 93, 99–101, *102*; rural mass scene, 94, 97–98; shot-reverse-shots

of, 94, 96; swamp reclamation, 103; visual rhetoric of, 118

theaters, Italian: class separation in, 38. *See also* movie theaters

Tilgher, Adriano, 255n36

Togliatti, Palmiro, 107

Tomkins, Silvan: on shame, 117

Tonini, Pietro: movie theaters of, 35

totalitarianism, European: importance of sea for, 139; national cinema in, 60

totalitarianism, fascist: bodies performing, 158; British hegemony and, 139; disciplined lives of, 145; experimental nature of, 62; neorealism and, 200; promises of, 80; rearticulation of sovereignty, 11

Toubiana, Serge, 20

Trains of America (documentary), 44

Trump, Donald: fascism of, 31; use of mockery, 177

Trump, Melania, 80

truth: in apparatus theory, 4; audiovisual force of, 26; body in, 25–26; force of ritual in, 25; racial order of, 208; state-sanctioned, 4; struggle over, 30; weaponization of, 1, 18–28

Übermenschen, Nazi, 79

L'Unione Cinematografica Educativa (LUCE) Institute: Blasetti on, 85; iconography of Mussolini, *3, 6*, 100; newsreels of, 8, 89

L'Unione Cinematografica Educativa (LUCE) Institute, groundbreaking, 1–2, *3*, 5–8; armed forces at, 6; askari at, *2, 6, 7*; biopolitical warfare and, 8; cinematographic apparatus of, 8; DUX sign at, 6; Italian people at, 6

United States: ethno-nationalist resurgence in, 137; hegemony over Italy, 230, 234, 241–43, 270n2; mechanization of, 49; as racial quasi-fascist state, 19; right-wing resurgence in, x; state violence in, 18; tempo of life in, 49; victim mentality in, 136

uomini che mascalzoni . . ., Gli (Camerini), 123–34, 172, 181; the abject in, 123; binary structure of, 123; class in, 116, 118, 125; critical reception, 261n19; desubjugation of workers in, 126; disciplined spaces of, 182; escapism in, 126, 131; fast pace of, 124; labor versus enjoyment in, 131; mannequin imagery of, 127, *128*, 131; POV shots, 126; proper/improper Italianity in, 123; sexism in, 127, 129–30; shoe imagery of, 124–25; skin tone in, 127, *128*, 129; spectatorial pleasure in, 183; technologized bodies of, 131; unproductive subjects of, 124; white spaces of, 125

Uomini sul fondo (De Robertis), 29, 137, 143–49; A103 submarine in, 144–45; airlessness in, 145–46, 147; anticipation of neorealism, 150; bare lives in, *146*; corpo-realism of, 150; as *film d'atmosfera,* 144; flesh/technology synchronism in, 145; heroic sacrifice in, 146–47; Italian bodies in, 144, 145–47, 150; Italian technology in, 145, 148; metonymic bodies, 147; montage of, 147; opening title, 147; postwar scholarship on, 137; POV shots, 145, 147; racial affect of, 138, 147; racial totality of, 145; sailor-actors of, 145, 147–48, 150; spectatorial body of, 147; subliminal pleasures in, 138; suffering bodies in, 147–48; survival in, 150

L'uomo dalla croce (Rossellini), 29, 138, 164–67; chaplain figure of, 164, 166, 167; Christian humanism of, 167; Communism in, 163, 164, 166; fascist Christianity of, 164; fascist redemption in, 166; Gravelli's work in, 164; just/unjust violence in, 166; masculinity in, *165*; national alibis in, 160; race war in, 167; racialized other in,

166, 167; religious microhistory of, 164; Russian campaign in, 159; salvation through Fascism in, 167; spectators' interpretation of, 166; spiritualization of war in, 166; visual rhetoric of, 167

"Vaffanculo Day" (2007), 177

Valli, Alida, 243, 244, 246

vampires, elites as, 99

Van Gogh, Vincent: *A Pair of Shoes,* 125

Vaser, Vittorio, 90

Vecchia guardia (Blasetti), 92, 103–8; authentic Italianity in, 104, 107; Blackshirts in, 105, 107; canonization of Fascism, 107; collectivity in, 106–7; Communism in, 104–5; ecofascism of, 107; education in, 105; fascist youth in, 104, 105, *106*; landscape of, 106; liberal Italy in, 104; March on Rome, 107; militia in, 104, 105; opening title card, 107; resentment against elites in, 92; rural Italy in, 103; socioeconomic justice in, 105; strike in, 104; subject positions of, 107

Ventennio: cinematic figuration during, 14; as momentary interruption, x, 5; popular culture during, 2; Rossellini's films from, 159–60. *See also* Italy, fascist

Venturi, Tacchi, 2

Verdi, Giuseppe: nationalism of, 221

Verdicchio, Pasquale, 9

Verga, Giovanni, 212; *I Malavaoglia,* 211; Sicilian novellas of, 209–10; Visconti on, 269n34

Vergano, Aldo, 86

victimhood: as affective mediation device, 136; comedians' use of, 177; imaginary community of, 136; in Italian Fascism, 139, 151; Italian imperialism and, 140

Victor Emmanuel III (king of Italy), 156

Vigo, Jean: *Zero for Conduct,* 194

Villa, Roberto, 174

violence: just and unjust, 166; white American, 135

violence, fascist: in national life, 13, 82; as political technology, 11

violence, racial: in colonialism, 23; permanence of, 24

violence, state, 18; popular condonement of, 22

Visconti, Luchino, 246; in Centro Sperimentale di Cinematografia, 205; at *Cinema*, 205; eco-cinema of, 92; homosexuality of, 215, 222, 224; melodrama of, 171, 220; patterns of affect, 167; on realism, 206; reality in works of, 236; remediation in, 201; on Sicily, 210–11, 269n34; sociosexual imaginary of, 199; on state-controlled cinema, 211; on Verga, 269n34

Viscontin, Luchino, works: "Cadaveri," 211; "Cinema antropomorfico," 211; *Morte a Venezia*, 214; *Rocco e i suoi Fratelli*, 235; *La terra trema*, 92; "Tradizione e invenzione," 211. See also *Ossessione*

visual culture, Italian: power systems in, 18

"vita create, La" (Pirandello), 56–58; cruel vitalism of, 57; support for Mussolini in, 60

vita ricomincia, La (Mattòli), 230, 243–46; admission of guilt in, 245; De Benedetti's treatment of, 243, 246; forgetting of history in, 243; forgiveness in, 246; ruined Italy in, 243–44, 244; self-exoneration in, 245–46; spectatorial pleasure of, 245; success of, 245; truth/justice relationship in, 243

Vittori, Rossano, 72

von Nagy, Käthe, 115

vulnerability, white, 135–36, 139

Wagstaff, Christopher, 233

warfare, biopolitical, 31; of colonial-capitalism, 7–8; "Italian theory" on,

8; racialized assemblages of, 8, 27–28; social bellicosity preceding, 25

warfare, ideological, 4

water: in racial modernity, 170; in Western history, 169–70

Watson, William Van, 222

Weheliye, Alexander G., 81, 146; *Habeas Viscus*, 8

Welch, Rhiannon Noel: *Vital Subjects*, 9, 251n19

Wertmüller, Lina, x

whiteness: deconstruction of authority of, 188; of Italian ethno-nation, 248; negative portrayal of, 202; northern European, 113, 162; racialized Other and, 16; reproduction of, 16

whiteness, Italian, 12, 15, 149, 248; in *Al Cinematografo*, 38, 41, 44–45; Blackshirt, 29, 88, 92, 158, 248; elites', 117; of Italian war machine, 150; majoritarian, 149

white supremacy: Blackshirts', 83–84; in fascist cinema, 201; in Italian Africa, 202; in the United States, 136

Williams, Allison, 99

Williams, Linda, 15, 151, 159

Wilson, Ruth Gilmore, 260n9; *Golden Gulag*, 83

women, Italian: as caregivers, 151; cinematic consumption, 151; *donna-crisi*, 94, 95, 99; laborers, 130; minoritization of, 184; model fascist, 134; resistance by, 191, 197

women, peasant, 95, 103; in fascist discourse, 98

working class, Italian: desubjugation of, 126; disciplined, 60, 71; racial profiling of, 127, *128*, 129; role in modernity, 115. *See also* labor, Italian; peasants, Italian

World War I, submarines of, 144

World War II: Allied takeover of Italy, ix, 230; as culmination of colonial conflicts, 139; as humanitarian intervention, 138; Italian entry into, 204, 232

Wreckers of the Limited Express, The (film, 1906), 41

writing: in French feminism, 183; power of, 181–82; as technology of self, 183

Wynter, Sylvia: "Beyond the Word of Man," 116

Zavattini, Cesare, 248; De Sica's collaboration with, 171; on liberation from cinema, 236

Zegna, Michela, 85

Žižek, Slavoj, 5

Zoppetti, Cesare, 124

LORENZO FABBRI is an Imagine Fund Arts, Humanities, and Design Chair and associate professor of French and Italian at the University of Minnesota. He is author of *The Domestication of Derrida* and founding codirector of the Twin Cities Black Europe Film Festival.

Printed and bound by CPI Group (UK) Ltd, Croydon, CR0 4YY

19/12/2023

08211617-0001